"Torment Me, but Don't Abandon Me"

"Torment Me, but Don't Abandon Me"

Psychoanalysis of the Severe Neuroses in a New Key

Léon Wurmser

A JASON ARONSON BOOK

ROWMAN & LITTLEFIELD PUBLISHERS, INC.
Lanham • Boulder • New York • Toronto • Plymouth, UK

A JASON ARONSON BOOK

ROWMAN & LITTLEFIELD PUBLISHERS, INC.

Published in the United States of America
by Rowman & Littlefield Publishers, Inc.
A wholly owned subsidiary of The Rowman & Littlefield Publishing Group, Inc.
4501 Forbes Boulevard, Suite 200, Lanham, Maryland 20706
www.rowmanlittlefield.com

Estover Road
Plymouth PL6 7PY
United Kingdom

British Library Cataloguing in Publication Information Available

Library of Congress Cataloging-in-Publication Data

Wurmser, Léon.
 "Torment me, but don't abandon me": psychoanalysis of the severe
neuroses in a new key / Léon Wurmser.
        p. cm.
 "A Jason Aronson book."
 Includes bibliographical references (p.   ) and index.
 ISBN-13: 978-0-7657-0470-2 (cloth : alk. paper)
 ISBN-10: 0-7657-0470-6 (cloth : alk. paper)
 ISBN-13: 978-0-7657-0469-6 (pbk : alk. paper)
 ISBN-10: 0-7657-0469-2 (pbk. : alk. paper)
 1. Neuroses. 2. Psychoanalysis. I. Title.
 RC530.W882 2007
 616.89'17—dc22   2006048034

Printed in the United States of America

♾™ The paper used in this publication meets the minimum requirements of
American National Standard for Information Sciences—Permanence of Paper
for Printed Library Materials, ANSI/NISO Z39.48-1992.

Contents

Prologue

The double title of this book implies an inner tension. The leading quote, "Torment me, but don't abandon me!", coming from a patient, expresses one specific meaning of all masochistic relationships, usually at least secretly coupled with its counterpart, "I beat you, but do not abandon me!" The subtitle seems to be a grandiloquent generalization and promise that refers to "the" severe neuroses comprising much of what nowadays is looked at as "borderline" pathology. The bridge between the two is formed by the centrally important phenomena of self-condemnation, self-criticism, self-contempt, and self-sabotage, mostly centering around intense feelings of guilt and shame and an injured sense of justice, assumed for large parts of psychopathology of any kind.

In many other patients, these phenomena are covered over by their opposite: a seeming shamelessness and absence of guilt, an arrogant attitude of transgressing all boundaries (known from Greek as "hubris"), a seeming flight from everything that would mean limitation and conscience. However such "flight from conscience" is complementary to the "submission to conscience" presented in this work and is the theme of a parallel book.

Yet still, this is surface. Behind it there is much hidden, though vehemently denied, gain and excitement accompanying the overt suffering, although such gain benefits only one small, but decisive part of the personality, a part that functions like a demon within the soul—an inner judge, prosecutor, and executioner. Theoretically, we may speak of this part as the archaic or sadistic superego. Many couch it in terms of inner objects or inner persecutors, rightly observing both that these are often multiple versions of

1

such a self-destructive agency within and that they perpetuate early relationships with important human beings. Yet to reduce this inner demonic force to "inner objects" limits its understanding, since much more goes into it than just the representation of "others," and the term "objects" already presupposes a spirit of "objectification" of self and others that may be inherently dehumanizing, although it is hard to avoid the term nowadays since it has become so engrained.

We have to add the great importance of chronic traumatization. Although usually part of "early object relations," the traumata are by no means restricted to them. Moreover, as we shall see throughout, trauma and conflict intimately belong together. They always complement each other, a little bit like the two ends of a rope or a ladder.

However, all this is hardly "a new key."

There is something more, although that something by itself again does not warrant such a proud claim: the very important role played by the conflicts between opposite contents and intents of this demonic force, or to put it now in technical terms, the "intrasystemic conflicts within the superego." This has been well known since the works of Hartmann and Loewenstein (1962) and Sandler, Holder, and Meers (1963). Yet, I have found that almost all the work I can observe through supervision and case discussions has overlooked its practical significance: the opposition of incompatible ideals, obligations, and values; the shame-guilt-dilemma; the loyalty conflicts within the person, and to a considerable extent on an unconscious level. The consistent attention to such antinomies of conscience is at least one part of what I claim to be a new key.

Such consistent superego analysis requires a constant effort not to be judgmental and authoritarian in the very core of approach. Paul Gray's recommendation (personal communication) "exploring instead of judging," and its reverse: the persistent attention to the self-defensive attempt on the patient's side of "judging instead of exploring" serve as a lighthouse shining its beacon through the fog.

The other part of this "new key" is emphasis on complementarity, in addition to conflict. But for that I have to broaden the vista.

DIALECTIC

The treatment of patients suffering from various forms of severe neurosis touches upon core questions of psychoanalysis and its central polarities: reality of the relationship versus transference and "as-if" quality of experience, emotional spontaneity and self-disclosure on the side of the therapist versus anonymity, gratification versus frustration and neutrality, insight versus suggestion and psychagogy, defect versus conflict, and the often disregarded but important question of psychoanalysis versus psycho-therapy. Also, the commonly and dogmatically held primacy of transfer-ence interpretations and of working in the transference needs to be ques-tioned: I continue to find also the focus on acute inner conflicts in regard to events and relationships outside of the treatment enormously helpful. The interpretive process may very well be seen like the three-legged chair of the Pythia in the Delphian oracle: transference interpretation, extra-transferential work on conflicts, and work on past traumatizations and conflicts. Moreover, as already stated, trauma and conflict belong always intimately together. There can never be an either/or of trauma and con-flict.

When I select the major points that have emerged from the work pre-sented here and from my extensive supervision, mostly in Europe, it has to be kept in mind that they have to be seen as part of a dialectic. Titus, Smith, and Nolan (1986) explain: "The dialectical process is a dialogue be-tween opposing positions . . . the dialectic is the development of thought through an interplay of ideas." Hoffman (1994, p. 195) uses Ogden's def-inition: "A dialectic is a process in which each of two opposing concepts creates, informs, preserves, and negates the other, each standing in a dy-namic (ever changing) relationship with the other (p. 208)." He postulates that "the relationship between psychoanalytic discipline and expressive participation is dialectical in that sense" (Hoffman, ibid.). "Psychoanalytic ideas are rooted in a belief in the dialectic," says J. L. Kantrowitz (in Greenberg, 2001, p. 404). However, this complementarity (I use this term interchangeably with "dialectic") "between the analyst's personal emo-tional presence and the analyst's role-determined behavior" (Hoffman, 1994, p. 197) is but one among a number of such complementary oppo-sites; some of the others I have just mentioned. Another relevant example is the dialectic between consciousness and unconsciousness, between drive and defense: "Each pole of the dialectic creates, preserves, and negates the other. Each stands in dynamic, ever-changing relation to the other" (Phillips, 2006, p. 150). "In general, a behavior is a defense in rela-tion to a drive more primitive than itself, and a drive in relation to a de-fense more advanced than itself" (Gill, 1963, p. 122–3).

Thus, the philosophy of conflict is complemented by the philosophy of complementarity. The old alchemistic wisdom and Niels Bohr's motto *Contraria sunt complementa* (Holton, 1973), that is that the opposites com-plement each other, seems particularly suitable for the progress of under-standing in psychoanalysis.

Intrapsychic and interpersonal understanding, conflict analysis and re-lational analysis complement each other in varying and subtle ways, but consistently so—in the sense of a continually evolving "research pro-gram," as postulated by Lakatos and Musgrave (1970): "*It is a succession of theories and not one given theory which is appraised as scientific or pseudo-scientific.* But the members of such series of theories are usually connected by a remarkable *continuity* which welds them into *research programmes*" (p. 132, emphasis added).

Yet, this movement from conflict to complementarity of opposites in treatment stands itself in polar opposition to the absoluteness of inner forces. Not only do the "drives" and affects show such absoluteness, but so also do the defenses and other corrective measures taken. And in particular, those functions that are subsumed under the superego concept partake in such absoluteness: ideas, values, obligations and commitments, guilt and shame, justice and injustice. Thus, the superego is the secularization of the idea of the godhead. It is a conscious and unconscious internal God. Ethics and value hierarchies are an important part of such a "God-system."

Yet, with such absolute demands and their irreconcilability we find ourselves in the domain of tragedy, the realm of the tragic worldview, and with that in the world of myths and mythical thinking. The world of absoluteness is the world of myth and of a mythical-magical understanding of the world.

It is the combination of all these epistemological tools and their application in a novel treatment approach that is the new key allowing the successful treatment of hitherto often untreatable patients.

Psychoanalysis is a separate field of symbolic forms, with its own lawfulness and its own form of empirical inquiry. Reducing it to other fields may become stultifying, always restricts its yield, and narrows its vision. Rather, it grows by gleaning from other fields whatever is useful: "Only what is fruitful is true" (Goethe, 1961, vol. 18. p. 63, in "Wilhelm Meisters Wanderjahre," 2nd book, "Betrachtungen im Sinne der Wanderer": "Was fruchtbar ist, allein ist wahr"), and yet it still retains its own identity, its inner coherence, and its uniqueness.

Its essence lies in understanding human nature from the vantage point of inner conflict and inner complementarity. One such complementarity is the antithesis of all relations to others and even to self of I-You and I-It, the great dialectic at the center of Buber's philosophy (1947). The intimacy of the human relationship as actuated in treatment cannot be reduced to concepts, and yet we cannot talk about it in any other ways except in concepts, to wit, in generalization. Deep encounter and objectification are inescapable dimensions of relating to self and others; they belong together and complement each other.

Melvin Lansky describes one such integration of viewpoints:

> the more transcendent, abstract language of say, the sixties, has been challenged with the more immanent language—the language of the actual

encounter—developed in the last several decades. My own remarks will presume that we need both languages, not one or the other. That is to say, that we can, should, must deploy a new language centered on the immanence of the analytic encounter, but that we are at great peril if we subtract a more transcendent explanatory language that conceptualizes how we view what we do and how the mind works. Otherwise, we are stuck in the concreteness of the dyad without a language of explanation of clinical phenomena and the tools for exploring treatment impasses and failures. (2006; see also Lansky, 2003)

SCENES, MYTHS, AND METAPHORS

Therefore, just as is the case in all the sciences, psychoanalytic theory cannot do without generalization and without abstract symbols for general categories. Yet, just as is the case in history and in the human sciences in general, psychoanalysis also needs the individual case in its incomparable richness, in its historical uniqueness, to demonstrate the essence of psychoanalytic insight and knowledge. Only a combination of these two forms of discourse—explanation by categorization and understanding as historical uniqueness—can lead to the fullness of psychoanalytic inquiry and is, of course, also didactically most helpful. The way leads back and forth between the individual case in its great depth, its intricacy, its complexity, and the ever-growing system of metaphors that make up the theory.

This back and forth is the dialectic approach used in the work presented in this book and in its parallel studies.

What do I mean by this concretely?

Off the bat, the detailed description of the cases (as before in *The Power of the Inner Judge* [Wurmser, 2000a]) illustrates the dilemmas faced and the self-critical review, step by step, of what appeared to be useful and what seemed harmful in the ongoing work. Several cases of paralyzing or self-destructive forms of neurosis were over a number of years successfully treated in intensive, psychoanalytic therapy. These were often patients that would commonly appear unanalyzable—severe obsessive-compulsive disease, masochistic-fetishistic perversion and character perversion, and "sociopathic" impulse disorder (the latter group has now been taken out and presented separately in *Flight from Conscience*).

During the course of therapy, it became evident that the various exigencies required a flexible approach, which was by no means always open to conscious scrutiny at the time when the psychoanalytic sessions were going on. But since all the dialogues were stenographically transcribed a much more thorough analysis and understanding in retrospect has been possible. The reader can follow and reexperience himself this process of gaining insight on many levels, step by step, and observe both the errors in treatment and the crucial breakthroughs.

I started out with the more or less traditional paradigm of conflict analysis: a careful study, moment by moment, of the "point of urgency" of conflict and affect, with a consistent approach from the side of the defenses and especially of superego functions, and as continually being recreated in the intersubjective fields with the analyst and with current figures in life. This attempt at consistent conflict analysis had, as usual, a kind of double focus: the transference, in particular the subtle and varied aspects of the transference of defense and of superego transference, and a reconstruction of the inner scenarios, of the sequence of compromise formations, both in the actual occurrence and throughout life history. I also recognize my own contribution to the analytic process: "No longer dominant is the myth of the analyst's total, somehow nonhuman detachment, with understanding and interpreting thought of as arising exclusively from outside the patient's mental state" (Poland, 1996, p. 87). And, at the same time: "Neutrality is the technical manifestation of respect for the essential otherness of the patient" (ibid., p. 92).

This inevitably entailed great attention to the construction of the history of childhood. On the one side, a number of salient scenes served as a kind of lens, collecting many rays of inquiry into a sharp focus upon recurrent images, "model scenes," as recently described by J. Lichtenberg (1989; Lichtenberg et al., 1996). These scenes serve as guiding myths for the inner history of these patients and for the understanding and resolution of the neurotic conflicts. Yet, no such model scenes can be understood as faithful replicas from the past. They are multiply refracted by series of layers of inner conflict. They are themselves coded messages from within, not trustworthy recollections (Lansky, 2006).

But beyond this, as the work progressed, it became more and more obvious that all these patients were severely and chronically traumatized and that they could only be understood when the nature of such traumatization was explored, as exactly as this proved feasible. Thus the focus on trauma had to be added to the centrality of conflict. I do not mean "trauma" in a trivial, universalized way, but in the sense of events with life-altering severity, intensity, and usually repetitiveness, like the killing of the mother by the father, repeated severe operations in early childhood, massive fighting between the parents, sexual abuse and other forms of physical mistreatment, but also some severe intersubjective harm, like chronic humiliation and systematic squashing of all individuality by "soul blindness" and "soul murder." The bridge between trauma and conflict consists in the overwhelming quality of traumatogenic affects, that is, their absoluteness and globality. Opposite affects of such totality inevitably clash with each other and are impossible to reconcile. Thus the concepts of "affect regression" (Krystal, 1988, 1998), of the breakdown of "affect regulation," and of the compromising of "affect modulation" had to be conjoined with those of "mastery," of "affect defense," of "ego control," and of the "totalitarian, regressive superego." These clinical experiences with the cases under treatment approximately paralleled the development within psychoanalysis, as a system of understanding and explaining, where the structural model had to be revised and complemented according to the increasing knowledge about early development. The often very archaic affect states, possibly from presymbolic and preverbal times, required a considerable revision of the therapeutic stance, again in the direction of great flexibility. Relational aspects like spontaneity, certain forms of self-disclosure, and intuitive responses that seem to contradict all precepts of standard technique (Hoffman, 1994), are on vivid display in the material, even occasionally the use of pharmacotherapy.

As becomes obvious in the work with the patients presented, there are central mythical-magical equations of great intricacy that lead to a fairly large catalog of core fantasies—a recurrent roster of dynamically central units of experience, combining imagery, affects, and self-states on many levels of development. They are found again and again throughout the spectrum of psychopathology, but with particular poignancy in obsessive-compulsive neurosis and in perverse sexuality. These mythical-magical equations are metaphors taken literally and experienced concretely.

The Jewish interpretive tool of the Midrash is another form of looking in concretized and often visualized form at metaphorical insight. But this is true for much of the literary tradition in general. The work with these patients has often demonstrated to me the great usefulness of referring to literature within the clinical dialogue. Literary prototypes can serve as wonderful symbols for those model scenes, for the inner myths, for the metaphorical equations, for the tragic irreconcilability of absolutes in conflict, and for the possibility of resolution by complementarity.

ALTERED PREMISES

This book is conceived of as a continuation and deepening of the work presented in *The Power of the Inner Judge*, which aimed at presenting a consistently conflict-analytic approach in the treatment of the severe neuroses. Yet, it also continues some explorations started in the earlier books, *The Mask of Shame* (Wurmser, 1981/1994) and *The Hidden Dimension* (Wurmser, 1978/1995). Although based on the case studies and their theoretical background published in Germany in the 1980s, much

newer material is added in this new book that should reflect the deepened understanding and more recent clinical experience in treatment
with such severely ill patients. One major focus remains the detailed
superego analysis as developed in the preceding volumes, but the complementarity of the technique of defense analysis and the less specific
relational aspects necessary for the work with the severe neuroses and
with that countertransference and the importance of my own contribution to what went right and wrong claim increasing attention. Nuanced
considerations of the core fantasies rival those of the core conflicts, complementing the superego-analytic endeavors.

This entailed some important enlargement of the conceptual framework: Some have pigeonholed my work into one category of psychoanalytic thinking and working—the structural model. This does not fit very
well anymore, if it ever did. It is certainly true that I was trained very
much in the structural paradigm and that I still use some of its language
and technique wherever it seems to me of the greatest utility, particularly
in regard to the cardinal and ongoing relevance of what is meant by the
concept of a "superego," or as I prefer to use it clinically often in a
metaphor coined by Kant of "the inner judge." To present how this concept proves relevant, in case after case, and with particular poignancy in
the work with the severe neuroses, is a major ongoing commitment, and
it is now for this book as well.

Yet, there is a second point I would like to make—again one that many
think is an outdated model: namely that the real center of psychoanalytic
understanding continues to be that of inner conflict. Psychoanalysis is the
science of inner conflict, in the words of Ernst Kris (1975). Everything else
is derived from it. The conflict nature of the human being is unresolvable;
it belongs to human existence, to man's very essence, as we read in Plato's
Phaidros (247b, [vol 2]): "There is imposed on the soul pain and extreme
conflict." And Kant says, "Man wants harmony; but Nature knows better
what is good for the species: she wants conflict" (1784/1983, section 4, pp.
38–39).

This dynamic model has, however, come to use a much broader theoretical background than the dual-drive theory of yore could give. It rather
means a flexible and changeable inquiry of how the various affects,
drives, values, and interests at any given moment stand in conflict with
each other. But at the same time, this thinking in terms of conflicts of
struggling forces owes more to the literary tradition in general, and to the
Jewish thought tradition in particular, than just to one segment of psychoanalysis.

Moreover, conflict is but one way how to conceive of opposite forces on
any of the levels mentioned. Their *complementarity* is its necessary coun-

terpart. It is mostly not an either/or, but a more-or-less, a balancing out that gradually comes into play during the treatment. "Compromise formation" is one of many expressions of such complementarity (I believe that what Anton Kris [1985, 1986, 1987] differentiates as *convergent* versus *divergent* conflicts corresponds to what I call the duality of conflict and complementarity). Especially in the final chapter devoted to technique, this idea of *dialectic* moves to the center.

Then there is a third point I would like to make: The attitude necessary to successfully treat the severe neuroses is probably often closer to that of the relational and self-psychological ways of practice and understanding than to traditional ego psychology. This also means that I give much more credence to the silent workings of countertransference and to the reciprocity of influence between therapist and patient (in this I was influenced by my long-term work with my German colleagues and friends, especially Heidrun Jarass). Moreover, in regard to theory and psychodynamic understanding, the approach chosen owes a lot to a deepened understanding of family dynamics and of early developmental research, especially the theory of affect development—as it becomes clear from my concentration on the deep problems of affect regression and affect regulation, and the role of shame and guilt in them, as well as on the genesis of a large number of other affects. The very important and exciting new findings in the interface between neuropsychology and psychoanalysis were somewhat outside of the purview of this work and have to await future study.

I add a fourth remark: To give a better feel for the technical and theoretical problems faced in this work I have found it helpful, rather than to give the usual brief vignettes, to focus very much on the inner complexity and therefore to present long, in-depth studies of entire treatments, based on verbatim notes of the clinical dialogue—again an approach that is quite unusual and has gained both positive and also some negative response. Many have found the self-critical review of my own interventions within that psychoanalytic dialogue—also a kind of ongoing dialogue within myself—helpful in their own work, because it keeps addressing technical questions that are often implicit, but unspoken, in their uncertainty with seemingly intractable patients.

In addition, and this is a fifth point, I combine this integrative approach with a strong and direct involvement of literary and philosophical themes and of cultural history, in my theoretical understanding as well as in my actual practical work—again something that may for some raise troubling questions.

All in all, I try my best to have this blend and integration of perspectives reflected in my writings.

LAYERINGS

Before I open the book itself, it is incumbent upon me to summarize a few pertinent ideas from the previous work, *The Power of the Inner Judge*.

One of its main theses is the structure of causality. Very briefly it states: The more severe the traumata, the more overwhelming the affects. The more radical and overwhelming the affects, the more intense the conflicts. The more intense and extreme the conflicts, the more encompassing (global) the defenses and the more totalitarian the contradictory demands of "the inner judge," that sadistic version of conscience. The trauma lives on in the severity and pitiless character of the conscience as well as in the split character of the superego (conscience, ideals, values, loyalties). The more extreme the aggression of the superego is, the more life determining are the masochistic and narcissistic fantasies and the more prominent the core phenomena of the neurotic process (compulsiveness, globality, and polarization), meaning: the broader the problems of "narcissism"; of "splitting of identity," or doubleness of the self; and of compulsiveness. In reverse order, the psychoanalytic path from description to explanation proceeds from the core phenomena of the neurotic process—compulsiveness, polarization, and absoluteness—as they typically are reflected in preconscious conflicts, affects, and self-protective behaviors. It uses with particular benefit the bridges of the core fantasies in order to reach the unconscious core conflicts. The recognition of them and the new attempt to resolve them bring about effective change; their place in the inner chain of causal connection is at the very center. Beyond the conflicts, we deal with core affects of a traumatic or physiologic origin, often determining the severity of the conflicts we deal with. Core fantasies and core conflicts are specifically set up to deal with, to defend against, central affects of a primary and global nature. Behind those four layers of psychopathology described—core phenomena, core fantasies, central conflicts, and main affects—there looms in almost every case of severe neurosis, the fatal power of trauma. A considerable space of the current work will be devoted to those core fantasies:

> Diagram: **Structure of Causality**
> Traumata
> Core Affects
> Unconscious Core Conflicts
> Central Fantasies and Preconscious Conflicts
> Core Phenomena of the Neurotic Process
> (compulsiveness, globality [absoluteness], polarization)

To repeat: The dichotomy of trauma versus conflict or deficit versus conflict is wrong. The two are always in a dialectical (complementary) relation with each other, with variable distribution of weight. Every conscious conflict is very often immediately equated with a reoccurring trauma; every new trauma gives rise to renewed inner conflict, often of an unconscious nature.

The total helplessness in front of the overwhelming and clashing affects, inherent in the concept of trauma, calls for an equally radical defense by a fantasy of omnipotence, and that entails the hope for a magical transformation of self and world. Because it is impossible that this hope be fulfilled, self and world assume a remarkable doubleness, a split quality, as a result of the complex inner conflicts engendered by traumatization. This doubleness has to be repeated in endless vicious circles. Thus the concept of "repetition compulsion" is central, but not referring to a metapsychologically elementary force; rather it is understood as part of dealing with trauma and unsolvable conflict by psychological means. As extensively elaborated in *The Power of the Inner Judge*, the repetition compulsion is an attempt to attain in symbolic ways regulation and conflict resolution; the attempt proves blocked because the affects and the drive needs evoked by them and, closely connected with them, the forms of defense and superego demands, are all of a *global* quality and therefore irreconcilable with each other, and the consistent endeavors to express them in symbols have to be defeated. Yet, the attempt cannot be given up, since it lies in the nature of the ego to attain inner unity, to overcome the inner contradictoriness, the doubleness of self and world experience. The need for synthesis, that is for psychical self preservation, is so important and so preeminent, that, in intensity and penetrating power, it corresponds to an "instinctual drive."

In short, massive traumatization and specific defensive efforts to deal not only with these traumata and the severe aggressions caused by them, but also with the resulting, usually intensive conflicts, especially also conflicts in the superego, play a great role in the understanding, explanation, and treatment of the severe neuroses. Among those defenses denial and repression; sexualization; turning against the self and from passive into active; projection; and externalization, especially by role reversal (Sandler, 1976a, 1976b, 1989, 1993), play a most prominent role.

A BRIEF PREVIEW

I would like to conclude with a short overview of some of the major contents.

The themes of "inner doubleness" and "demonic" quality of the "force to repeat" very destructive life patterns, which formed the nucleus of the preceding book, thread through the following studies as well. After some deepened studies in chapter 1 of the relevance and meaning of the superego concept and the origins of what is subsumed under it, chapter 2 deals with the issues of the "broken self," as result of severe and chronic traumatization, and the various layers of trauma-togenic shame.

An especially important form of treatment-resistant "repetition compulsion" can be found in perverse sexual activities that are set up, as experience shows time and again, to protect against massive self-condemnation and thus indirectly defend against the frighteningly overwhelming primary affects behind that hypertrophy of the superego. With the greatest consequences, such destructive repetition plays a cardinal role in what has aptly been called "character perversion." This term refers, in Arlow's words (1971), to "the distortion of behavior or character [that] takes the place of what had once been a perversion or a perverse trend" (p. 334). It is particularly fetishism with its doubleness of acknowledgment and denial of the anatomical difference and the warding off of castration anxiety that serves for Arlow as paradigm. Later authors, like Cooper (1988, 1991), Renik (1992), Lee Grossman (1992, 1993, 1996), Reed (1997, 2001), Bach (1994), and Jack and Kerry Kelly Novick (1996a, 1996b, 2003a, 2003b), extended the concept, partly by including other traumatic perceptions that are being warded off by character traits, partly by also including sadomasochistic and exhibitionistic forms of conflict solution. Renik and Reed speak in fact of the analytic process having become a magic action whereby the analysand transforms the analyst's intervention about his avoidances into a fetish that unconsciously contradicts his worry. I try, with the help of a number of cases and the theoretical issues raised by them, to deepen the concept of character perversion by stressing the causative role of the superego in it, in particular of the conflicts between different superego functions or structures.

Furthermore, much of drug addiction appears as a special case of character perversion. And even beyond this, as I will explain, the dynamics of character perversion can be considered an important dimension of the dynamics of the severe neuroses in general, rather than that they would form merely a distinct nosological entity. Moreover, the understanding of this group of clinical phenomena can help us also in the comprehension of large-scale sociocultural processes, like religious and ideological fanaticism, with its horrifying expressions in the form of genocidal anti-Semitism and the current wave of global terrorism. (These aspects will be taken up in a separate study, see also Wurmser, 2001, 2002, 2004b).

After a theoretical introduction into the issues of double reality and character perversion in chapter 3, the field is prepared for a detailed study of the cases and the clinical and theoretical problems raised by them. In the following chapters the focus will lie on obsessive-compulsive symptoms and character traits and on various aspects of masochism, including very much the sadomasochistic variant of character perversion. The questions of the virulence of self- and outward-directed aggression, the resentment vested in the "inner dwarf," and the phenomenology of split identity will arise with particular poignancy in chapters 5 and 6. Chapters 7 and 8 give the opportunity for a thorough study of core fantasies and primary process equations that form a finely woven web linking the severe neuroses in their depths. In this connection it should be noted that our literature shows very few careful descriptions of successful analytic treatments of obsessive-compulsive disorder and obsessive-compulsive personality disorders (Bristol, 2001). These chapters do just that.

With all this I do not mean, however, to reduce the various psychological and psycho-pathological dimensions of masochism, narcissism, or obsessive-compulsive disease to this one category of character perversion. The latter is just one aspect besides others in these cases, and one which plays a role in strongly variable strength; it is merely a valuable perspective that opens up new ways of understanding particularly difficult cases of various forms of severe neurosis.

In a concluding chapter (9), I present some of the major conclusions for the technique of treating patients with severe neurosis, but also the great importance of seeing the *fundamental dialectic between a technical and theoretical view of psychoanalysis and a philosophy of the basic human relationship* always at work in the intensive encounter that is a prerequisite for a good analysis. "Transference-countertransference" and "relationship" are two different ways of looking at what is happening. There is legitimacy to both perspectives; they complement each other. We could also say that there is an analytic-scientific approach to human nature, and there is a dialogic-philosophical one, and both require each other. To use Buber's terms: the former is an I-It relation, the latter is an I-You relation. Using one without the other is like clapping with one hand, as the Talmud says.

I turn now to a deepened presentation of one of the two main features of the "new key."

1

Sleeping Giant or Fossil?

IS THE SUPEREGO CONCEPT STILL RELEVANT TODAY?

Is the concept of the superego still relevant today, or is it just part of the stranded whale of metapsychology, the skull of the carcass of structural theory?

Indeed, there are many today who find the concept of a "superego" and much of what it refers to in clinical observation not very relevant anymore, outdated, and its systematic study and use not worthwhile (e.g., Brenner, 2002; contributions by Milch and Orange, 2004, and Lichtenberg, 2004 appear in Wurmser, 2004a). I could not disagree more and am convinced of the cardinal and ongoing relevance of what is meant by this theoretical construct, or, as I prefer to use it clinically often in a metaphor coined by Kant, by the "the inner judge":

> The consciousness of an *inner court* within the human being ["before which his thoughts accuse or excuse each other"] is the *conscience*. Every human being has conscience and finds himself observed, threatened and held in respect [. . .] by an inner judge, and this power that watches over his inner laws is not something that he *makes* by his own free will, but it is embodied in his very essence. It follows him like a shadow when he intends to escape from it. He may numb himself by pleasures and distractions, or put himself to sleep, but he cannot avoid at times to come to himself or to wake up as he perceives its dreadful voice. In his utter perverseness he may achieve a state where he does not pay any attention to it anymore, yet he is unable to avoid *hearing* it. (Kant, 1797–1798/1983, A100–102, "Metaphysics of Morals," my translation)

Kant speaks therefore about the "twofold personality," "the double self: on the one side, standing trembling before the bars of a court, yet one that is entrusted to himself, on the other side, holding the office of judge, by inborn authority, in his own hands." This inner judge has to be seen both as a "herald of the heart" (*Herzenskündiger*) as well as "universally committing" (*allverpflichtend*), that is, as representing God.

I find the superego concept in Kant's first sense—namely as "herald of the heart," yet as an inner agency that is largely empirically grown and analyzable—indispensable and of invaluable help for the work with the severely ill patients. I see a concept like this as crucially important for the task of developing a differentiated approach to the intricate dynamics involved, and I am often amazed in my supervisory work or in my readings to what extent these problems still seem strangely overlooked and neglected, no matter how strikingly helpful clinically their understanding and tackling would be and, in fact, how obvious their presence is. To show how they prove to be so, in case after case, and with particular poignancy in the work with the severe neuroses, has been a major commitment in my earlier publications.

Many suggest that, together with the concept of the superego, the dynamic model of psychoanalysis, namely the view that the real center of psychoanalytic understanding continues to be that of inner conflict, is also outdated. This dynamic model has, however, come to assume a much broader theoretical background than one based only on the dual drive theory. It now refers to a flexible and changeable inquiry of how the various affects, drives, values, and interests, at any given moment and of varied levels, stand in conflict with each other. Among the attempts to give some encompassing order, I have found Lichtenberg's model of the motivational systems heuristically helpful, precisely for a revised dynamic model (1989).

At the same time, this thinking in terms of conflicts of struggling inner forces owes more to the literary tradition in general, and to the Greek and Jewish thought tradition of a dialectical approach to truth in particular, than just to one core segment of Freud's theory and ego-psychology. Moreover, as already brought forth in the prologue, conflict is but one way to conceive of opposite forces on any of the levels of the life of the mind. The complementarity of these forces is its necessary counterpart. It is mostly not an either-or, but a more-or-less, a balancing out that gradually comes into play during treatment.

Similar questions are raised about the continued usefulness of the structural model altogether, especially of the detailed study of defenses and of other major ego-functions, like the self-observing part or of cognition— and of course with special emphasis the concepts of superego encompassing its major parts of conscience and ego-ideal, be they conscious or unconscious (or rather, the many shadings in between). It should be kept in mind that the structural model, just like the dynamic model, is a reformulation of concepts of the soul that have accompanied Western literature throughout, from its Egyptian, Greek, and Jewish origins onward. It has to be at least one important way to understand the life of the mind. Just as inner conflict is depicted in ancient Egyptian documents (e.g., "The dialogue between the self and his ba" in the Middle Kingdom, around 2000 BCE [Assmann, 2002]), in Homer and the Greek tragedies, in the Talmud and the Midrash, as conflict between contradictory strivings of the mind or of opposite impulses, or "drives" (in Greek *epithymíai*, in Hebrew *jetzarím*), we find hints of the superego throughout ancient writings, beginning with ancient Egyptian literature, both in the overriding and central principle of *Ma'at* as immanent and transcendent, as social and intrapsychic principle of "connective justice" and in the *Ka* ("conscience, social self" [Assmann, 2002]). Moreover, we find a juxtaposition of two opposite aspects in the superego in the Egyptian "structural model" (to be sure, to call it that is a stretch because what we find are the different parts of the personality as they were thought to dissociate during the long, drawn-out process of dying and being reborn):

> Like the heart, Ka belongs to the moral and, with that, to the social aspect of the person. . . . Ka refers to the moral personality, the "normative" double, almost kind of a superego to which the social categories of honor, dignity and status are joined, just as the categories of virtue and justice are connected with the heart. (Assmann, 2001, p. 137)

We can recognize in this doubleness of moral aspects of the personality the shame part and the guilt part of the superego.

We encounter superego equivalents in Socrates's quiet inner voice of the *daimónion*, the "little God," and comparable terms in the Rabbinic tradition (*bat qol*, "the daughter of a voice" or "the little voice," and *demút de'iqón*, "the likeness of an image," an externalized representation of the warning conscience as a fleeting apparition). Yet, there is another important way of viewing the superego's precursors: the concept of *God* or of the gods. What we subsume under the superego functions can all be found in the varied forms divinity takes. In the Judeo-Christian conception of the godhead, the emphasis lies very much on the conscience part of the superego: on justice, sin, condemnation, forgiveness, and redemption. In the Graeco-Roman conception of the godhead the focus is far more on the ego-ideal part of the superego, in different virtues and skills (*aretái*): artfulness and ingenuity; and power, beauty, nobility, and pride; and with that the importance of visibility, hiddenness, and shame; punishment by metamorphosis; and upholding and defense of honor. This duality and dialectic of the shame part and the guilt part of the superego, their contradictions and dialectic, have been vastly neglected in psycho-analytic superego analysis.

In fact, we can say *the* superego is the secularization of the idea of the godhead, somewhat in Voltaire's sense: "Si Dieu n'existait pas, il faudrait l'inventer" (If God did not exist, he would have to be invented, "Epître à l'Auteur du livre des trois Imposteurs," quoted in Büchmann, p. 155). It is a conscious and unconscious internal God, as we see in Kant, quoted above. Ethics and value hierarchies (e.g., in the value pyramid the German philosopher Scheler worked out in great detail about eighty years ago, see Scheler, 1916/1954) are indeed a very important part of such a "God-system," but still fall far short of the entire superego construct.

Similar antecedents can be found for the structural model as a more encompassing system of ordering inner, especially also out of awareness processes: Its historical nexus does not point back just to the later Freud (or even to the earlier Freud's topographical model), but very much to the Platonic tradition. The model of the soul in the "Republic" is a structural model par excellence, and so it is in the *Phaedrus*. The analogy is not stringent, since Plato's structural model is not entirely identical with Freud's, and we cannot so clearly tease out one agency that would strictly correspond to the superego. Still, through the ages, the similarity and usefulness of the "structural" concepts of the powers of the soul—one part, the *epithymíai*, are the desires; the second part the moral-ethical aspirations, passions, and ideals, or *thymós*; and the third part is *noûs*, the elevated spirit of Reason and contemplation, as they can be seen written large and studied in the "State"—is striking: their *democratic* concert with its "checks and balances" or of the *despotism* of *one* part.

Moreover, we encounter in the *Zohar*, as a presupposition extremely important for the Kabbalah, the threefold nature of the soul (based, of course, as it is basic for all mysticism, on the unquestioned assumption of the soul's immortality and preexistence), or, as we would see it, the tripartite nature of the soul. The lowest form (or part) is *nefesh* (*nafsha*), the vital soul, the one animating the body, also will and desire. Blood is *nefesh*. The middle form is *ruach* (*rucha*), the spirit, the rational soul. *Ruach* is breath and wind. The highest soul, the transcendent, meaning giving soul, the one near to God, is *neshama* (*nishmeta*); she is the pure, mystical soul that is unable to sin. This threefold nature is akin to Plato's tripartite model of the soul. Especially the Spanish Kabbalah of the late thirteenth century was a dramatic Platonic answer to the rationalistic and empirically oriented philosophy of Maimonides (Rabbi Moshé ben Maímon, "Rambam," 1135–1204) who was deeply influenced by Aristotle. Thus, we can recognize in these two main trends of medieval Judaism a resurgence of the dialectic between the Platonic and the Aristotelian worldviews.

Moreover, this fundamental, tripartite system strongly reminds us of Freud's structural model of id, ego, and superego. Freud gave them simply a clinical varnish and a method for their systematic study.

Certainly, the similarities of these three psychologies (Plato's, the Zohar's, and Freud's) are by no means complete, their divisions differ, but still the parallels are striking. Together with such a structural model, there goes the centrality of an understanding in conflicts; all three versions are radically dynamic models, that is, thoroughly conflict oriented. Therefore, Plato speaks in this context of *agón éschatos*—extreme conflict.

Yet historicity of an idea is no warrant for its truth or its usefulness. The Ptolemaic system, astrology, and alchemy are good examples for such superannuity. The magical-mythical understanding of soul and world is prevalent even today. Rather, the question is: How does any experience-based theory of the mind cohere with the rest of our knowledge?

There is no question that all these concepts and models require a thorough reappraisal in the light of the great expansion of knowledge, especially thanks to the new developments in infant and early childhood research, in neuropsychology and cognitive psychology, in family theory and relational psychoanalysis, and, not to forget, in primate research.

The question remains if the actual psychoanalytic work (including the psychoanalytically oriented forms of psychotherapy) would not lose more if the earlier models were simply thrown overboard in favor of some summarizing concept, like self-regulating functions for superego or executive functions for the ego. It is akin to the older fashion of subsuming much of psychopathology under the then new heading of "borderline." We might wonder whether we do not lose much specificity and differentiation by these replacements, without gaining much in return.

One way of defining psychoanalysis is the method of exploring and objectifying subjectivity from the vantage point of systematic conflict analysis. The sorting out of those objectivations requires equally systematic constructs of symbols that prove to be useful, thus fulfilling the pragmatic criterion for truth. All scientific constructs are based on metaphor. Especially, the systematic study of the mind has to rely on those metaphors that are most useful for the task at hand (Wurmser, 1977). It seems to me that the new findings in the adjacent fields require their own most suitable forms of symbolization and that for them the traditional psychoanalytic models are at best marginally useful, and sometimes not at all; new conceptualizations are imperative. What is, however, centrally useful for clinical work in psychoanalysis must not take a backseat to these necessary new theoretical formulations. Rather, they have to be continually tested *within* this clinical method and its variations; indeed, they have to be deepened, amplified, and revised according to the needs of this work itself, while at the same time, they have to prove their compatibility with the new explanations arising from these neighboring fields. No scientific endeavor can arrogate to itself the overthrow of central tenets of another field, ruled by other methods of gathering evidence, as long as there are no fundamental contradictions in explanatory power between the two; in particular, it cannot do so without accounting fully for all the empirical findings and pragmatic needs gained by the old theory. The reverse is just as true: the traditional field cannot impose its canons on new avenues of inquiry.

THE CONTENT OF THE SUPEREGO CONCEPT

Moral systems can either be symbolized conceptually, abstractly: as values; as ideals; as affective systems; as duty, loyalty, and responsibility; as restraints; and as functions—or they can be directly experienced affectively: as empathy and sympathy, as regrets and remorse, as shame and guilt, as a sense of justice and injustice (resentment)—or they can be studied as quasi-mythical metaphors: as intrasubjectively and intersubjectively effective constellations of images and voices. All these approaches are important; they also complement each other. In this overview I select just the few that are in this context most important and approach the question first from the side of the imagery of the superego, as metaphors and scenarios; second, from the side of the felt emotions and the unconscious, mostly denied affects; third, from the functional side; and fourth, from the deep dynamic connections and origins, giving the other three inner coherence and representing an attempt at a causal explanation. All four viewpoints seem to me important and necessary; all are of great relevance both to the clinical practice and to the refinement and possible revision of theory.

The Imagery of the Superego: Metaphors, Scenes, and Scenarios

The phenomena are uncontested and highly relevant for actual clinical work, not just in psychoanalysis *sensu strictiori*, but also in psychotherapy. Beyond that, their relevance for the social and cultural sciences, for history and, of paramount importance, for religion and philosophy is self-evident. The question is rather: How can we best order them with the help of symbolizations, and how can we best developmentally, culturally, and perhaps even phylogenetically and neurophysiologically explain them? Since I have no expertise in the latter two, they have to be omitted, and also to the former two I can give only some attempted answers based on my own experience.

I give now a more detailed dialogue of a session where some of the issues are illustrated.

"The Heart of Stone"

A colleague from overseas in her sixties recently asked me for some telephone consultations for severe panic attacks and underlying chronic anxiety after triple bypass surgery that was followed by a life threatening pulmonary embolus. She ascribed the underlying anxiety by and large to the recent ordeal she had gone through and to her traumatic youth: child of a Nazi father, an SS man; flight from the Russians; long separation from her mother, who was not able to flee from East Germany when the father smuggled the children at night over the border; in adolescence severe fighting with her authoritarian father, both about his Nazi ideology and his devaluation of her as girl and woman; throughout life a strong inclination to demand highest performance from herself, to reconcile the requirements of raising an only child and carrying full obligations as physician. She had for many years been living together with a colleague whose patience in regard to her physical limitations was quite limited.

At the time of the following dialogue, we had had only a few long-distance sessions, but what had helped quickly was a refocusing of her attention as to the immediate cause of her panic from her real recent trauma to issues of inner conflict, especially those centering around her wish to abide by the demands of the inner and reexternalized judge, commanding her to be strong again, as opposed to her deep anger at such imposition and her rebellion against such unreasonable hardness and harshness.

Thus, her unreasonable, unfeeling father, whom she had equated in her childhood and youth with Hitler and with Evil is not only repeated in her partner's impatience and anger, but in her own inner authority that shows little caring for any weakness. She was surprised to discover (in the second session) to what extent her fear of death had something to do with the severity of the inner judge who is omnipresent and always ready to pounce on her with utter disapprobation and reproof—in fact, to such an extent that death seems to be the lesser evil, the smaller threat, than to be sentenced within. In fact, the loss of approval by the inner judge was being equated with death. Death was an immediate presence and confirmed to her: "If you are guilty, if you do not pass muster before the inner judge, you are guilty of capital punishment (*todesschuldig*), and now you know what that means." She said that during her severe illness she did not have as much anxiety as she had expected. The anxiety appeared only at home. In the hospital and the rehabilitation center, a mild outer authority allowed her to rest and to be kind to herself. In the following, we heard much more about her defiance against this unreasonable figure of power, her father, her own inner judge, her partner, and about the intensity of her rage against it: the conflict between oppression and indignant revolt: "you must" against "I don't want to." But in the face of such irrational inner authority, she can only fail.

The terror of her father must reach very far back: she remembers the terrifying soldier in uniform and boots when he came home on furlough, but also the yearning for a better father later, for the mellowness and understanding he showed when dealing with his grandchildren.

In the fifth session, she starts by saying she had been awakened by a nightmare, followed by strong anxiety. This again against the background of a discrete enduring anxiety and loneliness; "I want to hide (*verkriechen*), to observe the beating of my heart, not go out. But I do everything in spite of it." She had planned for Saturday to drive with her younger brother to the mountains, and also to visit a peasant woman who takes care of their little vacation home and to bring her Christmas presents. She likes very much being together with her brother and was looking forward to the long ride with him, but then she got afraid because there were warnings about icy roads and snow. In this worry she had the dream: "I am with my daughter. She is adult. I kept having to do things for her, but I am under a lot of pressure because I am on call in the hospital. I keep running back and forth."

I interrupt: "Two opposite obligations."

The dream continues: "Suddenly, I am in the clinic, in a dark corridor, everything with tiles. Somebody is lying on a gurney entirely under a linen cover. As I am passing it, surprisingly a hand came out and wanted to grab me. I was horribly frightened and woke up in a panic, with angina feelings (*Herzenge*). It passed after 5–10 minutes. What came to my mind was that after the death of my father I had a dream that my father came out of the coffin and held me."

"So it is clearly a ghost who wants to pull you into death."

"Covered over." (I believe she refers to the body covered by the linen, but also to the disguise.)

"And the fear of death (*Todesangst*) appears in the context of the conflict of conscience about your daughter and the night call."

"This was in fact so then (*es war auch früher real*), and I still have guilt feelings about it."

"*Contradictory loyalties that are being punished by death.* The question is what is *now* the loyalty conflict?"

"I had heard in the evening that the temperature will plummet and that there will be snow and slipperiness (*Glätte*). I wondered whether I should call him and ask to postpone the trip. On the other side, I wanted to go there. It is also a beautiful landscape, and beautiful being together with my brother and bringing the present. I did not want to say No to my brother (*absagen*), he had kept the day open and was prepared for it. I was in conflict, but it was a beautiful experience [the going with him]." She describes the impressions and experiences of the outing more in detail, but reiterates that she did have much anxiety during the trip. He offered to stop for the night, but she did not have her medication with her. "That was the conflict."

"It is also an important inner postulate: to worry about safety, and it escalated from the anxiety in the conflict or the fear of conscience to fear of death."

"But why was it so threatening? Not to please?"

"And being weak. Your first thought after the dream was about your father who threatens you when you are weak."

"For giving in."

"It is worthy of death."

"The worst: worthy of contempt."

"The core of the Nazi-ideology."

"And also of his father; he was terrible, uncannily severe and hard: all was discipline." Parenthetically speaking, the patient's father had a huge fear of his own father and of all authorities, all through life. His conflict between submission and rebellion was covered over by the idealization of Hitler, the consequences of whose racism he appears to have covered over by denial. He had had a Jewish friend and showed great respect for Freud, and was very proud of her when she started studying psychoanalysis. In his sudden rages, there was horrendous power: she saw "glowing red eyes." She continues now: "For him it was hardness against himself, always demanding from himself what is hardest, except for music, that was the only thing, also literature."

"That was victory of form over suffering."

"And weakness was what he despised; failing was the very worst thing."

"So what triggered the dream: by all means not to be weak."

"I would like so much not to go on when I cannot any longer, but then come always the guilt feelings."

Picking up on what I have learned earlier, I ask, "I wonder if there were not also guilt feelings that you did not spend the time on Saturday with your partner."

"That is always a problem. He does not like it at all if I undertake anything with anybody else."

"Here you have the loyalty conflict within you, between your brother and your partner."

"Years ago this was an open conflict about these two [loyalties]. It has abated somewhat. But when we drove off he [her friend] was not friendly, was very curt, and the same when we returned."

"Jealousy is a passion that eagerly seeks what hurts (*Eifersucht ist eine Leidenschaft, die mit Eifer sucht, was Leiden schafft*) [a wordplay attributed to the philosopher Schleiermacher]."

"When I try to be autonomous (*selbständig*)."

"That is the essence of jealousy."

"It always is a battle, and I tend to give in."

"Your father was also somebody jealous."

"He found it self-evident that my mother was only there for him, and she completely submitted to him. She never fought against it. But when he was not there anymore [during the war, then when he was a prisoner], she developed her abilities."

"And afterward went back [to the submission]."

"I often wonder: how can she have made it: with a newborn baby, driven out, in a typhus epidemic, no heat, nothing to eat. Many killed themselves, out of fear of the Russians, many among their friends, whole families, killed themselves. But she was a devout Christian. She tolerated it all and carried us through. I thought: How could she have done this? I had thought she was so weak. We were so identified with father."

"With his judgment. Also toward you he was very possessive."

"Although he had studied pedagogy and psychology he had no idea that a child would not automatically love him. I had not known him, and he expected that I would seek his love and closeness. I was just observing him from afar."

"This intruder."

"Because we were very close to mother, we had much freedom and warmth and closeness with her. And all this stopped immediately. Although I have fought against this, I have internalized a lot of it."

"And it is being repeated in your relationship."

"I am identified with my mother: it is so much more comfortable and simpler not to fight, and yet, it still happens all the time. Not to battle, that is by my head, but I still do battle constantly, within and without." She has just mentioned here her double identification: with the judgmental part of her father and with the masochistic side of her mother, a doubleness continued now: her inner judge and the victim self, the guilty and ashamed self.

I say, "The conflict is only seemingly resolved, it continues within and without, and as trigger to the dream it is: 'With whom should I be, with my brother or my partner?' And this [acute conflict] against that background, and added to it the anxiety about your physical health."

"My partner then withdraws, hardly greets me when I come back. This is the same as when my father said that I am a cold child. I found that very cruel. With that he has struck me very deeply."

"Struck you in the heart."

"Again and again, it was very terrible, a sword into the heart. I had a very close and warm relationship to my brothers and to mother. I could not understand why I suddenly should be cold."

"It was so unfair."

"I probably did believe it because I was cold toward my father. Always this anxiety, it always emerges—that I abandon my partner by going with my brother, the guilt feelings from my childhood."

"And then it goes to the heart, the anxiety about the heart (*Herzangst*). Even if the illness is hardly a symbolic expression, it still seems fatally connected."

"I know heartache also from earlier times, as something psychosomatic, very much with that coldness, that I have a cold heart."

"A heart of stone. This then is the reproach in the background of the dream and the punishment for it. Thus we see four layers of conflict, expressed by the dream: as immediate trigger, the conflict between wanting to go on the trip with your brother, having a good time with him, and the old peasant woman, but against this the physical danger, the safety concerns. Second, the conflict between wanting to be with your brother, but fearing the wrath of your partner. Third, the conflict about your professional obligations while raising your child. And fourth, the closeness to your mother and brothers against being the cold child with your father, the guilt feelings of being 'cold' toward him, and the identification with his hard judgment."

"My father has punished me a lot, but that remark was very horrible for me. I know exactly where I was standing, very disconsolate (*ratlos*). I was nine years old, beaten, defeated: 'Now he has hit me mortally.' And my mother was not loyal toward me. My brothers were friendly toward my father. I was the only one who refused it. And my mother reproached me and increased the feeling that I was false and cold."

"You felt it was so unfair toward a child."

"He thought that I should have wooed him (*um ihn werben*). For him it was self-evident that I would accept him."

"Submission and rebellion (*Unterwerfung und Empörung*)." Again, parenthetically speaking, the amount of suppressed aggression is very important in this. She had actual physical battles, fist fights, with her father.

"Always this battle, and with much anxiety. It was very frightening, very taxing. I was unhappy in his vicinity; I had to make an effort to do [what he wanted]."

"We see how in a simple dream all these layers gain their expression (*zum Worte kommen*)."

"I notice how I was in that situation, when my father told me for the first time: it hits me even today still horribly." I ask her to describe that situation more in detail. "We wanted to go on a walk, on a Sunday. I should take his hand, and I did not want that. I wanted to go with my mother or the brothers."

"Again a loyalty conflict. 'I should but I do not want to. I belong to the mother, not to the father.'"

"He said: 'Then you do not need to come with us at all. You are cold.' I felt very bad, abandoned."

"Rejected."

"A bad human being. When I see myself standing there, I am sad. That has sufficed for an entire life, with this pain, with this annihilation."

"It was an annihilating judgment."

"I keep seeing this hand stretching out from the coffin. And now that in the clinic, the hand that yet tries to pull me across. These experiences from early childhood never cease."

"The early pain continues (*der frühe Schmerz wirkt nach*)."

"One cannot get rid of it for life. It is good that I do feel the pain, also the sadness and do not crush (*erdrücke*) it."

"There are deep relations between the heart disease and this pain."

"I often thought that also. It often does become a heart pain, that the vessels contract."

"A causal connection cannot be dismissed."

Shortly thereafter, it came to a strong fight with her partner, who again could not accept her physical limitations and put them all on anxiety. She experiences his importuning her as abusive. She withdrew in spite and pouting as she had done with her father. But such defiance is a last-ditch protection against shame: "If I let this be done to me I would be ashamed. By withdrawing I have protected my self. But I felt badly about it, as if I had done something forbidden."

"It is the dilemma between shame and guilt."

"I have thought a lot about it: that I feel guilty then. The claim for autonomy is ultimately not permitted. I need to defend it, and it is so hard to defend: 'You are not permitted to do this!'"

A little later I mention a slight variant of this shame-guilt-dilemma: "Shame about failing (about being weak), guilt about the rage in defending yourself. . . . Self-protection is forbidden."

In this case vignette and dialogue the multilayered and complex nature of some of the superego aspects, in her case mostly on the guilt side, but also the intrasystemic superego conflicts, are impressive. It is also important to note to what extent attention to these can be very helpful in short-term focal psychotherapy, not only in long term psychoanalysis.

The Superego Affects

As we have just seen in these sequences, the affects of shame and guilt appear like weapons in the hands of that spirit of self-scorn and self-blame. I only briefly summarize what I have written elsewhere (Wurmser, 1981): I see shame as covering three affective meanings: the anxiety about impending exposure (shame anxiety), the depressive realization that such exposure has occurred (shame depression), and the protective attitude against exposure (shame as reaction formation). Both shame and guilt have a subject pole: the part of the self that is being judged, and an object pole: that authority in front of whom one feels judged. The subject pole may be broadened and externalized; the object pole is typically internalized in the form of that inner authority. The yardstick used for such measurement and judgment may be an ideal image of the self in the case of shame, or that of a code of actions to be committed or omitted in the relationship with others in the case of guilt. In shame it is usually some form of failure, of weakness, of lack of control, in guilt it is rather some abuse of power toward the other, something that hurts and violates others. The aggressive charge in the affect of shame is prominently contempt, depriving that which is judged of all value; in guilt it is rather the wish to inflict pain: anger and hate. Both affects may be defended against with an array of other affects, or with outward aggression in the form of wild rage, or by externalization, that is, with the attempt to turn it around by making the other feel guilty or ashamed, or by projection of the judgmental part: that one feels ridiculed or accused by others; or efforts at massive denial within and lying toward the outside are used, or magical restitution attempted.

I refer also to Lansky's reference to Freud's early concept (in *Studies on Hysteria*, 1893/1895) of the "incompatible idea":

> An "incompatible idea," then, is an idea that, in anticipation of the pain of moral emotions emanating from conflict with the dictates of the conscience, is being banished from consciousness. . . . One major advantage of the model of the "incompatible idea," centering as it does on the psyche contemplating scenes of its own actions, is that it keeps a firm focus on the balance between what one *is* (or is exposed as being) and what one *does or fails to do*—that is to say, such a perspective gives us a splendid balance between moral judgments that involve shame and those that involve guilt. (Lansky, 2005a, p. 870, 872)

As mentioned earlier, there are other important affects directly reflecting the tension between the superego systems of ideals, prohibitions, and commandments and the rest of the personality, but also between these systems: for example, regrets and remorse. But another one stands out because of its importance: the affective sense of justice and especially its reverse: the affective sense of injustice, the burning feeling of resentment. Its French cognate, *ressentiment*, is even more emphatic and has, mainly due to its centrality in the philosophy and psychology of Nietzsche and Scheler, assumed great importance in political philosophy (see chapter 5 in this volume). "Ressentiment" is not simply synonymous with disappointment or insult, with shame and envy, with jealousy and vindictiveness, although all these play a part in it and in fact form the broad foundation on which it rests. Rather it is the sense of unfairness that dwells at its core. The more intensive the claim for justice, the higher the demands, at least originally, toward oneself, but the higher also the claims to receive one's desserts from others. One important consequence of such resentment consists in blaming: the attribution of guilt to the other. It leads to a distortion of the recognition of inner causality: outer and inner conflict are forged into a stereotypical accusation of having been shortchanged (Wurmser, 1997, 1999a, 2000a; 2002, 2003a).

The Functions Covered by the Superego Concept

What are the main functions of the superego? They are:

1. various, partly contradictory sets of expectations, especially moral commands like duty and responsibility, the ego ideal, that is, an ideal image and code of ideal actions, leading values and ideals;
2. the evaluating and judging self-observation;
3. self-criticism and self-condemnation, if there is a shortfall, compared with these expectations;
4. self-approval, self-care, and self-protection;
5. the protection of the inner and outer boundaries, limitations, and barriers; and
6. stabilization of mood and regulation of affects.

How these functions of the superego and their experiential contents are defended against, mostly by denial, and how they return in strongly regressive and distorted form can be seen with particular clarity in compulsive substance abuse, in antisocial behavior, and in perversions (see Léon Wurmser, *Flight from Conscience*, forthcoming).

The values and ideals in the sets of expectations can be divided in at least two large groups of particular psychodynamic importance, and thus, shame and guilt form the basis for two value scales, two systems of what is seen as right and wrong, two ranges of judgment that to some extent contradict each other (I dealt with this in some detail in Wurmser 1999c, pp. 317–18): the values of pride and honor versus those of consideration for the rights of others and acceptance of the needs of others—the parallel scales of shame and guilt values. In the former the fear is of weakness and failure; in the other the fear is of abusing one's power and hurting the other.

The understanding of, and working with the dialectic between guilt and shame, and with that one form of conflict within the superego, is, as the first case vignette showed, psychodynamically particularly helpful and important, but there are other salient conflicts and complementarities

within the moral system, "the superego": those between opposed loyalties, those between contradictory values, commitments, and obligations.

I would like to insert another example illustrative for loyalty conflicts
here.

It is another colleague but one whom I have had for years in treatment,
again mostly by telephone. She is in her mid-fifties, divorced, without
children. Her father had fought in the Wehrmacht in Russia and Poland
and had come back severely disillusioned and bitter, chronically depressed, burdened with nightmares, flashbacks, and chronic headaches.
His parents had been and remained ardent Nazis. There were massive
fights between her parents and the grandparents who, in spite of this,
were partly entrusted with taking care of the child (the younger of two
girls). She has had severely sadomasochistic relationships with men and
is deeply ashamed about her bondage to a partner who keeps humiliating
her and feels himself humiliated by her. He is the dysfunctional son of an
SS man and has very much taken on some of the traits of his abusive father. Her own family has become opposed to her liaison with this man.

It should be added that there are clearly oedipal conflicts, strong jealousy toward her often absent mother and anger at her father, who took
her in his bed when the mother was away, but then kicked her out upon
her return, with some intimation that she was to blame for their closeness
and her tenderness toward him.

I focus here only on one brief excerpt from a session (349; refers to number of session). The patient describes first her shame about the repetitiveness and the back and forth with this partner and goes then on to speak
of the feelings about my Jewishness and her being German, "my guilt
about the Third Reich, the Holocaust." She is reminded of a dream she
had when she came to see me the first time: "I was sitting in the airplane,
and in my hands there were ashes. I was very upset to come to you, and
on my hands, guilt is clinging (*und an meinen Händen klebt die Schuld*),—
that I have taken over the whole thing and I have to expiate this."

"By these fatal relationships."

"And the hope that I can resolve and repair (*gutmachen*) this. And at the
same time it is impossible: I cannot make up for it. The whole old guilt is
weighing down on me."

"And precisely with a man who has so much in common with this
past—an attempt to expiate it by suffering, and it never succeeds." She
mentions that it was important for her selection of going back into treatment that I am Jewish. She confesses some jealousy about a close friend of
hers who had also consulted with me from time to time and who is
daughter of a Holocaust survivor: "You would have to prefer her over
me." And then she bursts out: "How the grandparents have dragged me
into a loyalty conflict, and my father also! They dealt with it on my back,

their ideological fights—what was true and what not! They had maintained the old ideas of the Stürmer. I was eight to ten years old. And I believed them. That I could play with those thoughts as a child! That I could have had doubts! If that does not mean a big guilt in my life?! What would have become of me if I had lived during that time? Could they have infiltrated me that way also?"

"Certainly. We all are much influenced by propaganda."

"There is a lot of guilt and shame." She talks then again about the man she is bound to and thinks: "If I could liberate myself from him—but that I am not allowed to be happier than my father, that I also have to carry my part of suffering. Mine is nothing, compared to what others have suffered." She continues talking about how her partner has turned his aggression against himself, as self-punishment, and that this is exactly what she is now doing, that she is carrying her father's aggression and guilt. "And this together with my anger at him because he has burdened me with it, and guilty that I do not even want to carry this suffering with him. . . . Now it is so with the friend: between him and me there is a struggle who the perpetrator (*Täter*) is, because he can under no circumstances be the perpetrator. The horrible thing is that through him this SS father torments me."

"And the Nazi grandfather."

"And this is my real atonement."

"And the judge within you embodies these persons—the guilt and the shame with which you hammer down on you. And this is then repeated on the outside."

"This is a central connection. I see the picture that my father showed me from the 'Yellow Star': these emaciated human beings on the floor! Where he remonstrated with me: 'You traitor! You waste a thought on what your grandparents tell you that there is nothing about these old wives tales [i.e., about the atrocities]! Here we have the proofs!' There was abysmal shame that I could spend a thought on that the grandparents could be right. And at the same time I had burdened myself with a whole lot of guilt because it had been possible for me to believe in it."

"And now you constantly endeavor to wash off this guilt and shame by suffering."

"And at the same time to put myself into new humiliation." She feels relieved about having talked about this.

The Origins of the Superego

From outside our field, I adduce two cursory considerations: There is now solid neurophysiologic evidence for the separate emergence of what we call the superego. Based on the current state of research, Gerhard Roth

sees the "ego" or "self" as "a bundle of different states," located in various, but localizable networks in the brain and developing at different
times during infancy and childhood. He distinguishes eight such "ego
states" or selves (in German he actually uses the word "Ich," or ego):

1. the body self, the sense of "my body";
2. the localizing ego, the self sensing its location in space;
3. the "perspectival ego," the sense of being the center of one's own
   world of experience;
4. the ego as the subject of experience, the "self-ness" of ideas, perceptions, feelings, etc.;
5. the "control or authorship ego," the sense of being the cause and the
   one in control of one's thoughts and actions;
6. the "autobiographic ego," the sense of inner continuity;
7. the self-reflecting ego; and
8. the ethical ego or conscience, the sense of having an inner agency or
   authority ("Instanz") that tells or orders what to do or to leave (p.
   326). This "ethical-moral ego" is found in the orbitofrontal cortex; is
   the last of the ego systems to mature fully, that process beginning in
   adolescence at about age 16; and functions to strongly inhibit the
   amygdala, the seat of the drives. Roth thus confirms "that the
   Freudian superego has several roots, some conscious, some unconscious," the latter rooted in the amygdala (the memory of emotional
   experience), the former in the orbitofrontal cortex (ibid., pp. 375–76).

There is also increasing evidence that the beginnings of "moral systems" can be inferred in apes and monkeys (Flack and de Waal, 2000; see
also Kummer 1977/1978), although there is much controversy about the
interpretation of the respective observations:

> Many nonhuman primates . . . have similar methods to humans for resolv-
> ing, managing, and preventing conflicts of interests within their groups.
> Such methods, which include reciprocity and food sharing, reconciliation,
> consolation, conflict intervention, and mediation, are the very building
> blocks of moral systems in that they are based on and facilitate cohesion
> among individuals and reflect a concerted effort by community members to
> find shared solutions to social conflict . . . advanced methods of resource dis-
> tribution and conflict resolution seem to require or make use of traits such as
> the capacity for empathy, sympathy, and sometimes even community con-
> cern (Flack and de Waal, 2000).

The authors add a "sense of justice" among the mechanisms that allow
cooperation even contrary to independent individual interests. Most important is reciprocity: "some form of calculated reciprocity is present in

primate social systems. . . . The existence of such rules and, more signif-
icantly, of a set of expectations, essentially reflects a sense of social regu-
larity, and may be a precursor to the human sense of justice" (Flack and
de Waal, 2000). They powerfully conclude that

> the research on the natural history and social behavior of our nonhuman pri-
> mate relatives illustrates how both our capacity and tendency to pursue our
> independent interests and our capacity and tendency to pursue shared inter-
> ests are natural and important, at least from the biological point of view. . . .
> This suggests that morality was not *devised* to subjugate the independent in-
> terests of individuals. Rather, a moral system *emerged* out of the interaction of
> the two sets of interests, thus providing a way to express both.

Both sets of studies, the brain development and the primate research, indicate, roughly speaking, the double origin of what we consider superego
functions in human beings: "1. the emotional reaction and intuition of
each individual that jumpstart the moral process, . . . [and] 2. the cogni-
tive-rational evaluations that enable the individual to determine what is
right" (Flack and de Waal; for a critical view see Kummer's comments in
the discussion of Flack and de Waal 2000, pp. 48–51).

If we turn now to psychoanalytic study, the "normal" superego—the
ethical-moral systems with their inherent polarities, conflicts, and compromise formations between ideals and values—is the outcome of complex developmental processes relying much on identification, idealization, introjection, and turning of aggression against the self. The hallmark
of normality is the sense of inner freedom: the more-or-less conscious
weighing of the inner options; the hallmark of pathology is its compulsiveness, the sense of inner unfreedom, its rigidity and absoluteness (Kubie, 1954; Wurmser, 1978/1995, 2000a). It appears that one fundamental
capability is of overriding presupposition for the development and well-
functioning of an "ethical-moral ego system" and for ideal formation: the
ability to put oneself into the other's feeling state, a kind of basic empathy for the other's joy and suffering, for the other's pleasure and displeasure. As basis for a "normal superego," it seems that the identification
with the other's pain may at least be as important as the introjection of the
other's approval and disapproval.

TRAUMA, AFFECT DYSREGULATION, AND MORAL
MASOCHISM IN THE GENESIS OF THE ARCHAIC SUPEREGO

In what follows, I focus on what we can infer from our psychoanalytic
and psychotherapeutic experience about the ontogenetic background,
specifically in regard to the archaic forms observed in the severe neu-

roses (cf. Wurmser 2003a and 2003b for two, more detailed case illustrations).

I do not claim at all that traumatization is the background to the development of what we subsume under the superego; but the origins of the archaic form so dominant in the severe neuroses (even in the "antisocial" personalities that seem to lack it) can best be analyzed as reaction to multiple severe traumatization and thus may give us some indications, albeit in exaggerated form, what its origins in general are (Wurmser, 2000a). The "normal" superego lacks this extreme peremptoriness and absoluteness and may largely verge into self-controlling ego-functions—the difference being between a dominance of inner compulsion and a dominance of inner freedom.

In the empirical work separately presented by the German authors Krause (1997–1998) and Fischer and Riedesser (2003), the concept of cumulative traumatizations assumes particular prominence, especially traumatizations that Gottfried Fischer (Cologne) and Riedesser (Hamburg) in their textbook call "relational traumata." Krause mentions that in 90 percent of the biographies of severe personality disorders, especially of "borderline" conditions, there exist severest traumatizations in childhood. He stresses the complementarity of within and without: "Traumata are always consequence of the interaction between the conditions of the surroundings and of the learning individual's capacity of working it through" (vol. 1, p. 40; also vol. 2, p. 88, my translations). Similarly, in their standard textbook of psychotraumatology, Fischer and Riedesser define trauma "as a vital experience of discrepancy between threatening situational factors and the individual's abilities of mastery, a discrepancy that is accompanied by feelings of helplessness and unprotected exposure and thus effects a lasting shock in the understanding of self and world" (p. 82); they reject therefore the term *"post*traumatic stress disorder" and replace it with *"(basal) psychotraumatic stress syndrome"* (pp. 46, 372). Trauma is an ongoing process, not simply an external event (p. 46), and they distinguish shock trauma from cumulative trauma.

The theoretical and practical omission of conflict are considered by all three authors a severe error. Trauma and conflict, or attachment (or object relations) and conflict, determine each other; they are mutually complementary concepts.

The three dimensions of the "basal psychotraumatic stress syndrome" are, according to Fischer and Riedesser and following Mardi Horowitz's (1986) research: "intrusive memory images, denial/avoidance, and the physiologic level of stimulation" (Fischer and Riedesser, p. 47). The extreme form of denial/avoidance is a "frozen state," the extreme form of the intrusion component is "an agitated state of overstimulation and of being helplessly flooded by traumatic stimuli and memories" (p. 47).

Extreme variants of the physiologic component of overstimulation are long-lasting forms with physical illness (p. 48). A whole spectrum of phenomena belongs to the syndrome, particularly dissociative processes. Of special interest is the individually specific *"trauma compensatory scheme,"* that should prevent the recurrence of the traumata. The breakdown of such compensatory mechanisms is the "central site of fracture" in the dynamic of later trauma (p. 58). If trauma is reduced to inner conflict, the patient is not being done justice, but in turn the traumatic process always centrally involves inner conflict (pp. 59, 63–64). It is especially valuable that the authors single out "relational traumata (*Beziehungstraumen*)," in particular, persistent double-bind messages that leave the subject completely entrapped. The authors also call it an "orientation trauma"—a confusion of cognitive categories (p. 70). These forms of trauma are at least as important as gross traumatization by sexual abuse and violence and cause a deep sense of shame and guilt.

Time does not heal all wounds.

> Traumatic situations end not according to objective time and when the traumatic event has past, . . . but only when the destroyed interpersonal and ethical relationship has been reestablished by acknowledgment of causation and guilt. . . . Recognition of guilt and reparation, but also questions of atonement and punishment are crucial. (p. 75)

"The 'revolution' of Freud's trauma concept from energy trauma to information trauma has been, largely unnoticed . . . , carried out by Mardi Horowitz," write Fischer and Riedesser (2003, p. 89). The reorganization of such discrepancy in information requires long time inner work (p. 90).

As already mentioned, of great importance in the authors' understanding is the "trauma compensatory scheme," "the conflict between trauma and compensation" (p. 130), largely unconscious illusionary constructs as defense against what happened and might recur, countermodels or "retrospective prevention," for example, "If I had been better, the parents would not have beaten me" or a constant endeavor to help and protect others—the omnipotence of responsibility, as I call it (p. 101). "Therefore, there exists a dynamic tension and a central conflict in the traumatic process between operations of trauma scheme and trauma compensatory scheme (or partial schemes)" (p. 102). One such scheme might be the "disillusionment scheme," a kind of negative ontology: "The world is unreliable and deceptive; you are unable to defend yourself; you are to blame for the entire disaster that hit you" (p. 102). Both sides in this largely unconscious dynamic tension show up in various compromise formations: for example, both overwhelming affect and interrupted rudiments of actions (trauma scheme) and choice of an area where control can be exerted (compensatory scheme). An example is anorexia, where the control over the taking of food gives at least symbolic control over relational trauma. Part of such trauma compensatory actions may be self-medication, and hence, addiction (p. 125). Conflicts and compromise formations vary between different dissociative states, or "partial personalities" (p. 111). The splitting may dissociate the traumatic experience vertically, into separation of various levels, or horizontally into separately held scenes and compartments of the "revolving stage" (p. 115).

As effect of physiological traumatogenic changes, there may be according to some a biologically caused "addiction to trauma" (van der Kolk, 1996, 1998). Fischer and Riedesser talk about "traumatophilia"—the masochistic reenactment of traumatic situations with the aim of turning passive into active. One version of this is well described when the parents demand that the child fulfill "spontaneously" their demands: "Since my own needs are not *my* needs (but those of the parents), I am only then myself when I act against my spontaneous needs, e.g. by neglecting myself, damaging my body and lastly by annihilating my body in a suicide attempt." In such formulations, the paradoxical trauma compensatory response to the traumatic process can be recognized (Fischer and Riedesser, 2003, p. 163). Also the "splitting" in good-and-evil representations is due to trauma compensatory activity (p. 302).

Another, individually, socially, and historically particularly important countermodel to the trauma scheme is the "glorification of power and violence and the contempt of weakness:" "A reenactment of traumatic experience on a huge scale could be observed in Europe between the two world wars. It was supported by a pseudoscientifically rationalized minimizing of trauma by German psychiatry." Instead of the war traumatizations being taken seriously, their consequences were subsumed under *"Rentenneurose"* (behavior due to the wish to be financially compensated) and the patients treated as malingerers and dodgers.

> This cult of strength and of the 'invincible genetic inheritance' ('what does not kill me, makes me harder') was being consistently continued in the Nazi-ideology and brought to a delusional peak. With the cult of strength and the denial of one's own weakness and vulnerability went the disdain and extrusion of the 'weak' and the 'genetically inferior', up to their physical elimination. At the same time, in a 'trauma compensatory' undertaking of gigantic proportions, Germany threw itself into the Second World War, in a war lastly against the entire world. (p. 168)

Thus, we may view trauma also as an overwhelming, unsolvable external conflict between self and environment, that leads to a conscious but unsolvable inner conflict. The affects battling each other overwhelm the capacity of the ego to master them, a failure that leads to the split between the groups of ideas, to the act of making the connections unconscious, about which Freud originally was speaking (1893/1895).

Severe, repeated traumatization means that every emotional experience resonates as if it were the recurrence of the trauma. It leads to the standstill, usually partial, of affective development: the differentiation, verbalization, and desomatization of the emotions are blocked, as Henry Krystal has so well described. Thus in traumatization, by definition, the feelings, once roused, very rapidly become overwhelming and get out of control; they are global ("dedifferentiated"), beyond symbolization ("deverbalized"), and are experienced as if they were physical ("resomatized"). According to Krystal, these three concepts of dedifferentiation, deverbalization, or hyposymbolization, and that of resomatization, represent affect regression (Krystal, 1988, 1998).

But there is something else of great importance, especially in the recurrent traumatization in childhood: These affects tend to appear in sexualized form. Sexualization is an archaic defense set up to regulate affect (Fraiberg, 1982; Coen, 1981, 1985). The affect flooding, combined with this very primordial defense by sexualization, leads to an overwhelming sense of humiliation and embarrassment: Not to have any control over one's own emotional life is just as shaming as the loss of sphincter control, if not more so. Aggressive wishes are then used to reestablish control, a form of further archaic defense to deal preventively with a further spiraling out of control, an important way of turning passive into active.

The result of such severe disturbance of affect regulation is an archaic equation we typically encounter in the intensive, long-term treatment of the severe neuroses. The following five states and contents are equated: (1) overstimulation by something on the outside which is experienced as traumatic, as intolerable, and to which one feels helplessly, passively exposed; (2) a too much of an affect of any kind, overwhelming, but usually contradictory feelings, the sense of bursting, "I cannot stand it anymore," the traumatic state (that inner state of passivity); (3) something devouring, consuming, that is, the imagery of orality, like rapacious animals or elements (fire, floods); (4) sexual excitement; and (5) aggressive fantasies and of violence, even cruelty (see also Shengold, 1989). Each of the five may be an entrance point into the equation.

Losing control over the affects, the collapse of affect regulation and the conflict between global, but opposing affects, is indeed a primary danger, evoking a most profound sense of helplessness, of "fragmentation" and "splitting," and thus deepening in circular form the basic anxiety and shame. In fact, the loss of control over one's affects is a primary, elemental form of shame, no less so than the loss of control over the sphincters or the motor functions. This archaic equation of traumatogenic affective storms, sexualization, and aggression is deeply frightening and humiliating, calls for equally global defenses, and eventually to massive counter-actions by the superego, in the form of pervasive and global forms of guilt and shame: "and conscience, turned tyrant, held passion by the throat" (Brontë, *Jane Eyre*, 1847/1994, vol. 3, p. 238)—what we know as moral masochism. A very specific aspect of this is of course the well-known aim of warding off aggression. Inderbitzin and Levy (1998) noted to what extent severe traumatization leads to massive inner conflicts about aggression. Thus, the overpowering superego has to serve as a necessary defensive barrier against the intolerably dangerous own aggressions. This is done by the readily observable defense of turning the rage, the hate, and especially the contempt against the own self.

There are, of course, many forms of traumatization, but of special importance is what we may call "soul blindness" and "soul murder": "Soul blindness" is a systematic, chronic disregard for the emotional needs and expressions of the child (or, more generally, of other people), a peculiar blindness to the individuality and hostility to the autonomy of the child (or one's fellow). It shows itself as the peculiar dehumanization of the other person, as what Francis Brouček (1991) has called "objectification" and postulated as the core of the shame experience. Put differently, soul blindness is a severe form of lack of empathy. As to "soul murder," Shengold (1989) defines it as "the deliberate attempt to eradicate or compromise the separate identity of another person . . . depriving the victim of the ability to feel joy and love as a separate person" (p. 2). It stands "for a certain category of traumatic experience: instances of repetitive and chronic overstimulation, alternating with emotional deprivation, that are deliberately brought about by another individual" (p. 16). The first term refers to something that is too little, the second to something that is too much; yet they cannot be clearly separated and belong also clinically closely together. Also, as already mentioned, trauma and inner conflict are complementary concepts.

I summarize the pathogenetic sequence that may be valid for most of the severe neuroses.

1) A series of *traumata* consisting of factual helplessness in the face of very severe threats, usually from the outside (including external conflicts of loyalty).
2) Caused by these traumata, *affect storms*, feelings like fear, panic, rage, despair, the control of which collapses, or the anxiety about the likelihood that all affects, especially rage, and the drive impulses connected with them, could escape control at any minor provocation.
3) An *archaic, resentment-ridden superego*, which has the task to restrain those emotional storms and drive actions with excessively strict and absolutely rigid control. Its demands are just as *absolute* as the danger

of helplessness in the affective storms is *total* and as the dangers of retribution appear overwhelming. The feelings of guilt, of shame, and of despair are therefore of the most radical nature and often can be obeyed only with the sacrifice of one's own life. At the same time, the yearning for an ideal that could offer protection against such a merciless conscience, is overmastering, the necessity of idealization is compelling, yet the disappointment comes without fail.

4) The measures of defense toward the inside and the outside are correspondingly rigorous, ruthless, and absolute—be they now in the form of turning against the own person, be it as turning from passive to active, be they as withdrawal and giving up of all interest, be it as global denial. The narcissistic fantasies, claims, and character attitudes are taken into service so that they would offer shelter against that unbearable self-condemnation. *Clinical narcissism is therefore a multiform defense strategy against a superego that rules with absoluteness.* Behind the shining façade of the "grandiose self" and of the idealization of the other, an entire hidden world is alive in dramatic motion, with many inner players, in many stories and sagas and in repetitive scenes of inner strife and reconciliation. In turn, *clinical masochism has at its core the fantasy of omnipotence, that is, a narcissistic conviction,* itself a defense structure protecting against traumatic helplessness and the accompanying affect regression and conflicts between global affects (cf. Novick and Novick, 1996a).

THE ROOTS OF THE ARCHAIC SUPEREGO

The world of absoluteness is a world of total affects, of total defense, and of a totalitarian conscience. Resulting from this, the fantasy world of omnipotence and total helplessness and the reality world of competence, respect, and love are treated as equivalent and alternately seen as real and concrete or as estranged (see Novick and Novick, 1996a, 1996b); they mean No and Yes, and thus create the confusion and the altered state of consciousness, the state of trance. It is because of those total affects and forms of defense, that in the states of dissociation, of "trance," the personality seems to disintegrate into small pieces, into fragments.

Besides this archaic defense against overwhelming, traumatogenic affects and impulses, much of the archaic nature of the authoritarian superego is readily understood and intuitively grasped as resulting from the introjection of cruel parental imagos. The patients are often very quick to blame the harshness and unreasonableness of their inner judge, its contempt and resentment on similar traits in the outer authorities they had, and often still have to contend with. Yet this is only a part of the story, and commonly not a very useful one as insight.

Furthermore and third, a good part of this hypertrophy of the super-ego can be understood as resulting from the *omnipotence of responsibility* as defense against the traumatic helplessness: "It is completely up to me to prevent all these horrors. If it happens again, it is all my fault, my guilt is total."

And then there is fourth a process we could call the "symbiotic circle." Every separateness is experienced, both subjectively and usually also accurately as family reality, as if it were something annihilating, murderous. Abandoning the other means to injure, if not to kill her or him. Accordingly, being abandoned is equated with unbearable pain or death. This means that with every step of independence one feels burdened with great guilt; every self-willedness, every success has to be punished as great temerity, first from the outside, then from within. Disobedience and defiance are declared mortal sins. This is what we can call "separation guilt." If one retreats from this daring step and submits to the binding other, one loses one's own self, one's dignity, one's identity. However, sacrificing one's own self in order to preserve a human relationship is looked at with withering self-contempt. The victim-self, the passive dependent self, is looked at with deep disgust, with searing shame. Sooner or later, this *dependency shame* has to lead to open or hidden rage and to defiance, to renewed breaking away, and thus the circle is closed.

To summarize this part: The archaic superego in its absoluteness has to serve as primitive affect regulation. It is an effective defense, but at immense costs. The aggression necessary for it, namely as the most massive self-condemnation, is easily turned from within to without—as hatred, as contempt, and above all as blame. In this externalization there are two possibilities: either the superego part is seen on the outside: "You despise me, you don't want to have anything to do with me, because I am bad and dumb," or it is the victim part of the self, the one condemned, the shame self or the guilt-laden self, that is seen on the outside: "It is all your fault! You do not help me. You are unable. Shame on you! It is an impudence what you have done to me! I will press charges against you!" The more we assume, in our technique, a stance of authority, the more we give substance and credence to the ubiquitous superego transference and tend to get enmeshed in very important transference-countertransference enactments of these superego figures, functions, and affects.

But something more needs to be said about the role of shame and its origin—this cardinal superego affect and a fifth major source for the (archaic) superego. I will deal with this in the next chapter.

THE ANSWER TO THE INITIAL QUESTION: "SUPEREGO" AS ABSTRACT SYMBOL FOR "CONSCIENCE," "INNER JUDGE," "MORAL SYSTEM," "VALUE HIERARCHY"

In short, the superego has become a great and encompassing symbol that cannot be abolished without a lot of concern. It is a symbol for the subjective experience of moral systems, as an inner part-person in conflict with other parts, a symbol for their various functions, affects, and contents, and a symbol for their objective genesis as discovered in introspective work and observation of children. It is neither a mythical symbol nor one usable in a natural science framework, but rather like an important literary symbol (as, e.g., in "the tragic sense of life" or "tragic vision"), or a philosophical symbol, like "the self" or "the object"—all, as we know, also appropriated by psychoanalysis. As with every symbol, we have to guard against its reification—to treat it as if it were a substantial entity. Rather, it is an ordering principle. Its images, like "conscience," "inner judge," "inner demon," are, however, mental contents of great evocativeness and of consistent importance through all our clinical and introspective work, I would say, of cardinal importance in every hour of my work with patients.

A concluding thought to the topic of the "annihilating force of absoluteness" in the form of an interpretation of the double story of creation in Genesis chapters 1 and 2. In the first version, 1.1, it is said: "God [Elohim] created heaven and earth." According to the understanding of the rabbis, the name Elohim stands for God as judge; in fact, in the Torah "elohim" is sometimes used for human judges as well. In the second version, 2.4, we read: "YHWH Elohim made the earth and heaven." (The Tetragrammaton YHWH itself is not pronounced in the Jewish tradition, but alluded to by "Adonai," my Lord, or "hashem," the Name). God's name YHWH stands, however, for mercy, compassion. The medieval commentator Rashi explains this doubleness: "At first it entered God's mind to create it [the world] in the dimension of justice (*bemidát haddín*), but he saw that the world could not endure, and he gave precedence to the dimension of mercy (*middát rachamím*) and joined it to the dimension of justice."

The following Midrash comments:

YHWH Elohim: This may be compared to a king who had some empty glasses. Said the king: If I pour hot water into them, they will burst; if cold, they will contract [and snap]. What then did the king do? He mixed hot and cold water and poured it into them, and so they remained [unbroken]. Just so, said the Holy one, blessed be He: "If I create the world in the dimension of mercy alone, its sins will be great; in the dimension of justice alone, the world cannot exist. Hence I will create it in the dimension of judgment and in the dimension of mercy, and may it then stand!" (*Midrash Rabbah*, 1983, vol. 1, p. 99)

I end this chapter with some words from the "little note" (*Tzettel Katan*) of Elimelech from Lyzensk (died 1786):

The Chassid "should each time tell all the bad thoughts and obsessions to his teacher in God's way and also to his faithful friend, the *chaver ne'eman*, thoughts that are directed against the Holy Torah which the Evil Drive (*yetzer haRa*) lets rise to his brain and his heart, be that at the time of Torah learning or of prayer, be that when he lies down on his bed or in the middle of the day, and he should not hide anything out of shame. And it happens by his telling all those things which he brings forth out of his energy towards action, that this breaks the power of the Evil Drive, so that another time, when he is away from the good counsel that he could get from his friend, it cannot overwhelm him that much. This counsel however is the path to God and something wonderful."[1]

NOTE

1. I am grateful to Mr. M. Weiss for having made me aware of this passage.

2

"The Wall of Stone"—Broken Self and Broken Reality

MAGIC TRANSFORMATION

With the help of the following case study, I would like to introduce an important polarity of human experience, one that is more of a literary and phenomenological than a psychodynamic nature: the antithesis of *magic transformation* and *tragic transformation*.

Our fairy tales and myths, our dreams and fantasies live from the wishes that magically we could change ourselves and the world we live in. The subject of enchantment delights us, but it also may indicate foreboding, if not terror, as when we hear the myth of Kirke in the *Odyssey*, Grimm's fairy tale "Jorinde and Joringel," or Prospero's "my ending is despair."

It is no less true that in almost every hour of psychotherapeutic or psychoanalytic work we encounter this hope for magical transformation that our patients set in various objects in the outside: in drugs, in money, in gambling, television, success, food, in our presence or in symbiotic union with others, and especially also in sexual gratification or religious ritual.

They feel supported in their hope for magical transformation by the spirit of our civilization. The expectation is ubiquitous that complicated problems could be resolved by simple technical means: a profuse assortment of medications, a panoply of abbreviated treatment approaches or of technical, even surgical manipulations. What would require patient labor, what would call out for self-confrontation with the painful conflicts of being human, is being replaced by quick methods, shortcuts, and the incessant request for ostensibly more cost-efficient measures. Alas, what is faster is not necessarily more effective. We are reminded of Mencken's words: "There is always an easy solution to every human problem—neat, plausible and wrong" (as quoted by the *Baltimore Sun*, February 28, 1988).

Freud writes in *Totem and Taboo* (1912), "Magic has to serve the most varied purposes—it must subject natural phenomena to the will of man, it must protect the individual from his enemies and from dangers and it must give him power to injure his enemies." Its modus operandi lies in "mistaking an ideal connection for a real one" (p. 79). It is based on "an immense belief [by primitive man] in the power of his wishes" (p. 83). "The principle governing magic, the technique of the animistic mode of thinking, is the principle of the 'omnipotence of thought'" (p. 85).

In the context of this book, I speak of course not literally about such magic, but about magical thinking in a metaphorical and broadened sense, namely the clinically observable ways in which one alters the perception of reality on the basis of wish, anxiety, and defense and then expects to achieve one's aims in such altered reality by concrete, technical means—on the outside, or rather: in an experience of self and world where the boundaries between inside and outside are not reliably maintained anymore, but are mystifyingly lifted or blurred. The defense against separateness and difference will be studied in many permutations.

An especially important hoped-for magical transformation can be found in perverse sexual activities which should, as experience shows time and again, protect against massive self-condemnation and thus indirectly defend against the frighteningly overwhelming primary affects behind that hypertrophy of the superego. It plays a cardinal role in what has aptly been called "character perversion" where, in Arlow's words, "the distortion of behavior or character takes the place of what had once been a perversion or a perverse trend." It is particularly fetishism with its doubleness of acknowledgment and denial of the anatomical difference and the warding off of castration anxiety that serves for Arlow as paradigm. Later authors, like Cooper, Renik, Grossman, Bach, and Reed, extended the concept, partly by including other traumatic perceptions that are being warded off by character traits of such splitting, partly by also including sadomasochistic and exhibitionistic forms of conflict solution. For example, Reed writes, "sexual gratification is used in the service of a defensive effort to avoid certain external perceptions" (Reed, 1997, p. 1154). Reed speaks in fact of the analytic process having become a magic action whereby the analysand transforms the analyst's intervention about his avoidances into a fetish that unconsciously contradicts his worry.

An extreme version of magical transformation can be seen in strongly regressed patients where what is alive appears dead, and what is dead appears alive. Artificial things turn into terrifying bugbears; the own self and others seem empty, meaningless, dead. Benedetti (1983/1987) has described this impressively in *Todeslandschaften der Seele* (Death Landscapes of the Soul) in regard to psychotic patients, but we can encounter this in the severe neuroses as well, as the expression of massive anxiety in conflict and about trauma.

In mythical form we know this concept of magic transformation from Ovid's *Metamorphoses*, in literary form from Ibsen's *When We Dead Awaken*, from Tolstoy's *Resurrection*, and from Kafka's *Die Verwandlung* (*The Metamorphosis*).

Yet, there is a counterpart to this concept of magic transformation.

TRAGIC TRANSFORMATION

The term "tragic transformation" was used by George Eliot, the great English author of the mid-nineteenth century and—beside Shakespeare, Goethe, Ibsen, Dostoyevsky, and Nietzsche—one of the great explorers of inner conflict and with that one of the predecessors of Freud. She employs the word in her last great novel, *Daniel Deronda*, particularly in regard to one of the two protagonists, Gwendolen Harleth. It is mentioned just in passing: Daniel Deronda is "awaiting the entrance of a young creature whose life had also been undergoing a transformation—a *tragic transformation* towards a wavering result, in which he felt with apprehensiveness that his own action was still bound up" (1876/1982, p. 836, emphasis added). I give just a few select quotes that follow this term and may illuminate it partly:

Mighty Love had laid his hand upon her; but what had he demanded of her? Acceptance of rebuke—the hard task of self-change—confession—endurance. (p. 842)

In fact, poor Gwendolen's memory had been stunned, and all outside the lava-lit track of her troubled conscience, and her effort to get deliverance from it, lay for her in dim forgetfulness. (p. 843)

That was the sort of crisis which was at this moment beginning in Gwendolen's small life: she was for the first time feeling the pressure of a vast mysterious movement, for the first time being dislodged from her supremacy in her own world, and getting a sense that her horizon was but a dipping onward of an existence with which her own was revolving. All the troubles of her wifehood and widowhood had still left her with the implicit impression which had accompanied her from childhood, that whatever surrounded her was somehow specially for her. (p. 876)

What George Eliot means by "tragic transformation" is therefore not, as our common usage would indicate, something sad, but a process of profound change brought about by suffering, through massive inner conflict (particularly conflicts of conscience), through insight, and through action, or active work, on behalf of somebody else or in the service of a great cause. The magical words spoken by (her "protoanalyst") Daniel Deronda eventually will complete her tragic transformation: "You can, you will, be among the best of women, such as make others glad that they were born" (p. 840). She repeats them herself: "I have remembered your words—that I may live to be one of the best of women, who makes others glad that they were born" (p. 882).

Originally, this tragic transformation is the "πάθει μάθος (pathei mathos)—learning through suffering" of Aeschylus (*Agamemnon*, v. 177).

Tragic transformation is a major theme of Greek tragedy as well as of the tragic plays of Shakespeare, Schiller, and Ibsen, of the tragic operas of Verdi, and more generally of the major literary works of the end of the nineteenth and the beginning of the twentieth century. Thus, the Russian poet and critic Ivanov uses the term "novel-tragedy" for Dostoyevsky's five large novels. In the words of Mochulsky, "Ivanov analyzes Dostoyevsky's novels in the light of classical and Shakespearean tragedy and demonstrates how his purposes, construction, devices, and the ultimate effects produced by his work follow the *patterns of tragic rhythm: suffering, death, and rebirth through purification*" (1947/1967, p. xviii, emphasis added). This tragic worldview that underlies much of what I am going to present suddenly and brutally imposed itself upon all of us in our daily lives on September 11, 2001.

The four steps of inner and often also outer suffering; of inner and also outer conflicts; of deeply affecting, even shocking insight; and of transforming this knowledge into an activity that is directed at others, that in the main has a serving function, also indicate what the essential process of change in an effective psychoanalysis or psychoanalytically oriented psychotherapy consists of.

Thus, the following studies revolve largely around a special type of magic transformation: the doubling of self and reality under the impact of massive traumatization, and the process of profound inner change during psychoanalytic treatment as a form of tragic transformation. They use for this purpose a number of detailed case illustrations where the dynamics of such a split in experiencing reality and the grave issues of magical and tragical transformation could be understood with dramatic poignancy. The one-sidedness of some of the case descriptions is outweighed by the almost poetic force in the self-recognition and self-presentation of the patients in their individuality and in their own specific creativity as emerging from the psychoanalytic dialogue. At the same time, many of the insights speak almost for themselves, without being in need of much theorizing, and yet are characteristic for many other patients with severe neuroses and massive traumatization. Still I will interweave the case excerpts with necessary theoretical digressions and, as in my earlier works, with literary examples that in different metaphors explore the same inner issues, often precisely from the vantage point of inner conflict.

SPLITTING OF EGO AND SUPEREGO IN SEVERELY TRAUMATIZED PATIENTS

In Dostoyevsky's *Adolescent*, one of the protagonists, Versílov, says:

> You know I have the impression that I'm splitting into two [*razdváyivayus'*]. . . . Really, I'm sort of split into two, mentally that is, and I'm terribly afraid of it. It feels as though my double [*dvojník*] is standing here next to me. And while I myself am perfectly lucid and reasonable, my double wants to do something incongruous, sometimes something extremely funny. . . . God knows why you want it; in fact, you want it without wanting it [*njékhotya khotítye*]; you resist your wanting with all your strength. (1874, English p. 508; Russian pp. 499–500)

Right after this he smashes an icon in an impulsive, yet preannounced outburst into two pieces, thus symbolizing externally the inner process.

Dostoyevsky's biographer, Mochulsky, comments: "Duality, antinomy of soul, is the final word about him [Arkady, the Adolescent] and about Versílov [his father]. However, they are not the exception, but the rule. *Every human consciousness is inwardly contradictory*" (1947/1967, p. 517).

Another quote from Dostoyevsky, this time from *The Demons*:

> As the disgraced old man Stěpan Věrchověnsky wanders out into the firered morning and encounters Liza who rushes to the place of fire and murder and towards her own death, he tells her under tears: "*I've now broken myself in two* [*tepěr' ja razbil sebjá popolám*]: there—a madman [*bezuměc*] who dreamed of soaring up into the sky, *vingt-deux ans*! Here—a crushed and frozen old man, a tutor." (1872, Russian p. 487; English pp. 537–38, emphasis added)

These are literary prototypes for clinical experiences. In many patients with severe neuroses, we encounter something like a broken identity, a split self and a fractured experience of the world. In some, it comes to a full-fledged dissociation and thus to the phenomenology of the multiple personality. As is well known, it is precisely the occurrence of such deep disruptions of identity and the underlying polarizations in extreme affects and value judgments that have been made into the criterion for "border-line pathology." Often placing these patients in that special and very broad category leads to the view that the therapy has to be radically altered in the direction of a much more confronting and interactive mode; they are seen as transitions to psychoses, and their dynamics are reduced by some to those of the various psychoses.

On the other side, it is also evident how important and extensive severe traumatization, usually throughout childhood, has been in leading up to such a "double reality." Often this causality is put in opposition to the explanation by inner conflict. In fact, traumata and inner conflict are always complementary; they are not an Either/Or. Those traumata are usually panphasic; they accompany the youth of these patients through all the developmental stages and continue their mysterious drumbeat into the present. Ultimately, this strange repetition, this fateful compulsion, forces itself into the center of our therapeutic effort.

However, when we intensively work with these patients, with a psychoanalytic approach that entails only few modifications, we find that these "splits," these experiences of doubleness, occur in many forms of neurosis and may often and fairly rapidly open themselves up to an understanding of manifold severe, unsolved, inner conflicts. This happens if, dependent on the type of neurosis, we pay particular attention to the main forms of defense and of superego aspects, both within and outside the transference (A. Freud, 1936; Gray, 1994). It is crucial that we see such "splits" as the result of complex defensive processes, not as expression of a fundamental, irreducible psychic element. Something similar holds true for "masochism," "aggression," and "narcissism": they are indeed important and helpful descriptive terms, but they are by no means explanatory as yet. Almost all patients with severe neuroses (and even those with less severe manifest pathology) have been massively traumatized, often chronically so throughout childhood, but also later on.

The relevant traumata usually have not been repressed; commonly, the decisive analytic work does not consist in lifting the traumata themselves out of any amnesia. I do not claim that the wholesale repression of trauma does not exist, but it has not been my observation. Rather, the main affects and the attempts to gain control over them, the main anxieties and wishes engendered by those traumata, certainly the details and their perceptual clarity, and with all that the conflicts derived from them, have become or remained largely unconscious and are at the center of our therapeutic work. Their transformation into words (and other symbols) and the resolution at least partially of those conflicts have clearly had the desired mutative effect and justify the psychoanalytic endeavor.

A STORY OF TERROR AND RESILIENCE,
OF RESENTMENT AND FORGIVENESS

The Traumatic Past

Agnes was a health scientist referred for depression and after two severe, possibly self-induced car accidents. Shortly before, she had broken off a long-lasting intimate relationship with her boss who had exploited and humiliated her physically, professionally, and emotionally. At work she was successful, yet her inner life was ruled by self-condemnation, by guilt and shame, by anxiety and depression.

Both during the initial conversations and then for a long time thereafter, the repetition of her moral masochism, her self-reproaches and self-condemnation, the dreaded jeering or rejection by others, and also by me, stood therefore in the center of our analytic work, together with the concern of being robbed by others of her identity and willpower. Another side of the same problem consisted in her failing ever to build up a lasting, satisfactory intimate relationship and family, although this had become her deepest wish. The men with whom she had tried were, according to her description, most of the time selfish and domineering, even paranoid, and devalued her eventually in the most painful way—outer masochism. Every rejection was just a new confirmation of her deep sense of shame: that she was "an outcast, strange, peculiar, the dirty, poor beggar child"; this was repeated in the transference as well. Beyond that, her shame was deep about having needs and feelings because they had always been disappointed and seemed to be "too much."

Generally speaking, global, overwhelming feelings are an important reason for chronic shame; for her this was particularly the case for her sadness and yearning for love.

But now to her history:

Agnes was born and raised in Germany, the middle of five children, and emigrated in her adolescence with her family to America. Her father had been a soldier in the German army during World War II and later a prisoner of war in Russia. There is good evidence that, as a member of the SS, specifically of the Totenkopf Division, he had taken part in Nazi atrocities, probably the extermination of the Jews. The patient's mother was killed by the father during an illegal abortion, as the patient was close to six years old. This killing was attributed by the father to his sister-in-law. "Always someone else is at fault, whatever happens," Agnes adds. Not long after that, the father remarried, allegedly to a prostitute; the woman clearly was clinically sadistic, gleefully tormenting the children and pitting them against each other. Both the father and the stepmother still today espouse vehemently their Nazi ideology, deny the Holocaust, and

blame the Jews for all evil in the world. Agnes distances herself decidedly
from the ideology of her parents, is particularly conscientious, treats the
suffering with great compassion, and opposes with much courage the
profit orientation in modern health care. She is a sensitive, warm, erudite,
but lonely woman.

The father did not intervene on behalf of his children but would chas-
tise them for provoking the stepmother. He also was physically violent
and instilled fear in the children about revealing family secrets. Constantly, there were severe punishments by beatings and systematic food
deprivation, by ridicule and shaming or isolation in the totally dark
smoking chamber or in the wet cellar. Once the younger sister almost
died from a burst appendix, under beatings and accusations by the stepmother, and only thanks to the vehement intervention by the oldest sister was she brought to the hospital and thus saved. There was at least one
life-threatening attack by the father on the patient's oldest sister—when
she refused to join the family in their emigration to the New World—during
which he tried to strangle her and repeatedly hit her head against the ce-
ment wall. This was witnessed by the patient when she was fourteen
years old. Every accident at home was punished as if it were a crime, and
there was no solace during pain. All the feelings had to be suppressed, all
the weaknesses concealed.

Correspondingly, she harbored an "inner Nazi," who did not tolerate
any weakness and ruthlessly wanted to extirpate it. Because she was not
allowed to play anymore after the stepmother's coming, she was thinking
out stories where she was in the forest and had animals as her allies. Also
to go to school, to learn, to know more, gave her a sense of liberation.

At age nine Agnes was sent away from home to another part of Germany, where for about five years, until she was fourteen, she was raised
by a priest. He functioned as a quasi foster- or stepfather, to whom Agnes
was much more deeply attached than to her parents. He had, however,
also been a soldier in the Wehrmacht and taken part in the separation of
women and children in the Warsaw Ghetto for their liquidation. His only
comment about it was: "It just had to be that way." He considered the
Holocaust as largely due to the obstinacy of the Jews, who had refused to
submit to God's will and grace. He also allowed himself some minor
physical intimacies with the girl.

Later on, in spite of the severe traumatization and against extreme resistance by her parents, the patient was able to assert herself by going to
college, studying, and becoming professionally remarkably successful.
On the other side, she has, as mentioned, never succeeded in having a satisfactory and lasting relationship with a man, and has not many close
friends either.

Thus it has not only become evident to what extent the patient and her siblings have been abused with extreme cruelty, how deep the wounds set in all children of this family have been, but also to what extent she had bought her great professional success with a complete cutting off from the suffering side of herself, her love-seeking part. She had been living an emotionally isolated life, was deeply lonely and much of the time depersonalized.

At first, we decided to deal psychotherapeutically with the severely traumatic life experience, on a twice-a-week basis, mostly by connecting the depression, the masochistic pattern of relationships, and the incessant self-condemnation, with the terrible events and the ensuing brutality of her conscience, of her "inner judge," by working through mostly cathartically and with clarifications the emotions connected with the traumata.

At the beginning, she really felt very relieved about being able, for the first time in her life, to share the terrible experiences with somebody outside her family and thus to oppose the superego pressure; she liked coming to the hours. In-between them she wrote poetry dealing with her memories and the affects connected with them. We asked ourselves about the extent of unconscious (and conscious) guilt in her father and the "borrowed guilt" in herself: "He always has to shirk blame, cannot take responsibility; there weighs a blood guilt on him."

I quote a poem she wrote, shortly after beginning psychotherapy, in English:

> *The Invisible Child*
>
> Like a hammer, blows fall with unstoppable force
> Soft and silk turned to bruised bleeding flesh
> Brutal words strike down down down
> That which might form into self
> Enslaved, bound
>
> The world around grows to vast size
> Moves close, to crush and suffocate
>
> Become small then, unseen
> Shrink back into warm soothing nothing
> If there be nothing the hammer cannot find its mark
> Bonds cannot bind what is not
> Mothers cannot trample what does not exist.

A Nightmare

After transient improvement, the initial depression recurred; and with a deepening realization of the severity of her traumatization in childhood and of the intensity of the identification with the aggressor (introjection of the traumata and traumatizing figures in her superego), with massive turning of the aggression against the self and blocking off of affects, there was an episode of suicidal intensity of her depression.

A few months after beginning, she came immediately before my departure for Europe, to a session (18)[1] with an extremely frightening dream (partly as elaborated later on): "The man stands hidden in the corner of a long hallway, a black man with very cruel eyes; he veils himself with his hood so that his face cannot be seen. He approaches me and tries to suffocate me with a blanket or a pillow. I cannot escape him; I'm in the trap, pushed against the wall. There is no way out but a little window high up with bars and out of reach. I cannot even scream. He turned around and looked at me, ugly, as if he wanted to kill me. The man was the father, the father who wants to kill me because I begin now to see that he needs to be thrown out of my life. Then he suffocated me. As if that would be more pleasant than always having the anxiety; it just had to be that way. This wish to be unconscious. . . . For me, love is connected with all the horror."

At first she spoke about her guilt feelings toward the wife of her former lover, but then she remembered how, after the fatal abortion, her father had asked the children to pray for the life of their mother. When she then died anyway, Agnes felt personally guilty for it because she had not given it enough effort. In what may have been a premature interpretation, I mentioned, perhaps alarmed by the intensity of her fright and her self-condemnation and under the pressure of my impending departure, how every child harbors aggressive thoughts against its parents, out of jealousy or envy, for example, might wish the disappearance of siblings or a parent, but at the same time would be deeply frightened by such impulses, because it is so dependent on the parents, and how horrible it is when such hidden wishes are suddenly and cruelly fulfilled. She reacted to this intervention with panic and despair and, after some hesitation, decided to call and ask me for an extra hour that evening. She said she wanted to kill herself; everything she had said up to now appeared to her like a big lie; things would never get better, and she did not deserve any better. She was convinced that I was condemning her and that she was not worthy of living. Everything in her life that she had built up, all her success, was only deception and lies, only surface. She was not sure whether she should ever see me again. When I suggested that hidden behind this there were deep inner conflicts that needed to be treated in psychoanalysis, four times a week, she immediately agreed. At that point she decided to switch to German: "In English I am lying."

For a long time the problems of superego anxiety and superego transference stood entirely in the center. A direct approach to any aggressive impulses, especially her murderous wishes against tormentors, or envy or jealousy, especially against her older sister, were terrifying. Thinking, feeling, and fantasies were judged and condemned as if they were actions.

But with this there came another observation, that of the inner doubleness.

The Phenomenology of Splitting

Thus there was a dramatic split in regard to the perception of reality, both without and within, as far as it concerned the death of her mother: "I was being treated as if I was dumb, like an animal. I knew that something horrible had happened, but they were joyful with me. I had to go on playing. I thought something was wrong with me because I knew too much. When I heard how my aunt was whispering to my uncle at night in bed that my mother had died, I wanted to tell it to my older brother, to reveal the secret. But he did not believe me; he became angry instead and said: 'You always are lying!' and he continued playing. I knew too much, and I was always alone with my knowledge" (65).

"The twins he had killed—it was three in one stroke; or it seemed like murder out of indifference when he endangered us. Thus it always seemed that I myself was not important at all, that very easily I could have been removed as well. If one is completely alone, not important to any other human being, life has no meaning; one need not live. That is what I sometimes think: the killing of my mother—it was as if she was unimportant, as if her life could simply be extinguished, without any effect. As children we were not important either. Nothing did matter. This again comes back to the destruction of the Jews. That's the same: that one man can decide if someone else exists or not, in soul or body. When I think of myself: to become really angry—that is almost impossible. I do not want others to see me as bad or as a human being who wants to destroy others."

"It rather is the opposite."

"Therefore it is so easy for others to demand everything from me; I never say No—even when I am indignant" (77).

She speaks about the harp player in Goethe's *Wilhelm Meisters Lehrjahre* and how he was eventually crushed by the guilt he had unknowingly burdened himself with: "I know now that I carry also this heavy (*dumpf*) feeling with me since I was very little, and I am not sure with what it has to do. When I look at Augustin, the harper, who had stumbled like a dumb child into the guilt, it is the same with me . . . as if this guilt that had been carried over from my father had tainted me also. He has fought it off and burdened his children with it" (80).

"I know I was afraid to speak about the mistreatments at home. I remember a scene: As I went to the first grade I had to walk 5 km to the school. I had no bicycle like the others. I had to walk all alone by foot, and it was bitterly cold. Also, I had no gloves. So the hands were all frozen through, and when I came to school and into the warmth they hurt me so much that I began to cry. My [oldest] sister held my hands between hers in order to help me. But it was so painful that I could not help crying. Then the teacher inquired why I was crying so much, and when I told her she said: 'How can one send a child the long way to school without gloves!' But with that, I was so ashamed that I had not been able to suppress it and that they noticed that the parents had done something that was not right. It was not so that I would have been indignant myself but that I was ashamed. I always felt that I could never show how awful things were at home"—the brutality, the filth, the stepmother who never washed herself and dreadfully stank and became grotesquely thick. "It is so as if all the children had conspired to keep the secret, to maintain the appearance that externally everything was alright. If one had known about it it would have been a personal failure: that one had to be ashamed of it oneself" (82).

For more than a year she had lived together with a Jewish colleague, the son of a survivor of the Holocaust. She is very shaken as she describes how she celebrated with his family on Friday evening the beginning of Shabbat and how her boyfriend's mother blessed the candles. Eventually she left him, "because I could not think of how my parents would sit there and laugh about it. This is the main reason why I have not married him. I simply could not do it." But then she thought of something else: "I have turned him down because I felt his inner pain; that it hurt him just as much as me."

"You have avoided your inner pain in his inner pain."

"I have done this all my life: to get away from what was hurtful. I have always turned away what was human, the weaknesses, or what I saw as that. In addition I tried more to be with people who were so much like my father, those who locked up everything in themselves and did not show anything of their inwardness." It was no different later on with her boss who mistreated her and exploited her sexually: "As if he was entirely successful and could not be touched by anything. In this there was much brutality."

The earlier boyfriend, however, whom she had abandoned had something soft: "And it was precisely this that I was afraid of: that he was showing his weakness," his vulnerability (87).

In session 88 she brings dreams where she is together with her family, and she unveils some of their secrets, or she wanders around in a building lost: "Wherever I come to, I do not belong." The topic of writing about secrets and keeping them to herself recurs. Toward the end she has an inner, also repetitive image where her mother is a horrible corpse floating in the pond, and at the same time also alive, then the memory of how her father was running after rats with a spade and killing them, together with her fear to be killed by him in the same way. In his outbursts of rage he screamed: *"Ich werde euch totschlagen!*—I'll kill you."

She opens the following session: "Since yesterday I have been thinking of my mother. I could not sleep well." The images were of her mother lying in the hospital, dying of sepsis. She would prefer not to have to think of her in this way. It hurts her so much. Suddenly she interrupts herself: "When my mother was still alive, it happened once, as we were scraping away the moss between the tiles on the garden path, that my mother looked directly in my eyes. For a few seconds it was for me that she was completely connected with me, that I alone was important for her, that she was glad I existed. It surprised me. It had never happened. And although the siblings were also present, in that moment it was only my mother and me. When she was lying in the hospital and I visited her [that happened one time] she was looking at me, and it was not the same, but that she was very very sad, as if she would not let me know everything, that she was not free."

"Also the secret of death."

"She probably knew it. I sat on the chair, very good and straight [*ganz brav und grade*]. The feeling now is: I should have climbed to her in her bed, but that was not permitted. I did not know that that was the last time that I saw her" [she cries]. "It seemed to me that it should not have meant so much to me, I should have forgotten it more easily. It is strange [*komisch*]: After the death of my mother we should not know what had happened. It could not be mentioned. It was as if nothing had happened at all. One or two days after the funeral we all went to the grave. It was all covered with flowers, and I should know that my mother was underneath. But they did not tell me. I knew it somehow, but nobody spoke about it. I knew it, it is obvious, but I was not allowed to open my mouth or ask."

I say: "It was a double reality, yes and no, knowing and denying." She talks about a German song of flowers, the grave with the flowers, then many memories of various flowers.

A little later I mention the Lao Tzu quote: "To die but not be forgotten—is that not true long life, immortality."[2]

She replies: "Then it is also so: if you absolutely want to forget, that this means death."

"To kill by silence [*Totschweigen*]."

Her life seems so accompanied and overshadowed by death: "I always thought that I have caused it that everything so decays. In my life, in my profession, I try to do things that remain, also the writing, doing research, the books."

"To reach in this way immortality" (89).

She is writing a book that deals with her traumatic childhood while listening to Verdi's Requiem: "It is as if the book itself were the requiem. . . . I should always be brave, told me my Oma and my father. But I did not want to. Secretly I imagined that my mother would be here again; and that was my secret, which I could tell nobody, not my Oma, not my father, and also not my siblings. For six or seven years I could not acknowledge that she would not return. It was like defiance. It is even today very painful when I think about that time."

"The unfinished mourning" (91).

"I was afraid to talk here about the mourning for my mother, the sadness: that I would lose her and you would want to take her away ['her' refers ambiguously both to mother and to sadness, *Trauer*, feminine in German]. And then you said that it was the memories that make up immortality, and I sensed that it is precisely the restoration of memory what it is here about, not taking them away. . . . The memory is a refuge for me, and I am afraid that this refuge would not remain. This is the judge within me, the destroyer who does not want to permit me to remember. . . . If I know it is the silence that destroys me, that can be changed. There is an inner struggle. . . . It was like my treasure. As long as I had the sadness she was not entirely lost." Clinging to the sadness meant clinging to her mother: the affect of loss came to substitute for the lost object (Valenstein, 1973). But this entailed a double reality: of knowing and denying the loss.

She turns now, in the same session (92), to another form of double reality, besides this one built upon the denial of the loss: "I thought how early I felt guilty. I was perhaps four years old; it was therefore still before my mother's death. My father had misplaced some important scrap of paper and could not find it anymore. He accused us of having done something with it, and he called us together and was horribly furious. We had to be at fault and had to get it. He screamed he would kill us. He completely lost it. Suddenly I had the feeling, although I knew I had not taken it away, that he was perhaps right and that I might have taken it away anyway. I did not know where, only that I was guilty. It was not true, but I sensed that I was guilty of it. Then he got so enraged that he smashed the chopping board on the table and ran out of the house. Later he found the paper, but did not say he was sorry. The important thing was that I persuaded myself that it was my guilt."

"The double reality."

"I didn't know anything else; it was right so. Always being afraid, always seeking for an explanation. And the explanation was always that I was the one or my siblings were the ones [at fault]. Sometimes I have shifted the guilt onto them."

"The double reality: the reality of perception and the reality of the inner judge, and finally, he is right."

"It was almost impossible—on the one side, I knew that it was so [that she was innocent]. But then I was so angry at myself that I did not know where the slip of paper was. And then the anxiety going with it."

"And you turned into the culprit deserving death."

"And I believed that. It is as if the destroyer would be within myself; that I would be the most dangerous one, that this great power were turned against myself" (92).

We witness in her here, as we do similarly with almost all severely traumatized patients, how it comes to a splitting of consciousness, of the experience of reality: One form consists in a splitting into a perceived reality, one that is confirmed by the ego, and a second reality that denies what has happened, in Agnes's case the death of her mother. In a second form the doubleness of reality pits the reality of perception versus the reality of the inner judge, in her case that inner Nazi, who eventually decides what the truth is. Thus the second reality substituting for the one based on perception is in the first instance set up in order to contradict a painful loss by denial, in the second instance in order to submit to the command of the superego. One is built upon a fantasy of denial, a wishful fantasy invalidating mourning, the other upon the yielding to the fear of punishment, from without as well as from within. It is especially this second type, the conflict between perceptual reality and superego reality, specifically in the sense of an omnipotence of responsibility, that leads to a dramatic splitting of self and world. It means to live in contradictory ego states and worlds of experience, a kind of double accounting (*doppelte Buchführung*).

There is even a third variant: When she was severely beaten by her father she suppressed her crying by convincing herself that it was not she herself who was being mistreated, but that she was standing at her side and observing herself from the outside. Similarly when for a whole afternoon and evening, she was imprisoned by her stepmother in the totally dark smoking chamber and she thought she would be forever forgotten there, she had the idea that she could flee as a very fine thread through the hole in the chimney. Here for a moment she succeeded in denying her painful and shameful self and substituting for it that of the curious observer.

Along the same line, there were many other magical thoughts offering her protection against acute unbearable suffering. I shall come back to this.

The Magic Circle of Connectedness

"The magical thinking: that when it was snowing, I went to my mother to tell her that the earth had been changed into something white. The same with the ice flowers [*Eisblumen*] on the windows: that the green flowers of summer had been transformed into white ones. I hid this astonishment. Also the magical imagination that the cows knew where I was and even knew what I was thinking, my being connected with them—something my father could not understand at all. When he got mad at me I thought he was very dumb and could not understand that the cows would never hurt me, but that was a secret and I would not tell anybody about it."

"Your great secret: the magical connectedness with the living beings."

"And not only with the cows, also with the cats and the animals in the forest, but that I could never enter with other human beings in this magical circle: that somebody would know who I was. The siblings were also excluded from it; they could not understand it. Therefore also the idea of researching nature: that that was my realm, something that I could understand if I only would listen and observe enough. . . . The fear was always that the others would make it clear to me that all this was only imagination. Keeping secrets was a protection, a securing" (283).

I and You

"When I was three years old I had at first to learn the distinction between 'I' and 'You.' That was hard for me. I found it difficult that my mother would call me 'you,' and I would also call her 'you.' It took some time until she understood. . . . It was in the kitchen, and I was kneeling on the bench. I called her 'I,' because she was saying to herself 'I.' I thought that was her name. She turned around and did at first not understand me. Then she grasped what the problem was. She pointed with her finger to me and said: 'You,' then to herself: 'I.' Then she took my hand and pointed with it to me and said: 'I,' and then to herself and said: 'You.' That she understood that the concept came from me, with my hand, that I had to turn it around. I can now for the moment almost see her face again . . . there is also a feeling, the question who I am and why I am: that the self is never changed: that there is always a core of a self that never is altered, the inmost self . . . also a feeling for eternity, and the disappointment that that is not true" (287).

We can see how this mother, in spite of her horrible existence and chronic depression, was not a "dead mother," but, to the contrary, quite able to impart to her child what we now, with Fonagy, refer to as mentalization: the ability to put oneself into the mind of the other. In contrast to the father, this mother certainly was anything but soul blind and thus able to endow her daughter with a deep sense of self and an ability to trust, a kind of basic trust.

The Omnipotence of the Inner Judge

The inner judge is like the father to whose arbitrary power she had to submit, in order to obtain his love, and this process is now incessantly being repeated in her inner life and in her relationships with men. It is as if she had to keep him, but why?

In the further course, the image of the tree in front of the house of her childhood imposes itself on her, a tree tossed and pulled by the storm, the leaves torn, then the scene where she had her crib in the parental bedroom. She could not remember the intercourse of her parents, only infer it as inevitable, but then she saw herself again lying in the bedroom of uncle and aunt when her mother was in the hospital, and thus heard about her mother's death when her aunt believed her asleep and whispered it to the uncle. During both occasions she had to be completely quiet so as not to be noticed as an observer. She remembers the storm and the tree and the circumstances at home, but in the middle there is, as it were, a hole, and this void is being filled now by the cruel judge. She imagines her father as a cruel, hairy beast, which terrifies her and elicits the picture of her depressed mother. The pregnancy was her (the mother's) fault; the father treated her with reproaches and cruelty: "As my sister was being born [Agnes was about four?], my father ran away for three days instead of fetching the midwife. He was so enraged at my mother when she asked for the midwife. I remember how my mother was in the bed and I was horribly scared, because she should not have done that, that she was having the child against my father's wishes, and that this was very bad." She, Agnes, was sharing then the condemnation of mother: "that he was right in his anger at her. 'If you had not done that he would not be angry at you. It is not his fault, but yours.' I knew that she was not really the guilty one, and still, it had to be that way, because my father was so mad at her."

"Again the double reality."

By putting the blame on her mother, she transformed her from the helpless victim into the perpetrator who in her fantasy had been rightly stabbed by her father. "If she had behaved herself and only done what he had wanted and had not gotten children, if she had existed only for him and had not given him any reason to be mad at her, then it would not have been necessary for him to kill her. . . . When the mother was guilty then she had control over everything. The same was true with Edmund [her earlier boss and lover]: I felt guilty, and thus not entirely helpless."

The inner judge was so brutal because in this way she was, although guilty, at least not entirely powerless. Guiltiness presupposed that she had the power to avert the disaster. This omnipotence of responsibility was a powerful defense, a protection against the traumatic state of complete exposure, a protection above all against the overwhelming affects of anxiety, even panic, of shame about her weakness and her absolute sense of worthlessness, of pain and impotent rage. With this claim of omnipotent responsibility went the totality of superego demands and the absoluteness of the judgments when these immeasurable claims went unfulfilled.

Yet at the same time, this harsh and implacable inner judge served as a guardian against the intense aggressive wishes of envy and jealousy that were warded off with so much vehemence that any mentioning of them by an inadvertent drive interpretation usually led to the threat of breaking off the analysis. What she had, probably correctly, ascribed to her father as jealous, even murderous possessiveness, was also part of her, but a most frightening, denied, and repressed part of hers.

The Central Fantasy of the Doubling of the Self

She speaks about the great fear of her father when she was lying in the crib, his black boots, and again sees the face of the dream figure pursuing her. "In that dream the man tried to suffocate me with a pillow. I always thought I would just imagine that [that it was only fantasy]. For a very long time I tried to fight against it. But it is perhaps just the reverse: that they [the images] were real, but that I cannot allow that. It is always again the fear of suffocating, already in early dreams about the *Buschemann* waiting for me [*auf mich lauernd*]. That was the fear with my father: that I should not have been awake, that he should not notice it. . . . When he was beating us up one after the other I at first did not cry, and he kept on beating until it hurt so much that I began to cry anyway. My brother said: 'You are dumb; if you immediately cry then he does not beat you so much.' But I had the feeling that I put myself entirely on the side, that I would not be there."

"A double self as protection" (352/353).

"When I was little I kept having this dream: I had a little potato in the hand, with its eyes. And it slowly became very, very big so that one could not see the eyes anymore, all uniform [*einförmig*] and white, so big, much bigger than I, so that I suffocated. The same happened with the *Busche-mann*: that he got very big and white, uniformly bright, but very, very big, too big for the door, an uncanny danger. That was before the death of my mother. And then, in that dream on the hallway (18), it was a man who turned around and tried to smother me. Or I am drowning. It is always the issue of choking [*Ersticken*]. Sometimes when I think of the analysis it is also connected with danger, and I am afraid to continue thinking. Day before yesterday I had the impression that I would push open the door with my foot and I would see a very bright light, entirely white, but in it there was a dark face, just like the face in the hallway. It has to do with my father. This keeps returning; I thought what this might mean: as if my father had done something to me when I was very small before I could properly remember. I know how he screamed at the little (half-)sister to be quiet when she was crying, and she fell entirely quiet and had her eyes wide open [of terror]. He told me he would not tolerate that anymore that she would awake him every night. . . . The children's bed was in the bedroom of the parents. It is well possible that I woke up and cried and wanted my mother, and that then my father got angry, and it is not improbable that he then took a pillow and closed my mouth, and that I got scared, the feeling of suffocating. Could it have been sexual abuse? This is very improbable. But then: perhaps he put his hand on my mouth and closed it? That too is not very likely. In all these dreams it always is something uniform and white and often soft. . . . I was afraid that you might not believe me. But yesterday that anxiety went away: it was much rather my feeling how all these things suddenly fit together [*stimmten*], that there was something very likely. . . . And with that I was not afraid anymore that you would not believe me. The anxiety before was that I would not believe it myself. But now I am pretty sure."

"And we might add to it that it might have had something to do with the parental intercourse."

"I had very much the feeling that I was disturbing [them] . . . that as a baby I wanted my mother, that that interfered when he wanted to have intercourse, but that I did not want this, that he got enraged at me and wanted to push me to the side, that she was there for him and not for me. In a poem, 'Asunder [*Entzwei*]' I wrote a few months ago: 'not to disturb the animal that might devour crying children.' . . . Thus I wanted to control everything; I needed this inner guardian, this not-saying, not-hearing, not-sensing: because I was afraid. If I had everything under control then nothing would happen. If I did not cry then I would be safe. In the same way I also should not show my longing for a connection (*Verbindung*); I push it aside in order not to suffocate."

"And we may also turn it around that you were choosing men for whom it would be too much, men who carry this prohibition."

"The longing is like a stone on my chest, that it is impossible . . . [she cries] the feeling that nobody can sense who I really am (*wer ich überhaupt bin*). It appears to me as if my entire life I had been outside, in the universe (*im All*) . . . in my family they could not see me, I was not there. The cow was there; foremost, when I was very little, the connection with the animals was much stronger. It was as if it was there that I belonged" (354).

We notice how intensively she is struggling with remembering, in the attempt to bring the overwhelming emotional experiences aroused within the hour into a context of meaning. Gradually, she herself establishes a kind of reconstruction, mostly of her inner experiences of then as they reemerge in the Here and Now in the form of fantasy. But we can learn more about this process of reconnecting of torn threads.

Remembering and Repressing

"There was a contradiction: what I expected was extremely different from what I got. . . . Often I get the feeling that if I thought differently from you that you would also reproach me, and of that I am very afraid. Because you are sitting behind me and you do not say much, that increases my anxiety a lot. . . . With my father it was very important to be very vigilant about doing the right thing [*genau aufzupassen, was richtig wäre*] so that nothing would happen. . . . When my father bought new plates for the roof [*Dachpfannen*] my brother teased me that I was too little and not strong enough to lift one of them. I wanted to prove to him that I could do it. It was terribly heavy, and it fell to the ground and broke. That terrified me. When I turned around my father was standing behind me. I still today can feel the horror that I wet my pants. He beat me and pushed me so that I fell down. He was angry about both. I thought he would not speak with me anymore for my entire life. . . . I was thinking that I was entirely bad, that he did not want me; I had to creep away [*verkriechen*]. It was not the fear of the beatings; it was more the feeling of guilt."

"And the shame that you were not worth anything."

"Perhaps it was more shame" (355).

"When I am lying here and think of these things [e.g., the scene in the smoking chamber], it is as if it was happening just this moment, and I am terrified. I know that it is not happening at this moment, but the feelings are so. . . . It seems to me as if the feelings were timeless: that what occurred at different times is being pulled together into one thing, that the same feeling keeps being strengthened . . . also that image of the open window (in her bedroom as little child), with the waving curtains." It had been, since the beginning of analysis, a recurring image of calm and peacefulness, then crudely interrupted.

"These 'beautiful' images belong together with the counterimage of the dream in the hallway."

"That image keeps coming back . . . and so does the other dream where I was in the cellar of our house digging up my mother's coffin and opened it and where this horrible creature sat on me. In the last few weeks I connect this figure more with the face I saw in the other dream, that of the furious father, very menacing, and that I am being forcibly held and choked."

"Or the childhood dream of the white potato with the disappearing eyes."

"That was a very powerful dream that kept returning, and each time with such immense anxiety. If I succeeded waking up completely it would disappear. The anxiety felt this morning was: that I should not remember; that doubles the threat. If I recognize what I am really afraid of, the threat would become doubly strong. What I connect with this is the rage of my father when I or anybody else tells him how horrible our life was then or that he should have behaved differently toward our mother. He can really not bear this. He becomes furious. It is even today so: as if he was guilty, then he gets uncannily enraged. The anxiety I feel about remembering how it was: that would trigger his rage. This anxiety means that one is not even allowed to think how it was; even to think of it is forbidden."

"Because it would mean a new, additional danger" (370).

She deals here with a kind of double defense: the anxiety about experiencing the pain and horror is one threat; the anxiety about remembering and putting it into words is the second threat. Both together lead her to repression; both anxieties reemerge in the session; and it requires long, patient work on her side that gradually she is able to reconnect what has been torn and that she permits herself to put it into words—in my presence and thus also to herself.

Yet there is something more which is very dangerous, hugely important, and significant for most other patients as well: sexualization.

The White Mare and Bloodroot—Sexualization and Magical Power

"What often frightens me: not only the wish for freedom, but also that I am searching for the horror. . . . Like, that something attracts me to the Holocaust, . . . precisely in the depression: when I occupy myself with the horrible things in the past; that I want to go precisely there where it was horrible, as if I wanted to cry and to feel the horror. And just in that there is a feeling of guilt that I should not do this. And it is my own guilt: that I am infatuated by the horror [*Und meine eigene Schuld ist es, daß ich in das Schreckliche verliebt bin*]."

"The intertwining of suffering with pleasure."

"I am thinking of Kafka's novel *Penal Colony*, the machine that is killing the man—this pleasure in tormenting, the observation of what is horrible, I notice. Also as a child I had the pleasure when I was tormenting the cat or tore out the wings of a fly. In the depression it is rather self-pity. When I think of the Holocaust, it is so that I would be connected with the people who were suffering, that I could understand them, that I belonged with them."

"The tormentor was the same—the figure of the cruel father"(357).

"What I was feeling this weekend again is a vindictiveness you can hardly imagine—against my father. There is also something sexual with it: I would have liked that he himself would be raped, and that he could not defend himself. At first I was thinking that it would have been good, then when he had that rope on the attic—[crying]. Somehow, it did not fit that he would hang himself, that would have been too good. I wanted to stab him with a knife. I wanted him to notice at first how much he hurt the others. . . . In the fantasy, he was lying on his belly and could not defend himself. . . . I was sitting on his back and kept on stabbing him, again and again, and I wanted to take his head and smash it against the ground, again and again, just as he had smashed my sister's head against the wall, that he would become aware how much this hurt. Moreover there is a feeling that he raped my mother, and that I wanted to kill him for it."

"And I am convinced that you were seeing more than you remember now consciously, and that it returns in your fantasies."

"There it is in me like a volcano that could explode."

"It is your own murderous rage that could explode" (364).

"Since yesterday I have this rage in me, a feeling I am strong enough, always again the fantasy to cut my own father to pieces, as if I saw the entire thing that frightens me so much in my father. . . . I do not want to have a man who would want to have me only if I am like a doll. I keep having the feeling that others want to hold me down [*festhalten*], to tell me what I have to do and think and how I should look. I have the image in my head of a wild white horse, a mare, beautiful and fierce that they want to hold in and pen in, and she fights against it, but could not free herself, until she got so furious that she would be strong enough to break down the stable and everything and to run away, to be free. I hate that sweetness, being like a doll. . . . Many men are afraid of this. I do not need to torment others in order to feel strong, but I do not want to allow my being oppressed. . . . Sadism is directed against the one who is already weak; revenge is directed against somebody who seems stronger" (365).

"I feel that I am inwardly much stronger, that it is not bad anymore to have this rage, this wish to destroy. . . . Now the little white flowers are blooming again; they are called blood root. Within myself it is so that I would like it most to dissolve my father in many little pieces, and that these million pieces would be buried and turned into these flowers. . . . Symbolically or really, but the anxiety is real: being suffocated by my father, not only bodily, but also emotionally. This is the greatest insecurity, because it is from the parents that security should come: being attacked by them is more than a betrayal: it makes life impossible. . . . I cannot remember a time where I would not have been terrified by my father. What I want to destroy are not so much his hands, his body, the genitals, but always the head, the face that frightened me so much. In that [earlier] dream: he was there in the corner; that face was horrible. . . . There was more to it: he was approaching me, with the pillow in his hand and wanted to suffocate me, and I became very soft, loose [*schlaff*], not strong, not that I wanted to get away. Somehow it was pleasurable if I did not do anything against him, although he wanted to suffocate me, but if I only let it pass over me. There was a sexual feeling with it, that that would then gratify me. It is the very opposite of what I feel right now: that I myself would be very dangerous and that he would be afraid of me, that he would see me as terrible, that my eyes could kill him—the opposite of what I felt then in the dream. At first it was the sexual feeling, then I noticed that it would lead to death, and then I woke up, and it was the anxiety that awakened me. At first I wanted the father, I wanted to be passive, I wanted that gratification. It was much too late that I noticed that it was not good at all and that he wanted to kill me."

"So it was a sequence then of (1) the passivity and the sexual gratification, (2) the anxiety, and (3) the magical power?"

"And this [the third] comes only now, two years later, not then. This [the revenge] I had thought out before, but against my stepmother. It was in the smoking chamber: the idea was that I could escape as a very thin thread through the hole in the chimney, although I remained in the smoking chamber: I myself would not be there anymore; she [the stepmother] could not hold me there. . . . Every time I think of it, it is not anxiety anymore, but triumph, that in spite of everything I did not remain there, although she thought she held power over me"(365/366). She adds that, in contrast to her victimization in front of her father's brutality, sexualization of her passive surrender had no part here: "In contrast: here it was indignation and hate against the stepmother from the first. I was locked up because I fought against her. Only then came incredible anxiety: I thought I was dead and that nobody would notice anymore that I existed at all. There was nothing gratifying in this, only in the fantasy that I would escape."

I remarked: "The doubleness was very valuable as protection for you: the magical thoughts of speaking with the [protective] animals in the cowshed and forest, standing outside of yourself during the beating."

"—or in the smoking chamber. When N [her stepsister] talked about it that it was there so dark, without any opening, I was thinking: the chimney did have a hole, and I had imagined that there my mind [spirit, *Geist*] would slip away."

"The mind against the body as a protective fantasy, the fantasy of doubleness, lets us better understand the entire past."

"It would have been impossible for me to get out from there [her family] if I had not had this. It also had to do with the future: these magical thoughts were helping me then so that it would be possible in the future. And this continues: in my research I see now the possibilities that others cannot recognize: to see what is hidden, and then to search for it" (371).

Thus we encounter at the other end of the spectrum of splitting the creative doubleness: what opposes the painful repetition of the traumatic experiences in memory and action is the mastery by an understanding and transforming self-figure.

Electra's Grief and the Identification with the Murderer

"I had a fantasy, and I wrote it down. It was horrible, about me and my father, but the strange thing was that I was not on the side of the little girl but on the other side. The father murdered the child. It was a *Lustmord*, a sexual murder. At the end the girl was entirely torn apart, and he was lying on top of her, sleeping, because he had been satisfied . . . it is not something my father would really do . . . and still it was close to the reality with the killing of my mother. . . . For me it is not so much anymore a danger from the outside, but the anxiety that I myself—[she breaks off]. . . . There was also his strangling me, and the pleasure before the anxiety. In the fantasy he was putting his penis deep in my mouth, down the throat, that I would choke to death, like in the dream when he tried to choke me with the pillow and I had such a sexual feeling [followed by overwhelming panic]. I don't want it, and yet it comes from me." She continues stressing that the murder would be for pleasure, and it resonates with her own excitement, accompanied by the feeling that I would condemn her for it. It would be important to displace these feelings of sexualized aggression, as something deeply feared, to the outside, to the father: "Usually it is so that I am the one who would be destroyed, but yesterday I was on the other side. I did it, as if I was myself in the figure of the murderous father, not in the child, although I was also the child,—" again the doubleness.

She compares this murderous self in her with Lagerkvist's "Dwarf" who sits chained to the wall of the underground cellar of the Prince, but can break out again, and to Kafka's *Penal Colony*.

In the following hour, she develops the fantasy further: "It does not mean that I was murdered, but only a part of me was. In the room where it happens, a figure is sitting which is big, horrible, vengeful, and this is me. . . . This figure in the corner, which had at first not been there, has the power. He did not know that he exposed himself to that revenge. And I see the stepmother who enjoys the blood; she lies down beside him. That gives her pleasure. It is exactly that which she sees as right. But she does not see what is sitting in the corner either. And in front of the door that has a little window the pastor is standing with the prayer book in his hands. He looks in and is also glad. And his housekeeper sits besides him and knows that something awful was happening, but she has a bottle in the hand and is drunk. The pastor looks and does nothing. But now it is not something that makes me sad, but angry. He did not resist the evil, he was passively participating in it. . . . At the end I am the one who is sitting in the corner, uncanny, mighty, and vengeful, that I have much more power than they all, and that I can destroy them. All were there, but not my mother. Yet she was not dead either, vanished but not dead [*gestorben, aber nicht tot*]. She is sitting high on a star, very great, very alive. Her eyes are glowing, her hair is dark black and is streaming through the Universe. It is as if she was taking in big parts of the Universe, and she sees everything. . . . She is like an ally for the child. But she could not do anything either as long as she was living; both had first to experience death. . . .

Weak as the child was, she could not go on living. It was so helpless, I had to let it die. Not that I did not have compassion for it, but it had to die and had to be created anew, just like mother. The way she was, she did not have enough power. They [mother and child] were not blind, they foresaw even everything that was happening, but they were not forceful enough to defend themselves, only afterwards. It was as if I created in the fantasy something which is much more powerful, not only that, but also much more evil. This is not a good child; it too is a kind of judge."

I say: "An Electra figure."

"I was thinking this morning: in the Christian Bible it reads, when Christ was hanging on the cross: 'Father, forgive them; they don't know what they do.' That makes me angry. This figure in the corner does not say this but it says: Don't forgive them, kill them, because it is their responsibility to know what they do. It is easy simply to say they were too blind or too weak. . . . The picture of the pastor standing at the door window [*Guckloch*] comes from reality. As I had my x-ray examination before the emigration I had to undress, and there was a small window, and he was observing me. That made me furious, that he was watching me without my permission. That seemed so hypocritical. He was preaching that we all are sinners and should be good and saintly. He too had responsibility and should have opened his eyes. . . . Men are very afraid of that: that just the most horrible things which happen are experienced as sexually satisfying. I felt that when I wrote down this fantasy. I think again of the *Penal Colony* where the tortured man recognizes that he will die and that he is being watched, and even children are there watching, and they look at it with pleasure."

She deepens afterward that earlier fantasy where she had imagined her father dismembered into million little white flowers, bloodroot, blooming in the forest. Now she wants to dismember specifically his face, because of the murderous eyes: "I had an incredible fear of him when I was a little child. He had only to look at me, and I fell silent. It was as if he could devour [*fressen*] me. . . . I was not allowed to show any mourning for my mother" (450–452).

As we saw, she herself had tried to deny that her mother had died, and at the same time held on to the grief as a treasure, the very sense and affect of loss as a substitute for the lost object. As long as she felt the sadness she still had her mother. It is like Electra's "cureless pain" (*améchanon álgos*), in evils beyond "deliverance" (*análysis!*, Sophocles, *Electra*, v. 142): "never shall I give over my sorrow" (v. 231).

This prohibition against the grief was itself, she now says, "an incredible beating down of my own dignity: that I am not important, that I should be glad, that I would not suffer, because I would see her again if I only were good and pious. This is such a lie, a disregard of myself." As

Electra says, "You don't know how to listen" (v. 629: *"oud' epistasai klyein"*).

Agnes stresses, like Electra, in this context the centrality of the intertwined themes of looking, disdain, shame, and murder, and the ultimate abyss when human beings are made into things: "His eyes were the worst, as if he would kill with his eyes, the way he looked at me. I was not even allowed to cry, not even to show when I was sad. . . . The stepmother teased him before the wedding that his confession had not taken very long: 'You have not told everything, have you?' It was more than a joke. He had to hide more: it was not even just the crime against my mother, but there was something much worse he had to hide which had turned into a joke between him and my stepmother, and to their alliance."

"Terrors compelled me, to terrors I was driven—*deín' en deinoîs enankásthen*" (v. 221).

The Wall and the Fence

In what follows, I return, with the help of some thoughts of Agnes, to a problem the recognition of which often might work like a magical key opening up severe, seemingly unanalyzable psychopathology: the problem of conflict in the superego, of intrasystemic conflict, the opposition of ideals, obligations, loyalties, and values—Ἄρης Ἀρεῖ ξυμβαλει Δίκα Δίκ v. 461, Aeschylus, The Libation Bearers:"Might clashes with might, right with right" [Ares Arei xymbalei, Dika Dika]).

She is speaking, in the middle part of her analysis, again about her cruel conscience and its compulsiveness: "I clearly feel this judgmentalness not as myself, although it does come from me; I sense it as something at my side, not part of the real self. . . . I tried to get away from it, to flee. . . . When I started the analysis it was clear that I had made a circle [around myself], that I could not get away from it, that it belonged to me although I wanted to get away from it. The other thing was that I built up a wall between what lay on the outside and what I was, in order to protect myself. Every time that there was a big attack the wall got strengthened so that it became very strong and smooth and I would not have to feel anything, but also so that no warmth could penetrate from the outside. Yet, the figure of Lagerkvist's Dwarf [*Dvärgen*] belonged also within it; I had not noticed this, during all the fleeing and wall building: that I had walled him in with me. He was not the same as my self, but an enemy."

"Like immured in the basement."

What she refers to here is the following passage about the Dwarf, this embodiment of resentment, being chained to the walls in the basement of the Prince's castle: "Here I am in my hole, living my obscure mole life, while he goes about in his fine handsome halls. But my life is also his, and his noble highly respectable life up there really belongs to me" (Lagerkvist, 1944, pp. 216–17). Behind the mask of power the malicious dwarf is hidden, and it is behind both that the bad conscience and the helpless self know to hide themselves. Yet both of them, Prince and Dwarf, are parts of our personality. *"Sin dvärg har man alltid bruk för*—One always needs [the services of] one's dwarf" (p. 171–82).

Agnes continues: "The anxiety in the image comes from the fact that this wall had appeared to me as protection, but then it becomes something that brings the dwarf much too close to me so that I cannot get away from it anymore, precisely because I had built that wall. The result was that the most disgusting thing [*das Scheußlichste*] in my life was connected with me without my knowing it."

"And what is this dwarf?"

"He stems from the old dream, the ghostly hands—where I found that coffin of my mother in the basement, and this ghastly little thing came out of the coffin, alive, and clung to me. In another fantasy it is connected with the stepmother, that I had to go back in a horrible cave that was very dark—the old life, the childhood, especially in the house of stepmother and father. In the middle of the cave, that hideous dwarf sits by the fire and laughs at me. In the beginning of the analysis I had the idea that the dwarf was stronger than I, but then that I would become much stronger, that he would not have the power anymore."

"Yet what is the dwarf? What does he mean?"

"The judgmentalness [*das Urteilhafte*]. But this is not entirely so. That there is something in my life that tries to destroy me, merely out of malice, without reason. Judgment would be if something came from me, yet this dwarf—there is something entirely different involved that I did not cause myself, but something very evil that tries to destroy me, only because it wants that, not because I had done something and I would have deserved it. Therefore it has to do with my stepmother; it is really out of malice."

"Again the *sin'at chinnam*, the baseless hatred." (I refer to this Talmudic concept that I will take up in chapter 5).

"And of that I am afraid."

"But it sits within you."

"At my side, much too close by."

"Walled in with you [*miteingemauert*]."

"But I fight against the thought that I have to get away from it in order to be safe when the malice comes."

"The inner [malice]."

"So that I could defend myself against it. If I let it be that way, I am in danger. Although I want to see it, it is not clear to me. Sometimes it seems to be so close that I am convinced the judgment comes from within, and it seems to me quite right: I am evil. When I think then about it it slowly clears up that this was not so, that it came out of baseless malice against me. I sometimes feel it as relief that it could easily be taken over by me."

"As an inner enemy."

"But it is so difficult because the enemy is often not distinguishable from what—. I sometimes do not notice how unjust the enemy is toward me, often not."

"Again the bad conscience, the inner judge, the superego, that is so baselessly bad" (470).

She had sought protection behind a wall of dissociation and withdrawal against all the hurt and shame and rage assaulting her from the outside, but then had noticed that she had taken the enemy within her own self: she recognizes the intensity of envy, jealousy, and resentment that had become part of her own superego, but now all directed against her own self—and of course, indirectly and much less accessibly to her consciousness, her own dangerous feelings.

Now she goes on (in the same hour) and makes a crucial distinction between the superego forces.

The Just and the Unjust Conscience

"I think sometimes about this conscience. The problem is that it is important. I would like to separate it into two parts. It is not a good conscience that shows me when I have done something right, but it would be a conscience that would be fair. It is therefore the matter of a fair conscience and of an unfair conscience. Good and bad are something very different. Being good means to submit; it is not just."

"This is a crucial distinction, also generally." ·

"Sometimes I am able to distinguish when the conscience is right, and when not; sometimes I deceive myself. And that is the problem; it is like a mirage. Slowly the light fades, and then you notice that it is not so. The deception goes back and forth; you are not quite sure. Like then, when I think about my father: to recognize clearly the evilness and to know that it is just to oppose it. But it varies, because even such a man may also have something good, although he has so turned against me" (470).

I will come back to this differentiation, but I now skip much material.

A Crucial Dilemma in the Transference

"The law was sacred. Yes, but rebellion might be sacred too . . . the problem [was] where the sacredness of obedience ended and where the sacredness of rebellion began" (George Eliot, 1862–1863/1994, pp. 441–42).

She opens session 740 with the wish to stop the analysis: that she just does not do any better. She has dreamed the night before that I had been naked and lay beside her on the couch while she was sleeping. When she woke up [still within the dream] I was ashamed and she as well. Now she would have to leave the analysis. It is a feeling of horror and betrayal, similar to the one with the pastor. The whole thing is a shame dream, one of exposure. She simply cannot shake off her sadness, this underground mourning. It brings her despair, she says, as long as she believes it would have to be abolished. I refer to the exposure of my own grief in regard to *Schindler's List* and the Holocaust (this had occurred much earlier in the analysis). Would it be "normal" not to be sad? I mention Aristotle's words about melancholia. She adds to it how all good actors have a deep wound and that this is what makes them good. "It is exactly what I felt the first years here: that it was okay, that I would not have to be ashamed of the sadness. But since the break with Gregor (a recent friendship where she felt betrayed) it is different; I am so much withdrawn since; then I feel the sadness." I add: "And probably also the connectedness with me, but with this also the fear of sexuality." A little later she says: "When I think of the Holocaust it seems to me as if these two opposites were fighting within me, very strongly, not secretly: that, without wanting it, I had received from my father the Nazi, and from my mother the Jewess. . . . Perhaps it would have been better if I was not existing, that my father did not have the right to have children. Then I think of my mother; she certainly did have the right. . . . Wanting to be just is, in spite of everything, good."

"And this is really the counterforce to the sadness, and both belong together, are complementary, not really standing in conflict with each other."

"I always am afraid of the other thing that I also feel, the hatred and the rage; I try to control it so very much, but sometimes hate and rage also belong to justice."

I later mention "the sacredness of rebellion," and she says: "This is very important for me; that gives me joy. . . . I do not believe that I have compromised my integrity."

A few sessions later (746) she again accuses the analysis. She complains about the one-sidedness of our relationship. She does not agree that it does not allow any friendship; it angers her. I refer to her inner conflict about it, specifically in regard to the nakedness dream, how uncomfortable she would be with the mixing of the two as much as she would wish it also.

She replies: "If I do not know what you feel it is just entirely one-sided. I cannot fully trust someone if I do not know what he feels. If you hide yourself completely, hide your feelings, then I am inferior [*unterlegen*] to you. . . . Not that you say anything for the sake of appearance [*zum*

Scheine] or that you are secretive and dishonest like Gregor, but you often do not say what you think. In this way it is anyway uneven."

"It is an inner conflict between two thoroughly legitimate needs: the wish for intimacy and mutual love, as against the consciousness that it would blunt my ability to help you—more, as in the nakedness dream, that it would be a breach of confidence."

"I know this conflict, but it lets me partition myself off [*abschotten*]. It is difficult to trust somebody when he is himself so locked shut [blocked off, *abgeriegelt*]. It is something that I sense as being expelled [*Verstoßene*]—with my father, my sister, with the pastor, the lover, with most of the people I know. I never feel that at times someone else would let me entirely enter into his thoughts, that he would trust me enough that this would be permitted. And this is the feeling that makes me so lonely. It is always the case of: 'So far and not farther'."

"The wall."

"And this does not come from me; it comes from the other. . . . I even think of the day when I saw my mother for the last time. I was enthusiastic that I could go in. . . . Nobody told me what was really going on, not even my mother. It was always the feeling: I have to find out myself what the matter is here, and usually it is very bad."

"And the same is feared here."

"Not so much that I would be afraid. How can I know what will be if I do not know what you think? For example, how can I know if you think that I will never be better? In the last session I was afraid that you could believe that the problem does not lie with the others, but that I am the one who excludes the others, that it comes from me. Driving here this morning I was thinking: My whole life I have wished I could transform the world so that other people would be better towards me, and I cannot do it."

"As we said some time ago: you seek the limitlessly trustworthy mother and always find the evil father instead."

"And not even my mother was so as I wished. Right now I feel: If I cannot have this I do not want to live. Life appears to me as a series of lies, of pretenses. Already for a very long time I have written in poems that I am very far away on the moon or in the Universe, so far away that I do not make the least impression on others at all, that it does not matter at all whether I am or not."

"The words 'Love means, I want you to be,' against the Universe of complete lovelessness."

"This is the wall with other human beings. The wall: 'This is not allowed to you; my love is forbidden; I keep it for myself.'"

"Every limit turns into the wall and into absolute rejection."

"Not entirely so. I do have friendships where I do not expect love in the sense of this very strong love. . . . It is not a genuine love where I would know that this other [person] would want to stay with me and share his life with me; and there where I have tried to have this love it has failed."

She returns to the conflict about the analysis, that she does not get what she wants. "I do not know if I can learn more about myself in the analysis which could help me. The problems are always the same: the deep sadness about what I have lost in my life, this hopelessness that I cannot attain it again, and also the recognition that most people have their own autonomy, and that limits exist between human beings, and that this remains so that there are people who feel very little about others and that they therefore, without even noticing it, hurt others, people who only bustle about for themselves and do not care what happens to others, and many who genuinely and simply are together with their family and friends, who have their lives, their children. Only I do not have that. I know all that; it does not help me, and I do not have the feeling that it ever will help me to make things better. . . . It does not make me any happier, only more effective; but happy, that I am not. . . . At the beginning of my analysis I believed—and that was perhaps some magical thinking—that I too could be loved by someone else, but I do not believe it anymore. What I do believe is that I can find passion in science and in my ideas, some of the time, anyway and that I do not need any other human being for that."

"But that intimate love would be denied to you."

"It is not so because I would not like it myself, but it does not exist, and if I keep searching for it without getting it I am only unhappy, and I do not want to search for something that cannot exist. Much rather: to have something where I have a little happiness and can be joyful [*froh*]. I am so angry about everything that people chatter around about love that I am excluded from, that I would like to continue alone instead of pretending what is only illusion. . . . How can analysis here still help?"

"What you have left out in all this is the condemnation and devaluation of that which is not absolute fulfillment."

"It is no condemnation, but it is just not enough for me. It is not so that I condemn imperfection, but because it does not fulfill what I wish. Therefore I have to go after what I can reach, and not after what is not fulfillable. I am angry that I cannot have what I would like, it is not the condemnation of others. . . . Only that I recognize that I have to get along without that which does not exist. It is a delusion; all these forty-five years I have experienced no real love. How should I believe that it could exist? This is no condemnation; it is the truth. And it does not come from a conflict, but out of knowledge and seeing what is; it does not exist. What I do want to condemn: I would like to curse God who has given me this feeling."

"This longing."

"And here I blame you too. The analysis has led me to sensing this yearning more. And when there is nothing that could fulfill this yearning it is cruel to open someone's eyes to perceive something that hurts, without that there could be anywhere any alleviation [*Linderung*]; this is cruelty. Now I think of the image with which I started the analysis: the little baby in the crib, as if life were somehow without significance for me."

"And the dark shadow of your father and the anxiety in the image."

"In the last few weeks I have often thought of that image. I have much more the feeling there that my father is hitting me. I was crying, and that he did not want that I cried, as if I could feel his hand."

And shortly thereafter (750): "I have thought more about how much I am ashamed in front of you. This may be partly the reason why I want to get out of the analysis: because my father was in the SS, and how much he has participated in."

The Raging River

The following excerpt comes from the final phase of the analysis and takes off from the feeling of being excluded, being a stranger, and with that from the shame and the aggression tied to it. In hindsight, I recognize now that this preoccupation with feeling excluded refers to intense, but largely repressed jealousy, the affect par excellence of the tragic character (see below).

She asks me at first why she likes so much to shape in writing what she is feeling. Sometimes it seems to her she should not do this because it serves only herself but this is not so: "I would like to communicate what I know within very strongly in order to create connection with others. It is then very shattering when I do not succeed with this. If I do it in writing it is at least safer. Then it could be that somebody I do not know would receive it anyway."

"Yes, there is greater safety with it, and it is very connected with the main feelings of your life: sadness, indignation, sense of injustice, longing, love."

"What keeps appearing is the yearning for connection. It has to do with the days when my mother died. It was as if I had been entirely excluded from what was happening. I was desperate and incredibly enraged about it: the indignation against my father, against the other adults, against God. Perhaps I feel it more now; as if they had done something without noticing how it hurt me, or as if they did not know that I existed at all. And I had to hold all this despair within. Had I talked about it, they would not have been capable to feel it. Now I imagine: they would have sent me away to a room where they could close the door, so that they would not have to look at me. It would have been too much for them. The connection to the other, that gives me the feeling that I do exist, while not being noticed gives me the feeling that I do not exist. I cannot quite call it love. Love is too mild. It is as if my own feeling that I am worthwhile is connected with it—that I matter. . . . The loss of his [Gregor's] love as man to the woman was not so great, not so painful, as the loss of being something altogether in his world. It is as if he tried to kill me by trying to have nothing to do with me at all. It is very much connected with [the possibility] to be able to talk about what goes on within."

She deepens the analysis of her problems of conscience and aggression by bringing up a conversation she had last night with her girlfriend in the Midwest. Preparing himself for Bar Mitzva, her son was protesting against the common interpretation of Abraham's sacrificing his son Isaak. Agnes reflects: "I was thinking about it: What would a woman have done in his place if God had commanded her to sacrifice her son? I would have said No. I would not have obeyed a God like this. My girlfriend says her son believes that Abraham had failed his test. He is certain, Abraham should have told God that it was his responsibility to refuse, to say No. When Abraham said Yes, God showed mercy by pointing to another sacrificial victim. Dan is now thirteen; he has exactly expressed what I was thinking: the idea that the human being is subject to God, instead that he could decide himself what is good and what is bad. This is a basic idea in religion. To be able to talk with her about this is very important; it touches on what is within."

"If we see in God the expression of the inner judge, we are very familiar both with the good and the cruel inner judge."

"The fair judge has to learn to think much more clearly than the sadistic one. To see the difference between what is right and what is wrong is often very difficult. Seeing right and wrong within oneself is one thing. However, when wrong is being seen on the outside as right, then it is not so easy. To place yourself in opposition to others and to say: No, this is not right—with that you are very much alone. I imagine that all the others might have seen it very differently from Dan: you have to obey God. In the Catholic religion it would not have been possible to state Dan's decision. For example, if I had said it to the pastor he would have replied: 'No, you are wrong. You have to obey God.' It is again the distance from everything that the others believe: Suddenly you stand there very much alone."

Changing briefly the focus from within the material to outside, I say: "In the Bible itself there is this polarity: on the one side this obedience of Abraham toward God, on the other side his protest against him, in regard to Sodom."

I allude here to the following Midrash, which Agnes knows, referring to the scene where Abraham pleads with God for mercy toward the people of Sodom. I quote it here, not in the session. The starting verse in the

Torah is this: "Far be it from You to do such a thing, to bring death upon the innocent as well as the guilty, so that innocent and guilty fare alike. Far be it from You! Shall not the Judge of all the earth deal justly?" (Genesis, 18.25). The Midrash comments, in the name of Rabbi Levi: "If You desire the world to endure, there can be no justice; if You desire justice, the world cannot endure.[3] Yet You would hold the cord by both ends, desiring both the world and justice. Unless You forgo a little, the world cannot endure" (*Midrash Rabbah*, 1983, Bereishit, 39.6).

Agnes continues (with clear transference implications, especially the transference of defense: seeing in me the wall against the feelings, the intellectualization, denial, and blocking of affects): "Being alive as human beings means not only to speak with each other about religion and philosophy, but about all that moves us within, not to have to deny it. That is the most beautiful thing in man, and in this I am very lonely. Most of the people I know cannot do it. It is this very sharp encapsulation from feeling so that nothing should be expressed of it and you exist only as a machine, and this is what my inside so much rebels against and why I am so furious at the world. . . . In my first year of analysis I often had the image: I am standing in a very great, very old cathedral in Germany, and I had the power, to destroy the church so that it would melt down around me, because of my rage, that the stones would not just crumble, but melt. And all the poor religious people—I could not entirely decide if they merely would see and recognize, or whether they also would have to die. This is ambiguous in the image. There is such a rage, a destroying rage. . . . The problem in my life is that my rage is so great that I want to destroy, while I also know that it certainly would be mostly unjust toward the people who could not see it. . . . And so, when I think of Gregor, I have an uncanny, almost murderous rage at him while recognizing also that he is too weak and too blind as that he could see what he has really done, and that it would therefore be unjust to destroy him. I do not know why it always comes to this: if a person [*Mensch*] knows that he does evil he deserves [that one takes] revenge [on him] because he knows why one should not do this. And yet those who do not know are often the worst."

"You think of your father."

"Yes. There is something else also. I often have the image: I see myself as a little girl in my nightshirt, and I run away from home after my mother had died. I run away out of despair, in the middle of the night. And outside is a storm, and it is raining very hard, and I am very wet in my nightshirt. After a while I come to a river, and this river is very full with water, all lashed up, and I cannot cross it. On the other side there is not this storm and it does not rain either, and two philosophers are sitting there, one who is not religious, and one who is very much so, and they debate those questions and do not notice that a child is standing there and wants to be consoled because its mother has died—that even these deep thoughts are blind to what is really important. This image is a fantasy I had when I was hearing Verdi's Requiem, *Dies irae*. The female voice that seems to lament very much, she stands near me, on my side of the river and she accuses philosophy and God: Why can something like that happen?"

"You should write about this. Everything what you have said in this hour—I would like to ask you whether I have permission to talk about this."

"I would like that. I do have it within. I know what I feel, but my words are sometimes too weak to really express it."

"I would not say this."

"I mean by writing. It pales. This is exactly what I meant before: To express it so that somebody else understands it, is the most important thing for me. The peculiar [*komisch*] thing is that it returns to what in life is not even so difficult: to love a little child. For that one does not have to say much; it is very simple. This is really love. It is true: this has much to do with the time when my mother died: That I was being put upon the Ocean on a little piece of wood, and that those to whom I really belonged simply set me adrift" (823).

At the beginning of the following session: "It is very clear: I am looking for someone who would see me. What you call soul blindness is the problem. This raging river between the philosopher and the child is the separation, the distance I feel. If I had someone who would accept me just as I am, without my having to change, and who knows with certainty I am okay, then it would be solved. . . . You know me better than all other people; why do I have even with you still a feeling of separation? It has to be so that you can only be somebody who helps me to find such a connection with others. It also lets me despair because I cannot imagine that anybody else can know me that well as you do. . . . It hurt me within but also angered me when all the others [after mother's death] pretended as if I knew nothing. The distance between the others and my self was even bigger because I was the only one who did not wear black clothes. . . . It was a symbol for them that I did not belong [*dazu*: to it, to them], that one did not want to tell me what I already knew though, and that one could not at all see my grief, that which I felt. . . . Everywhere there is the red thread of this blindness toward what is real."

"It is the key experience, especially the blindness toward grief" (824).

This blindness of others vis-à-vis her sadness is certainly a key experience that had contributed much to her traumatization. The allusions to the transference are also obvious, both the stimulation and the distance, both the recognition of the affects and the fear they might be too much, too overwhelming, but also the transference of defense by intellectualization (induced by my diversion immediately before to a focus outside of the immediate material) and the ensuing massive aggression. I think in retrospect that I kept throughout the analysis a certain caution, an inner reserve, about tying her intense affects too closely with me, in the fear that they would overwhelm her and compel her in rage and shame to break off the analysis, as in fact she had repeatedly threatened to do, usually when I directly addressed some form of aggression. What would have been possible though, as I recognize now, was to express more strongly my own countertransference, specifically the fear just mentioned.

But back to the session: "What I wanted to attain with studying and working—partly it was out of enjoyment of science, but partly it was that I wanted to prove that I am an equal, that I am not that dirty, poor beggar child, and a German one to boot" (827).

"It is as if, when I was a little child, they had put on me a dress I had to be ashamed of. It should exactly have been the opposite; it should have been beautiful, something that I could be glad about. You call it contempt; in me it is to a large extent self-contempt. Within me there are always two thoughts: In my consciousness I do not disdain myself. I think, in my clear consciousness, that I am a good person, it was also so at the beginning of the analysis. But against this, in my unconscious, there is always this feeling that I have to withdraw, that I have to try to change things, always to take the guilt upon myself, to see me as the one who is less, the masochism. That has not only occurred since earliest childhood, but that plays a very strong part in the religion which I have grown up in. Religion is not without this very strong command that one has to despise oneself, that one is not good if one does not disdain oneself and mankind. It emerges clearly from the prayer said before communion in the church: 'Lord, I am not worthy that you enter under my roof. But say only one word and my soul heals.' The sacred has to come from the outside because one has from the beginning a sick soul. This is very destructive."

"The opposition between truthfulness and humiliation."

"In a religion which is good the human being should have the feeling that he himself has dignity, that he himself is sacred, and not do things that have one lose one's own dignity, and also do nothing to others that would deprive them of their dignity. . . . If it comes out of the thought of self-contempt: to do good for others in order to improve oneself it does appear to me like a bell that has a crack. Although it resonates it does not sound from wholeness; it cannot bring forth the right beautiful tones. I see it that way with the self-contempt: if one does not see oneself basically as good, but from the beginning on as sinful and imperfect and small and little then all the things that are done for improvement are only done to improve *oneself*. If one is whole within it is different: then the good things are done out of a wish for joy and for what is great. What one then does causes joy. If one feels not worthy one is always ashamed and does the good in order to remove shame, to take off the bad dress and to take on a new one, to hide oneself so that it would not be seen. If one feels whole [*heil*] then the good serves to give joy, and not to hide shame. The resentment also comes from shame. If one feels oneself to be worthy and whole (*heil*) one does not have to be ashamed nor to envy others" (829).

In the sessions afterward (830/831), the hatred flames up even more consumingly: "Whenever there is a new problem, the hate blazes up so strongly that I can think only about this. In spite of six years of analysis I tell myself: I am not allowed; this hate is too strong because it makes my own life miserable. . . . This reaction is so uncannily strong in me because I have learned it as a child. . . . My hatred of Gregor is so strong because he shows no humility, as if he were God. He has attained all he wanted: He is at the top of his field, has a wife and child; he can brag. He treats everybody around with contempt. I hate him for it. . . . [The administrator] said [in regard to dismissals]: 'For me all is just a question of the bottom-line.' What kind of person is that who can say something like this without noticing that it is only part of life and should not be determining?"

"The golden calf."

"He did not notice it. He said: 'This is my task. It does not matter to me what happens to the people.'"

"The complete objectification [*Verdinglichung*] of the other."

"There was not even malice with it. It is simply so as if we were machines. This is also a contempt of the human being. . . . What I have not learned is to bear this hatred in myself [against Gregor]; that it is entirely natural" (830).

"At the beginning of the analysis I had the hope that suddenly everything will be good again, a quick recovery"—the magic transformation. "It did not happen that way. But I do feel better even if I have these ups and downs. Yet, all in all I am much more stable and much more adult. And even if I have those feelings of hate I am not afraid that I would do something terrible. . . . I have often wondered why you can have so much patience, for example, with me. I do not believe that I could do it: for such a long time, and not give up."

"I do not know the answer."

"It must be very frustrating: to see, now it again goes badly. In spite of that, it does help me. If you do not give up, I do not have to do that either. That would be the worst if you gave up."

"To answer your question: I believe that an important part in it is my wanting to understand, to work it through in writing, to see the connections, and to transmit it."

"At first, I was surprised that you wanted to know all the names. . . . Now I know that without them it would not be possible at all. One cannot talk about the individual life without the names. . . . One would not talk about the things that are very personal, but so much more generally. That is the exact opposite of what actually occurs. This is the most valuable in it: because I got the feeling that I am important myself, my history, not what is general. I was not one among many anymore."

"It is like in history, not like in the natural sciences—history where it is always a matter of what is individual."

"It happens more and more also in medicine that way: not to treat according to a protocol for the many, but every individual [the single one] gets his treatment, and that with much greater success, although most still treat generally. It becomes important anyway to treat the individual, also in the physical [area]."

"Medicine is not only a natural science, but also a historical one; the history of the individual. Freud has been criticized that psychoanalysis is in its essence not a natural science, but he said himself there are basically only two sciences: natural science and psychology."

"What I recognize in my own analysis: one part that is valid generally, also for other human beings, versus another part that consists in what I am and what makes me special as a human being. The comical thing is: what makes me similar [to others], for example, the hatred: I notice that that reaction is almost biological even if the reasons are different: it has to be expected if one injures the other very much, that he reacts so. One can count upon it that that will be his reaction, that he will not simply tolerate it. But this understanding gives me no feeling of joy, only that of comprehension. In contrast to this is the feeling of specialness, that my history was entirely different from any history of anyone else: this gives me the feeling of joy. This is being self, the psychical. The emotions appear more the biological. In this sense, Freud was right: there are many reactions and emotions that one finds again in all the others, many."

"The kind of conflicts, the defense."

"This is very important as a starting point . . . that it is only natural science that counts, that the psychological is *hokuspokus* [a swindle], even in psychiatry" (831).

The Wall

She refers to a powerful poem of Rilke I had shown her:

> Ach wehe, meine Mutter reißt mich ein.
> Da hab ich Stein auf Stein zu mir gelegt,
>   und stand schon wie ein kleines Haus, um das sich groß der Tag bewegt,
>   sogar allein.
> Nun kommt die Mutter, kommt und reißt mich ein.

Sie reißt mich ein, indem sie kommt und schaut.
Sie sieht es nicht, daß einer baut.
Sie geht mir mitten durch die Wand von Stein.
Ach wehe, meine Mutter reißt mich ein.

Die Vögel fliegen leichter um mich her.
Die fremden Hunde wissen: das ist DER.
Nur einzig meine Mutter kennt es nicht,
mein langsam mehr gewordenes Gesicht.

Von ihr zu mir war nie ein warmer Wind.
Sie lebt nicht dorten, wo die Lüfte sind.
Sie liegt in einem hohen Herz-Verschlag
und Christus kommt und wäscht sie jeden Tag.[4]

"If I think of father and stepmother it was exactly like in the Rilke poem: one had to keep them away by making oneself invisible. One has to keep them at a distance. The wall in the poem is like mine when I still wrote a lot: Here was the wall that I had built up, and it was so smooth and white so that one could experience [spüren] nothing even if one put the hand on it. I think of the dark smoking chamber where I was locked up and the contradiction with my wall: there I wanted to get out; here I needed it in order to keep others away, in order to protect myself. Yet the bad thing is that both come down to the same thing: whether it is for protection or for a lock-up, one is alone and imprisoned all the same. When I think of how I make myself invisible I have it still, but it is not universal anymore. . . . I have the feeling that I now know my mother so well after all those years that this love for her has reestablished itself, instead of only being sad about her loss" (835).

"I had then the fantasy of the little girl: that in the wall the door would open up, and there is the garden where the sun is shining, and she [es] is at first afraid to move lest this beautiful image vanishes, and suddenly the puppet moves and becomes alive. The girl decides to go there anyway and steps over the threshold, just like the high threshold out from the smoking chamber. And then she is in the garden and has a cat, and she finds milk for it [sie] to lure her out into the garden. Now they are cat, puppet, and she herself, bushes where raisins and almonds grow. She takes both. She knows she is not allowed to eat that; it does not belong to her. She calls the guardian of the garden and asks whether she is permitted to eat. She is so very hungry. She does not get any answer, but it is rustling in the tree. Suddenly there sits a beautiful white bird on the tree, with blue eyes. It [he: er] has a piece of bread and lets it fall into the hands of the girl. It is sweet and good. He tells her: 'One can nibble [naschen] in this garden. Everything that can be found here can be eaten. And there are no garden guardians here, and the sun is here to make it warm.' But the bird says he is afraid of the cat: 'Cats from the cold world eat birds.' Then a little mouse stirs under the bush: 'And they eat mice as well.' It is another animal that is afraid. The girl cannot stay in the garden because the cat is too dangerous. I tell her: 'We have to go back; the animals should not be eaten.' The girl tries to find the door through which she has entered and cannot find it anymore. The cat drinks something and does not need to eat the animals. In this way the fantasy came onto the paper. I could live myself entirely and clearly into these fairytales and stories, with a feeling of happiness. This also happened when I was suffering—especially then."

We notice the shift in the story first from the neuter to the feminine, from the little child to the female identity, then the representative of conscience that changes from guardian to the giving bird. There is no evil inner judge anymore. At home she was often condemned to starving because she had "nibbled." The children had altogether a lot of hunger while, as far as she remembers, the parents gorged themselves. The hunger for nourishment as well as for warmth and love and respect was, at least within her, relabeled as something sinful, evil, and greedy, because she felt so starved: the threatening cat. It was a counterbalance against the horror, the creativity as a cure for her chronic traumatization. "I knew that it was fantasy but then I was as if disappearing from the cold world" (836).

"I asked myself about that cat that could eat the bird. I know that it represents aggression, but in a good sense. I feel that it belongs there, that the girl would never have left the other world without the cat, and not only as a protection, but that she never should be left alone on the other side. For me, it is very strongly marked, that feeling: to bring along who is faithful to me and to whom I am faithful; that it is not possible simply to pack up and leave."

She talks about the split in her between gladness and being depressed, after I had quoted Schiller: "Des Lebens ungemischte Freude ward keinem Irdischen zuteil" (Life's unmixed joy has been given to no earthling, *Der Ring des Polykrates*, Schiller, 1911, vol. 1, p. 73): "What appears prominent about me is this inner courage."

I add: "And honesty and the will to creativity."

"When I think of how I make myself invisible"—
Thoughts about Traumatic Shame

Kilborne (2002) describes how "too much unbearable shame leads to a loss of the self, and a loss of self generates more shame. And unconscious shame leads to greater dependency upon both what others see of us and what we imagine they see" (p. 92).

We find (in Agnes and more generally) the feeling of shame in its multi-layeredness and depth as prominent among the frightening affects induced by trauma. In many cases, much of psychoanalytic work may consist in listening to the sense of current slights that seem to confirm the feeling of one's own unworth. In fact, the analysis itself can be traumatizing as a repetition of this original link between trauma and shame within the transference, or rather, within the real relationship with the therapist. What is this link however?

1) One root may indeed be massive shaming as part of the trauma, and that seems to be a self-evident connection. But there is far more that we uncover in our analytic work.

2) Very commonly it is the shame about the intensity of feelings in general, the great anxiety to express them, and the anxiety of inner and outer loss of control. It is so often the premise in the family, supported by cultural prejudice, that it is a sign of disgraceful weakness and thus of vulnerability, to show, or even just to have, strong feelings. This causes a very strong tendency to be deeply ashamed. The body, especially sexuality, may be far less strongly shame-inducing than this alleged weakness of having strong feelings: feelings of neediness, of longing, of tenderness, of being moved, of being hurt. Many look then for a partner who is an anti-shame-hero: someone emotionally untouchable, impenetrable, invulnerable, a disdainful ruler. Looking for the acceptance by such a figure and merger with him or her would remove the shame of feeling and wishing too strongly, but it means an almost incorrigible masochistic bondage, and a renewed and deepened sense of disgrace.

3) Then shame is caused by the experience that one has not been perceived as a person with the right to one's own feelings and will. The soul blindness of the other evokes the feeling of great worthlessness; the contempt of the other expressed by disregard for one's own inner life is matched by self-contempt. I mentioned how analysis itself may be shaming and thus inadvertently repeat the traumatogenic shame. There are many ways of doing this: Sometimes it may be the silence to a question, sometimes a sarcastic comment, often direct drive interpretations, and, what I see particularly in my supervisions in Europe, the unempathic, forced relating of every aspect to transference. All this can be felt to be soul blind. Incomprehension and tactlessness are experienced as a renewed deep insult and shaming.

4) Typically in severe traumatization in childhood, sexualization is then deployed as an attempt to regulate affects. Both the flooding with affects and the very archaic defense by sexualization leads to an overwhelming feeling of shame. On an additional frontline of defense, aggressive wishes, impulses, and fantasies are thrown in as means to reestablish control; they should stop the further tumble in that regressive spiral.

This archaic equation of traumatic affect storms, sexualization, and aggression leads, on the one hand, to global forms of defense, above all of denial, externalization, and projection, and as a result to the observable dissociative phenomena and, on the other hand, to massive countermeasures by the superego in the form of the same absoluteness and pervasiveness of shame and guilt. Much of this hypertrophy of the superego consists in the dominating fantasy of omnipotent responsibility set up as protection against traumatic helplessness.

5) Every kind of excitement turns, as affect regression, into overexcitement and overstimulation, and this has to lead inevitably to a crash, to a painful disappointment. This traumatic, passively experienced process is again and again turned around into something actively reenacted. How so? It happens in that way that every joy, every gratification, every expectation, everything good has to be broken off and changed into something negative and bad. It may seem as if it were unconscious guilt that would make it appear as if one did not deserve to be successful. This may certainly contribute. But that dangerous, mortifying, shame-laden excitement appears to be more important: "It is too dangerous to sense pleasure and joy; it will be abruptly taken away or it will become unbearably intense and totally unfulfillable." Thus the inner judge, the archaic superego, has to prevent all pleasure.

6) Closely connected with this is a sixth reason: that of the intrapsychic passivity. David Rapaport (1953/1967) wrote about the passivity of the ego. Often, what appears as ordained from the outside, is in truth an inner passivity in regard to affects and drives, but also and no less so a passivity vis-à-vis the threatening and hammering superego. There is not only profound anxiety about being helplessly delivered to these inner powers, but also shame for such inner ego-passivity. Outer victimhood is very often its externalization: a repetition on the outside in the vain attempt to resolve it within.

The Trauma of Objectification and Man as His Own Purpose (*Selbstzweck*)

In the context of this depth of her shame proneness, Agnes herself mentions the importance of soul blindness. This obtuseness toward the emotional interests and needs of the other, and soul murder, treating the other as a thing, exclusively as a tool for one's own gratification that can simply be discarded when not needed anymore, are found whenever man is not treated as aim and purpose in itself, but solely as a means to an end. However the human being that is used as a mere means, man as an instrument, as a dehumanized being, stripped of his or her individuality, senses the humiliation expressed in the depersonalization and reacts with a sense of unworth, of shame, and eventually with helpless rage to it. Finally he directs the full force of this resentment against the other.

Or it is turned, as we have witnessed in Agnes, against the self—in the form of a sequence of severe traumatization with empathy lacking, leading to shame and self-hate, with a sadistic superego part claiming omnipotence. That entails the great practical importance of the connection of trauma and aggression. Lawrence Inderbitzin and Steven Levy in their important paper "Repetition Compulsion Revisited: Implications for Technique" (1998) criticize the literature on psychic trauma for its onesidedness, especially for the disregard of the severity of conflicts about aggression:

> In our view, what is regularly absent from such formulations is a consideration of the intense frustration and ensuing aggression such trauma generates and the opportunities for aggression provided by 're-experiencing trauma.' The trauma appears to take on an instinct-like role that really belongs to the aggression created by the trauma. (p. 41)

Therefore, the manifest disturbances are then ascribed to defect and damage, instead of conflict and compromise:

> We wish to underline the vast, complicated array of defenses against aggression that are poorly regulated and integrated when trauma has significantly interfered with ego development and object relations. In such instances, fantasy cannot be utilized to transform the traumatic disturbances. In the stereotyped victim and victimizer repetitions that ensue, turning of aggression on the self, and identification with the aggressor are central. (p.45)

Part of the appropriate technique consists therefore in the "systematic interpretation of the massive defenses against aggression." Repetition compulsion, postulated as an elementary force and a basic cause, is a pseudo-explanation.

I fully agree with this. It is the conflict about aggression, as it shows itself moment by moment in the analytic work, that needs to be addressed again and again: the fear of envy, jealousy, vengefulness, rage, and hate—much more than the inferred aggressive affect or drive itself. As already mentioned, Agnes reacted to any such direct interpretation of aggression by immediate deterioration and withdrawal.

Cordelia Edvardson, a survivor of Auschwitz who had been transported there as proxy and sacrifice for her mother, the prominent German poet Elisabeth Langgässer, wrote in her book *Burned Child Seeks the Fire* (1998):

> The rage of the survivor that becomes the fear of her life. Year after year, the young woman hid the fierce rage; it completely filled her, it almost choked her; but these two, the woman and her rage, never got acquainted with each

other. The rage was too overwhelming that she could have dared to meet it; it would have burst her, and it would have turned into a flashing knife for the thrust into her mother's heart. But she did not dare the mother murder. It would have also extinguished Cordelia, the chosen one, the selected one, the one who had kept her vow of loyalty. (I quote from the German translation of the Swedish original, p. 114)

Double Reality

The patient has become far wiser, more stable, much more successful, but often also much sadder and even lonelier. The conflicts grounded in profound traumatization are very deep and encompassing, as we have met them in many forms. To select but a few of these conflicts:

- between overwhelming, traumatogenic affects and archaic, global affect blocking;
- between her unbending truthfulness and the recurrent processes of denial and idealization;
- between an archaically cruel superego versus the wishes for revenge and the feelings of hatred and resentment;
- between bitter despair and the will to protect, to save others and fight for their rights, although not for herself;
- between the wish to remain faithful to her own conscience and insight, and the fear to be rejected by everyone for her self-loyalty;
- between standing there defiant and alone and being submissive and accepted;
- between separation guilt and dependency shame;
- between the sadistic, brutal superego (the "unjust judge"), based in the omnipotence of responsibility and the introjection of the father and more generally of the traumata altogether, and a more tolerant, friendlier superego (the "just judge") that lastly coincides with a rational ego.

The result of those traumata and inner conflicts is a double reality within and without: On the one side there is a world of omnipotence and impotence, full of magical expectations and experiences, a basic masochistic attitude and world orientation (Novick and Novick, 1996a, 1996b), that is determined by the omnipotence of suffering and the omnipotence of responsibility. On the other side we encounter the world of competence, of real power through mastery of problems and resolution of conflicts.

In the extreme case we see the alternating invalidation of the feeling of reality. At one time, that whole first world of omnipotence and helplessness is experienced as unreal, like a shell. Only the second world, that of competence, of work, of creativity, retains its character of reality. Only this adaptation is felt to be good; it permits her joy and protection. It is like a railing holding her back from falling into the abyss. Then a massive disappointment occurs, a "narcissistic crisis," and now it is the reverse: only the world of global affects and of the radical Either/Or dilemmas is experienced as real, and with that the centrality of global guilt and global shame. It is, in the words of the Novicks, *"the conflict between the magical and reality systems of thought"*(p. 92, emphasis added).

This encompassing conflict between the world of trauma, omnipotence, and defect and the world of competence, of mastery of tasks, and solution of problems, is carried out mostly in the inner world, and yet it has to be again and again externalized.

Such a split in the experience of reality presupposes the force of denial, and with that the search for magical transformation. The cause of the inner split, the dissociation that has been put in the center of attention also by non-analysts like van der Kolk, is to be found in the experience of trauma: The total helplessness in front of the overwhelming and clashing affects calls for an equally radical defense by a fantasy of omnipotence, and that entails the hope for a magical transformation of self and world. Because it is impossible that this hope be fulfilled, this doubleness of self and world has to be repeated in endless vicious circles.

The Power of Symbolization

I try now to finally tie some of the main thoughts and experiences together.

We recognize how important it is both in the child's development and in therapy to open up the symbolic world, to impart a language for the inner world, and to put the life of inner experience into the great context of symbolic forms. It appears that among these symbolic forms particular power of binding global affects belongs to the word symbols. It is with their help that continuity is created in the psychological self. Target and Fonagy write (1996, p. 466) "that the active involvement of parents or siblings helps the child to accept two realities, internal and external, without needing to split his ego functioning to maintain a dual mode of thinking . . . the capacity for mental containment (reflectiveness) of the infant's mental states enhances his confidence in her [the mother's] capacity to assist with overwhelming affect and thus the infant turns to her in states of distress and overarousal."

This is, however, also at its most essential our task, and what helps us the most in this is the free unfolding of fantasy, that is, of the play of the mind.

Agnes would not be who she is, in spite of the extreme traumatization, without her continuous, trustful, nourishing relationship to the mother of her early childhood, in spite of many indications that the mother was often, if not chronically, depressed. I believe it is this relationship and to some extent its continuation for a while by the older sister that have made it possible to build a very strong sense of self, of identity, a feeling of inner continuity and self-loyalty, an image of an inner world, in spite of those delimited splits of ego and superego that I have outlined. She has not needed to develop that profound compromising of integrative functions that has been aptly described as "character perversion" (see next chapter). More and more the insights, the relationships, and especially the creativity have allowed her to grow out of her neurosis. Measure has more and more replaced absoluteness. The conflicts, particularly about aggression, mostly related to the many traumata, and the fantasies of omnipotence and exaggerated idealization of self and others have become largely conscious and been worked through: in inner experience and insight, not in the form of acting out within the sessions or outside.

The traumatogenic splits, the doubleness of self and world, were a form of adaptation that made possible her survival, but it also expressed itself in the creative transformation of that which is into something that should be: something that is right and just. With that I do not mean only her own poetic attempts or the recreation of literature in reading, but especially also her research where she has found significance and recognition.

She herself alludes to that tragic transformation when she made me aware of a passage in *Daniel Deronda* (Eliot, 1876/1982, p. 508): "'Take the present suffering as a painful letting in of light,' said Deronda, more gently. 'You are conscious of more beyond the round of your own inclinations—you know more of the way in which your life presses on others, and their life on yours. I don't think you could have escaped the painful process in some form or other.' 'But it is a very cruel form,' said Gwendolen, beating her foot on the ground with returning agitation. 'I am frightened at everything. I am frightened at myself.'"

May it be true for Agnes what Pylades tells Iphigenia (in Goethe's *Iphigenie auf Tauris*):

Das Leben lehrt uns, weniger mit uns
    Und andern strenge sein; du lernst es auch.
    (Life teaches us to be less strict with ourselves and with others; you will learn it also.) (Act IV, Sc. 4; my translation)

NOTES

1. The parenthetical numbers refer to the number of the session during the treatment. With . . . I indicate the elipsis of material, with—interrupted speech.

2. Translation by R. G. Henricks, of chapter 33, according to the newly discovered Ma-Wang-TuiTexts, p. 85.

3. "Im olám atá mevaqésch, en din; we'ím din atá mevaqésch, en olám."

4. I am very grateful to Dr. Ursula Engelhard, Dossingen, for making me aware of this poem (*Sämtliche Werke*, vol. 2., *Poems*. Frankfurt: Insel, 1956, p. 101). I try to translate it by staying as close as possible to the original:

Woe to me! My mother tears me down. Here, I have put stone upon stone to myself and I already stood here, like a little house around which the day moves, even alone. And now comes my mother, comes and tears me down.

She tears me down by coming and looking. She does not see that somebody is building. She walks straight across my wall of stone. Woe to me! My mother tears me down.

The birds fly around me with greater lightness. The strange dogs know: this is That One. Only my mother does not know it: my face that has slowly grown (has become more).

From her to me, there never was a warm wind. She does not live there where there is free air. She lies in a high heart-planking, and Christ comes and washes her every day.

3

Character Perversion

The complex dynamics of multiple and massive traumata, the global quality of affects and defenses, and the absoluteness of conscience, mostly in the meaning of moral masochism, and its replication in masochistic outer relationships calls for a theoretical deepening and broadening, both in clinical dimensions and into the area of broader cultural concepts. Most of all it is the centrality of doubleness, as we saw in the inner experience of Agnes, that has to serve as the starting point for our deepened inquiry.

This investigation has to begin with the defense by denial, the phenomenon of splitting, and the dimension of character perversion.

DENIAL AND CHARACTER PERVERSION

The starting point for the following theoretical introduction is Freud's comment (1940b): "The view which postulates that in all psychoses there is a *splitting of the ego* could not call for so much notice if it did not turn out to apply to other states more like the neuroses and, finally, to the neuroses themselves. I first became convinced of this in cases of *fetishism*." He then generalizes the observation:

It must not be thought that fetishism presents an exceptional case as regards a splitting of the ego; it is merely a particularly favorable subject for studying the question. Let us return to our thesis that the childish ego, under the domination of the real world, gets rid of undesirable instinctual demands by what are called repressions. We will now supplement this by further asserting that, during the same period of life, the ego often enough finds itself in the position of fending off some demand from the external world which it feels distressing ["peinlich," more properly translated as "embarrassing, shameful"] and that this is effected by means of *disavowal* [*Verleugnung*] of the perceptions which bring to knowledge this demand from reality. . . . The disavowal is always supplemented by an acknowledgment; two contrary and independent attitudes always arise and result in the situation of there being a splitting of the ego." (pp. 202–4)

Freud concludes the chapter with the statement: "Whatever the ego does in its efforts of defense, whether it seeks to disavow a portion of the real external world or whether it seeks to reject a drive demand from the internal world, its success is never complete and unqualified; the outcome always lies in two contrary attitudes, of which the defeated, weaker one, no less than the other, leads to psychical complications" (p. 204, modif.).

This defense by denial (disavowal) is not only a mainstay of the dynamics of the sexual perversion, but of what has been called "character perversion." This term refers, in Arlow's words (1971), to "the distortion of behavior or character [that] takes the place of what had once been a perversion or a perverse trend" (p. 334). Just as is the case in sexual perversion itself, the focus is on the denial of a traumatic perception and the fixation on a reassuring detail in the external world which seems to refute that danger; and just as it is specifically true for fetishism, a screen reality is magically being created to counteract the traumatogenic anxiety. For Arlow, as for Freud, the decisive anxiety is that of castration, the traumatic observation refers to the female genital, and accordingly, the protective fantasy needs to be the reassertion of the female phallus. Arlow describes three such character types: (1) the *unrealistic* character who misperceives reality in a systematic and often pseudo-stupid way in order to invalidate that traumatic observation; (2) the *petty liar* for whom the lie covers up the reality like a veil or fog in order to protect him against the perception itself, an ambiguity and illusion that corresponds to the fetish as a "screen percept"; and (3) the *practical joker and hoaxer* who frightens others with his pranks and then enjoys unmasking the deception, with the meaning: "What looks so terrible is not real; it is just a joke" (p. 330). In accordance with the dynamics of castration anxiety in response to the perception of the lacking penis in the woman, Arlow restricts this category of character perversion to male patients. It is particularly fetishism with its doubleness of acknowledgment and denial of the anatomical difference and the warding off of castration anxiety that serves for Arlow as paradigm. We may, therefore, speak of a "fetishistic character perversion."

This concept gets decisively broadened by Lee Grossman (1993). Like Freud, he also sees neurotic defense as being directed against wishes whereas perverse defense is used against perceived reality: ". . . in neurosis, the wish is renounced, disguised, or otherwise inhibited, out of respect for dangers perceived in reality; whereas in perversion, the perception of reality is altered, and the wish retained" (p. 423). The perverse treatment of reality is, however, not restricted to openly sexual perversions, but manifests itself as a general attitude of "disavowal, distraction, and illusion [as] defensive maneuvers directed against a threatening *perception*, which remains available to consciousness in some form" (p. 427), that is, concurrently with the acknowledgment of the perceived reality. It is what Freud demonstrated paradigmatically for fetishism: the split between No and Yes. The border between truth and fantasy or dream becomes blurred and vanishes. This also holds especially true for the insights in psychoanalysis: they are seemingly accepted, but then invalidated, deprived of their emotional significance. Functions both of the ego and the superego are in that way compromised. Grossman understands this process more broadly than Arlow insofar as quite generally perceptions of a threatening or painful reality are robbed of their felt meaning (not just in regard to those pertaining to castration anxiety).

Accordingly, in another article (1992), Grossman adds that "character traits may support the denial in fantasy of intolerable perceptions in women as well; and that depressive affect can motivate the formation of such traits" (p. 581). In the described case, it is, however, again the topic of the missing penis, although as a depressive concern. Ultimately, it still is a narrow version of the perversion paradigm since it is based on a phallocentric concept of gender and sexual development.

This is not so in a later work of his (1996): Grossman suggests that the distinction between "psychical or inner reality" and "material or outer reality" can be misleading. What we mean with psychic reality is not reality, but a persistent unconscious fantasy. The real conflict therefore exists between "tested reality and untested fantasy" (p. 510); "if the concept of 'psychic reality' elevates fantasy to the status of an alternative 'reality' in the mind of the analyst, the outcome may be collusion with the patient's pathological blurring of the distinction between fantasy and reality . . . there is a large group of patients whose pathology rests on their tendency to suspend testing the reality of their perceptions" (ibid.), and who, for defensive purposes, actively confuse fantasy and reality. They deny unwanted perceptions in order to avoid in that way having to question relished fantasies. This is what he calls "the *perverse attitude towards reality*." It is a regress to a developmental level where thoughts cannot be reliably distinguished from actions, nor wishes from deeds, nor inside from outside. The fetishist directs his attention to a peripheral detail to distract himself from the intolerable observation of a penisless female genital. At the same time, he persuades himself that the fetish is something that women possess, and thus he obliterates the difference between fetish and penis. In his cross-dressing the transvestite implements his wish that the woman's appearance is only an illusion and hence the view of the female genital is also illusory. In all these cases, the importance of a specific perception is discredited. "The pathology is in the license he grants himself to *keep his treasured beliefs untested. . . . He treats dreams as if they were real and perceptions as if they were dreams*" (p. 512; emphasis added). This perverse attitude vis-à-vis reality is by no means restricted to the sexual perversions but affects a much wider range of patients "whose solutions to intrapsychic conflict center around the persistent and widespread disavowal of troubling perceptions of reality" (ibid.). "Perverse" means the extensive defense against reality. In Grossman's opinion "it is imperative that the analyst be prepared to speak for the demands of reality" (p. 515). If the analyst fails to call a spade a spade and bows to the so-called psychic reality of the patient he fails in his own responsibility to help the patient meet the world in such a way as he knows it really is.

The following work by Alan Bass (1997) brings, I believe, a further deepening of the understanding of this "perverse attitude toward reality." He refers to patients who fail to make use of interpretations because, in Jacobson's expression (1957, p. 73), they tend to "handle intrapsychic conflicts as though they were conflicts with reality" (Bass, 1997, p. 643). This "infantile concretization of psychic reality . . . permits persons who employ this defense to treat their psychic strivings as if they were concrete objects perceived" (Jacobson, 1957, p. 80; Bass, 1997, p. 643). The questions posed by Bass are how we can understand why the patient has to defend so strenuously against the possibility that one thing might mean another, that it is being used symbolically, and how to approach this technically. He sees the answer in the *"defense against differentiation"* (p. 645, emphasis added). "To use interpretation therapeutically, psychic organization has to be not unduly threatened by the possibility that one might be different from what one consciously thinks oneself to be" (ibid.). It is therefore his thesis that "persistent 'concreteness' is the result of complicated defenses against the possibility of differentiation itself" (ibid.). This means, *eo ipso*, of course that the ability to symbolize is compromised (p. 646). As Grossman had stated, fantasy and reality are not separated from each other. Fetishism is a prototype for this merger: a perceptual identity is created between an external object and a fantasy, "the concrete, visible thing . . . has to be *perceived* in order for the man to be potent" (Bass, 1997, pp. 654–55). Bass revises Freud's observation of the "splitting of the ego," noting that the oscillation of the fetishist between the view of the woman as castrated and as not castrated is one between two fantasies: *"Perceived castration is a fantasy"* (p. 657), and he continues that "castration and noncastration are both clearly fantasies that substitute for the reality of sexual difference itself . . . *the reality the fetishist disavows is the reality of sexual dif-*

ference" (pp. 657–58, emphasis added). The fetishist constructs the genders in the sense of a phallic monism, as a fantasy of one sex and of its absence. The doubleness of reality and fantasy, the "oscillation" between them, consists in that the sexual difference is seen, but denied and replaced by that fantasy of phallic monism (p. 658). Thus we deal with a primary split created by denial, namely that between the registration of differentiation and its replacement by wish fulfillment altogether and the undoing of differences, and a secondary split between those two fantasies, that of "castration" and that of "noncastration," which "substitute for the differentiation lost to defense" (p. 658). Such denial is, however, a kind of negative hallucination. Thus Bass arrives at his central thesis: "concreteness in general is a result of the process that produces the primary split in the ego, a split between any differentiation that has become too anxiety provoking and the defensive use of hallucinatory wish fulfillment to substitute for it altogether . . . differentiation itself always raises tension and is therefore always potentially traumatic" (p. 659). "One can understand concreteness as a 'fetishistic' compromise formation between differentiation, on the one hand, and 'primary wish fulfillment and defense' on the other" (p. 660). In all this it is by no means just an issue of sexual difference. Rather, this concreteness may be derived from conflicts about differentiation on all levels of development. Every possibility of differentiating between inside and outside, between self and objects is experienced as a traumatic increase in tension (pp. 672–73).

Renik's (1992) and Reed's (1997) articles already show by their titles that fetishism continues being the lodestar for the understanding of character perversion, and with that also, though not exclusively, castration anxiety and the depressive admission of one's own genital deficiency (in my view: "castration shame") as a lead motivation for perversion in general, and for character perversion in particular. A magic fantasy has to replace the frightening or painful view of reality, as expression of that characteristic splitting between denial and recognition, between No and Yes: "A final judgment between contradictory ideas is never made: at times one holds sway, and at times the other, with equal power" (Renik, 1992, p. 549). This crack of doubleness stretches through wide areas: the patients avoid deciding whether certain significant observations are realistic perceptions or wishful fantasies (ibid.).

Arlow (1971, p. 333) writes about a "superego subverted by anxiety" or, as Grossman adds, by any intolerable affect (1992, 1993, 1996); the latter author concludes that "perverse defenses depend on a form of dishonesty, a disordered conscience that allows the subject to *act as if* he were unable to distinguish fantasy from reality." Therefore, "the superego's contribution to perception and reality testing . . . is compromised in the perverse view of reality" (Grossman, 1996, p. 513). Renik speaks, in the same sense, of "an overall deficit in the patient's conscience functioning" within analysis, "the lack of a particular discipline necessary to psychoanalytic self-investigation: the patient does not persevere in the pursuit of truth in the face of unpleasurable affect" (1992, p. 551). Also outside of the treatment situation, we observe astonishing irruptions of irresponsibility. In Renik's opinion, pedagogical turns given to interpretations can therefore not always be avoided. The transference is more and more shaped in a way that the patient sees the own self as defective and the analyst and the analytic interventions as offering something that is lacking, as a substitute for what is missing in the self, as replacement of one's own skills; that means, however, that the treatment is used fetishistically: "she [a given patient] was unable to think clearly without me" (p. 555). The patient's pleasure that she could trust the analyst to know her secret thoughts "revealed her fantasy of merger with a missing part—an idealized, omnipotent conscience, personified by her analyst. I supplied capacities to think and to judge reality that she believed she did not have and could not develop herself. No surprise, then, that she hoped analysis would last forever" (p. 556). The patient's aim is therefore that the analyst replace a missing part; it is not the process of self-exploration. The enactment of such a restitutive fantasy serves the defense against the depressive affect about loss: the defense against mourning. Thus, analysis becomes interminable, in the service of that magical expectation.

Gail Reed (1997) continues this line of thinking. Above all, she "explores the transference dynamics and underlying fantasies of analysands whose characters have been shaped by conflict solutions common to perversions. Giving the impression of a serious engagement for therapeutic ends, these individuals live out in the treatment a sexualized engagement in which the analyst's interventions are transformed into a fetish. This enactment is designed to support a defensive effort to avoid external perceptions that trigger certain fantasies of danger, including that of castration. It is designed also to cancel out interventions of the analyst that become equated with these frightening fantasies. Since the analyst's efforts to explore and interpret this enactment are also turned into a fetish, such a transference poses grave difficulties for the analysis" (p. 1153). She suggests that the analyst focus on the contradiction itself, on the operation of disavowal, on the fantasy of the danger that is persistently denied and on the "underlying, often vengeful and envious wishes that contribute both to the undermining of the analysis and to the content of the fantasies of danger that provoke so much anxiety" (ibid.). "Sexual gratification is used in the service of a defensive effort to avoid certain external perceptions" (p. 1154).

However, the main danger against which this fetishistic form of transference is set up to defend is in her view, as in that of Bass, the terrifying observation of differences—the difference of presence and absence, meaning both the danger of separation and of the anatomical difference of sex. Still, for her too, it is the perception of the missing penis and the aggression evoked by this, that stand in the center of the defensive efforts. The analytic process must again subserve magical restitution and thus offer security against anxiety or depression in the form of the protective fantasy: "Just as the fantasized danger situation is triggered by an external perception of difference, the perverse fantasy that replaces it requires the presence of an external object. Conflict is not only externalized; there is also a partial failure of symbolization, in that the transference object to be possessed, reduced to a fetish, stolen from, merged with, or interchanged with must be present *in fact* to sustain the illusion of reality" (p. 1170). The technique should therefore consistently and actively counteract those contradictions and the anxiety avoided by them and thus assist in shifting from "the magic of illusion" in the transference to an "awareness of its as-if quality" (p. 1178).

In a later paper (2001), Gail Reed above all describes more precisely the consequences for the transference: The analyst only exists to support the illusion, to blur the differences, a fantasy of omnipotence and magic. One consequence of this is the radical discontinuity within the analytic process: rapid, disconcerting, mystifying shifts, leaps, breaks, in particular also rapidly alternating exchanges of roles that leave the analyst perplexed and helpless and evoke intense aggressions in the countertransference. The as-if quality of the transference disappears, the therapeutic ego split between experiencing and observing ego becomes impossible, the interpretations are ineffective, and the treatment itself turns chaotic and stagnates. Gail Reed proposes to focus in these cases entirely on these discontinuities and the repetitive contradictions. The knowledge of difference itself is for these patients traumatic and is replaced by a fantasy of eternal sameness and togetherness: they use the analytic frame to live out a fantasy that disavows the difference between patient and analyst, at the same time as they obliterate the analyst when he/she does not satisfy their wishes for eternal togetherness and security. The progress of analysis largely depends on how far the analyst recognizes and is able to articulate the anxiety about the helplessness entailed: "Thus the analyst first must represent the patient's discontinuity to the patient in the hope of initiating a process that will end with *the transformation of a breach in continuity into a carrier of meaning*" (p. 929, emphasis added).

Just as Gail Reed speaks, in accordance with André Green, about severe early trauma as creating the experience of the "black hole," a traumatic absence without representation, the German psychoanalyst Küchenhoff (1990) writes in regard to early trauma,

in contrast to later trauma, it does not remain external to the psychical apparatus, but becomes part of it. In other words, the traumatic experience becomes a transcendental part of the categories of experience, a subjective *a priori* of all possible experience. In this regard, the early trauma poses an entirely different psychodynamic problem. Its assimilation is so total that the trauma becomes the image of self and world whereas later trauma remains a foreign body for experience which could still infect all other forms of experience. It is the early trauma that is therefore used for the formation of identity. (p. 18)

We should therefore rather speak of "traumatic identity or traumatic identity formation," instead of "early trauma," he says, manifest in a basic sense of unpredictability.

Dependent upon the development of identificatory ego-functions, this identity formation will vary. Due to a trauma in the first months of life, the development of basic trust may be interrupted; no memory image of a good breast arises that could form the background for any possible experience; the trauma becomes incorporated like a bad and unpredictable breast, leading to the basic conviction that life unfolds within a basic unpredictability. (ibid.)

This early trauma can be defended against by "personification in the traumatic object," the bondage to an evil object as fundamental to life and perpetuated in the archaic superego (with the alternating solutions of submission to it or triumph over it), or by "rejection of the relationship to the traumatic object," the "attacks on linking," and the establishment of *"the phantasma of the empty space"* (pp. 23–25), or in the parlance of André Green, again as a defense, "the *disobjectalizing function* leading to an *absence of representation* rather than to depression," "the pathological negative" or "void" (1993).

Richard Zimmer (2003) expands on Freud's concept of the "splitting of the ego" as being characteristic for fetishism and then for broad swathes of psychopathology (including what I am investigating right now as character perversion), by stressing the doubleness of perverse thought:

The forms of thought I am discussing are organized around a split in the ego rather than around repression. In this split, one part of the ego embraces the reality principle and is capable, within its circumscribed purview, of mental activity that takes into account external reality and the limitations inherent in the ego's relation with it. The other part of the ego rejects some piece of external reality and its own limited capacity to control and understand it. In so doing, it reverts to a primitive form of mental activity in which somatically represented projective and introjective fantasies regressively substitute for reality-oriented thinking particularly in the form of concretization (p. 908–9).

Again in line with all the more recent authors, he goes far beyond the model based on defense against castration anxiety:

Theoretically, I believe that this mechanism—that is, the splitting of the ego into progressive and regressive parts and the establishment of a false integration between these parts—is a fundamental mechanism of perverse psychic structure, one that, from a developmental point of view, most probably precedes and contributes to the intense castration anxiety that typically characterizes perverse structure. (p. 910)

Finally, the conceptualization of character perversion is expanded in very important ways by Sheldon Bach (1994) and by Novick and Novick (1996a, 1996b, 2003a, 2003b) by also involving narcissistic, sadomasochistic, and exhibitionistic forms of conflict solution.

Bach's book is perhaps the most comprehensive study of the topic of character perversion. He opens by stating that

perversions are attempts to simplistically resolve or defend against some of the central paradoxes of human existence. How is it possible for us to be born of someone's flesh yet be separate from her, or to live in one's experience yet observe oneself from outside? How are we able to deal with feelings of being both male and female, child and adult, or to negotiate between the worlds of internal and external stimulation? . . . For various reasons they have not developed the psychic space that would allow them to recognize the reality and legitimacy of multiple points of view. Thus they tend to think in either/or dichotomies, to search for dominant/submissive relationships, and to perceive the world from uniquely subjective or objective perspectives. (p. xvii)

Here Bach points to the basic differences of human existence: union and separateness, subjectivity and objectivity, male and female, child and adult, inside and outside, fantasy and reality. Although all his patients have the oedipal beating fantasies, the problems of separation and individuation are just as important, the former reflecting the disturbances of the latter (especially of object- and self-constancy). The denial of shame and of death assume a particularly important position in these disturbances. "Sadomasochistic relations . . . arise as a defense against and an attempt to repair some traumatic loss that has not been adequately mourned" (p. 4).

One form of such grandiose denial is the overobjectification and with that the dehumanization of the person (p. xix). Cooper spoke earlier (1988) in similar terms; in my formulation, perversion is dehumanized sexuality and sexualized dehumanization. This archaic equation holds true with particular force for character perversion.

Bach also specifically asks why the sight of the female genitals would be so traumatic and replies:

From my perspective, one may surmise that in some cases the *whole* mother and not only her genitals has been traumatic or, to put it more concretely, that some of those children who find the sight traumatic have discovered *not only a fantasied gap in the genital area but also an actual gap in relatedness,* and that the child's *entire psyche has been mobilized to deny and to patch over this gap* [emphasis added]. In certain cases one can regard this fantasy of a frightening genital nothingness as the ultimate body metaphor for a series of developmental losses culminating in the fear that there is *no one there* to love or be loved by and no possibility of finding some libidinal connection behind the screen of technical relatedness. (1994, pp. 11–12)

In sadism, the sadness is avoided by sexualization of rage; the female phallus and the existence of a loving and idealized mother are both confirmed and denied. Masochism is the bond to the idealized mother of pain, sadism both a denial of his need for her, yet at the same time a primitive identification with the omnipotent, aggressive, and androgynous mother of pain (p. 14). "It is sometimes as early as infancy that the fateful choice to live in pain rather than lose the object may already have begun" (p. 15). The masochist says: "Do anything you want to me but don't leave me"; it feels pleasurable because the partner is still present: "*The pain of suffering defends against the greater pain of loss*" (p. 17, emphasis added)—in the words of several of my patients (Elazar [see chapter 4 in this volume], Albert [see Wurmser, 1993, 1999b]): "Torture me, but don't abandon me!" In contrast, the sadist proclaims: "I can do anything I want to you and you'll still always be there!" (Bach, 1994, p. 18).

In order to deny castration, loss, shame, and death, the sadomasochist pays the price to remain frozen in a lifeless stereotype; no progression is possible:

This fantasy of part-objects manipulated without loss unfolds in a world that the sadomasochist has split off or dissociated, in an altered state of consciousness characterized by extreme sexual excitement, sharply diminished reflective self-awareness, and a diminished sense that his acts are his own and under voluntary control. While in this altered state he feels as if hypnotized or in an *erotic haze,* and under its spell events take on a hyper-real and hallucinatory quality that make them seem larger and more compelling than reality itself. What I call the *erotic haze* serves to deny that reality is not in accord with fantasy. (Bach, 1994, p. 19)

One of the marks of perversion is the inability to think metaphorically and to tolerate paradox and ambiguity (p. 57). Instead, there is the absoluteness of judgment. Enactment is sometimes the only genuine communication the patient is capable of (p. 64). The other no longer exists as an object in his or her own right, but merely as a carrier for the not-me (p. 67).

In earlier books of mine I have stressed how helpful the work of Jack and Kerry Kelly Novick has been for me and how it continues to assist me in my clinical tasks with these severe clinical problems and in some of the theoretical formulations ordering those experiences. In the current context I would like to quote some thoughts from their recent manuscript "Two Systems of Self-Esteem Regulation" (2003a):

> In our work we have emphasized that we do not view omnipotent beliefs as part of normal development, nor as equivalent to oceanic feelings, grandiosity, egocentrism, or primary narcissism. *Omnipotent beliefs are created in response to reality failures in order to protect the person from physical or psychological trauma. We define such defensive omnipotence* [emphasis added] as a conscious or unconscious belief in real power to control others, to hurt them, to force them to submit to one's desires, ultimately probably to force the mother to be a "good enough," competent, protective, and loving parent. Repetitive, resistant, self-defeating functioning, stalling or impasse in the clinical relationship—these form the arena for most analytic endeavors. We are suggesting that what is at work in regulating the self-esteem of patients at such times is a *closed, omnipotent, sadomasochistic system* [emphasis added], in which the active search for pain and suffering has transformed experiences of helplessness into a hostile defense. The organizing belief in this defense against overwhelming, even traumatic, anxiety, guilt, and helplessness is one of magical power to control the object.

Instead of seeing sadomasochism as a separate diagnostic entity, they suggest that it is, together with its core beliefs of omnipotence, present in all cases, "in some more visibly and more persistently than others." All the ego's abilities and gifts are being put in the service of the conviction that they themselves represent an exception from the rules of reality, from both the laws of society and of nature; moreover, because of their suffering they feel fully entitled sadistically to force others to fulfill their needs.

At each point of development, another system opposes this sadomasochistic-omnipotent one, a system of self-esteem regulation that aims at competence and efficacy and is based on mutually respectful, pleasurable relationships. These are formed through realistic perception of the self and others, are open toward inner and outer experiences and thus permit creativity in life and work. They quote Freud (1923, p. 50n): "analysis does not set out to make pathological reactions impossible, but to give the patient's ego *freedom* to decide one way or the other," and Rangell (1982), who suggests that the goal of treatment is choice. I have put the same thought at the center of my considerations of normality and pathology, and hence of treatment goals, in *The Power of the Inner Judge* (Wurmser, 2000a).

The Novicks propose then, corresponding to the two systems of self-esteem regulation, "two kinds of technique, one that elucidates closed system functioning, another that enhances open system functioning." They explain:

> Closed system phenomena require the classical approach of transference and resistance analysis, with the aim of putting the patient in the active center of his pathology. But defense and transference interpretations of open system functioning can pathologize and drive away competence. Mirroring, empathy, reconstruction, validation, support, and developmental education . . . link open system phenomena with the analyst's functions beyond serving only as a transference object. These techniques applied to closed system functioning, however, may be at best a palliative waste of time, at worst, may serve to reinforce a passive, helpless, victimized stance on the part of the patient.

Summarizing some of the ideas of the Novicks and applying them to the cases that follow, we can say: The result of these developments is a *double reality* within and without: On the one side there is a world of omnipotence and impotence, full of magical expectations and experiences, a basic masochistic attitude and world orientation (Novick and Novick, 1996a, 1996b), that is determined by the omnipotence of suffering and the omnipotence of responsibility. On the other side we encounter the world of competence, of real power through mastery of problems and resolution of conflicts.

In the extreme case we see the alternating invalidation of the feeling of reality. At one time, that whole first world of omnipotence and helplessness is experienced as unreal, like a shell. Only the second world, that of competence, of work, of creativity, retains its character of reality. Only this adaptation is felt to be good; it permits joy and protection. It is like a railing holding the person back from falling into the abyss. Then a massive disappointment occurs, a "narcissistic crisis," and now it is the reverse: only the world of global affects and of the radical Either/Or dilemmas is experienced as real, and with that the centrality of global guilt and global shame.

These patients live clearly in a double world, with a double self: a world of rationality, of professional mastery, and often impressive competence, and even sometimes loving relationships where there seems to be at least partly the attainment of an integration of inner and outer reality, where their feelings are under control and they can exert considerable power over their own life and the life of others. In this area of existence, concrete reality and symbolization are clearly distinguished and at the same time integrated so that they can function at a very high level of competence, differentiation, and integration (Fonagy and Target, 1996).

But then there is that other world in which everything seems polarized, fallen to pieces, split into opposites, and dominated by compulsion, a realm of being where everything always, even quite consciously, turns into a matter of either omnipotence or total helplessness, of either perfection or total shame and vulnerability, of either absolute purity or equally total vileness, of global sexuality and equally global aggression. There may be outbursts of ruthless rage out of the sense of suffered injustice, followed by abysmal guilt. It is what Fonagy would describe as the mode of mental equivalency—or what Jack and Kerry Kelly Novick stress: the central delusion of omnipotence as a complex form of defense in traumatic states and as core of the masochistic personality disorder. In that way, split and radical conflict between fantasized omnipotence and idealization against real competence and mastery move into the center of the psychoanalytic work:

> One of the aims of treatment is to help the patient become aware of the system he is using, to face the way in which the omnipotent system destroys the reality of his capacities and achievements, and ultimately to realize that relinquishing the omnipotent source of self-esteem will not leave him with nothing. As the patient laboriously gets in touch with the alternative sources of self-esteem available through competent, empathic, and loving interactions with others, a conflict arises between the systems. (Novick and Novick, 1996a, p. 68)

This is "the conflict between the magical and reality systems of thought" (p. 92). It is what I called in the prologue the antithesis between magical transformation and tragic transformation, and one we observed while accompanying Agnes on her long path.

This encompassing conflict between the world of trauma, omnipotence, and defect and the world of competence, of mastery of tasks, and solution of problems, is carried out mostly in the inner world, and yet it has to be again and again externalized.

In the first world a feeling of compulsiveness dominates, up to a sense of complete paralysis of will. In the second world, thought and feelings are translated into decision and action, and with that the patient is in charge of what is subjectively felt as willpower and inner freedom.

The often huge work consists in effecting a gradual shift of the inner equilibrium from inner compulsion to inner freedom; but this is finally only possible if the two ways of being can be reconciled. This work is a matter of insight and art and requires enormous patience and persistence on both sides, in order to break the iron grip of compulsiveness.

Two recent works on this topic are noteworthy, both by analysts working in Israel. Ruth Stein (2005) writes that two features are common to both sexual and nonsexual perverse relations: (1) seductive and bribing aspects; and (2) its means-ends reversal:

> Perversion as a mode of relatedness points to relations of seduction, domination, psychic bribery and guileful uses of "innocence," all in the service of

exploiting the other . . . perversion, whether sexual or otherwise, is the use of the ends of sexuality as the means to control the other and to destroy intimacy when intimacy is experienced as threatening. Perversion is the induction of helplessness . . . and the perpetration of hostility and cruelty in the name of love and caring. Perversion is the psychic act of penetrating without being penetrated. . . . Perversion is the active replacement of intimacy by a sexualized, enticing "false love." (pp. 781–82)

It is "an implicit contract signed against reality" (p. 793).

Ofra Eshel (2005) stresses the massive trauma and psychotic regression warded off by the perverse relation:

severe perversion registers and freezes a haemorrhaging traumatic core experience of self-with-significant-other. The perversion embodies the *specific experiential-emotional key quality of the traumatic situation*, and stops at the near-hit, last impression before reaching the full intensity of dread, annihilation and psychic deadness—*making present the imprint of the past destructive experience*, over and over again, concretely, unremittingly. (p. 1079)

It is the last-ditch attempt to halt the fall into the abyss. Central to this defense is the radical inner split; Eshel calls it autotomy, cutting part of the self off in "massive dissociative splitting into two disconnected parts, alien to each other, as a means of psychic survival" (p. 1078). In short, she regards "perversion as a defense organization—through splitting, externalization, and compulsive sexualization—against a violent, devastating, unbearable, deadening early past situation," a "sexualized manic survival; not the 'disavowal of castration,' but the 'disavowal of annihilating destruction'" (p. 1080)—not Oedipus, but Pentheus. Ostensibly, she focuses on sexual perversion, but what she writes applies with equal strength to character perversion.

DEFINING CHARACTERISTICS OF CHARACTER PERVERSION

Turning now to my own study of this large subject, I would see great merit in enlarging the concept of character perversion so that it follows not only the paradigm of the fetishistic perversion, but also that of sado-masochism, of exhibitionism-voyeurism, and of the narcissistic perversion. I also very much concur with Cooper and the Novicks, seeing this more as a *dimension*, a *perspective*, rather than merely as a nosological category. Minor aspects might very well be a ubiquitous part of our inner life and of all neurosis, but I find its conceptualization as a major structure of inner dynamics and of relatedness particularly helpful for the understanding of large segments of the severe neuroses.

I already noted that some of the authors mention how this aspect of pathology compromises superego functioning. I would go further and state that superego pathology is an essential part of what underlies character perversion, not just its consequence. The main defenses certainly are specifically set up to deal with more or less severe traumatization and the conflicts dealing with such trauma. But it is decisive that severe superego problems, especially in the sense of conflicts within the superego, play a cardinal, I would say indispensable, part in those traumatogenic conflicts, and much of the access to an understanding of the main features of character perversion can be gained by technically working through those absolute demands of the "inner judge" that are in contradiction to each other (as we just saw in the opposition between the "just judge" and the "unjust judge," but also as I have described in chapter 6 of *The Power of the Inner Judge*, Wurmser, 2000a).

Guided by my experiences I would therefore stress the following criteria for character perversion:

1) As all the authors postulate, there is the centrality of chronic severe trauma, both physical and emotional, often, but not necessarily sexual. In the traumatic background, the main family factors are chronic shaming directly or by soul-blindness, massive violence, and an atmosphere of resentment, "injustice has been done to me." But physical defects, severe accidents, and operations may have a similar longtime effect. The trauma itself creates new psychic and physiologic reality, including strongly altered brain functions: "extensive experience with an affectively misattuned primary caregiver creates a growth-inhibiting environment for a maturing corticolimbic system . . . affect pathology reflects a regulatory dysfunction in the orbitofrontal structure" says Allan Schore (1997, p. 830).

2) With Freud, there is *splitting*, in the sense of the doubleness of the denial of traumatic perceptions and their acknowledgment, of Yes and No, and with that the dominance of the defense by denial, I would now add, and more radically, of *dissociation* in the character (Eshel, 2005), together with the necessity of countervailing fantasy. We witnessed precisely this prevalence of the defense of dissociation in Agnes, both as a protection against externally induced trauma and the accompanying pain or grief, secondarily, against her own reality perceptions at the behest of the superego, and then thirdly, against much of her inner world: all the "too-muchness" of her feelings and wishes. She was quite clear about the doubleness of Yes and No, the parallelism of acknowledgment and disavowal described by Freud.

3) With Renik and Reed, we encounter the persistent attempt at *magical* realization of this fantasy that should counteract those threats, as

wish fulfillment and illusion in the relationship to the analyst or psychotherapist. At the same time, the remarks of the therapist are often
tuned out: one does not want to see and hear what would touch on
the traumatic anxiety or on the superego anxieties. The same is valid
of course for external reality in general: it too has to keep being
screened out in a self-destructive fashion.

4) With most of the authors, I also stress the *sexualization* of the underlying traumatic experiences, of the dangers and losses (Coen 1981,
1985). The various forms of anxiety and depressive affects are being
changed in very early times into pleasurable excitement (Fraiberg,
1982). Other defenses are then specifically used against this sexual
transformation. The outcome is a strongly erotic character, without
having to be directly sexual, but rather idealizing, infatuated, ecstatic, covering over intense hatred. A very deep and prevalent form
appears to be the predominance of phallic conflicts, of castration
anxiety, castration shame, and penis envy. In line with what Bach
proposes, we can see how the traumatically experienced "hole" in
the human relationship: the lovelessness, the affective coldness and
soul-blindness of the environment, is filled with a preoccupation
with the supposed anatomical "hole" and the seeming anatomical
defect when there is no penis. Ultimately, then image of the genital
"hole" and its "plug" may be attempts at representation for what
eludes symbolization, the "black hole" referred to (Reed, 1997, 2001;
Green, 1993; Küchenhoff, 1990; Bach, 1994) where "knowledge of
difference is traumatic" (Reed, 2001, p. 928). Thus, the phallocentric
orientation and with that the frightening difference between the
sexes is a sexualizing defense against deeper affects of anxiety,
mourning, and pain, rooted in the traumatic original relationships of
early childhood (Hägglund et al. 1976).

5) With the experience of soul-blindness, there is a general atmosphere of *dehumanization* of relationships in general, of sexuality in
particular. In line with what Sheldon Bach (1994), Arnold Cooper
(1988,1991), and Ruth Stein (2005) observed, I repeat that perversion is dehumanized sexuality and sexualized dehumanization.
Dehumanization is a special form of aggression, expressing deep
contempt and hate. In many, especially in intellectuals, we notice
a fascination by all that has to do with death. This enthrallment by
what is dead implies a glorification of the dehumanized personal
relationship by its aesthetic and sexual transformation and distancing. Creating distance by aestheticization is not only a defense
against the fear of death and castration by denial, but also against
the entire traumatically experienced reality; it serves above all the

disavowal of one's own pain and of the yearning for love by the other.

6) We always find the *doubling of the self*. Typically, a sadomasochistic and a depersonalized, although seemingly functioning part-identity alternate in bewildering ways (Eshel, 2005). As the Novicks describe in detail, corresponding to this doubleness of the self, the experience of the world is also split, namely into a universe of omnipotence, impotence, and suffering, where power through mutual humiliation and suffering becomes the main aim, that is, the sadomasochistic dimension, and a universe of competence and mastery, of respect and love. Part of such doubling is the prominence of brief trancelike states, states of *altered consciousness*, which Bach calls "erotic haze." Often in these states, there occur stereotypical impulsive action sequences (Lansky, 1984, 1992).

7) Very important is the *splitting of the superego*, especially in the sense of overwhelming shame versus overwhelming guilt, or of opposite loyalties or values, and hence the narrowness of the path between these two abysses of self-condemnation—a walk on a thin crest between abysmal guilt and equally abysmal shame. This points to the crucial role of the superego in the pathogenesis of this disorder. An important pathogenic way of dealing with such an archaic, split superego is the denial of important segments of reality in order to reconcile those irreconcilably contradictory inner demands, those opposing claims for absoluteness that otherwise inevitably lead to a sense of fragmentation, of "falling to pieces."

8) As Lee Grossman, Bass, and Reed describe, the *denial of the most important differences* is central: between inside and outside, between fantasy and reality, between concrete and symbolic, between animate and inanimate, between person and thing, between the whole and the part, and, of course of particular dynamic significance, between male and female, between a phallically understood sexuality and a far more differentiated and comprehensive understanding of sexuality.

9) Finally, also the flow of *time*, its ebbing away, and hence *change* altogether, have to be denied. Time and change and their delimitations may for example be denied by not wearing or having any watch. This guardian over time, the centerpiece of modernity, can serve as a powerful symbol for the superego in its limit-setting functions. In their place, there is unending union instead of separateness, there is "the eternal return of the same," as Nietzsche put it as the foundation for his "will for power," in his own struggle against his most painful isolation. Those central wishes for merger, for the lifting of

all boundaries and *denial of limitations*, lead into the vicious cycle of symbiosis described in chapter 5 of *The Power of the Inner Judge* (see also chapter 8 in this volume).

❉   ❉   ❉

Such a split in the experience of reality presupposes the force of denial and dissociation, and with that the search for magical transformation. The cause of the inner split, the *dissociation* that has also been put at the center of attention by non-analysts like van der Kolk, is to be found in the experience of trauma.

The magic transformations sought relate in one way or another to the nine points elaborated above; the most important among them are those deployed to lift crucial borders and limitations, to hide the contradictoriness (allowing the Yes and the No side by side) and, clinically of the utmost significance, to change the significant other from being the harshest judge to being one that forgives, accepts, and admires.

Yet there is one more shift in perspective in our study of the severe neuroses, another dimension that resorts more to a literary metaphor, and yet it is also a valuable way of looking at the phenomena we are dealing with—once more a view complementary to the one just given. But I defer its introduction.

We turn now to a deepened study of how such magical transformations, blurring of boundaries, and discarding of limits and limitations clinically occur, and how the processes of tragic transformation in the treatment dialogue slowly emerge, evolve, and progress. Knowledge is a powerful weapon against despair and fright. A saying befitting such deep inner change and the daring journey of psychoanalysis comes from one of the famous Chassidic masters of the early nineteenth century, Rabbi Nachman of Bratzlav: "The entire world is a very narrow bridge. The main thing is not to be afraid."[1]

NOTE

1. "Kol ha'olám kulló gesher tzar me'ód; we ha'iqár lo lefachéd klal." Quoted in Abrams, 1999, p. 111.

4

∗

The Way from Ithaca to Golgatha—The Analysis of a Masochistic Sexual and Character Perversion

THE QUESTION

"How would it be possible, how could it be possible for any human being to respect himself, if he tries to find pleasure in the very feeling of his own humiliation?"[1]

This question of the "autobiographer" in Dostoyevsky's *Notes from the Underground* (1864/1982); I quote from the 1982 Russian edition; all translations are mine), is an important, but also multilayered riddle.

On one layer it alludes to a problem that has accompanied psychoanalysis from its inception: How can it be understood that anybody would draw satisfaction and even sexual pleasure out of pain and sorrow, out of humiliation and shame, and that he would, because of this, directly seek out such suffering, draw it upon himself, provoke it? Does not that directly contradict everything we would expect on the basis of that basic teaching about mental functioning, one that had already been proffered by Plato in the *Protagoras* and then was elevated by Freud to the fundamental principle: the primary motive of seeking pleasure and avoiding unpleasure—that is, the pleasure principle? Does it not also contradict other psychological theories, like those proposing that the primary human motive is increase of benefit to oneself or self-preservation, the will for life, for power? This is the superficial riddle of masochism. It is relatively easily answerable and has, again and again, been solved in the literature.

Much more difficult is the next layer, the second obvious question: How can the pain addict, the seeker of humiliation, respect himself? Should he not be ashamed of finding pleasure in the very fact of his abasement? Does not the shame about the shame—more exactly: the shame about the pleasure hidden in the shame—give additional suffering, leading into an unending vicious circle, an unbound regress of self-degradation?

Moreover, we may also see on this second level a problem of the kind that we nowadays might, in some broadly understood sense, call counter-transference: How can we others respect someone who behaves in this way? In fact, the 1960 English translation of the Dostoyevsky passage has accordingly changed its meaning: "How can one, after all, have the slightest respect for a man who tries to find pleasure in the feeling of humiliation itself?" Others, not he himself.

Yet for therapists the riddle goes still deeper; it is still more difficult to resolve than those two layers of the question. Dostoyevsky does not pose it in in the quotation, but it is at least implicit in the rest of the novel: How could such a mental state be cured? How can one help a person so addicted to pain and insult out of his shame and suffering?

For us, the riddle means therefore: We know only too well how extraordinarily difficult it is to approach the issues of masochistic character, masochistic symptoms, and masochistic sexuality, the problem of how to revise them in any lasting and fundamental way, how much patience the treatment requires both on the side of the patient and on the side of the analyst or therapist, how regularly every success leads to a setback, has to be paid, as it were, by defeat, how much torment there is in the relationship between therapist and patient. The real riddle is therefore: What do we have to do, how can we understand better the underlying dynamics in order to bring about any lasting change by our intervening?

In the solution of this riddle we are well aware of Nietzsche's statement (although he refers to the opposition of the modern self-understanding to that of the ancient Greeks): "If we wanted to, and dared to, [build] an architecture according to *our* mindset (although we are too cowardly for that!)—the labyrinth would have to be our example!"[2]

We will now get up our courage and enter the labyrinth.

In one of her haunting stories, "Herr Arnes penningar"—(Mr. Arne's Money), the great Swedish writer Selma Lagerlöf (1858–1940) uses the image of bloody footprints in the snow to symbolize blood guilt threatening as a ghost from the outside ("att han går med nakna fötter och satter blodiga fotspår på snön"; 1904/1989, p. 58). It is the story of a girl, Elsalill, the only one who had survived the massacre of the priest's family that had been sheltering her. Unknowingly she falls in love with one of the three murderers, noblemen from Scotland, and as she slowly discovers the horrible truth, alerted by those ghostly tracks in the snow (the spirit of her foster sister), she feels torn between her loyalty toward the murdered foster sister and her love for the murderer. She betrays him, but then tries to help him to flee, yet finally, "in murderous hatred"—("det dödligaste hat"), draws the weapons of the arresting guards upon herself, thus trying in vain by her own death to block his escape: Love stands against love, loyalty against loyalty, betrayal against betrayal, guilt against guilt.

It is these bloody tracks in the snow that we want to follow now—the tracks of conscience and self-induced suffering, set off, just as in the story, not so much by actions as by intentions and inclinations, by veiled and split loyalties, by contradictory voices within conscience, by deeper conflicts of great complexity and on many levels between love and hate, between idealization and murderous hatred, between overwhelming feelings and desperate attempts at controls.

DEFINITION

For a long time, partly in conjunction with my work on shame as well as with that on the addictions, it has struck me to what an extent the clinical issue of masochism is one of the most prominent, and yet also most vexing problems in the practice of psychoanalysis and psychotherapy, how problems of masochism permeate most treatments in one form or another, and that an in-depth understanding of its underlying dynamics could elucidate much of what is most recalcitrant in the treatment of the "severe neuroses." In fact, it struck me more and more that the study of superego problems, that is, issues of shame and guilt, of resentment and loyalty is one side of the coin; studying the dynamics underlying masochism is the other side of the same coin.

I say: "underlying masochism." It is immediately clear that the term "masochism" is purely descriptive; by itself it does not as yet explain anything. The work begins with it, it does not end with it. The phenomena so described are the result of complex inner processes on all developmental strata: "At present, it has become evident that masochism is a term of little precision and that its value is descriptive and evocative. . . . Masochism cannot be usefully invoked to explain complex clinical phenomena. It is an aspect of various kinds of pathology that also requires explanation" (Grossman, 1986, p. 381).

What do we mean with this *descriptive* term masochism?

It usually means the compulsive need to seek suffering, pain, and humiliation, and to sabotage one's chances and success, in order to obtain love, attachment, respect, and secret power; the preconscious motto is: "Power through suffering; torment me, but do not abandon me!"

If we put this strictly in object-relation terms, "masochism means loving a person who gives hate and ill-treatment" (Berliner, 1947, p. 460).

This is obviously only one way of stating it—one far too narrow, as we shall see.

> Masochistic fantasies are recognized by a preoccupation with combining something the subject regards as pleasurable with something he regards as unpleasurable . . . the essential point is that in the fantasy the combination is obligatory. . . . The interchangeability of roles between subject and object is also characteristic of such fantasies, as is the attachment to objects that are loved ambivalently or hated, but cannot be given up. (Grossman, 1986, p. 387–88)

"The term masochism will be most usefully and understandably applied to those activities organized by fantasies involving the obligatory combination of pleasure and unpleasure, or to the fantasies themselves" (p. 408–9). Grossman summarizes his paper of 1986:

> the term "masochism" lacks specificity except when used to refer to a *scenario combining some kind of sexual gratification with something (generally thought to be painful or) unpleasurable, and presented in conscious or unconscious fantasy, or in manifest perversions that are the enactment of such fantasies*" (1991, p. 33, emphasis added).

All that I have so far encompassed is a wide definition.

However, we can hardly talk about masochism if there is not also a sexual connotation to such suffering: in Arlow's view the term "should only be employed when pain and unpleasure occur as the necessary conditions for sexual gratification"(quoted in F. G. Maleson, 1984, p. 337).

Accordingly, Helen Meyers (1988) distinguishes the limited definition: "states of suffering with a clear linkage to sexual (genital) pleasure, conscious or unconscious," from the broader one:

> the gratification need not be only sexual. . . . It may indeed be gratification of sexual or aggressive drives or their derivatives; or it may be an ego gratification, such as maintenance of object relations or self-definition or self-esteem enhancement; or it may be appeasement of the sadistic superego's need to punish. In the compromise formation of masochism, the price of pain pays for gratification and avoids attendant anxiety and dangers of damage, object loss or loss of self-esteem or identity. Whether the pain itself also is experienced as pleasure, either by libidinization of the destructive instinct or simply based on the physiologic prototypes of excitement associated with any strong stimulus (Freud's, 1924b, "erotogenic masochism"), or whether the pain is only the prerequisite for pleasure is still a matter of debate. . . . It is the motivation of *seeking the unpleasure* and the satisfaction in it that is the key [p. 178] . . . pain serves an unconscious function in achieving some need satisfaction. (p. 179)

However, I believe this distinction between the wider and the narrower definition may in fact be more apparent than real: While the erotic quality seems to be often missing, the deeper study of the phenomena of an ostensibly nonsexual search for suffering usually brings ample evidence for such sexual (or at least sensual) meaning, as is shown for example in the way Brenner expresses it:

> Masochism is best defined as an acceptance of pain and suffering as a condition of libidinal gratification, conscious, unconscious, or both. . . . Self-imposed unpleasure is, in a child's mind, a way of avoiding object loss, loss of love, or castration by appeasing the parents, or it is a way of winning their love, or it is both at once. . . . Masochism plays an important role in normal superego formation and functioning. (Brenner, 1982, p. 127)

It is very important that, as already Fenichel observed, the pain is not the aim in and of itself. In Brenner's words: "in all cases of masochism which have been observed analytically, pain is the condition rather than the source of sexual pleasure" (1959, p. 205). With that we have, however, gone beyond the descriptive use of the term and advanced a dynamic explanation. However, before I present some of the recent attempts to cast light on the underlying dynamics I would like to conclude this part on the phenomenology by stating that I have found it useful to differentiate the following four forms of masochistic pathology: (1) *outer masochism*: the main relationships with others seem to reflect an incessant search for and clinging to tormenting partners and a need to end up as the victim; (2) *inner or moral masochism*: the tormenting is mostly carried out by the conscience and directed against the self; (3) *sexual masochism, masochistic perversion*: sexual gratification is bound to symbolic or concrete pain and humiliation; and (4) *masochism covered by a sadistic-narcissistic façade*: what appears as outwardly directed cruelty and selfishness must hide the acting out of a masochistic core fantasy ("counter-masochism").

These four forms of manifest pathology (1, 2, and 4 belong to the range of character perversion, as outlined in chapter 3) are not sharply separated from each other. In reality they usually coexist, albeit in different strength. Dynamically they form *one* connection, *one* texture with varied patterns. These patterns themselves are universal. Only insofar as they are of a *compulsive* quality are they pathological. There is just as much normal masochism (of all four kinds) as there is normal narcissism or normal aggression. The distinction between normality and pathology follows separate criteria (Wurmser, 2000a, chapter 6).

Thus I concur with Brenner when he states that:

> masochistic phenomena play a part in the lives of all of us, the normal as well as the neurotic. . . . A need or wish for punishment, as opposed to a fear

of punishment, is in itself a masochistic phenomenon. . . . A need for punishment, whether it be a conscious or an unconscious one, is invariably a
part of normal superego functioning. It follows therefore that some degree
of masochism is ubiquitous. (1959, p. 206)

THE DYNAMICS OF CLINICAL MASOCHISM

Cooper (1988, pp. 119–20) summarizes very well Freud's theories trying
to explain "these puzzling phenomena"; I give them in abbreviated
form:

1) excess of stimulation = pain + pleasure
2) sadism as primary, turned against the self
3) masochism as primary instinct, component of death instinct
4) need for punishment, out of excessive harshness of superego
5) suffering as condition for pleasure, not as source of pleasure
6) masochism related to feminine characteristics and passivity.

Helen Meyers stresses the underlying dynamic complexity and the
complementarity of the various explanatory models:

Thus, to my way of thinking, the very differences in the many contributions
to the theory of masochism, rather than being obscuring and contradictory
(Maleson, 1984), add valuable components to the whole picture. Each contribution, clinically valid, yet addressing a different function of masochism derived genetically from a different developmental level, adds another piece to
the puzzle. . . . Each piece is necessary for completion of the puzzle." (1988,
p. 175)

She advocates various technical emphases as complementary to each
other:

Masochism and guilt: "payment for forbidden, unacceptable oedipal de-
    sires and aggression." "The sadistic superego is appeased and feels
    pride in its punishing, the ego feels pleasure in its suffering—moral
    masochism" (p. 179).
Maintenance of object relations: "appeasing the aggressor mother and
    buying her love with suffering," "seduction of the aggressor" (p.
    180), getting better would mean the loss of a vital object-relation.
Masochism and self-esteem: "There is pride in pursuing one's own course
    even if it is painful. There is pride in being special as a victim of fate.

'I am in control. I want to be pained. I asked for it. I enjoy it. I can handle it. I have more discomfort than anyone" (p. 182).

Masochism and self-definition: "The adult masochist's 'I will, too, be self-destructive and you can't stop me' asserts his control, but also defines him as an independent agent, separate, autonomous, and individuated. 'I am the sufferer' defines his identity, though a negative one," against his wish and fear for merger (p. 184).

An encompassing attempt at a dynamically explanatory definition is the one given by K. K. Novick and J. Novick: "Masochism is the active pursuit of psychic or physical pain, suffering, or humiliation in the service of adaptation, defense, and instinctual gratification at oral, anal, and phallic levels" (1996a, p. 46).

In the dynamic explanation particular weight has been given to the role of narcissism inherent in the masochistic pathology.

Already in 1947 Berliner comments:

These two forces and their ambivalent interplay are responsible for the great perseverance of the masochistic character: the need for the affection of a frustrating love object and the drive to punish the object. The beloved partner, or his proxy who is to be punished, has to be provoked and put in the wrong and simultaneously the illusion of being loved by him has to be maintained. It is this magic thinking, obstructing any test of reality, that makes the condition so persistent. (p. 467)

This is amplified in the Novicks' book (1996a):

There is more to a masochistic fantasy than omnipotence, but the delusion of omnipotence is a necessary part of it. The classical view is that the failure of omnipotence forces the child to turn to reality. In our view it is the *failure of reality that forces the child to turn to omnipotent solutions*. Competence is rooted in the attunement between the child's signals and the caretakers' responses. Repeated failures are frustrating and, as research with infants has demonstrated, soon lead to expressions of helplessness and confusion (Papoušek and Papoušek, 1975). Within a month from birth, it can be observed that such failures produce signs of discomfort or psychic pain and are soon followed by signs of anger, such as gaze aversion. This is followed by denial of the source of pain, and denial is maintained by the transformation of pain into first a sign of attachment, then additionally a sign of specialness and unlimited destructive power, then a sign of equality in every way with oedipal parents and omnipotent capacity to coerce parents to gratify all infantile wishes. By school age the magic omnipotent system has been established and the possibility of an alternate system of competent interactions with reality is undermined by the child as each realistic achievement is experienced as due to omnipotent magical behavior. (p. 61)

There is therefore throughout what the Novicks call "a *delusion of omnipotence*":

> Pain is the affect which triggers the defense of omnipotence, pain is the magical means by which all wishes are gratified, and pain justifies the omnipotent hostility and revenge contained in the masochistic fantasy. (p. 64)

> In the fantasies the subject is an innocent victim, who achieves through suffering reunion with the object, defense against aggressive destruction and loss of the object, avoidance of narcissistic pain, and instinctual gratification by fantasy participation in the oedipal situation. (p. 47)

Similarly, Arnold M. Cooper (1991) stresses the "narcissistic base of perverse development," and postulates as underlying core trauma the preoedipal experience of terrifying passivity in relation to a mother who is perceived as dangerously malignant, malicious, and all-powerful and arousing sensations of awe and the uncanny (p. 23). "The development of a perversion is a miscarried repair of this injury, basically through dehumanization of the body and the construction of three core fantasies designed to undo the intolerable sense of helpless passivity." (p. 23). These three fantasies are: (1): "I need not be frightened because my mother is really nonexistent; that is, she is dead or mechanical, and I am in complete control." (2): "I need not be frightened because I am beyond being controlled by my malicious mother because I am myself nonhuman—that is, dead and unable to feel pain—or less than human, a slave who can only be acted upon rather than act." (3): "I triumph and am in total control because no matter what cruelty my squashing, castrating, gigantic monster mother-creature visits upon me, I can extract pleasure from it, and therefore she (it) is doing my bidding." Put differently: "1. She doesn't exist, 2. I don't exist, 3. I force her—now a nonhuman 'it'—to give me pleasure" (p. 24). He defines as perverse "the extent to which they dehumanize actual relationships" (Cooper, 1991, p. 31). "To the extent that narcissistic-masochistic defenses are used, the aim is not a fantasied reunion with a loving and caring mother; rather it is fantasied control over a cruel and damaging mother" (Cooper, 1988, p. 128).

Cooper takes a *dimensional rather than a categorical view* of perversion (1991, p. 33) and stresses the common psychological mechanism at work in all those situations in which, however briefly, the body is dehumanized and in which mixtures of those three defensive fantasies—mother is not human, I am not human, and I enjoy victimization—are constructed in the effort to avoid the fear of infantile passivity (p. 33). He concludes that the

perversion dynamic is present whenever an action or fantasy is dominated by the denial of unconscious passivity through the triple fantasies
of dehumanizing the object, dehumanizing the self, and securing
masochistic pleasure (p. 34).

Sexualization as a defense against traumatization from without and
frightening aggression from within is emphasized by Stoller and Coen.
Speaking of perversion in general, Stoller calls it "the erotic form of hatred": "The hostility in perversion takes form in a fantasy of revenge hidden in the actions that make up the perversion and serves to convert childhood trauma to adult triumph . . . the harm done is an act of humiliating
in revenge for one's having been humiliated" (Stoller, 1991, p. 37). He
speaks of "fantasies of harm/humiliation/ revenge/triumph without actually harming/humiliating/revenging/triumphing over others" (p. 54).

Coen (1988) states: "Erotization tames destructiveness" (p. 45), "hatred
drives the couple apart; fear of separateness and loneliness forces them together" (p. 46ff.), and he speaks of the "seduction of the castrator," as a
variant of Loewenstein's term, "seduction of the aggressor" (1957, p.
53ff.).

It is commonly stated that clinical masochism is always linked to severe
traumatization, in the meaning of living "in pain rather than lose the object" (Bach, 1991, p. 84). "The pain of suffering defends against the greater
pain of loss" (p. 86).

The role especially of early trauma is described by Valenstein, Blos, and
Grossman:

> Primitive affect states occurring during periods of marked regression are
> likely to be as far as it is possible to go therapeutically toward the recovery
> of the events or circumstances of the preverbal period. And such primitive af-
> fect states appear to be consequent to the propensity of such individuals to
> relive in later life and in the intense transference recrudescence what they
> cannot cognitively remember, namely, the aura of early experience including
> the *sense* of self and self-object. This is especially so if, as is usually the case,
> they are strongly fixated to early trauma associated with pain; then they
> readily regress to primitive affect states characteristic of such trauma. (Valen-
> stein, 1973, p. 375)

> I believe that such affects are emphatically held to because they represent the
> early self and self-object. Giving up such affects, coincident with mostly cor-
> rect, but insufficiently deep interpretations would be equivalent to relin-
> quishing a part of the self and/or self-object at the level which those affects
> represent. (p. 376)

> In this regard the negative affect state represents the primary object, i.e., the
> mother. (p. 387)

Blos (1991) ties together the central fantasy of omnipotence with the defense against painful affect: "the regressively displaced libidinization of the anal area along with the particular modality of anal-phase thinking—yes/no, magic, omnipotence, and omniscience—can serve as a continued resistance to the resolution of oedipal conflicts," that is, to the "relinquishment of the fantasy of bisexuality and omnipotentiality" (p. 419).

> There is a process very like mourning over the loss of an illusion that had seemed so essential, real and true. When these conflicts are preeminent, the anal position appears to provide a haven wherein nothing has to be given up, bisexuality is still possible, ambivalence reigns, and holding on gives satisfaction and a sense of security. That is—*all is still possible*. (p. 420)

He thus focuses in the treatment on

> the patient's utilization of sadomasochism in the analysis as a transferential defense against reexperiencing and remembering painful affects. . . . This fantasied hope of reversibility is sustainable only so long as the sadomasochistic position is maintained. When this is analyzed as fantasy, not reality, the patient experiences a loss as though something valuable has been taken away. It is this painful affect of loss, with its accompanying fearful rage, that the sadomasochistic position defends against and that reappears with its associated guilt in the symptoms. (p. 421)

The link between trauma and self-directed aggression in masochism is most explicitly and comprehensively stated by Grossman (1991). He views pain and painful affects as "sources" of aggression (p. 26) and understands the psychological effects of trauma in connection with the development and functioning of the capacity to fantasize:

> I suggest that to the extent that fantasy formation is possible, some transformation and mastery of traumatic experience is possible. Severe trauma impairs the capacity for fantasy . . . , leading to a failure to transform the traumatic experience through mental activity. Instead, repetitive behavior and intrusive imagery that repeat or attempt to undo the traumatic experience are possible consequences. (p. 26)

Inhibitions, avoidances, and withdrawal could thus be seen as alternate attempts to avoid painful, repeated occurrences of a traumatic state. Repetitions in fantasy may contribute to the mastery of trauma (p. 26). "From early infancy on, there is a capacity to respond to traumatic treatment with destructive and self-destructive behavior" (p. 28). His hypothesis is that "pain and painful affect (anxiety, shame, guilt, humiliation, fear) are ordinarily occurring sources of the aggressive drive, though perhaps not the only ones" (p. 39). Accordingly, any somatic pain might be thought of as a somatic source of the aggressive drive, much as stimulation of the erotogenic zones can be regarded as sources of libido. . . . Pain and painful affect evoke aggression toward those people who are perceived as the perpetrators." To preserve the relationship, the expression of aggressive impulses must be modified:

> In some cases, sexual activity is utilized, as are other pleasurable experiences. Sometimes, the sexual activity itself may be a part of an enforced relationship, and its pleasurable quality may be ambiguous. In childhood, as well as in the traumatic situations of later life, pleasure-unpleasure fantasies become another vehicle for the management and channeling of aggression leading to some familiar forms of sadomasochistic fantasies. (pp. 39–40)

He even postulates very early inner conflict:

> In the early cases, the issue seems to be self-control out of fear in conflict with the caretaker. . . . The early self-control generated out of fear and pain may perhaps be considered to be the precursor of inner conflict occurring at a presymbolic, sensorimotor level of development. It may not be conflict at the level of tripartite structural, but it may be conflict. (p. 45)

His views accord very well with my own and are, I believe, borne out by the case to be presented.

❋   ❋   ❋

In the rest of this book, especially in chapter 8, I stress the importance of *core fantasies* as bridges from the phenomenology to the underlying *core conflicts* (see also Arlow, 1969a, 1969b; Person, 1995). Accordingly, the Novicks write: "Suicidal pathology, masochistic perversions, certain forms of hypochondriasis and psychosomatic illness, and moral masochism have in common an underlying fantasy structure. In our view, this fantasy structure is the 'essence of masochism' (Freud, 1919a, p. 189)" (Novick and Novick, 1996a, p. 47). In fact, in the case to be presented, much of the analytic work was anchored throughout in such a central fantasy.

The treatment of masochism requires special attention to certain technical issues. It is above all the question I dealt with extensively elsewhere (Wurmser, 2000a, chapters 1 and 2), namely how the analyst, as far as possible, should avoid becoming a superego figure *in reality* and thus promoting a *real sadomasochistic relationship*—instead of being able to explore this twin issue of superego transference and masochistic propensity *within the transference* and to work it through patiently and diligently.

Because of the general importance of this problem, it might be rewarding to study a case in detail where there was the combined presence of an

explicit masochistic perversion with a clearly masochistic character structure, in the form of "moral masochism," and with many of the hallmarks
of what I have outlined as criteria of character perversion—a case moreover that has been studied in great depth and a patient who has considered the analysis as having been, all in all, a great success.

HISTORY

The patient Elazar was thirty-five years old at the time of entering treatment, a civil service official, married, with one stepchild. He first entered
psychotherapy, which three months later was changed into psychoanalysis, because of severe marital problems with a deeply depressed and phobic woman and difficulties in raising his stepson, mostly in the form of
outbursts of rage against the youngster. His wife blamed him for the marital malaise, and he tended to accept the guilt quite readily. Moreover, he
thought that his creative and philosophical gifts and interests were
stunted because of his neurotic problems. He felt detached and anhedo-
nic, generally unfulfilled and unhappy.

He was the younger of two children of a marriage that was very unhappy. His father was a lawyer who had begun his career brilliantly, including his work for a rescue mission to Russia during the 1920s; he apparently had married there, but had to leave his wife behind. Many years
later he married again, but his work as a lawyer faltered, and he turned out
to be an abysmal failure, largely sustained by the financial support brought
by his wife. This woman, from a quite well-to-do and moderately prominent, politically ambitious family, had been married before too. After she
had broken up with her first husband, she had abruptly left her child from
that earlier marriage for six months with her own mother, so that she could
go on some lengthy trips abroad. Apparently the marriage with her second
husband was not much better. There was much bitter fighting, and the
mother treated her husband with open contempt and her sons with little interest. Thus there was for Elazar no tenderness and warmth with the rest-
lessly driven mother, and until much later no real motherly substitute figure. Only deep into the analysis he remembered how in early childhood he
used to bathe with her—in a memory filled with fascination and horror,
tenderness and repulsion. There are, however, fond memories of how his
father used to, at times, to take care of him; yet that too appears to have
been quite haphazard and unreliable, as when he repeatedly left the little
boy, alone and deeply terrified, in the car on city streets. Later on he vanished as caretaker even more than the fickle mother.

The family moved aboad for several years where the father had been
given a rather important position; yet this too was soon given up, "be-

cause he could not learn the language." At that time Elazar was between five and eight years old. Finally the strife became so severe that the parents separated and eventually, shortly before the death of the father, got divorced. The father died after a series of strokes and years of isolation and depression. The older son of the couple had a similarly promising career, which gradually fizzled out because of his involvement with an extremist political group.

It is thus evident that childhood and youth of the patient were quite traumatic, the more so as the mother repeatedly left the little child behind when she went on some of her jaunts; for example, once she had the three-year-old stay with strangers in a European mountain village for several months.

Another source of severe trauma was the fact that Elazar suffered from congenital cataracts on both eyes. He was operated on at ages five and eight and repeatedly later on, but one eye had become almost completely blind, and the other also was and is not fully functional. This problem crippled him in his social functioning even more than the loneliness of growing up with two self-absorbed, quarrelsome parents; he lived constantly under the shadow of the threat of surgical intervention and pain.

After a minor traffic accident in late youth he gave up driving a car because of his dangerously impaired vision. That made it necessary during part of the analysis for his wife to at least pick him up, and often also to drop him off (at times he could make use of an bus connection). About halfway through the analysis he developed an ingenious design for eyeglasses that would allow him to use the rest of his visual capacities. He had the design patented and had a model made for him to his specifications by a company. This model allowed him to do the driving himself—except somewhat during inclement weather and at night.

Apparently he had also suffered from encephalitis as a small child, which left him with insufficient muscle tone of his bladder. Because of beginning kidney insufficiency he was forced to rely on self-catheterization as the only means for voiding his bladder.

In spite of all these impediments and handicaps, he proved successful in his education and studied philosophy and literature with much interest. One day a former girlfriend of his, who had left him and had at that time a serious problem with drinking, appeared at his doorstep, pregnant by another man, and asked him to marry her. In his loneliness and detachment he felt someone was truly reaching out to him because she needed him. He agreed, but the marriage was much burdened by the often paranoid accusations of his wife and his outbursts of rage when she kept accusing him and when his stepson interfered with his wishes for orderliness and discipline. She eventually entered treatment, and, although not improving very much, prevailed upon her husband to get himself into therapy—which he did.

At work he is, in spite of his handicap, excellent and has received some important awards and advancements.

The treatment was successfully terminated after six years (962 sessions). Catamnestically he continues doing very well; the gains have been sustained in spite of serious adversities (new operations and disease). He has been able to use the insights in particularly creative and socially highly effective ways.

THE CORE FANTASY

It became only gradually evident that he engaged in masochistic-fetishistic acts with his wife, mostly in the form of his being bound with leather straps and her wearing leather shoes and gloves during intercourse. Yet his masturbatory fantasies showed his masochistic inclinations much more floridly—scenes of being savagely mistreated by women who trampled all over him with stiletto shoes, humiliated him, nailed or stapled his scrotum to the table, whipped and rode him, tortures to be followed by an effusion of love and acceptance. The following version was especially pleasurable: "Two women staple my scrotum to the table. This makes it impossible for me to pull myself away. I could not tear the staples out. I was forced to sit there spread-eagled, fixed to the spot. It was not done in anger and did not give me any pain. They just wanted to keep me there because they liked me. They were kissing and stroking me and were playing with my penis and stimulating me." At the same time there was deep shame accompanying these fantasies. In fact, an important reason why he was seeking treatment was not that he wanted to get rid of those fantasies and wishes but of the shame about them.

Here I shall mainly focus on the teasing apart of the necessary and sufficient conditions for the dynamics of the masochistic perversion. Before I give an account of those nine constituents, I would like to open, however, with a fairly detailed excerpt from those hours that provided the decisive breakthrough in the analysis, about five and a half years into our work, half a year before termination. It should also give an impression of the problems of transference and countertransference encountered in the treatment of masochistic character pathology.

MASOCHISTIC TRANSFERENCE, THE ISSUE OF OMNIPOTENCE, AND THE PROBLEM OF COUNTERTRANSFERENCE

"The treatment of masochistic character problems has long been considered one of the more difficult analytic challenges," writes Helen Meyers (1988). "The fixity of masochistic trends and their self-defeating nature in life and treatment, as well as the related counter-transference reactions, are major constituents of this difficulty. But a part is also played by the complexity of the genesis and variety of functions of masochism" (p. 175).

There were of course many instances in Elazar's analysis where he tried to provoke me to despair or to attack him angrily, where he "depersonalized" and "dehumanized" our relationship, or where he tried to enlist me in his various outer conflicts. I must say though, the difficulties encountered with him in the interaction were minor compared with those in many other patients, whose severely masochistic character pathology was far more pronounced than the manifest sexual masochism, the perversion. It appears as if the latter provided a certain shield against the former.

In other words: There is a kind of *triple stratification* in development and inner depth: First and on the surface, we find the sexual perversion where sexual gratification is largely bound up with physical or emotional torment. Second, one layer deeper, we find the character perversion, in the sense of prominent moral masochism and with all the criteria outlined in chapter 3. Third and deepest, we find severe chronic traumatization with affect regression, and with sexualization and mobilization of aggression as important defenses.

This sequence even represents a rank order of clinical importance, the third being the most important (this is also one reason why I started this book with Agnes, not with Elazar).

The analysis is resented by Elazar: "I want love without having to pay for it. What I want is love, not analysis. To that extent I find the analysis unfulfilling and disappointing. Regardless [of] how much analysis I will do, it will be ultimately unsatisfying. I don't feel loved here" (877). "The amount of anger and resentment about the injustice is so great, and the sense of being a victim so deep that no analysis can ever get rid of that" (881).

In the session right after a short break during the Christmas holiday (879), he reports in detail several dreams and gives a quite intellectualized "interpretation" of them. After a while I interrupt him and say that we have not heard what had been going on since our last session five days before and that it reminds me of an image he had used at the beginning of the analysis—that he was flying detached from the earth, 30,000 feet in the air, in a radar plane as an observer. He responds very angrily that this, the feelings in the dreams, is the important thing for him. He and his wife and son have been visiting the in-laws for the holidays, but that has been absolutely unimportant and boring.

In the following sessions his anger is increasing. He says it is about time to break off the analysis, that there is such an intensity of rage in him that he is not willing to confront it. At least he is glad that he has decided to cut back the sessions to three times a week, after the first of the year. I indicate my misgivings about this reduction but also agree that we have so decided and, upon his question, that the fourth session is not available anymore (at the usual time at least). He complains that I am cold, that what he really wants is to be loved, to be accepted and made to feel "that I'm the greatest person who ever lived. I want to be accepted and respected and admired and loved. I never felt that my mother really respected or loved me or thought highly of me. And in [his mother's] family, shame hung like a pall over everything: that my mother had married this 'nebbich' about whom she could not be proud. That permeated everything—that shame that they felt about each other. And she felt it about me. It is too painful, and such intense anger about it. . . . Therefore I want to be special for you. It's hard to overcome my fear of you—to see you without seeing my grandfather. He could put you down. . . . Angry to submit . . . to any restrictions or controls."

He comes to the last hour of the year, Friday (882), with deep resentment: "This morning I'm very angry at you, that I have to submit to the control over this analysis. That you are a pompous ass, and that I want to quit. That I cannot work with you. But that would not work, it would be running away from the analysis. And therefore I am here: to confront my anger and to fight it out with you. It is an issue of control. I was irritated Tuesday, that you were chiding me because I was speaking about the dreams and not about the weekend. I never can satisfy you. When I speak about one thing you want me to speak about something else. If this is your analysis, tell me! Either you or I! I'm angry about the struggle. There is a deep element of resentment, that I cannot have what I want—"

"—[that someone else] controls your bowels—"

"I guess so, it's on that elemental level. I did think about the rescheduling. I found it good, it makes my life less hectic. But I also have misgivings about it [the cutting down]. It is exhausting. I resent that I have so little time for myself. And yet I have to confront this anger, instead of running away from it and from you. It has been helpful, but I'm still uncomfortable with you. There is the basic identification of you with my grandfather—a man disconnected from reality, whom I resent because he tries to control me and does not know reality himself. He kept himself apart, yet he was a successful businessman, an effective manager, and a good listener, but very reserved. So are you. And you are pompous, you don't have contact with people on a working basis or deal with bureaucracy or with management conflicts [as he does]. You are very theoretical, just like my father, who avoided dealing with everyday conflicts like the plague. That's why I'm so adamantly against anything theoretical, even if I tend to use intellectualization to avoid my conflicts. Yet dealing with theory is no solution. I'm obsessed with what is practical, and that's why I left Academia. "

At that I go back to the Tuesday session and read back to him the major associations to show him their theoretical character.

"That was my reaction to the dream; it was a very intensive dream, very exciting, more real than anything that had happened. It was the most real of those five days. And as you reread them to me just now I re-experienced it. And it makes me so angry that you are intruding in it, that you are denying me the reality, that you can tell me: 'This is unimportant.'"

"Which means: 'That which is real for me is what I dream and fantasize, not the outer reality.'"

"Exactly! That dream meant more than the other five days. Those five days were not real, they were boring, unpleasant."

"It matches what you said yesterday: 'I want to be the greatest man.' To abolish reality for a fantasy of omnipotence."

"I don't understand."

"'Those five days were not real—'"

"Like in the dream?"

"Not *in* the dream, but how you dealt *with* the dream: *the dream is the reality, and the five days do not count, they are not reality.* This is very important."

"It does not make sense to me."

I comment upon the split between perception and denial: "It is something we never really addressed before: how the *fantasy is set up to dispense with what you saw, and replace it by a dream.*"

He angrily retorts that I try to control him, what he should feel, that he knows very well the difference between reality and wish, and that he certainly wishes to escape reality, but it angers him that I am telling him what is important and what not.

I counter: "Not that one was not important, but I tried to point out that the fantasy of omnipotence is an important protection, as part of the masochistic fantasy: that women really do have a penis, and that pain really is pleasure."

"That I can accept, that makes sense. There is certainly an element of omnipotence in that, I want to control that."

"And how very specifically the masochistic fantasy was set up to rescue your mother by your power, perhaps to help her in her depression."

"It was a failed attempt to rescue. And now I wanted to provoke you into kicking me out of the analysis. And then I could be angry at you. The failed attempt to provoke you is like the failed attempt to rouse somebody out of her depression, to make her angry, to get her attention: if not by kindness, then at least by anger."

"And that also the request of the reduction in the hours, besides the realistic factors, had that meaning."

"I think that also. It was a provocation. I came with objective factors when I was angry at you, the resentment about the amount of work and the tiredness, and yet it served to reenact the masochistic scenario." He then refers to the masochistic sexual play with his wife (again using sexualization and concretized aggression as defenses in the analytic process, right at this point of angry conflict with me and about his life's frustrations)—"threatening to beat each other, tying each other up, biting, pinning down, tickling, but most of all tying up, the threat of violence without [actual] violence."

I interpret: "'And when I provoke her to anger and she beats me up, then everything will be good.'"

"And that brings me back to the issue of omnipotence: that I rescued her and she loved me. It was a self-centered fantasy."

"It holds true for your wife as well as for your mother."

The following session (883) he feels again angry about my "drawing some conclusions about omnipotence." He adds: "I don't have to love or like you in order to work with you. I don't feel very loving toward you, but also not so hateful, I don't despise you as much."

"Despise me?"

"As a defense against fear."

"Let's perhaps look first at what the despising entails before we rush to an interpretation."

"I don't know what to make of it."

"Let's see what it is."

"I don't know—they are words that don't mean anything for me, they are just said for the sound effect."

"To use words to create reality when it does not exist—isn't that the omnipotence we were talking about?"

"Yes, that's true. I like to do that, this is very true. I do that at my work: *creating reality which does not exist.* If it is truthful or not becomes a legal question. I'm a spin doctor, and I enjoy it: creating illusions. It's a form of control. Facts are not immutable; they are there to be interpreted. This is supported by modern philosophy, by phenomenology, the construction of perception. . . . That is my fascination with writing and literature: a creation of illusion, of a new reality. I agree with you that I indulge in creating reality. The question which is not clear to me: What is pathological about that? What is wrong with that? Also why would that be morally wrong? Perhaps this is itself pathological that it is not clear to me."

"It's difficult in human discourse if the meaning of words is simply changed according to wish, like in 'Alice in Wonderland': 'I decree what it means!' As it happened just now in regard to 'despise.'"

"This is something central. I don't understand how to get agreement between people. This seems magical to me, it bugs me—this indifference about speech, the cynicism about language. Like with my parents, their lack of discourse. So it is between you and me, the problem of communication. I don't understand it."

"We had an example early in the analysis, in regard to the fee." He agrees.

This refers to the fact that at the beginning of the analysis I agreed to a considerable reduction in fee, based on his own moderate income, the expenditures for his wife's therapy and her resumed college studies, and the tuition of the son in private school. In fact, it seemed that the analysis was only feasible because his oldest (half-)brother, a very successful businessman, was considerably contributing to the outlays because, having been himself for a very long time in analytic treatment, he was very much in favor of analysis. Only much later, perhaps two or three years into treatment, it turned out that the patient had concealed from me the fact that he had inherited from his grandfather a sizable endowment/trust fund, which he intended to leave untouched for times of real need. I stated at that point that the time of real need had arrived.

"When I was saying that I despised you, I had that feeling perhaps only for one moment. Love and contempt are almost back to back. To pin down the words with feelings—as soon as I say them they don't exist any longer. It *is* like Alice in Wonderland: 'What did I mean with this?'"

"Is this not similar to Friday's: 'What is real to me, is what I dream and fantasize, not the outer reality. Those five days were not real because they were boring and unpleasant'?"

"I don't know, I don't see anything wrong or unusual about it. . . . I have to deny much reality, but everybody else does it too, in order to live, to get up in the morning. . . . I agree that I manipulate reality, I do distort reality. . . . I cannot face absolute reality."

"What you say: 'I have felt so much anxiety, felt so helpless that I needed those fantasies of omnipotence to deny much of what I knew and felt.'"

"That makes a lot of sense. I know one thing: that reality is very confusing, very plastic, very shapeable, flexible. For me facts are not immutable. That has to do with the intellectual tradition I grew up in. For my father as attorney it was: 'Reality is what a good argument says it is.' And so it is in [Plato's dialogue] *Theaitetos*: 'What is knowledge?' At most it is the right opinion. It is a legalistic view of reality, finding loopholes in it, wriggle room, because nobody knows what is real: 'What is real is what we say that it is real, or that we can get everybody to agree on.' . . . Perhaps that's how I was brought up, that I had to deny what I saw. That is the attraction of philosophy, that philosophers can be omnipotent: they can create realities."

We return to the contempt: "For me it's the confusion that is so upsetting—despising all permanence, or statements of reality, or truth."

"Confusion?"

"That my feelings and perceptions are confused, that the world feels very much in flux and unstable and very frightening."

"And then you use words to create safety."

"Exactly! Like God!"

"'*Yehi or wayehi or!*'" ["There be light, and there was light!" from Genesis 1.3; the patient knows Hebrew].

"Exactly!"

In this excerpt one thing becomes clear: The first form of the interpretation, which dealt directly with his fantasy of omnipotence, with the high and mighty exclusion of reality, in other words, the *direct drive interpretation of his narcissism* was being experienced as a reproach and had to be rejected with a rising torrent of rage. It was only its reformulation as a defense against anxiety, and with that the interpretation of the entire conflict about traumatization and defense against the overwhelming affects engendered by it, which opened up insight and acceptance. The first form of interpretation was a mistake, an acting out of my own countertransference—my impatience, my "knowing better," my annoyance about the resistance by intellectualization we had so often worked through, also my wish to work out my own emergent insight into the close connection of masochistic phenomenology and underlying narcissistic dynamics (I had been made aware of this by hearing the Novicks presenting their understanding of sadomasochism). This direct drive interpretation only increased the resistance. I can see only modest mutative significance in the outburst of rage *within the transference*. Rather, what was decisive was pointing out the relationship between his sense of helplessness and the narcissistic fantasies as a defense against the affects engendered by that helplessness. In that way we succeeded in short order in breaking through to the underlying structure of the masochistic core fantasy and the central conflicts, as will now be presented.

"THE ALCHEMIST'S DREAM"—THE RECONSTRUCTION OF THE DYNAMICS OF THE CORE FANTASY

Those nine factors representing the dynamic "causes" for the core fantasy—its necessary and sufficient elements—will be presented in the form of characteristic quotations from the hours, occasionally also in the form of quasi-quotes or summarizing statements. I also use relevant quotes from sessions earlier in the analysis.

Internalization of the Trauma, Repeating It in Order to Master the Overwhelming Affects, and Turning of the Aggression against the Self

"A psychic traumatic experience is one in which the individual is subject to such severe internal or external stimulation as to render him unable to utilize his usual defenses adequately" (Glenn, 1984, p. 357). Traumata, and the related affects, drives and defenses are "precipitated" into the superego; conjointly they exert their power through the "inner judge."

Elazar not only reexperiences the dreadful anxiety about the eye operation of early childhood, but also the loneliness and despair about having felt abandoned, left alone by his parents. There might have been a nurse who had taken care of him—as protective figure before and after the operation; it was not a distinct memory, but rather a reconstruction, at least in the form of an important fantasy figure.

In some dreams the castration anxiety appears almost without disguise; but mostly the anxiety appears to be so much more pervasive, much more unfocused, mostly about traumatogenic affect flooding with attending fragmentation. Sometimes he thinks his mother had wanted to get rid of the child-invalid, perhaps had tried to abort the pregnancy and thus caused the damage. Behind that, the "anxiety about a destructive angry chaos" is lurking, one preceding the operation by a long time, "a very primordial feeling—an exploding star—parts are being hurled out into space, thrown at me—endangering my life, my stability. A real sense of danger, of violence, my fascination with the atomic bomb. This violent eruption, that I lived with an atomic bomb in our house, and that atomic bomb was also in me." They are feelings that cannot be put into words, "powerful eruptions of violence" (484).

He continues: "The wish to identify with my mother as a source of strength and power, and yet the struggle with her. *By submission I gain control over her*. . . . A violent, self-mutilating fantasy: that I'm tied to a car and dragged behind. The function of self-hatred, of anger turned against myself, wanting to get rid of myself. My shame is my father's shame. I'm his mirror image: as my mother despised him, she despised me. I was ashamed for both of them. And we were right: I use the fantasy to gain control over my hatred against myself."

"By using the 'strong woman' within for it."

"And mastering it is something sexual. That's the crux. In the fantasy the woman does my bidding, what my mother never did. I internalized all the desirable features of this powerful woman and turned them to my own service."

"And doing that changed anxiety and anger into pleasure."

"What I feel I have to do: to transform this woman into myself."

"To acquire her strength" (474).

All value was being seen in that exalted female figure while he saw himself as weak, contemptible and shame-laden—the helpless little child. Now the traumatizing force had come to reside in his conscience, personified by the woman who would humiliate and torment (beat) him, only in order to eventually accept him—as supreme magical transformation. He

perceived himself as the traumatized victim. The traumata that had become part of his superego were: the coldness, detachment, and untouchability of his mother, her depression and withdrawal, all the terror and
pain surrounding the memories of the operations, and the battles between
his parents, which filled the house of his childhood. The fear of castration
was easier to bear than the real traumatizations and the sense of total
helplessness, confusion, and anxiety, frequently repeated in the sessions,
though without concrete memories.

It is decisive that the connections have been torn between those multilayered traumatizations and his rage, and between his rage and those
threatened immense consequences (as punishments not only on the level
of mutilation, but on all levels of dangers): "The connections are very
weak between the feelings and what is happening." It is the defense by
isolation, corresponding to his strongly obsessive-compulsive character
traits (480).

And, as a counterpoint, there emerged shortly after the operation, already at age five, the lustful fantasy that he was being tied down by a girl
(475): "that's how I deal with the anger and the resentment, that I turn it
against myself, as part of it" (889).

Magical Reversal of the Affects and Denial of Perception

> At the highest level, the humiliation or suffering represents a punishment,
> symbolic of castration but precluding castration . . . a token "punishment"
> under the patient's absolute control and staging of the performance. Seduc-
> tion of the castrator, a variant of Loewenstein's (1957) term, "seduction of the
> aggressor" is an apt way to describe this attempt to change the woman's im-
> age from aggressive and threatening into accepting and participating. (Coen,
> 1988, p. 53ff.)

The masochistic-perverse fantasy reflects defense by *reversal of affect*
and *sexualization*, accompanied by intense *denial* and *repression*. In this
context what Anna Freud wrote in regard to such reversal of affect is also
relevant: "Her ego made use of the defense mechanism of reversal, a kind
of reaction formation against the affect, at the same time betraying its obsessional attitude toward the instinct" (1936, p. 40). This fits very well to
the observations with Elazar: reversals of affect as well as of drives
proved to be a kind of Ariadne's thread.

An important sequence we could observe in relation to his wife in the
present, but traceable to the relationship to his mother, was this: (1) "She
is depressed and anxious, and that frightens me because I feel so dependent upon her." In fact he was and remained unable to seriously consider
any separation from her (his wife), in spite of all the unhappiness and tor-

ment. In spite of it? Rather because of it! (2) "It is I who has caused her depression by my anger; I'm to blame, I'm guilty." (3) The anger is split off: "The other is the attacker." For example, he accuses me of attacking his wife when I pick up on his conflict about his own criticism of her. "And I am the rescuer and savior of the suffering woman. I need her for survival, because I am completely dependent upon her: 'Let out your anger on me, and you will feel better.' I see myself as the victim taking upon myself the depression and the shame of my mother." (4) "I have failed in the rescue mission"—with all the shame and guilt that entails (457). He compares himself with Christ, with the lamb that takes the sins of the world upon himself, with the humiliated, tormented victim.

This may explain, at least partly, the general masochistic attitude, especially if we add to it the intense rage and the feeling of helplessness looming behind that sequence. Yet why the peculiar sexual perversion—the pleasure bound to suffering, abuse, and shame?

"I was thinking of the masochistic fantasy—that I'm making in it a kind of transition from myself as the victim to me as the perpetrator, as the tormentor, and that in womanly disguise I'm getting rid of the weak me, identifying with the anger of the mistreating woman. That I wanted to get rid of that weak helpless child that I was and to be strong like my mother, to be independent" (468)—again the magical transformation.

"The struggle with my mother was a no-win situation: If I tried to assert myself I risked her anger, her turning her back to me; and when I submitted to her she ignored me. Bowing to the will of someone else, offering oneself and submitting, and then to be ignored, to be treated as mull, that is humiliation. And that became *transformed* in the fantasy: I am the one building the fantasy, I am in charge of the scene. All that happens is under my control. I have extracted the pain, and I rebuild it as something pleasurable—in order to make it bearable. How do I defeat my mother, how can I get control over her? *I turn my pain into pleasure!*" (473).

He had also tried to master the severe trauma of the operation by endowing the perceptions immediately preceding and following the operation with pleasure, as a defense against the panic: "This powerful figure who was tying me down and giving me an injection will be the one who will protect me. Instead of the anxiety and the terror of then I now experience sexual attraction and pleasure" (432). So much of the core fantasy reflects elements of that trauma: being strapped down, stripped, mutilated, the role of underwear, terror, and protection.

It took a long time to deepen this concept of the magical transformation. Only in the last part of the analysis we arrived at its concise formulation:

"And that is the reality where I was powerless, and where I am now obsessed with power. This is so in the masochistic fantasy, all those transformations are there for one purpose: that I as the victim am the one who is controlling" (884).

"And all this is possible with the *denial of reality, to undo what was so traumatic.*"

"There is no doubt about this . . . it is a compulsive need to repeat over and over again that scenario of punishment and love, in a desperate search for constant love, and the equally compulsive need to punish myself. This seems to me to be the essence of my masochism: the goal can be attained only by twisting reality around, by converting pain into pleasure—"

"—and helplessness into power, and torment into love."

"—and passivity into action."

"—and revenge into orgiastic union" (886).

"It finally dawned on me, the point about the fantasy of omnipotence, that it is a shift from a fantasy of punishment to a central fantasy where I can change pain into pleasure—the alchemist's dream—"

"—and loneliness into love, and shame into elevation and admiration."

"Right."

"And rejection into acceptance. I think this is the central meaning of the fantasy" (889).

The endpoint of the core fantasy is not to remain the victim but to become the one who is really loved (891). Degradation and humiliation, beating and pain are but the means to an end: "The identification with my suffering mother, that is the key, why I went that route. To demonstrate my commiseration with her, my comradeship, to share it. . . . It can become a very powerful mystical experience: redemption through suffering."

This *magical transformation hidden within the masochistic beating fantasy* (Freud, 1919a) is indeed the most important element: through suffering and humiliation, through the beating, the patient tries to achieve love and respect on many developmental levels: "Only through pain can I preserve attachment, love, and sensuality." Most poignantly, the patient thus tries to alter magically, omnipotently, reality and bring about a series of massive denials and reversals: "By my suffering I transform suffering into pleasure, anxiety into sexual excitement, hatred into love, separation into fusion, helplessness into power and revenge, guilt into forgiveness, shame into triumph, and many more." In the masochistic character and sexual perversion the suffering is conscious, the aim of the transformation is unconscious, whereas in other forms of self-destructive acting out, in the so-called "impulse neuroses," for example in "countermasochism" and in substance abuse (see the parallel book *Flight from Conscience*) the suffering is successfully warded off, only the triumph and the narcissistic entitlement appear in manifest form.

Splitting, the Two Realities

The double identification with tormentor and victim is known from the literature on masochism, for example: "The patient identified with both parties in their squabbles. He accepted the role of attacker and attacked, and defensively shifted between sadistic and masochistic positions" (Glenn, 1984, p. 361). It is, as we saw, one of the criteria of character perversion.

"The interchangeability of roles between subject and object is also characteristic of such fantasies, as is the attachment to objects that are loved ambivalently or hated, but cannot be given up" (Grossman, 1986, p. 387–88).

In Elazar there existed three, relatively separate self-figures: the crucified savior, the contemptuous, mistreating woman, and the raging avenger. These three can be understood as parts of an inner sequence: "If I show my murderously jealous side, I have to atone for it by subjecting myself to the punishing, strong mother, and I will be accepted by her only if I make myself, by my suffering, into her rescuer. Yet the punishment for the wishes to assert myself is so frightening, the retribution which I have undergone in reality such a threat and factually so mutilating, that I preemptively make myself to the avenger against myself and counteract the intense anxiety by atoning in suffering and humiliation for these wishes, as a condition for lust and union" (quasi-quote).

Yet that longed-for protective figure was not his mother, as he had really experienced her; quite to the contrary, it was an idealized woman who was, in contrast to the real mother, not humiliated, not powerless and passive, and above all not withdrawn and "castrated": "I was ashamed for my weak, incompetent parents, and I was ashamed about myself in the family of my grandparents. I felt profoundly inadequate; the personal sense of shame threatened my identity, and in addition there was my physical defect. And the rage was directed at my parents because they were unable to protect me against the humiliation inflicted upon us."

In contrast, the woman of his fantasy is not humiliated, but humiliating, not castrated and clumsy, but endowed with the phallic hallmarks of boots, leather tools, and stiletto heels. She represents a specific denial of shame and castration: "That makes sense. I have never seen it so that there was no penis in my family. And metaphorically, my rescue mission was an attempt to give my mother my own penis. It was not the figure of my mother but of the nurse who took care of me during the operation—powerfully protecting me at a moment of extreme panic." With that there is the basic attitude: "I am already passive and prostrate, I give up all power, all revenge, all rage and rivalry, but please, don't mutilate me. It's reassuring that you are neither impotent nor mutilated, in contrast to my parents. If I can merge with you, I shall succeed in acquiring also your strength and pride" (quasi-quote).

The imago of his mother had broken apart into a dark and a luminous figure, into a dangerous and a loving, a devouring and a consoling, a biting and a gently rocking woman—and both sides were now strictly separated into two beings (867).

The dilemma was (and is): "How should I decide—should I be like my father, a humiliated man with a penis, or should I rather be a powerful and shaming woman without a penis? What do I want to become? The answer is: I can be a humiliated man but one who experiences his shame as pleasurable, and at the same time I also want to be a powerful woman but one who also owns a penis—and both at the same time" (727).

Thus he always tries to live in two realities—in a rational reality with the acceptance of his physical handicaps, the vulnerability of his eyes and his penis and the anatomical difference of the sexes, and in a fantasy-woven reality based on denial in the terms of which he may give in to his envy, where he can wipe out his resentment about the injustice, can satisfy his revenge, and yet always can assure himself that he may keep his phallus and victoriously overcome any danger of mutilation. Yet this double reality entails a disregard for the nature of others. He feels unable to express fully his need for love and especially for giving love. Others become two-dimensional; his life is impoverished.

Fantasy identity and fantasy object replace the real relationship between him and others, particularly also real satisfaction during intercourse. The multiple defenses "split" his world.

Sexualization as Defense against Helpless Rage and Castration Anxiety—The Centrality and Erotization of Power

In this context, I found a thought of Janine Chasseguet-Smirgel especially illuminating: Speaking of patients with an "uncommon craving for trauma and internal and external excitations" she states:

> Those concerned, in my view, need to transform the narcissistic wound (which cannot be melted away) into sexual excitation which could be discharged, self-regard being preserved through the accompanying fantasies of revenge, hatred and self-affirmation . . . sexuality becomes the fundamental means by which self-respect is preserved in a triumphant victory full of hatred over the primary object. (1988a, pp. 150–51)

It seems to me that a special power resides in masturbation itself: (1) one can bring about satisfaction at a time where there is despair, anxiety, and overwhelming exposure; (2) one can bring about the illusion of the other as both quasi-real and as ideal in a concretely experienced presence; or (3) the body itself magically changes and powerfully responds in its physiology, thus helping to wipe out much of the unpleasure caused by reality.

The meaning breaks through in a dream about a nurse who examines him rectally and then hugs him in a mixture of eroticism and humiliation: "—to cling to that woman in a moment of need and panic, to experience her as soothing and benevolent, to have her instead of my mother, to get rid of my mother . . . the essence is that I want to replace my mother. That is the bottom line. I punish myself for these thoughts, because they give me pleasure—because that woman was strong. The pain she was inflicting on me came from love. Pain is converted into love, and I derive pleasure from the pain. That is the gymnastic feat: to transform an act of pain in an act of love. She brings me the soothing a male doctor cannot give me; and the sexual attraction is at the heart of it that enables me to make the transformation [of anxiety and pain into pleasure]." He compares me to that nurse (481). "No guilt, no pain, no anxiety, no mutilating interventions—everything is lust and love."

"I remember how I was sitting together with my mother in the bathtub. Do you think that the 'crime' consisted in my having 'taken' the penis from my mother? . . . I remember her anger at men, her distance and coolness toward men, and that I felt guilty and ashamed to possess a penis myself. My wife talks very openly about this, that it is a source of resentment and animosity for her that she has no penis. It makes the man vulnerable." He adds: "What's unfair: that she wants mine. And there it is where the hurt innocence comes in: Why should I be the one to give up mine? It is not my fault."

"And yet somewhere it is felt to be your fault" (516).

A particular aspect of his aggressive fantasies is anal defiance: "The temptation to shit in my pants must have been great, enormous. It was defiance against my mother, to make her angry." It comes up in the context of another very important affective memory: "—the connection between sexual excitement and anger. I can clearly identify my giddiness and excitement when the parents had their arguments or between them and my brother. It's a hysterical defense against the fear and anxiety . . . the giddiness enabled me to deny to myself that I was the agent provocateur, but then the punishment is justified by it. Being the cause gave me a sense of power" (842). "I clearly have the image that I was controlling their fight by setting one against the other, as an expression of my anger, and then the denial: my innocent amusement about their fighting" (849). "Yet any anger and defiance was tremendously dangerous because my mother seemed so fragile. I would push her over the edge. Instead I had to blame myself" (856).

"The sexual attraction was to the power, to [my] mother's body, to her legs, whatever was controlling me. What is sexualized is the power and my lack of power—the fetishes: the leather clothes, the high heels, the bondage, the whip. The sexual excitement harnesses the power."

"It transforms power into pleasure."

"I don't know from where it comes. As far back as I can remember I was involved in a power struggle and in anxiety—lying in the crib and being frightened of monsters peering through the window, feeling helpless and powerless, and my mother would not come and take care of me, nor would my father. It was so frightening. They had their party, and I wanted them to be with me" (891).

He: "Power brings pleasure; the ultimate pleasure is sex."

I: "Or in turn: sex gives the ultimate sense of power against helplessness."

"Sex is a very powerful narcotic. When everything is so miserable, the only power is sex."

"Masturbation is the ultimate consolation" (858).

How to account for the sexual link—especially since the masochistic fantasy seems strongly attached to the vision of the legs of the woman? The answer is inescapable: Very importantly he links rescuing his mother in fantasy and sexually loving her with his bathing together with her in the bathtub throughout early childhood and his seeing her without a penis, "an excitement tinged with revulsion" (891)—a powerful mix of overstimulation and rejection, of exciting sexuality and feared castration.

Painful Touch as Defense against Being Separate and Isolated

"The pain of suffering defends against the greater pain of loss," explains Sheldon Bach (1991, p. 86).

In the words of the Novicks:

[in one of the cases presented] the need for the object overrides the need for pleasure . . . safety resides in an object that induces pain rather than pleasure. . . . We could speculate that externalization of blame, failure, and devalued aspects of the self onto the child served as a major and early mode of relationship and may have become the "primary fault" (Balint, 1968) leading to the evolution of masochistic structures. We suggest that the first layer of masochism must be sought in early infancy, in the child's adaptation to a situation where safety resides only in a painful relationship with the mother. (Novick and Novick, 1996a, pp. 20–22)

In Elazar's words: "All those feelings of shame, the obsession, the paranoia come down to the anxiety about the basic shame of being touched. . . . Being touched, enveloped, surrounded by water, merging with the water, and the water is mother. . . . In the bathtub both were together, being fondled, having sensual feelings, the warm being together, but also her black spot, the hole."

I add later: "And perhaps also the fantasy: mother doesn't touch me because I'm such an angry child; it's all my fault—and as counterpoise the bathtub memory: mother does touch me, hence I'm good, not bad; now it's not my fault anymore" (916).

The deep anxiety of being abandoned and remaining alone is fought off with the help of the core fantasy: "Torment me, but don't abandon me; punish me and forgive me then, but never leave me again" (670). The punishment becomes "the avenue of union."

And most specifically: "If I cannot be touched lovingly, then it is better to be touched violently and painfully than not being touched at all, and the paraphernalia substituted for the close physical contact I lacked. . . . Much of the masochistic fantasy was a desperate search for this touching. . . . And the whole process became depersonalized: I hated the person, I wanted to get rid of her" (919). "All the fantasies of bondage and pain were manufactured to fill the void of physical feelings, of physical contact. I never imagined how big a need I have to have a very concrete, physical sense of feeling about myself, beyond words and images, an immediate physical connection with the ground, no mediation, just touching. There is no substitute for it" (916).

Counterfantasy: Idealization of Invulnerability and Phallic Completeness

"The defensively idealized, omnipotent, all-good object or self-object is needed to merge with and shore up a defective or bad self" (Meyers, 1988, p. 181).

> We found that all of the children in our sample dealt with their aggression by denying any sign of hostility between themselves and their mothers and struggled to maintain an idealized image of mother as loving and perfect. This included denial of the mother's castration, which Bak (1968) considered an important factor in perversions. (Novick and Novick, 1996a, p. 28)

Thus it is essential for Elazar that the strong, abusive woman of his fantasy is not a replica of his mother, not even of the mother of ancient times, but an entirely "idealized figure who is active, invulnerable, invincible, omnipotent, and 'intact,' that is, not 'castrated.'" "I felt I had to endure things, to suffer, in order to get the love." He surrenders himself to her in the hope that: "If I submit to her and merge with her, I can partake in that power and become like her—and avoid dealing with my anger and the guilt" (894).

The ideal, imperious, phallic woman is in truth a synthesis of idealized versions of mother and father—a synthesis patterned not after their reality, but after two mighty figures of his past instead: his own nine-year-older brother and his virile, sport-loving aunt (the wife of his mother's brother):

"The really very important thing is to recognize my emotional investment in this impervious ideal woman as my solution—"

"—who actually is the counterimage to your mother."

"Absolutely! And to myself! And that is the crucial insight: that this woman possesses everything I feel I lack: power, strength, security, sexuality, imperviousness, stability—"

"—invulnerability, impenetrability, and a penis."

"And these were very much the attributes I ascribed to my brother and to my aunt, and these are all things I want to be."

"And the power to shame the other and not being shamed yourself, to be shame-proof."

"In control. In control of meting out the shame and to be impervious to shame" (896).

This whole effort rests squarely on the equation: being together sexually = being punished and loved = merger. It is an archaic fusion fantasy (895). And this entails another equation, about the ideal person whom he aspires to merge with: love = invulnerability = omnipotence.

Pervasive Guilt Founded in Omnipotent Responsibility

"I had a strange masochistic fantasy and afterward a dream repeating the same scene: The fantasy consisted in that I was being tied down by a woman; she threatened to cut off my penis and my testicles. I found that very exciting. In the dream I was being beaten by a man with a stick and then by an Amazon woman with a bullwhip. I said that I did not want the man but the woman to beat me. He denied it to me, but then the woman appeared. I was scared, and yet also excited. . . . This juxtaposition of castration and pleasure is so absurd, absolutely crazy and 'verkehrt.' I have to atone with this for my anger. In that way she controls me. It is a sin to be angry. Yet with the guilt there is the resentment, a sense of unfairness: why should I be guilty if my mother does not have a penis?" He ruminates about the confusion created by all this and the use of his intellectualizing, his philosophizing to create clarity. "Yet this does not explain the gnawing feeling of having done something wrong—except for the anger and the resentment."

Here I venture a direct interpretation: "—and the fights between your parents, your conflict of loyalty between both of them, the built-in betrayal, a conflict we often have had a chance to observe here also, namely in the form of the apparent loyalty conflict between your wife and me." I refer here to his impression when I comment upon his masochistic attitude toward his wife that I am "against her."

He thinks about this for a while: "And the wish to castrate myself—that this would solve the problem? That it would bring peace? If my mother were appeased she would leave my father alone?"

"And that this could be accomplished by such an archaic blood sacrifice?"

"It could have been plausible: then she would not be angry anymore, the family would be at peace, and there would not be any divided loyalty—"

"—if magically the 'injustice' was removed, 'even if I had to renounce upon my masculinity.'"

"Then I would be the savior" (517).

"When I am together with the woman I become the woman, especially the strong (phallic) woman without losing my masculine identity, that is, without being castrated. In the fantasy I can be *like* a woman without being a woman. I do not lose the penis. It gets close to it, but then I do keep it after all. Everything else may happen to me, but the danger is averted. To the contrary, it is a joy and a strengthening" (540).

This is the masochistic core fantasy forcing him symbolically to repeat again and again his self-castration: "It is like a ritual: to have this large organ, handing it over and presenting it to the woman and thus to achieve reconciliation and love. And that is repeated with my brother: the wish to be tender and kind and feminine toward him" (518).

Clearly also: if the rage is global and the wishes for revenge and destruction omnipotent, then the punishment for it has to be equally total. And, as he adds, "the omnipotence is in inverse proportion to the helplessness. It's a Napoleonic complex—the hubris for which I would have to be punished. But I don't quite feel the terror of the helplessness."

"I believe the severity of the imagined punishment blocks off the magnitude of both terror and the wish for omnipotence."

"The rescue fantasy: I can pull wife, mother, father out of their depression; when I'm Christ-like, when I suffer, then I can save my mother" (889): "to transform the helpless mother into someone powerful, and more importantly: the detached, uncaring mother into a loving, protecting one."

He refers to dreams of murderous rage—"exciting, but also very terrifying." And he goes on: "With the power goes the responsibility."

"Therefore the intensity of the punishment" (891).

"In the chaos of my childhood, that hurly burly of argument and retribution—there was the need to keep everything still, in a fixed position, in order to understand it. If things are not perfect, the Universe will collapse, meaning my parents would fall apart and I would be blamed for it; I would be guilty and responsible for it" (913).

There is more to this globality of guilt: I refer to the depth of his loyalty conflicts throughout his growing up and even continued into the present (e.g., as he perceives it: between his wife and me), and with that his role as *mediator* who has to take everything upon himself. Of course, it is a doomed effort—loyalty to one means disloyalty to the other, and requires the denial of how irreconcilable the two loyalties prove to be. It is in fact part of the rescue scenario: "The masochism was the result of the failed rescue effort, it was a shame, a humiliation."

Isolation, Deanimation, Dehumanization

"This is obviously the core of perversion—to become the passive, manipulated, dead, and deformed object of the malicious female" (Cooper, 1991, p. 26).

Elazar had felt treated as an object by women—"treated like a piece of furniture" by a "detached mother who would not touch me, and when she did, it was and is lifeless and cold"; so he wants to treat women like objects now, he says, that is, without respect (893).

"Thinking of all the fetishes—the boots, the high heels, the leather—they are all part of that process of objectifying, and with that of that quest for power, the love of myself and of others as objects. To deny the pain by objectifying it, by transforming the human being into an object, treating the woman as a thing just like myself. There is an element of denial: 'It is not really my mother who is hurting me, but an inanimate object'" (893).

After a dream where he was terrified among strangers he states: "It adds something to all my masochistic fantasies—this estrangement. . . . That woman chains me to the bed and forces me to have cunnilingus with her. The relationship to the woman is always mediated by the attachment to mechanical devices—straps, and chains, and leather clothes, boots, something mechanical that creates distance, something that is forced upon me. Something distancing, removing, cutting off of feelings, replacing intimate contact like hugging with these artificial things. The understanding of these symbols would be so important: they are there to cut off the intimate feelings of love and hate, to substitute for the real feelings. That whole image of oral sex is mechanical, compulsive, repetitive. That's what struck me. It's how to deal with affect. That image of bondage—why is that always there? As a substitute for hugging or being embraced. It is a kind of artificial, unfeeling hugging. . . . It's by these instruments that the love is conveyed, how it is made concrete and specific, by all these contraptions. The love is embodied in all the paraphernalia. This is the definition of a fetish: that love is invested in these inanimate objects. It's intentional that the human element is excluded. Bondage becomes the object of love, the woman becomes the life force that animates these objects—the chains and the boots and straps and whips and tacks and the nail gun, the rape fantasy. That power is the ultimate aphrodisiac" (914).

In my formulation: "'If mother deals with me in such a mechanical and hating way—the only way of experiencing love is if it is associated with being mechanical and with hate. But now it is under my stage management and under my power, and it will end up differently.'"

"Consummated."

I: "Transformed."

He: "This transformation is very important—it's made concrete."

"Transforming something mechanical into real love and power—yet another *reversal*."

He adds that the counterpoint to this mechanization and depersonalization of love consists in the wishes of sexual excitement with the mother in the bathtub, fantasies of merging with her—"the dangers of depending on her, the fear of the monsters of the deep" (915).

The lead symptom of his perversion, this form of "depersonalizing," as he used to call it, is clearly a compromise formation:

"It entailed a double goal: attaining the sense of love by the instrument and expressing the hatred against your mother by removing her."

"The human figure was a function of the instrument: to operate the machine!" (919).

How "depersonalizing" his mother could be in reality was shown around that time (toward the end of the analysis). He called to tell her that he and his wife were planning to visit her in two weeks (she lives in a distant city). Her reply was: "Fine, if I don't have anything more important to do."

"Isn't our trip important too?"

"You know what I mean. I need to go out, and if there is something special."

He adds: "I thought about that depersonalizing of my feelings, that cutting off in the masochistic fantasy, the love for the inanimate objects: I was cutting myself off from my mother to protect myself, so that she cannot hurt me anymore. It's futile to seek her love, and still I'm left with a residual resentment" (921). "Yet the sexual aspect of the fantasy was very personal."

It was a form of undoing: the mechanical eventually does become personalized. "I don't think of my mother as a person; I cannot feel great sympathy for her, and often I also have not had sympathy for myself. This is also a kind of depersonalizing" (920).

This process of denial in the specific form of *deanimation* and *mechanization or "depersonalizing"* was an important addition in the reconstruction of the dynamics of his perversion. This is in fact *the most specific factor, the most characteristic aspect of the development of a perversion* instead of that of a neurotic symptom. It is probably akin to what Chasseguet-Smirgel and Grunberger refer to as the anal denial of differences in the perversion, the process of nivelization (leveling) in the anal universe.

This is the place too to insert an important insight into the transference—we could call it *the depersonalizing transference*, as one form of the transference of defense.

A little while before the end of the analysis he expresses his astonishment about the peculiar "detachment" toward me, the sense of estrangement in the sessions. He feels unloved: "As if I were touched and treated with instruments, by a machine, not by human contact. My wish is that you love me as a son or as a lover. I need strong expressions of feelings and confirmations. This here is so restrained; it should liberate my feelings and thoughts." He feels ignored and wants to provoke me. The situation here resembles the core fantasy where he also would like to evoke anger or love. He would like to sense more mutual dependency. "What I missed so much with my mother I am missing now also with you, although in many regards you are entirely different from her, so enthusiastic and joyful. I have a deep need to hug you. And yet I know very well that your neutrality has been very useful for our work. It is the measure of the success of the analysis that it has brought me to those realizations how much I need contact, hugging and kissing."

I remark that he is touching on a very deep issue: to what extent the limits had been blurred at home—bathing together with his mother, having a father whose masculinity had been an object of scorn and who had been described as if he had not had any penis—how also in the core fantasy the boundaries were blurred and transgressed, while here clear limits were maintained, that this is something he both wishes and rejects. He immediately agrees and mentions the sexual ambiguity of his identity in the masochistic fantasy. He also adds how the parental authority had been exerted by grandfather, uncle, and brother, but not by mother and father. I comment: "You are looking to me for what you are painfully missing in your intimate relationships, in spite of your increased inner freedom—the lifting of the boundaries and the feelings of love and power" (936).

The Claim for Omnipotence

After some rather gross expressions of rage against a coworker—"I could have strung her up on her tits!"—he finds: "The connecting tissue in all these aspects is being omnipotent, being in control, at the center" (891).

I have given already extensive credit to this ninth factor in the detailed description of the "good hours"—the hours of the breakthrough.

THE HIERARCHY OF CONFLICTS
UNDERLYING THE PERVERSION

Summarizing the clinical findings in a kind of pathogenetic, ultimately etiological hierarchy, we notice that which is applicable to the psychodynamic structure of other types of severe neuroses can be found again in this case of clinical masochism and character perversion, a case showing both "erotogenic masochism," the masochistic-fetishistic perversion, and "moral masochism," the tyranny of inner and outer authority, and leading to a concern with a largely unconscious, but powerful pursuit of punishment of himself and others: a series of conflicts. I proceed from the most archaic and global to the more recent and differentiated layers.

Conflicts between and about Global Affects

There is the preeminence of the problems of, and therewith the conflicts about, affect regulation. Grossman writes (1986) in regard to the masochistic perversion that "this control of the adult serves indirectly as a kind of regulation of the child's affect to the extent that it limits behavior upsetting to the child" (p. 403), and that "behaviors that appear self-destructive to an observer may be organized to serve a variety of functions having to do with the regulation of unpleasurable affects, pain, and aggression" (p. 408). This is certainly noticeable in the case of this patient.

"I am so angry that I could blow up the whole world. . . . It is so frustrating to confront this anger. It always eludes me. It is totally devastating, a nuclear bomb. Hence my constant fantasies about a nuclear holocaust. That goes back to the earliest childhood. I'm not hopeful that I ever can solve this analytically. It is very dangerous and very destructive. I avoid it like the plague. To feel crazy with anger, to feel out of control. It is always there, underneath; a constant anger about my plight, the chronic pain. I try to ignore it, I don't notice it. But it is always there in the background. . . . I like the idea that I erotize my anger; that's a good way to handle it, to channel it. I cannot imagine any other possible way of living" (880).

Statements like this accompanied the analysis; it will also be remembered that it was his uncontrollable rage that had been a main motive for his entering analysis in the first place. Similar comments were made about anxiety and terror, about pain, loss, and loneliness.

These affects impart to all later conflicts their own intensity and radicalism. The anxieties engendered by the conflicts are particularly overwhelming, hence especially fragmenting (Rangell, 1982). Fragmentation is prominent in Elazar's self-experience—"the pieces of an exploding star hurled out into empty space." The sense of losing himself in those affect storms of rage, guilt and panic is specifically being dealt with by the core fantasy and its derivative enactments.

Conflicts between Union and Separateness

"It's more than the right of having one's own life that matters," says Elazar, "what means even more to me is: having the right to feel my own feelings and to trust my own feelings, to live them out and to accept myself in those feelings. That is at the core of the neurosis: that those feelings are wrong, bad, and destructive" (488). His global identification is that of the victim trying to turn rescuer, a pattern preformed in his family, one whose suffering and self-punishment should serve to bring about love and to appease aggression, then and now. "There is the control of the adult's aggression by the affective display of the child" (Grossman, 1986, p. 403)." The permanent wish to please the once rejecting, introjected object causes the person to lose his identity" (Berliner, 1947, p. 468).

Elazar also mentions himself the "inability to separate myself from the world, of establishing sharp boundaries" and his problems about "limits" of any kind (895). We heard also his identifying to the point of merger with the figure of the idealized, invulnerable woman.

Conflicts about Sphincter Controls

The dichotomies ruling Elazar's fantasy life are remarkable. The main polarity is that of being weak, overwhelmed by feelings, mutilated, shame-laden versus the ideal object's being powerful, impenetrable, emotionally impervious, shame-proof, and phallic. Individuality becomes submerged by such rigorous categorizing according to an *axis of power and shame*. Prominently this polarization is represented by anal qualities— messy versus orderly, stubborn withholding and defiant control versus submission and abject yielding. There is that which Chasseguet-Smirgel and Grunberger describe as the "anal universe," where all boundaries separating genders and generations are wiped out.

Triangular Conflicts—The Way from Ithaca to Golgatha

By triangular conflicts, I mean emphatically more than just oedipal conflicts in the usual understanding. We have to consider the great relevance of jealousy in siblings' rivalry and clearly distinguishing this focus from oedipal rivalry. Franz Wellendorf, who devoted a valuable study to this neglected topic (1995), summarizes this by saying: "Looking at the history of psychoanalysis one is struck by the discrepancy between frequent and

intense sibling conflicts among psychoanalysts and the neglect of this issue in the psychoanalytic literature. One can find this discrepancy already
in Freud" (p. 309).

Elazar's competition for the love of his brother against father and
mother, and second, the competition for the love of his father against
mother and brother, were much more pronounced than the triangle of the
"positive" Oedipus conflict and rivalry for his mother. He says: "I have
to understand more clearly my obsessional wish to provoke punishment.
It is the nub of my masochism. Why do I have that wish? What am I so
angry about? It has to do with my anger at my father, wishing him dead.
It's different with my mother. There is real love and hate with him. With
my mother it is rather that I want to get her power. I want to control
women, but I wanted to humiliate my father, not to control him. I saw my
father as susceptible to women, that he preferred women over me. And
what kind of a woman! One whom I hated. How could he have found that
bitch more attractive than me? That's the reason why I want to control
women, that I want to have their power: to get father—because he preferred her over me." It is clearly then a triangle in which the mother is the
rival whom he wanted to be *like*, whose power he wanted to acquire, and
whom he wanted to eliminate as a rival.

"And that means all my obsession to become like a woman without
losing my balls, that castration anxiety. If I became loved by my father, I
would lose my balls," as it emerged from very strong homosexual
dreams. What I have just quoted him saying in regard to his father is, I
believe, even far more relevant and far more pronounced in his idealized relationship to his brother and hence to the triangle with brother
and parent—perhaps more in the form of the triangle of patient, father,
and brother than of that involving the mother. On many levels the
brother appears to have been the main oedipal object, coming closest to
that idealized figure already mentioned (the powerful hermaphrodite—
a term he actually repeatedly used). All this is powerfully repeated in
the transference with me, as will be inescapably manifest in the following dialogues.

A daydream (in session 476): "The homecoming of Ulysses to Ithaca
and the contest with the bow—something about blood—blood on the ar-
row."

"The bloody contest with the suitors, who all were slaughtered?"

"Wanting to overthrow my conscience, that's a bloody battle, to subdue
it. Ulysses defeats them by guile, not by direct confrontation. I felt the
same: that my conscience cannot be overcome by sheer force, but by getting it to relinquish its control by trick. This is analogous to analysis. It does
not seek a direct confrontation with the conscience, but tricks it into a sense
of security and allows it to reveal itself, so that its vigilance decreases and

it exposes itself; thus it can be defeated. It is a covert attack, instead of a direct frontal assault, a Trojan horse."

"Or are you not also saying: that behind the conflict of conscience a bloody competition between you and someone else is looming? . . . But: 'It is too dangerous to compete. I can gain love and attention and power only if I am the victim and show myself as the rescuer.'"

"With the brother for the attention of the parents. Passivity instead of aggression—because I could not compete with all these other aggressive people. This is true."

"Yet the fantasy was: like Ulysses to kill off the rivals. That was however too dangerous. Instead of that you saw yourself as the one who got crucified. The way led from Ithaca to Golgatha."

And thus, from behind the Crucified, Barabbas emerged, the murderer (actually also the murderer of his father).[3] Only at that point he ventured to enter into the depth of his rage, a really murderous fury. He had mentioned once before that these episodes represented a kind of altered state; that he partly would lose his consciousness and his relationship to reality, and that it was afterward difficult to remember what had been going on. Certainly he wanted to kill but he never had gone so far as to seriously harm his stepson, as much as his wife had dreaded this.

However, he added, his resentment was profound: he felt chronically cheated, unfairly treated, painfully burdened by restrictions and frustrations, a sense of unfairness he was trying to vent by his rage. Not only was this going back to the overstimulation by intrusiveness and the disregard for his private space by his mother, but to the severe and real infringements in the form of his physical impediments (504).

Yet there is a deeper competition with his brother, a kind of triangle self—brother—brother's penis.

I refer to the envy toward the big brother who had been bragging with his big erect penis and intimidated his little brother with his held back anger—an envy (penis envy) and a homosexual attraction that he had to defend against by the image of his subjugation to the phallic woman. It was above all his fear of his envy and the defense against that envy, in particular the shame as a powerful defense against envy (by affect reversal, but the reverse is true too: envy as a defense against shame) that lent itself to the analytic working-through. It verged into the compound, strongly superego determined affect of resentment (see chapter 5): "I begin to feel the connection between damaged eyes and damaged penis; both involve mutilation" of a vital organ. "I would see the link between my mutilated eyes and this very strong penis, to see this large penis through my damaged eyes." He had dreamed that he had participated with his little (three- to four-year-old) son (who in reality is an adolescent) in a robbery, but that he is concerned about the vulnerability of the child (that he would be caught and hurt). While it is on the one side the always so prominent identification with the victim, there are behind that "intense feelings of wanting to rob and to steal, to take what is mine, that I have been cheated, that I only take what is properly mine. We have talked about the fee here and my reluctance to pay a higher fee, to dip into the savings. That this (the trust fund) is properly mine, why should I give it up? This is very much in the background, vague whispers of a feeling. I'm not sure if that is envy. It's more: to get what I deserve to compensate for the loss."

"The resentment—the envy combined with the sense of injustice that is so stressed."

"That I am the victim, and I take only what is properly mine. And the brother is certainly the person with whom I am competing and against whom I harbor that feeling. He could do the things which I could not do, both because of his age and my handicap. . . . I think of that, my sense of victimhood, and very much unconscious resentment, and also very much conscious resentment" (623).

Superego Conflicts—The Rescue Mission

As to the severity of superego conflicts: "I always come back to that inner accuser—instead of self-worth it is self-accusation. The principal basis for all my guilt comes from that aggravated, exaggerated conscience. It transforms petty mistakes into big deals, so that my wife's blowing up of small mistakes to a state's crime turns into my blaming myself, not forgiving myself. It is beating up on myself, not letting it go by, harping on it, over and over again" (900). "In turn, I resent the accusation. It is not fair. . . . I have a deep resentment of anybody who offers judgments of others. . . . My parents and grandparents were extremely judgmental, to the point of prejudice" (897).

More specifically, we encounter again (as in Agnes and as stressed in chapter 3) the importance of intrasystemic superego conflicts: In the masochistic core fantasy the polarity of guilt and shame is represented by two opposite ideals—that of the Savior who suffers, versus that of the "Triumphator" who kills the weak: Christ versus Ulysses. In the fantasy the two opposites merge into one; their contradiction is negated. Suffering means power. The "illusion of perfectability" (Rothstein, 1991) combines with the "delusion of omnipotence" (Novick and Novick, 1996a) to bring about a logically irreconcilable duality of ideals that are being united by the process of reversals inherent in the masochistic scenario.

In addition to such intrasystemic conflict in the form of the guilt-shame dilemma, I referred in the clinical material repeatedly to the massivity of the patient's loyalty conflicts. "There was a very narrow path to walk between both parents. It was a mistake to favor one parent over the other, and it caused an enormous feeling of guilt. It meant alienating the other. Always to remain impartial! This plays very neatly into the omnipotence fantasy: that I had such power over them, that the smallest thing I did would make them hate me for life"—or rescue them from their despair and bring about peace, by reconciling them (900). But also: "Whom did I originally accuse? All three of them. I felt betrayed by each one of them" (897).

In his fantasy life, he very often, especially during the earlier part of treatment, identified the victim in the core fantasy (the "I") with the pathetic father, the tormentor with the abusive mother. Rothstein speaks of the "representation of the self as object" versus the "representation of the self as agent" (in Panel, 1988; Rothstein, 1991)—the self as "killed," versus the self as "killing." By taking the suffering upon himself, Elazar hoped to mediate between the fighting parents, to reconcile the two loyalties: "It is all my fault." Just as Berliner writes that "he [the masochist] is stigmatized with unwantedness and displays his stigma as his bid for affection" (1947, p. 468), so one crucial aspect of Elazar's "stigma" is the cruelty inherent in the family discord and the family shame, the deep schisms and opposed allegiances in that family. He has identified with the splits in the family. His perversion is an active reliving of that pervasive duplicity, an attempt to master the play of passivity under his own active stage management. Its actions explicate, though symbolically, what is hidden behind the overt strife and value contradictions.

Therefore, I do not believe that the perversion is, as Chasseguet-Smirgel and Grunberger postulate, something radically different from the neurosis. It is merely another attempt to solve neurotic conflicts by compromise formation, in addition and parallel to character and symptom neurosis. And, just as in all neuroses, the severity of conflict is reflected in the "narcissistic" phenomena of trying to disregard "boundaries" and "limits," of "idealization" and "grandiosity," and very centrally in the inexorable demands to live up to an unreasonably harsh "inner judge" demanding perfection and omnipotence. And, also as in all neuroses, the severity of conflict more or less directly corresponds to the massiveness and frequency of trauma. And trauma is, by definition, always connected with a defect of affect regulation and hence of affect control, with attending cognitive and emotional regressions.

THE NOBILITY OF SUFFERING

Finally, in this context of the sexual perversion and character perversion and against the broader question about masochism in culture, I quote from a brief interchange between the patient and myself (890): He raises the issue of suffering and martyrdom in Christianity and Judaism (he himself is Jewish): "Is this not all then masochism? Doesn't this [our analysis of the underpinnings] take away the nobility of suffering?" He poses the question in order to retreat from the insights into *his* masochism. "The acceptance of suffering is not masochism," I respond. "Masochism is the seeking of suffering as the only way to love and to acceptance by others and to self-acceptance."

We talk about the difference between the message of love versus the message of masochism in (Christian) religion, whereby in the latter the sacrifice becomes the important element, not the message of love. "It is one thing to believe very strongly in certain values, even if it entails the risk of being killed," I reply. "It is another thing when the self-sacrifice becomes the overriding goal."

"Only through sacrifice I could find importance and worth." Love and respect were bound to his being beaten or humiliated.

THE SACRIFICE

I repeatedly mentioned Elazar's fantasies about the ritual sacrifice of his penis or his masculinity, his identity and will to appease his mother.

Novick and Novick write (1996a, p. 58):

> It would be interesting to explore the connection between obsessional symptoms and masochism. One link appears to be the delusion of omnipotence. . . . The obsessionality was an attempt to defend against rage and death wishes experienced as omnipotent. In many instances the obsessionality involved a "bargain" with God, whereby, in return for keeping mother or father alive, the child promised to do something or say something in a particular, usually painful, way. Often the ritual also involved a sacrifice; in a number of cases the child made a deal with God to trade his own life, or years off his own life to keep one or both parents alive.

The material previously presented bears this out also in regard to our patient.

In this context I would like to digress briefly and refer to one of the novels of the Swedish author Pär Lagerkvist, the strongly autobiographical *Gäst hos verkligheten* (1925/1982; Guest in Reality), in which the connections just made are born out with particular lucidity:

This autobiographic novel describes how a small boy is warned by the supervisor of the city park (*källarmästaren*) against digging a hole in the ground of the gravel way because it would mean someone in his family was going to die. This arouses a panic in the little boy—an early and overwhelming form of fear of his conscience. This terror changes in the course of the years to an obsession with the fear of death: only by magical actions of an unmistakably masochistic nature, most of all by his kneeling and praying at a private altar, far out in the forest at a half hidden stone, could he hope to avert the disaster. There he pleads that nobody, absolutely nobody would die—he enumerates them all—more: that nothing, really nothing at all would change—that there would be "no difference" (see chapter 3 in this volume). Only the atonement achieved by his personal sacrifice and toil could relieve him briefly from the obsession with death, meaning, as we would infer: with "unconscious" guilt (to the narrator this connection does not seem to be unconscious at all, as the construction of the narrative shows). However, as it happens that his grandmother falls sick and eventually dies, his world breaks apart. He is convinced he would soon die himself; everybody else is therefore avoiding him and they seclude themselves from him, so he thinks—he is standing in empty space. Only his mother does not want to let on anything, just wants to show him that he is still dear to her and that she keeps thinking of him and caring about him. Yet her tenderness and kindness is especially intolerable for him. (We might add: how could he deserve it—after those thoughts!?) If he could only hate her! He feels closed in, trapped, stifled, one would have to break out (p. 96; I quote from the Swedish edition; all translations are mine). Yet such breaking out from the heaviness and stickiness—what would that mean, what would that consist in? In the sweeping away of God, in the acceptance of that very meaninglessness which the "Dwarf" (in Lagerkvist's like-named story, see below, chapter 5) takes to be the basis of existence. Only anxiety and emptiness would then have any existence. "The anxiety was gnawing and gnawing, was eating a hole within." Still he can also be glad and cheerful; he is at least like two beings who have nothing to do with each other.

Yet it is clear to him that this anxiety about dying is something inhuman, that in the crazy clinging to life there is something that is hostile to life itself.

For the analyst, it is likely that there are above all (omnipotent) wishes to kill, to have somebody die, which must be kept under tight control by such an overly strong conscience and become evident in the form of the excessive and incessant preoccupation with death and the anxiety about it. And since these fears appear for the first time directed at the father, right after the warning by the "källarmästaren" (himself a father figure), the original target is also probable. One can assume therefore that, behind these obsessional symptoms, behind this ego restriction and ego split, there are oedipal conflicts with strong jealousy and death wishes, conflicts marked by great ambivalence. However, these do not come up explicitly; their explicit presentation certainly would also interfere with its artistic value.

THE RECONSTRUCTION OF THE
SPECIFIC PSYCHOANALYTIC CAUSALITY

"One frequently hears the opinion that masochistic character disturbances have a poor or hopeless prognosis," says Brenner in his important
paper of 1959 (p. 216), and he continues:

> success was not achieved in a crucial analytic hour or by a single, crucially
> important piece of analytic understanding suitably interpreted to the patient
> . . . in the majority of masochistic patients what seems at least to be of vital
> importance for a satisfactory therapeutic result is the steady day-to-day
> work, always with as clear a view as possible of the conflicting forces at work
> within the patient's mind. (p. 217ff.)

While I have selected a number of verbatim statements and inter-
changes from particularly "good hours" (Kris, 1956, in Ernst Kris, 1975:
"On some vicissitudes of insight in psychoanalysis," pp. 252–71) that allow the "reconstruction" being presented here, I have to concur with
Brenner that the majority of the work, even with Elazar, has rather been
of a cumulative nature and, I would add, has also had much of the nature
of an "emotional corrective experience"—what in the final chapter I will
address as the "real relationship": to be listened to without being judged
and condemned, to be "seen" and "heard" in regard to his individual,
though opposing needs, feelings, and impulses, in his value discords and
divergent loyalty commitments. These *unspecific* therapeutic factors (the
"psychotherapeutic" aspects of the treatment in Gray's [1994] sense, the
same or "supportive interventions" for Wallerstein [1997]—"suggestions"
for Gill [1991]) have worked in conjunction with the *specific* "psychoanalytic" factors of reconstruction by insight. These insights were achieved
not so much by distinct, selective interpretations, but by the whole intricate *interpretive process*, the conjoint working out of interpretations: the
restoration of the torn connections in the dialogue of the collaborative inquiry. It also needs to be stressed that such restoration referred by no
means just to transference interpretation, but to the back and forth and
weaving together of transference, extratransference, and historical connections, with a nonobtrusive use of countertransference.

In this whole reconstruction, particular importance was given to the
magical transformation ("the alchemist's dream") achieved by the
masochistic core fantasy: the power of victimhood to omnipotently alter
reality. Among the underlying conflicts, special attention was paid to the
conflicts within the superego and to those between overwhelming affects
and between these and the ego's attempts to reestablish control. Viewing
the treatment from the perspective of the traumatization causing the pathogenic conflicts, we gave much weight to the chronic traumatization by

"soul blindness," as shown by his surroundings, most of all by his mother, and by "soul murder."

"EYES THAT LOOKED AT HER WITHOUT SEEING HER"— "SOUL-BLINDNESS" AND "SOUL MURDER" IN LITERATURE

We find hints of the concept of soul-blindness[4] in the biblical terms of the "heart of stone" ("lev ha'even," Ezekiel, 36.26) or the "hardening" of Pharao's heart in Exodus ("wayyechezáq lev-par'oh" or "wayyachbéd et-libbó").

I would like to give here a few excerpts from two of the greatest writers of the nineteenth century who presented this twin issue very eloquently—George Eliot and Henrik Ibsen. The latter is usually credited with coining the concept "soul murder" in his last works. Strindberg actually used it in a review of Ibsen's *Rosmersholm* (1887). Yet it goes back to Goethe's time and to its use by an early contemporary of his, Jakob Michael Reinhold Lenz (1751–1792), who used the concept in a drama, *Der neue Menoza*, about Count Camäleon, who commits an incestuous rape: "I want to tear the guts out of this soul murderous dog."[5] We are also reminded of a quote from Goethe's autobiography, *Poetry and Truth*, referring to a close friend of his family, a prominent physician of his time, Zimmermann: "His harshness against his children was a form of hypochondriasis, a partial insanity, continuous soul murder (*moralisches Morden*) that, after sacrificing his children, he eventually turned against himself."[6] Shengold (1989) has already pointed out the use of this term by Anselm von Feuerbach in his work on Kaspar Hauser (1832).

But first the relevant excerpts from George Eliot's *Romola* and *Daniel Deronda*, in regard to the first concept, "soul-blindness."

The trauma of having lost trust, both in husband and in Savonarola, is shattering for Romola:

> No one who has ever known what it is thus to lose faith in a fellow man whom he has profoundly loved and reverenced, will lightly say that the shock can leave the faith in the invisible goodness unshaken. With the sinking of high human trust, the dignity of life sinks too; we cease to believe in our own better self, since that also is part of the common nature which is degraded in our thought; and all the finer impulses are dulled. Romola felt even the springs of her once active pity drying up, and leaving her to barren egoistic complaining. (Eliot, 1862–1863/1994, p. 473)

She gives herself over, in a passive kind of suicidality, to the wide ocean:

> Memories hung upon her like the weight of broken wings that could never be lifted—memories of human sympathy which even in its pains leaves a thirst

that the Great Mother has no milk to still. Romola felt orphaned in those wide spaces of sea and sky. She read no message of love for her in that far-off symbolic writing of the heavens, and with a great sob she wished that she might be gliding into death. She drew the cowl over her head again and covered her face, choosing darkness rather than the light of the stars, which seemed to her like the hard light of *eyes that looked at her without seeing her*. Presently she felt that she was in the grave, but not resting there: she was touching the hands of the beloved dead beside her, and trying to wake them. (p. 475, emphasis added)

"Eyes that looked at her without seeing her": This was a form of chronic traumatization she had experienced with her father. His physical blindness was like a sign of his "soul-blindness." In his own words:

For me, Romola, even when I could see, it was with the great dead that I lived; while the living often seemed to me mere spectres—shadows dispossessed of true feeling and intelligence. . . . My path . . . has closed in now—all but the narrow track he [the son who had left him and returned to religion] has left me to tread—alone, in my blindness.

Romola was "stung too acutely by her father's last words to remain motionless as well as silent" (p. 49–50).

He could not recognize her needs; she was only a tool for his scholarliness. The same chronic traumatization is described for Tito Melema, Romola's treacherously opportunistic husband: "he [Baldassarre, the foster father of Tito who had rescued the child] was constantly scrutinizing Tito's mind to see whether it answered to his own exaggerated expectations;" Tito was but "a radiant presence for a lonely man to have won for himself" (pp. 95–96), a false self. There was, however, not only this "being blinded by images" ascribed to Baldassarre, but this foster father had saved Tito from physical abuse ("I took him when they were beating him," p. 423).

In *Daniel Deronda*, the steady traumatization by soul-blindness and soul murder inflicted by Gwendolen Harleth's sinister husband Grandcourt and her ensuing helplessness and humiliation becomes ever more insistent: "He generally observes the forms; but he doesn't listen much" (1876/1982, p. 487). [His secretary] "Lush . . . was as much of an implement as pen and paper . . . he had been so accustomed to this human tool" (p. 657). It is due to his total lack of empathy, particularly into the inner conflicts of others: he "lacked the only organ of thinking that could have saved him from mistake—namely, some experience of the mixed passions concerned" (p. 657). He is only able to see the narcissistic side of her, "her personal pride," not "the remorseful half," the side of obligation to others: "Grandcourt's view of things was considerably fenced in by his general sense, that what suited him, others must put up with. There is no escaping the fact that *want of sympathy condemns us to a corresponding stupidity*" (p. 658, emphasis added). For Gwendolen, hubris had turned into nemesis: "Any romantic illusions she had had in marrying this man had turned on her power of using him as she liked. He was using her as he liked" (p. 659).

Turning to the main hero of the novel who had also been raised by a foster father, Sir Hugo Mallinger: Twice there is a statement about the latter that refers to this issue of "soul-blindness." Once at the beginning: "The mistakes in his behaviour to Deronda were due to that dullness towards what may be going on in other minds, especially the minds of children, which is among the commonest deficiencies even in good-natured men like him, when life has been generally easy to themselves, and their energies have been quietly spent in feeling gratified" (pp. 213–14). The second time toward the end: "he was beguiled into regarding children chiefly as a product intended to make life more agreeable to the full-grown, whose convenience alone was to be consulted in the disposal of them" (p. 781). Both statements refer to a basic lack of empathy, a "soul-blindness," similar to the one in Bardo de' Bardi, Romola's father, and in Baldassarre, different from the "soul murder" by Tito Melema and Grandcourt. The major manifestation of this enduring traumatization of Daniel Deronda is the sense of falsity, the "secret of his own birth," "this dread of utterance about any shame connected with their parents. . . . The terrible sense of collision between a strong rush of feeling and the dread of its betrayal . . . others probably knew things concerning him which they did not choose to mention . . . he was feeling the injury done him as a maimed boy feels the crushed limb" (pp. 206, 209). He came "to regard concealment as a bane of life, and the necessity of concealment as a mark by which lines of action were to be avoided" (p. 435).

Now to Ibsen: Already Brand (in the like-named early verse drama) proclaims: "If man is to be used, he must be killed" ("Skal mannen brukes, må han dødes"; 1866/1991, p. 149; my translation).

A deep paradox goes through many of the plays: The pursuit of one high value, living life for one ideal, the insistence upon a high ethical principle becomes itself a deadly peril; it destroys both the protagonist and his immediate surrounding. The ideal itself turns murderous by overshadowing and extinguishing in its one-sidedness all other needs and by making the people around into mere means in the service of this purpose: the other human being is sacrificed for this main goal. It is the case of a particular form of soul-blindness—the needs of the other are not seen, he is treated as mere object. This, however, means: the border between animate and inanimate becomes blurred (see Kafka, 1989), man becomes more and more a thing.

In *The Lady from the Sea*, Ellida's stepdaughter Bolette says about her: "There are so many things this one doesn't even *see*. Or maybe she doesn't *want* to see—or *doesn't care*" (1989/1966, p. 73).[7]

The exclusiveness with which Rita Allmers (in *Little Eyolf* [1989/1966]) claims her husband's love, the obsession with his task on Alfred Allmers' side—both are fatal, they eventually become a kind of murder of their child. It is the jealous absoluteness in pursuit of a goal that is unveiled as a kind of deadly sin.

Already in the first realistic dramas (as it had been also in *Peer Gynt*) the basic sin is a kind of soul murder: that the other is not being recognized and treated in his identity, in his self, as his own purpose (*Selbstzweck*)—and thus in fact is crushingly degraded, humiliated, shamed.

For power's sake, for the sake of obtaining, with the help of his rival for Ella Rentheim's love, the position as bank director, Borkman (in the play *John Gabriel Borkman* [1989/1966]) forsook the woman's love for him and his own for her in order to marry her sister Gunhild. Late in life, when he has lost his entire position and all his property in a scandal and utter disgrace, Ella confronts him:

> That time I didn't know yet your big, horrendous crime. . . . I mean the crime for which there is no forgiveness. . . . You are a murderer! You have committed the big mortal sin. . . . You have slain the love life in me. Do you understand what that means? In the Bible there is word about an enigmatic sin for which there exists no forgiveness. Never before could I understand what that might be. Now I understand it. The big sin without mercy—that is the sin of murdering the love life in a human being. . . . You betrayed the woman you *loved*! Me, me, me! What was dearest to you in the world you were ready to give away for the sake of profit. *This* is the double murder you are guilty of! The murder committed against your own soul and against mine![8] (pp. 543–44)

And again toward the end: "And you crushed this human heart. . . . You sold it for—for—" And he finishes her sentence: "—for the sake of the realm [the dream land of technical conquest]—and of the power—and of the honor—you mean?" (p. 562)

In Ibsen's last drama, *When We Dead Awaken*, (1989/1966) the same point is made by Irene, the model of the sculptor Rubek, who had spurned her, failed to recognize her love offering, who had used her self-giving as his naked model only for his artisanship—to him who had revered her as ideal image, but ignored her as human being: "You have killed my soul, and then you model yourself in repentance and atonement and self-accusation, and with that you consider your account settled."[9]

"Yet *I* was a human being—at that time! And *I* had also a life to live—and to fulfill a human fate. Look, all that I threw away, I sacrificed it in order to subordinate myself to you. O, that was a suicide. It was a deadly crime against myself. And that crime I never can expiate" (p. 590, my translation). That he had sacrificed her to his art and his artwork—that was the unforgivable sin, the soul murder: "You committed a crime against what was inborn in my inmost self" (p. 577).

"I gave you my young and living soul. And now I was standing there and within I was empty.—Soulless. That was it what I died from, Arnold" (p. 580).

Rubek's guilt is overwhelming; he tells Irene: "You have a shadow tormenting you. And *I* have my heavy conscience" (p. 587). This guilt has deprived his life of its authenticity, has destroyed his creativity and emptied and debased his life with other people: now these others appear to him as mere "animal snouts behind masks" (pp. 584–85).

"What cannot be made good again, we recognize only then, when—when we dead awaken—" (p. 593), says Irene. "We see that we never have been alive" (p. 594).

Yet, to deepen our understanding of character perversion and, in particular, of the tragic character who "forever remains sitting in his hell," we have to turn now to the psychodynamics of resentment.

NOTES

1. Ну разве можпо, разве можпо, хоть сколько-нибудь уважать, себя человеку, который даже в самом чувстве собствеппого нижения посягул отыскать наслаждепие (Эаписки из подполья, p. 144).

(Nu, razvě možno, razvě možno chot' skol'ko-nibud' uvažat' sebja čelověku, kotorij daže v samom čuvstvě sobstvěnnovo uniženija posjagnul otyskat' naslaždenije?)

2. "Wollten und wagten wir eine Architektur nach *unserer* Seelen-Art (wir sind zu feige dazu!)—so müßte das Labyrinth unser Vorbild sein!" (Nietzsche, 1886/1976, *Morgenröte* [Dawn], 169, pp. 145–46).

3. See Lagerkvist's 1950 novel of the same name.

4. I have defined the concepts of soul-blindness and soul murder already in chapter 2.

5. "Sein Eingeweid will ich ihm aus dem Leib reißen, dem seelenmörderischen Hunde." I thank Dr. Friedrich-Wilhelm Eickhoff in Tübingen for this valuable information.

6. Goethe (1961), *Dichtung und Wahrheit*, Bk. 15; dtv vol. 24, p. 196.

7. "Der er så mangt og meget som denne her ikke *ser*. Eller som hun kanskje ikke *vil* se,—eller ikke *bryr seg om*" (p. 354).

8. "Det er dobbeltmordet som du har gjort det skyldig i! Mordet på din egen sjel og på min!" (Ibsen, 1989, *Nutidsdramaer*, pp. 543–44).

9. "Du har drept min sjel,—og så modellerer du deg selv i anger og bot og bekjennelse,—og dermed er ditt regnskap oppgjort, mener du" (p. 590).

5

Superego as Herald
of Resentment

"CAUSELESS HATE" AND THE STORY
OF QAMTZA AND BAR QAMTZA

In the Talmud tractate Shabbat (32b) we read: "Rabbi Nechemia said: As a punishment for causeless hate [*sin'at chinnam*], strife multiplies in a man's house, his wife miscarries, and his sons and daughters die young." In tractate Yoma (9b) it is said:

> Why was the first Sanctuary destroyed? Because of three [evil] things which prevailed there: idolatry, sexual immorality, and bloodshed. . . . But why was the second Sanctuary destroyed, seeing that in its time they were occupying themselves with Torah, [observance of] precepts, and the practice of charity. Because therein prevailed hatred without cause. That teaches you that groundless hatred [*sin'at chinnam*] is considered as of even gravity with the three sins of idolatry, uncovering of the genitals, and bloodshed together. (*Talmud*, 1962/1936)

Chinnam is translated as "causeless, senseless, in vain." The word is derived from *chen*, "grace, loveliness, pleasure." Thus we can translate *Sin'at chinnam* also as "hatred that is just for pleasure, arbitrary, frivolous." We know though that behind that appearance of frivolity a lot is hidden. As analysts we cannot stick to the phenomenon of seemingly groundless, frivolous hate, because it is here that the inquiry only starts.

The close conjunction of shaming, resentment, and revenge, and with that the inner history of senseless hate is shown with particular impressiveness by the following story from the Talmud (Gittin, 55b/56a; I follow with minor modifications the translation by Isidor Epstein 1936, and the Hebrew/Aramaic original, 1962 edition):

Rabbi Yochanan said: What is illustrative of the verse (Proverbs, 28.14): "Blessed is the man who always fears the Lord, but he who *hardens his heart* falls into trouble" [*umaqshé libbó yippól bera'áh*]? . . . The destruction of Jerusalem came through Qamtza and Bar Qamtza in this way. A certain man had a friend Qamtza and an enemy Bar Qamtza. He once made a party and said to his servant: "Go and bring Qamtza!" The man went and brought Bar Qamtza. When the man [who gave the party] found him there, he said: "Since this guy is a master of calumny, this mister here, what are you doing here? Get up, and get out! [*Qum, puq!*]" The other said: "Since I am already here, let me stay, and I will pay you for whatever I eat and drink!" This one replied: "No!" "Then let me give you half the cost of the party!" This one said: "No!" [Bar Qamtza] replied: "Then let me pay for the whole party!" He still said: "No!" and he took him by the hand, had him get up and threw him out. The other said: "Since the *Rabbanan* [the teachers and dignitaries] were sitting there and did not stop him, this shows that they agreed with him. I will go and inform against them to the king." He went and said to the Emperor [*Qeysar*]: "The Jews are rebelling against you." He asked: "How can I tell?" [Bar Qamtza] said to him: "Send them an offering and see whether they will offer it [on the altar]." So he sent with him a [third? a three-month-old?] sacrificial calf. While on the way he [Bar Qamtza] made a blemish on its upper lip, or as some say, on the white of its eye, in a place where we [the Jews] count it as blemish, but they [the Romans] do not. The *Rabbanan* [our masters, our Sages] were inclined to offer it anyway in order not to offend the authorities. Said Rabbi Zecharia ben Avqulas to them: "People will say that blemished animals are offered on the altar." They then proposed to kill Bar Qamtza so that he should not go and inform against them, but Rabbi Zecharia said to them: "Is one who makes a blemish on consecrated animals to be put to death?" Rabbi Yochanan thereupon remarked: "Through the scrupulousness [*anwetanút*, piety, humility] of Rabbi Zecharia ben Avqulas our House has been destroyed, our Temple burnt and we ourselves exiled from our land."

Later on (in Gittin 57a) we read: "It has been taught that Rabbi El'azar said: 'Come and see how great the power of shame is [*bo ur'éh kamá gedoláh kochá shel bushá*], for the Holy one espoused the cause of Bar Qamtza and destroyed His House and burnt His Temple.'"

Clearly, this is not just a story of humiliation and inner shame, of revenge and retaliatory massive destruction; but something specific in attitude and affect is added here: the deep sense of aggrievement, of injustice, of helpless rage about that shaming, in short: resentment.

As far as I know, there is no psychoanalytic in-depth study of this affect and attitude. Closest to it come, however, what Melvin Lansky (2001) writes in regard to unforgiveness, Jürgen Körner's brief essay on "resentments and counter-resentments" (2004, as part of a very valuable collection of essays *Ressentiment! Zur Kritik der Kultur*, a special edition of *Merkur*[1]), and John Steiner's chapter in *Psychic Retreats* entitled "Revenge, Resentment, Remorse, and Reparation" (1993, see below, chapter 8).

Friedrich Eickhoff (1996/2001), in "Moral Masochism and the Affect of Resentment," explores the intimate connection between masochism and resentment: According to Bela Grunberger's concepts, Eickhoff sees the boy's wish to castrate the father projected onto the "evil" mother and the self placed in the position of the innocent victim that wallows in the role of the guilt-free, but deeply aggrieved and much suffering victim: "Do not castrate me; I am already castrated" (see also Wurmser, 1981, chapter 13). His guilt is thus successfully warded off, and he can self-righteously (i.e., with good conscience) blame the outside world for all his misfortune and arrogate to himself the right to correct the balance of justice. Decisively, this victimization is sexualized; suffering means lust, as proof for his innocence. Eickhoff applies these insights to the movements of protest in Germany in the last forty years. I think we may be able to extend this psychodynamic explanation if we widen the notion of the castration wishes to shame and envy of the feminine power of mother ("womb envy," "birth envy") as well as of the masculine power of men, and this in both genders: "I am already humiliated, do not humiliate me anymore!"

We can extrapolate much of these findings, as well as what I am going to present, to terrorism—a sociocultural phenomenon that is cardinally understandable on the basis of resentment and moral masochism (see Wurmser, 2004b). In fact, it is probably no exaggeration to say that resentment is the main motivational force in all phenomena of fanaticism. Could they be looked at as synonyms? Not quite: On the one side, the realm of resentment is far wider than that of fanaticism, but fanaticism is, I believe, always carried by extreme forms of resentment. On the other side, something else enters in fanaticism, just as in "narcissistic rage"(Kohut, 1972) that goes beyond resentment. I shall come back later to this issue.

A Google search of "resentment psychoanalysis" gives no fewer than 4,450 references, but I failed to detect any in-depth study of it. Before we try to analyze this feeling state more in depth, let us look at the broader connections.

HUMILIATION, REVENGE, RESENTMENT, AND FORGIVENESS

In every human relationship we encounter a fairly typical sequence of external events and inner processes that accompany them: We feel unjustly treated, not recognized in who we are and how we want to be seen, not appreciated in what we really meant, shamed for something that we have offered and given in good faith, and rejected and fooled in the trust that we have shown others. The feeling of humiliation can become completely overwhelming. At least we feel deep hurt and sadness about what we have experienced as a break in the relationship, a kind of betrayal. If we are entirely honest and open toward ourselves, we sense, hidden behind this grief, also rancor and wrath. And if the humiliation is only deep enough, soon also vengefulness, the lust and greed for revenge (*Rachgier, Rachelust, Rachsucht*) emerges, a seemingly addictive craving for reparation (*Wiedergutmachung*). Such "redress," such retaliation, only seems possible if the other would suffer the same injustice, no, if it were paid back to him in multiples. It is against this that a fundamental commandment of the so-called Old Testament is directed (Leviticus, 19.18; I quote from the Hertz-Bible, but modify some of the translations): "You shall not avenge, nor retain any grudge against the children of your people, but you shall love your fellow man as yourself: I am the Lord" (*lo-tiqóm welo-titór et-bnei amnécha we'áhavtá leré'achá kamócha, aní Hashém*)—the demand to respect and accept and to understand the other as yourself. Immediately preceding this basic obligation (R. Aqiva calls it the central postulate of the Torah, *ze klal gadól batorá*, Talmud, Yerushalmi, Nedarim, 9, 3), it is written: "You shall not hate your brother in your heart: although you should rebuke him, you should not burden yourself with guilt for him" (*lo-tisná et-achícha bilvavécha hokéach tokíach et amitécha welo-tisá aláw chet'*). Rashi, the great medieval commentator (1040–1105) interprets this so: "Though rebuking him you shall not expose him to shame [lit.: make his face grow pale] in public, in which case you will bear sin on account of him." This means: Robbing one's fellow of his dignity and honor is a very great sin. Correct the other person, but do not humiliate him or her (the feminine is very explicit in the Talmud, Bava Metzia, 59a: "A man should always be careful about his wife's honor, for blessing is found in a man's house only on account of his wife"; Steinsaltz, 1989–1999, vol. 3, p. 234). Be honest, but respect the other and his self-esteem.

Returning to the sentence, "you shall not avenge yourself or hold a grudge," Rashi explains the difference between revenge (*neqimá*) and grudge or resentment (*netirá*) in the following beautiful parable:

> If one says to another: 'Lend me your sickle!', and he replies: 'No!', and the next day he [the latter] says to him [the former], 'Lend me your hatchet!' and he retorts: 'I am not going to lend it to you, just as you refused to lend me your sickle'—this is avenging. And what is 'bearing a grudge'? If one says to another, 'Lend me your hatchet!', and he replies 'No!' and on the next day he says to him: 'Lend me your sickle!', and he replies: 'Here it is; I am not like you, because you would not lend me'—this is called 'bearing a grudge' be-

cause he retains [*notér*] enmity [*eivá*] in his heart although he does not actually avenge himself. (Siphra, Yoma, 23a)

After humiliation and revenge or resentment, there is the difficult problem of forgiveness that is continually posed to us as a great task. If we very deeply love the other, such forgiveness is usually not too hard to come by because we try to understand them and can empathize with them; we follow his or her thinking and feeling and repeat it within ourselves.

However, if such empathy is disrupted, a black shadow falls upon the love. We may feel betrayed and cruelly misunderstood. The grudge keeps gnawing at us more and more deeply and may break through in vindictive acts. And then forgiveness becomes harder and harder. *Unforgiveness is resentment.* We slide into the well-known vicious circles where misunderstanding, blaming, and inflicting of injustice on both sides keep accumulating, and where also the attempted dialogue keeps being stuck in blame and reproach. Then there are deeds whose enormity makes it appear that forgiving is impossible, especially if there is no repentance.

MEASURE FOR MEASURE

In this broad context a further thought is relevant, especially in view of wide prejudice. How do we understand the often-quoted saying from Exodus (21.23–24): "Life for a life, eye for an eye, tooth for a tooth," at least the way traditional Jewish interpretation of the last 2,000 years has understood this? The word "tachat" usually translated as "for" (*nefesh tachat nefesh, ayin tachat ayin, shin tachat shin*) is taken as "substitute for," meant as compensation for damage (R. Mitnick, pers. comm.). To this there are detailed discussions in the Talmud tractate Bava Kamma (83b): "Why [pay compensation]? Does not the Torah say an eye for an eye? Why not take this literally to mean the eye? Let not this enter your mind! . . . Compensation (*tashlumin*) is to be paid." Rashi states there is indeed a controversy about "life for a life," but in regard to the other issues it is clear: "If one blinded the eye of his fellow man he has to pay him the value of his eye, i.e. he pays him how much his value would be diminished if he were to be sold as slave on the market. And the same holds for all the other cases: it does not mean the actual cutting off of the offender's limb." Rashi himself points however to the controversy in regard to the first of these parallels, "life for a life" (or "soul for a soul")—whether it should be taken literally.

Thus it is clear from the context that it is value for value, the obligation to replace the value as decided by a court of law. The Talmud (between

200 BCE and 500 CE) is very determined in this. The more general underlying principle is *"midda keneged midda—Measure for Measure."* Shakespeare, however, took this literally and concretely in his play with the same title: "'As Angelo for Claudio, death for death!' Haste still pays haste, and leisure answers leisure/Like doth quit like, and measure still for measure." The man who hastily and unjustly wanted to execute his rival should be subject to the same summary execution.

I am not certain myself if this exegesis of "eye for an eye" held already one or two millennia before the Mishna, but there are other sentences in the Torah speaking for the later understanding. The same may hold true even for its parallel in the legislation of Hammurabi in Babylon, around 1700 BCE; were it taken literally, there probably would not have been many surviving physicians or two-armed citizens in Mesopotamia, and all work would have come to a standstill. It is fascinating, however, that both before the time of Hammurabi, namely in the Sumerian cities Eshnunna and Ur-Nammu, and a little later with the Hittites, exactly the same interpretation explicitly occurs as we find in the later rabbinic exegesis: namely that it is not meant concretely, but that it was a matter of compensation (Pritchard, 1958, pp. 221–24).

"THE SLAVE REVOLT IN MORALITY—A DISGRACE OF MAN"

Here again there is a much deeper dimension than just resentment as conscious attitude and affect: resentment as hidden motive in ethics. Nietzsche was the first to draw attention to the degree of resentment that animates the morality of the West, particularly that of Christianity:[2]

With the last phrase of the above heading I refer to the passage in the *Genealogy of Morals* (1887/1976, I, 11, p. 269): "All those instincts of reaction and resentment . . . these 'tools of culture' are a disgrace of man."

On this subject of resentment, "das Ressentiment," Nietzsche says much that is relevant and expresses even more without directly putting it into words. In deep misrecognition of historical truth, he ascribes it to the "priestly people of the Jews. . . . ; The Jews were in turn that priestly people of the ressentiment par excellence" (1887/1976, I, 16, p. 280, all quotes are my translation). "Out of powerlessness their hatred is growing into something immense and uncanny, into what is most spiritual and most poisonous; it gets satisfaction against its enemies and conquerors at the end only by a radical transformation of their values, thus by an act of the most spiritual revenge"(1887/1976, I, 7, p. 259). They replaced the aristocratic value equation of good = noble = powerful = beautiful = happy = loved by God, by their opposite "held by the teeth of the most abysmal hatred," namely that "only those who are miserable are good, the poor, powerless, lowly ones alone are good, the suffering, deprived, sick, ugly ones are the only pious ones, the only ones in God, only for them there is blessedness" (1887/1976, I, 7, p. 260). With this value revolution the "uprising of the slaves in morality begins" (ibid.). In truth, as Gustav Seibt (2004) observes, Nietzsche's postulate of an antithesis of Jewish slave-morality and the Roman principle of power, is without foundation: "The Jews were the only people in the giant Roman Empire that took up the fight against Rome in open field battle which had to be oppressed in the most brutal way" (pp. 800/801, my translation).

Nietzsche's double message of resentment gives some answer to the question why his philosophy came to develop an effect of such horrendous brisance and destruction.

There is, on the one side, a most trenchant analysis of the pernicious effect of resentment—an "analysis" not so much only of the "Jewish" resentment as it is the resentment hidden within Christian ethics and metaphysics that is its real target, and even beyond that: the entire old morality, the traditional conscience altogether—the superego as we know it. Most succinctly he describes it as "the attempt to sanctify revenge under the name of justice" (*Versuche . . . die Rache unter dem Namen der Gerechtigkeit zu heiligen*; 1887/1976, II, 11, p. 305).

Yet, on the other side, his own analysis shows all the influence of resentment—it is a bitter accusation of an insidious poisoning of the Western world by a Jewish conspiracy of more than 2,000 years' duration, of a most cunning, skillful, and success-crowned emasculation of "noble man," the degradation of "tragic man," the sapping of the strength of the enemy, in short his humiliation and defeat, by the most elegant means of revenge— the self-castration with the help of a magic symbol, the cross. It is the accusation of the power of resentment by the very means of a magic exerted by the appeal to everybody's own, deeply buried sense of unfairness.

This is what I mean by Nietzsche's philosophy of resentment at its purest, over and beyond his most intelligent descriptive analysis of resentment: the prescription of the overthrow of "Christian" (= Jewish = anti-aristocratic = anti-noble = shame- and guilt-evoking) morality. (1887/1976, I, 10, p. 265).

Untruthfulness, inner and outer deception, and, most of all, a passive outward orientation, all born out of pervasive weakness and impotence, carried by a vicious spirit of relentless but insidious revenge and couched in terms of poison, dissolution, decay, and narcosis—these are the shameful attributes of the "Mensch des Ressentiments" (the man of resentment), this countertype to the man of nobility. He sketches this "man of resentment": "His soul squints; his mind likes hiding-places, devious ways and backdoors, all things hidden appear to him as *his* world, *his* safety, *his* relief"(1887/1976, I, 10, p. 265).

This then is the new ethic, this is the new antithesis, this is the inner conflict conjured up by Nietzsche in ever new images and proclamations, in steady shifts back and forth between most skillful description and equally skillful, yet ultimately extremely dangerous prescription—a prescription followed eagerly by all those prompted exactly by that very resentment so masterfully drawn here by a magician of the language.

DEEPENED ANALYSIS OF RESENTMENT

Resentment, "ressentiment" in Nietzsche's parlance—its French form is, even as a loanword in other languages, stronger than the English "resentment," nor does any other language seem to possess an adequate equivalent for it ("bitterness," "rancor," and "grudge" come close to it, the same in German *Verbitterung, Groll*, and the verb *Hadern* [see F. Eickhoff, 1996/2001], in Swedish *agg*, in Russian *zloy* and *zlost*, used very frequently by Dostoyevsky). *Menis Achilléos*, the "wrath of Achilles," the words with which the *Iliad* begins, could best be understood as resentment. The same seems to me the case for what King Saul showed toward his son-in-law, consoler in his melancholia, and more popular rival, David. It is said (1 Samuel, 18.9–10), that he "kept a jealous eye on David" (*'on 'oyén*) and that an "evil spirit of God" (*rúach elohím ra'áh*) gripped him. This too might be close to what we would call "ressentiment." I already spoke of the Hebrew word *netirá*.

The German philosopher Max Scheler concurred partly with Nietzsche's analysis, but tried to ascribe the sense of resentment within morality to a perversion of Christianity, not to its true and real spirit. It needs hardly to be doubted though that the dark shadow accompanying Christianity throughout its history—anti-Semitism—represents a particularly virulent form of resentment; we may also be able to understand it better if we find access to a deeper dynamic comprehension of this affect.

"Ressentiment" is described by Scheler (1915) as a "mental self-poisoning" (*seelische Selbstvergiftung*), "caused by the systematic pushing aside [repression] in the discharging of certain emotions and affects." While it is "vengefulness, envy, jealousy, scornfulness, pleasure about the other's suffering and malice" that underlie resentment, these only lead to the formation of resentment if "a yet more pronounced sense of powerlessness impedes such action or expression" (pp. 38–41)—again what we encountered in Nietzsche's analysis as "passivity."

Left out in Scheler's description is the relationship to the sense of justice, inherent in the affect of resentment and found in the definition of the French root word: "le fait de se souvenir avec animosité des torts qu'on a subis (comme si on les ressentait, ou les 'sentait' encore)" (Robert, 1985).[3] However such an injured sense of justice can only occur once the value of justice itself, in whatever version, has not only been accepted, but asserted as a central, if not all-consuming, concern.

The conjoining of these several motive forces determines yet another essential element—that of the mask: Pretense and disguise, deception and lying appear to be indispensable accompaniments of resentment. This holds true especially when the resentment is largely concealed from one's own self-observation because of its odious connotation, when it has to be denied and rationalized away. It is felt, but not perceived.

Another attribute of resentment appears to belong ubiquitously to it: Precisely because of the violated sense of justice it happens that the rancor and vindictiveness inherent in this affect of "ressentiment" is generalized and displaced from the original object to substitutes. In fact, this occurs to such an extent that one can just as well talk about the mood and the attitude of resentment as about it as an affect.

Thus it is not simply synonymous with disappointment or insult, with shame and envy, with jealousy and vindictiveness, although all these play a part in it and in fact form the broad foundation on which it rests. Rather it is the sense of unfairness that dwells at its core. The more intensive the claims for justice are, the higher the demands are, at least originally, toward oneself, but also the higher the claims to receive one's desserts from others will be.

One important consequence of such resentment consists in blaming: attributing guilt to the other (see Lansky, 1992). It leads to a distortion of the recognition of inner causality: outer and inner conflict is forged into a stereotypical accusation of having been shortchanged. Now it is used to inflict pain and insult on others.

Thus we have six qualifications to define resentment:

1) aggressive wishes and feelings, above all envy, jealousy, and vengefulness;
2) these have been aroused by a perceived violation of justice and presuppose the feeling of the importance of the value of fairness;
3) the sense of impotence, of helplessness about achieving the aims inherent in those aggressive impulses, namely of redressing the balance of justice;
4) the need to conceal the envy and the vindictiveness behind some mask of innocence, hence to engage in lying and deception, not least against oneself;
5) the readiness to generalize the sense of suffered injustice and to displace the wish for revenge onto other objects, both eventually amounting to a mood and an attitude; and
6) the claim of absoluteness of right and wrong, and with that the depersonalization and dehumanization of the other.

As we saw in the Nietzsche quotes, it is of decisive importance that the most virulent and pernicious power of resentment becomes vested in the superego, a mighty figure of defense dominating not only the individual but typically whole families, if not entire cultural or ethnic groups. Thus, resentment may come to resemble a ghost that binds the generations in shame and hatred to each other. It is the spirit of the vengeful inner judge demanding the absolute. This connection of morality and resentment is clinically confirmed over and over again. In our analytic work we keep observing how value judgments and the underlying value attitudes are many times permeated by a spirit of resentment. In the inner life of the patients, resentment may show itself in double form—on the one side in the superego: as a yelling inner voice of self-beratement and self-condemnation, on the other side in the ego: as enduring bitterness, in the simmering indignation about others, the world, or fate, that suddenly breaks out in impulsive actions and in defiance against the expected or perceived condemnation from without.

In this way, one gains the impression with quite a few patients, as if their conscience had become such an "evil dwarf," who, like the mythical figure in Pär Lagerkvist's *Dvärgen*, incessantly cries for "*straff och hämnd,*" for "punishment and revenge." It is an inner figure obsessed with the anal aims of power, possession, and revenge, a petty, vengeful "antihero" (as Dostoyevsky calls the "Underground Man")—the pre-oedipal, specifically anal-sadomasochistic superego operating in absolute polarities (cf. Shakespeare's Iago [*Othello*] and Edmund [*King Lear*]; Balzac's *Cousine Bette*; Pär Lagerkvist's *Dwarf* [*Dvärgen*; see below]; and Dostoyevsky's "Underground Man" [*Notes from the Underground*] and Smerdyakóv [*The Brothers Karamazov*]).

It is that evil that wraps itself in the cloak of the good conscience, entirely convinced that it only wants and accomplishes the best for everyone, and is absolutely on the side of Right and Justice. In its beginning it is just this: the power and authority of conscience that secretly uses its violence and self-righteousness against the own self, and does that absolutely, categorically, not tolerating any other view from within or without. Insight into the deep doubleness of our life is made inoperative. Now there are only those absolute dilemmas of Either/Or, the postulates of absolute Right versus absolute Wrong. It is the categorical demand of conscience that becomes inhumane and refuses to tolerate any other needs besides its own. Such a resentment-laden superego becomes the carrier of a deep narcissism, which rises in rebellion against the humiliation and helplessness experienced by all. The representative of such a regressive superego is a symbol of revolt against being treated as things, as mere means for some aim. That revolt though, as is typical for such revolutions, just turns the tables; it aspires now to make everyone else into means of his aims.

I think we have to add to this analysis the central role of moral masochism in the genesis of this affect and attitude, that is, what I outlined in the beginning section in regard to the concepts of Grunberger and Eickhoff: the sequence of castrating or, more generally, envious wishes, turned against the self as the aggrieved "innocent victim," which now seeks to redress the balance and rectify the supposed injustice.

Now is also the moment to deal with the questions of "narcissistic rage" and "fanaticism." As to the former, Kohut defines it thus (1972):

> The need for revenge, for righting a wrong, for undoing a hurt by whatever means, and a deeply anchored, unrelenting compulsion in the pursuit of all these aims which gives no rest to those who have suffered a narcissistic injury—these are features which are characteristic for the phenomenon of narcissistic rage in all its forms and which set it apart from other kinds of aggression. (p. 380)

He adds the importance of the defense of "turning a passive experience into an active one," in this instance specifically in regard to shame, and describes it as "the active (often anticipatory) inflicting on others of those narcissistic injuries which he is most afraid of suffering himself" (p. 381). If the fulfillment of these aggressive wishes of the grandiose self run up against the limits of reality we witness "the gradual establishment of *chronic narcissistic rage* [italics in original], one of the most pernicious afflictions of the human psyche—either, in its still endogenous and preliminary form, as grudge and spite; or, externalized and acted out, in disconnected vengeful acts or in a cunningly plotted vendetta" (pp. 396–97).

From this description it becomes clear that the great difference between narcissistic rage and resentment lies in the factor of activity versus passivity. We might be able to say: Narcissistic rage thwarted, narcissistic rage plus helplessness lead to the affect and attitude of resentment—just as Kohut intimates about chronic narcissistic rage that it leads to grudge and spite.

Now to "fanaticism": André Haynal in Geneva has studied fanaticism, which always underlies terrorism (Haynal et al., 1980). Fanatics see themselves as the possessors of the one and only truth—a narcissistic overvaluation. "Every possibility of doubting or questioning—that is, every analysis of (external or internal) reality—is blocked. . . . In the regressive state of the fanatic everything is reduced to simple alternatives: there is good and evil" (Lindau-lecture in German, unpubl., 2003). He speaks of the fanatic's sense of happiness as long as he (or she) remains within the system of fanaticism. I would interpret it as the replacement of the archaic, absolutistic superego figure within by an external, concretely and as ideal experienced authority. This externalization is felt to be an enormous liberation—the more so because in this way one can be counted among an elitist group, the chosen ones. The fanatic feels free, says Haynal—freed from his superego, free in his surrender to this god-like agency represented by the group and its leader. Haynal quotes Arthur Koestler, and Eissler wrote earlier something similar, "that in modern history it was not the aggressive drives as such that exacted the highest costs but the so-called 'non-egotistical devotion.' As Karl Kraus noted: the opposite of 'good' is 'well intentioned.'" Again resentment is very much the swamp out of which this poisonous plant of fanaticism grows, but the two are not the same; the decisive difference lies once more in the factor of activity, of externalization, of helplessness tran-scended.

"MAN AS AN END IN ITSELF" AND RESENTMENT IN SOCIETY

Soul-blindness, the blindness toward the emotional interests and needs of the other, and soul murder, treating the other exclusively as a tool to one's own gratification, which can simply be discarded, are found in the wider frame of society and culture, and represent one root of *Sin'at chinnam*. I use these terms to refer to the "alienation" caused by large-scale institu-tionalization or bureaucratization. Life seems to become overrationalized. In one-sided pragmatism, human values are reduced to what is quantifi-able and usable; utility becomes the peak of the value pyramid. Goethe's saying: "What is fruitful alone is true" (*Was fruchtbar ist allein ist wahr*, in "Wilhelm Meisters Wanderjahre," Goethe (1961), dtv, vol 18., p. 63) is sub-tly transmuted into "What is useful and countable alone is true."

Similarly, religious institutions and ideological movements, even par-ties, can have the same effect: "The end sanctifies the means."

Moreover, bureaucracy in particular, and political administration in general, needs to deny, on behalf of technical control, what is individual, personal, particularistic. The logical consequence is the bureaucratic elim-ination of those whose individuality does not fit into the system. It is this denial that, as presented by Rubenstein (1978) and Lifton (1986), was a presupposition facilitating the Holocaust; in a way it made it "logical."

A literary work, appearing in the same year as Hitler's assumption of power, 1933, highlights this peculiar suffusion of conventional morality with resentment: Aksel Sandemose's *En flykting krysser sitt spor* (A Refugee Crosses His Track"; in Norwegian). The "law of the town of Jante"—*Jantelagen*—gained currency throughout Scandinavia as a phrase that marks this pernicious alliance of small-minded envy and vindictive-ness with morality and Godliness and grows in ponderous weight to be-come an absolute ethos of conformism, the value of adaptation to mediocrity and narrowness proclaimed supreme.[4] As such it has universal applicability. Every university and each professional association, not to mention political and religious groupings, runs the risk of implementing their own version of *Jantelagen*.

The balance between political and social organization and the individual has always been precarious. As Aristotle said, if one or the other is given too much power, the state itself becomes sick (*Politics*).

We recognize to what extent the "use of the other" not as an end in itself, but exclusively as a means to an end, entails the denial of the other's individuality and subjectivity, hence of his or her creative abilities, of originality and privacy. Buber's basic pair of I-You (*Ich-Du*) is completely replaced by I-It (*Ich-Es*). The human being used only as a tool, as a dehumanized creature senses the degradation entailed in this "depersonalization" and reacts to it with a feeling of unworth and shame and finally with helpless rage. Such denial leads to anarchic revolt and self-sabotage, a reaction well known to us in our clinical work. The stricter the cultural demand for submission, self-negation, and conformity, the greater in secrecy is the rebellious force and the stronger is the concealed rage against those who are seen as carrying the main values (Freud, 1930). First this rage may be directed against oneself, but eventually, it is turned in the full vehemence of the resentment against the other.

The more intense this indignation is, the more likely it is that the ultimate victor over the original ethical restraints will himself resort to totalitarian counterblows—totalitarian because of the absoluteness of the forces at play: denial and shame, self-condemnation and self-surrender, envy and resentment, rage and revenge.

In this way, the flight from conscience, the revolution against the superego, that is, the wholesale denial of inner demands put on the self, the magical fantasies accompanying this denial, and the violent defiance in action contribute mightily to events of terrorism and mass annihilation that seem otherwise senseless—*sin'at chinnam*.

One of its manifestations is malignant ethnocentrism, where "the ethnic particularistic consciousness turns evil" (Tugendhat, 1995). Such destructive nationalism has developed out of a patriotism of pride in one's cultural identity, or perhaps rather: is a deviant mutant of it. Instead of living by Gottfried Keller's saying: "Respect every man's fatherland, but love yours!" this form of "pride" leads to a radical aggrandizement of state or nation (or now again of fundamentalistic religion) and above all to its mythical transformation, where what is one's own becomes absolutely good, and what is different, foreign, becomes absolutely evil. What are root and ground of this growth? Wherefrom this fusion of narcissism and aggression, of compulsion and polarization, that goes along with the destruction of all higher ideals, of all those ideals that are not entirely centered in power and annihilation of what is seen as weak or "other"? We have seen it: The infernal axis leads from shame and degradation to irrational self-condemnation and self-hate, from that to a gnawing resentment, and from this to cruelty against everyone who deviates from an ideal of absolutely posited power and invulnerability, a state of being where no inner conflict can be tolerated. Insecurity of self and fear may contribute to such one-sidedness and mythical absoluteness.

The extreme form of this denial of the other's humanity, the gravest form of such "depersonalization" and its greatest peril, is when the other is purely a thing or insect, when "every stranger becomes the enemy" (Primo Levi, quoted by Tugendhat, 1995): when the other is treated exclusively as a means to the end of the extinction of one's own guilt or shame. The other has to be eliminated like vermin, so that the perpetrator can escape from his own annihilating self-condemnation. The mythical denial goes along with the equally mythical projection of what one feels ashamed about or guilty of. This is the absolute evil we have experienced at its most enormous in the Holocaust. The absoluteness and implacability, the one-sidedness of conscience allies itself with the vengefulness and hatred that have their origin in shame, and out of this horrible combination grows that demon of destruction.

Evil thus becomes recognizable as the unleashed force of conscience—the turning outward of the needs for power and assertion and the impulses for revenge that originally contributed so mightily to the formation of the archaic conscience.

The described absoluteness of demand, the archaic, radical, and global nature of the superego, goes through all totalitarian systems, be it now the family, be it religion, be it a state. One patient reports about her Nazi father and her childhood: "Everything had to be under control, everything was absolutely regimented [*reglementiert*]; there was no freedom."

The absolutistic, totalitarian thinking, carried now by the superego rooted in severe traumatization, takes concrete what is symbolic; it is the *cognitive regression*. The axis of traumatization, especially by soul-blind humiliation and shaming, envy, resentment, and revenge, is the *emotional regression* that lies behind the phenomena of ideological absolutism. There are mild forms, there are highly malignant forms. Yet, these reach only their full virulence when family, society at large, or state share these features—from violence by clan or gang to dictatorship in the state. The resentment is directed against every authority, especially also the authority of reason and order. Arthur Miller describes it in regard to the violence he observed in adolescent gangs in Brooklyn: "They drew a certain perverse sense of dignity from the very purposelessness of their wars, a gallant kicking over of society's tables of loss and gain. The spirit's logic was the mind's irrationality" (Miller, 1987, p. 360). This is the sovereign logic of the resentment.

Behind resentment, we usually find some form of shame and humiliation. The unbearability of shame—remembered, continually feared, or re-experienced in fantasy—drives vindictiveness on and blocks the possibility of *forgiveness*. In order to allow forgiveness in therapeutic work, Lansky (2001) urges "the exploration of shame fantasies" because it

> provides necessary details about their unbearableness. . . . If attention to this shame is bypassed in analysis in favor of attention to more visible rage or re-sentment at the transgression of the betrayer and the guilt that attends that rage, this many-faceted model of forgiveness is oversimplified. Inexact inter-pretation . . . is the likely result, and with it an over-focus on rage, control, and guilt at the expense of the dynamics of shame. (pp. 1030–31)

The vicious cycle (*circulus vitiosus*) of shame, resentment, revenge, clini-cally resulting usually in massive condemnation of self and others, is re-placed in therapy by a process, a "corrective circle" (*circulus correctivus*) that gradually leads to forgiveness. This process requires, however, a de-tailed working through of the dynamics of hidden shame.

DVÄRGEN: "MY POISONED BLOOD"

Pär Lagerkvist's *Dwarf*, the ostensible diary of a dwarf at the court of a Re-naissance duke in Italy, is "ressentiment" personified in a mythical figure, a kind of pure culture of resentment.[5]

What does this figure of the dwarf mean, this person who, seeing him-self as a witness for posteriority, writes his journal, but makes himself into the spokesman of indubitable meaninglessness and of an ostensibly ab-solute lack of ideals? A figure who, despite his atrociousness, is able to captivate our intense interest? Is it simply the fascination of Evil?

The novel is, superficially viewed, a powerful critique of the epoch. It was written during the high tide of Nazism and appears in many pas-sages as a condensation, both as persiflage and as exploration, of the spirit of resentment as the most powerful driving force of that movement: "I long for the day when there will be war again!" (1944, p. 60, my transla-tions). "I crave blood!" (p. 71).

I assume that one of the starting points for the imagination that created the dwarf, consisted in observing that revolution of the *Spiessbürger*, the rising to unrestrained power over life and death of that narrow-minded and resentment-laden philister, who could only think along conventional tracks and hated everything original and individual, as was the case in

National Socialism. There the spirit of the "little-bourgeois" (*Kleinbürger*) could very well be combined with excellent intelligence and a technical dexterity, even cunningness. His abilities devoted to thing-oriented planning, his complete obtuseness in the face of the inner world of others and toward the richness of his own feelings, and the intensity and cruelty of his resentment formed that characteristic triad, which historically led to the "Absolute Evil."

He derives his particular pleasure, to demolish the values and the ideals of others, out of his profound resentment. This urge to "overthrow all the values" ("*das Umstürzen der Werte*," in Nietzsche's work) out of his resentment emerges most poignantly in reversing the scene of the eucharist: "I eat his body which was deformed like yours. It tastes as bitter as gall, for it is full of hatred. May you all eat of it. I drink his blood, and it burns like a fire which cannot be quenched. It is as though I drink my own. Savior of all the dwarfs, may thy fire consume the whole world!" (pp. 26–27).

It is not only the suffered humiliation and nonrecognition of the right to be oneself, it is not only its turning around in the form of a lack of feeling for the human environment, a disregard for others as persons, but it is also above all a deep self-contempt and self-hatred: "It is my fate that I hate my own people. My race is detestable to me. But I hate myself too. I eat my own splenetic [gall tainted, *gallspr ängd*] flesh. I drink my own poisoned blood. Every day I perform my solitary communion as the grim high priest of my people" (p. 28).

The entire massive self-contempt and self-hatred of the Dwarf is again and again turned outward, directed against the outer world. The world of the others is despised as the carrier of what he is afraid of within himself and what he therefore has denied and repressed. He wants the punishment and the extermination of all what could tempt him, as if to say: "No one has the right to have something that is forfended to me or what I prohibit to myself."

With that we have arrived at a main sign of his resentment (and perhaps of this affect altogether?), namely the wild contempt and the conscious hostility and bitterness (*gallspr ängd*!) against ideals. Yet behind all ideals lies some form of love.

This resentment, this consuming hatred against everything human and against the ideals of humanity culminate in an orgy of revenge and "punishment," the massacre in the hall of celebration. After he assassinates the invited guests he revels in the sight of his horrendous deed:

> [I] stood there, frenzied with excitement, surveying the tremendous results of my work; the extirpation by me of this loathsome race which deserves nothing else. I saw how my mighty sword went forth over them, pitilessly de-

structive, demanding vengeance and punishment for everything. How I dispatched them to burn eternally in the fires of hell! . . . Why should these lying dissemblers and braggarts exist, these lustful shameless creatures whose virtues are even viler than their sins? May they burn in the fires of hell! . . . I felt my temporal power with a joy greater than I had ever known, and so acute that I nearly lost consciousness. I felt how the world had, through me, been filled with terror and doom, and transformed from a brilliant feast to a place of fear and destruction. . . . For after my drink they forget all the beauty and wonder of life and a mist enfolds everything and their eyes fail and darkness falls. I turn down their torches and extinguish them so that it is dark. I assemble them with their unseeing eyes at my somber communion feast where they have drunk my poisoned blood, that which my heart drinks daily, but which for them spells death. (pp. 152–54)

Yet what is the psychological background for this "straff och hämnd" (punishment and revenge), for this hatred against their "reveling, laughing and loving"?

We dwarfs have no homeland, no parents; we allow ourselves to be born of strangers, anywhere, in secret, among the poorest and most wretched, so that our race should not die out. And when these stranger parents discover that they have begotten a creature of our tribe they sell us to powerful princes that we may amuse them with our misshapen bodies and be their jesters. *Thus did my mother sell me, turning away from me in disgust when she saw what she had borne, and not understanding that I was of an ancient race* [emphasis added]. She was paid twenty scudi for me and with them she bought three cubits of cloth and a watchdog for her sheep. (p. 15)

He is a piece of tradeable goods, a toy, an object one can employ for general amusement. He is not treated as a human being with a right to his own individuality. It is the denial of individuality, it is the rejection of the right to be oneself, to own one's feelings, to trust one's thoughts and perceptions, which induces such all-pervasive shame and thus indirectly that burning resentment, such an all-consuming sense of injustice. Added to it is the humiliation of being treated solely as a "thing": "She got twenty scudi for me!"

Standing naked in front of the painter and seeing the *Last Supper*, his hatred and resentment is unbounded:

I rejoiced to think that soon he would be taken, that Judas, sitting huddled in his far corner, would soon betray him. I thought: "Now he is still loved and honored, now he still sits at his feast—while I stand here in my shame! But his shame is on its way! Soon he will no longer be sitting there with his followers, but hanging alone on a cross, betrayed by them. He will hang there as naked as I am now, as humiliated as I, exposed to the stares of all, mocked and defiled."

Why should he not? he asks. And his answer cuts to the core of the sense
of injustice underlying and feeding this ardent *ressentiment*:

> He has always been encompassed with love, nourished himself on love—
> while I have been nourished on hate. From my birth I have sucked the bitter
> juice of hate, I have lain at a breast filled with gall, while he was suckled by
> the mild and gracious Madonna and drank the sweetest mother's milk that
> ever was. . . . That is just why they cherish their *secret rancor* toward him, just
> because of that miracle. Mankind does not like to be violated by God.
> (pp. 46–47)

He is the stranger who has learned to despise himself and has made the
scorn of others into a protective shield and disguise. Thus he tries to protect
himself against shame in two ways: on the one side by taking over from the
parents on a large scale the denial of his true identity—that is, by building
up what Winnicott has called "the false self"—and on the other side by acquiring a "narcissistically" exaggerated counterimage, as if to say: "I am
something very special, exceptional, I am myself a Savior, and incredibly
important and powerful. I know everything, understand everything, don't
ever show any weakness, have always justice on my side, and am lastly untouchable, irreplaceable and always needed." And above all: "I want to be
alone. I don't want there to be anybody else except me" (p. 31).

This basic "narcissistic" attitude, especially as protection against
shame, as well as the "splitting off" of everything that could lead to the
dangerous "real self"—love, relatedness, trust, inner conflict—can be
found throughout the character formation of the Dwarf: "I delight in
nothing" (*jag har inte glädje av nånting*; pp. 20–22).

We can look at the Dwarf as something like an inner figure effective in
all of us. With many patients I have, in fact, the impression that their conscience has turned into such a malicious dwarf who incessantly cries for
punishment and revenge. He let himself be used quite well as a metaphor
during some psychoanalyses for this petty and vindictive inner tyrant
that keeps haunting and tormenting the patient without relief—*the superego as herald of malignant resentment* (see chapter 6).

It seems to be the sexual power of the woman that is experienced as the
great temptation and hence as the most terrible threat—the (inferred, not
literally demonstrable) fantasy of the woman as a witch who devours soul
and body. It is her dangerous womb (*sköte*), it is her bodily nature that
needs to be fought off as something monstrous, as something nauseating
and terrifying, and against which he directs his whole rage and cruelty—
again dynamics not rare in clinical observation.

Behind the mask of power the malicious dwarf is hidden, and it is behind both that the bad conscience and the helpless self know to hide

themselves. Yet both of them, Prince and Dwarf, are parts of our personality. "One always needs [the services of] one's dwarf" (Swedish/English, p. 171/182).

And its antithesis is equally true: "But as soon as I saw Giovanni I knew that love was the only reality in the world and that everything else was nothing" (p. 187/199), as Angelica, the true opposite figure to the Dwarf, recognizes. It is in the one great tension between these two poles of love for oneself (for power) and of love for the other (or self-surrender) that human life moves. If life is pulled too much toward one of these two extremes, if it wants either power or love absolutely it becomes crippled and it must succumb. Only in the mixture and in the middle lies, as Aristotle (*Nicomachaean Ethics*) postulated, virtue and wisdom. The absoluteness contradicts the survival both of the individual and of the community. No matter how much the dwarf in us, this representative of all that is Either-Or and categorical, may sneer about it: "Human beings like to see themselves reflected in clouded mirrors!" (p. 211/225).

In that deepest sense the Dwarf has become the persecuting shadow of man. "I follow him constantly, like a shadow" (p. 10/7). Together with the Hangman, the Eternal Jew, and Barabbas he represents one counter-figure to the Crucified, the grimace of a demonic counterreality that dwells in the inmost core of Christianity: "Pilgrim and criminal. Pilgrim on mankind's pirate ship to the Holy Land" (Lagerkvist: *Det heliga landet*, another novel, in *Pilgrimen*, 1966, p. 257). How this has become the tragedy of the Christian occident, how this inner and unsolvable doubleness has led to a break within this world, and how Europe's self-betrayal in the twentieth century is rooted in the counterreality of a resentment cloaking itself as morality—the exposure of this and its overcoming by a particular form of love of life and world, namely by stepping beyond the Either/Or, appears to have been the central issue for Pär Lagerkvist. It culminates in the wonderful confession: "det enkla och enhetliga är inte sant, kan inte gärna vara det. Bara det sammansatta kan möjligen tänkas vara det" ("what is simple and unambiguous is not true, it can hardly be it. Only what is complex may be thought to be it" [*Det heliga landet*, p. 230]).

NOTES

This is an expanded and strongly revised version of a paper with the same title submitted to *Psychoanalytic Inquiry*.

1. I am grateful to Mrs. Elisabeth Imhorst in Cologne for having made me aware of this volume.

2. See my paper "Nietzsche's War against Shame and Resentment" (1997), and my extensive treatment of the topic in chapter 13 of *Das Rätsel des Masochismus* (Wurmser, 1993).

3. "The remembrance with animosity of suffered instances of injustice as if one still or again felt them."

4. I translate the ten commandments of "Jantelagen" from the Swedish translation:

1. You shall not think you *are* anything. 2. You shall not think you are as good as *we*. 3. You shall not think you are more intelligent than *we*. 4. Don't imagine you are better than *we*. 5. Don't believe you know more than *we*. 6. You shall not think you are more noble than *we*. 7. You shall not believe *you* are of use to anything. 8. You shall not laugh about *us*. 9. You shall not think that anybody cares about *you*. 10. You shall not think that you can teach *us* anything. (1933/1980, p. 75 of the Swed. transl.)

(I am grateful to Dr. Anders Ryberg for having made me aware of this work and its ideas.)

5. I give here only a strongly abbreviated version of my analysis of this work (see Wurmser, 1987, 1989).

6

＊

Tragic Character and the Devastating Power of Absoluteness

"You are too absolute."

—Shakespeare, *Coriolanus*, Act III, Sc. 2

From our personal and from our professional life, most of us know a certain type of personality. I try here to outline its traits, at least in one version of it: Everything good, every joy or pleasure has to be devalued, blocked, or destroyed. Every frustration turns into a catastrophe, into a tragedy, and, at least for some, every catastrophe turns into someone else's guilt. The fault-finding is foremost and overwhelming, but often is sought somewhere else. Thus some may come to see themselves in a glorified role of victim while turning into secret perpetrators. In that way they exert much power over others by making them explicitly or implicitly feel guilty. Blaming becomes a large part of their lives and fills much of what they have to say. They justify their own existence by this attitude of blaming (cf. Lansky, 1992).

However, what is consistent is the victimization repeated in reality—brought about unwittingly and unwillingly, but again and again.

Their demands of others and, in a more hidden way, of themselves, are clearly of an absolute character. Their conscience is of a rabid cruelty, but often, though not always, prefers to turn its unfulfillable requests for the ideal against others and draws from this the justification to discharge the cruelty of the inner judge against the other person. Instead of "Love your neighbor as yourself!" it becomes then: "Condemn your neighbor as yourself!"

177

They may fling presents, either literally or at least metaphorically, into the face of the giver—or, at least inwardly, they have to devalue them, just like everything else that is good and joyful. Secretly, the other person's success excites envious scorn and leads to attempts to provoke him or her to rage by new accusations, thus to lose his composure, falling prey to shame and contempt.

The demand for what is perfect may refer to various values that are in and of themselves of highest dignity: Truth and honesty, or honor and recognition, or unreserved self-sacrifice to the point of renouncing one's own will. Such ideals are fanatically asked for and pursued.

Closely related to this *absoluteness of conscience* is what we may call the *taboo of exclusivity*, itself a theme in cultural history of preeminent force: "Do not revere any gods besides me," is the religious paradigm. However, I rather address here an inner truth: only *one* love, only *one* essential bond, only *one* fidelity is being allowed. Often (though not always), any breach of this taboo calls for dreadful revenge—vindictive jealousy, or a furious inner conflict about such jealous inclinations flames up, fueling even more self-condemnation and the need for self-punishment. If other people do not bow to such exclusivity, the person I describe may be deeply offended, and shame and resentment lead to an unquenchable irreconcilability. In a hidden or open way, the vindictiveness simmers on and on, until it erupts into wild rage.

I would like to call this personality type a tragic character because their life is haunted by calamity, but the star of disaster shines over their inner life. In our diagnostic scheme we would most likely talk about a masochistic-narcissistic personality disorder with paranoid features. Yet, I do not refer with this to a specific diagnosis but rather to an inner constellation, traits of which can be found in all of us. I rather plead for an openness for new metaphors that may let our psychoanalytically empathic and introspective experience appear in a new light.

The description given is vastly oversimplified: "And one man in his time plays many parts" (Shakespeare, *As You Like It*, Act II, Sc. 7). Usually this personality figure is masked by another part that is in its own way just as authentic and real: sometimes by a figure of often high competence, at times also of graciousness and friendliness, even submissiveness. Or it is a conventional overadaptation that hides the main figure. Or there may be drugs and alcohol, there may be money and power, there may be small and big lies concealing the tragic drama. Again in others we find a bigoted overreligiosity or an inclination to what is esoteric, to mysticism. All these features can be understood as *anti-tragic* forms of defense, as protection against the main personality and its inherently tragic fate.

Thus the tragic personality is always double. As it is stated about Don Quixote: his ways are so confusing because now he is very reasonable in his thinking, *cuerdo*, and then again he is entirely crazy, *loco*, in his actions. Not only is the self somehow broken, but the experienced reality appears to be double.

The patients described up to now have some aspects of such tragic character as well, but with a very strong counterforce predominating against this part.

Behind all the absoluteness of what one desires and of what one ought to do hides an existential woundedness that eludes simple representation or lurks entirely beyond words. Sometime it appears as a deep, unquenchable longing, conjoined with a yawning emptiness and meaninglessness of existence. At other times, it may rather be a core feeling of pain, sadness, and loneliness—especially of being the outsider, the excluded one, the stranger: "A stranger I came here, a stranger I depart again."[1] Then again it is a nagging feeling of shame and an attitude of being easily offended because they are easily convinced that they are not worth being loved and respected. The rancor, the sense: "Injustice has been done to me," is always present and very close to the surface. The helplessness accompanying these feelings calls for counteractions: the tragic character keeps trying to escape from passivity—basically an inner sense of being subject to forces beyond control. It is this feeling of an *incurable wound* that points to deep, usually chronic traumatization.

Before I deepen this study, I would like to discuss a brief case study that also links up quite manifestly with the previous chapter. The patient herself experienced the pernicious power of what we came to see as the "Inner Dwarf," lurking behind the tragic features of her life. This figure served as a metaphor for the redeployment of aggression and narcissism entirely in the functions of the superego and directed against the self.

"CLOSED OFF IN A CLOSET, IN DARK RECESSES, SITS THE REAL ME"

Regula, an academic professional, divorced, in her later middle age, had since her youth suffered from severe depression. She looked much older and almost cachectic. She was seen for many years in psychoanalysis.

Her father, a physician and politician, had suddenly died of the consequences of his alcoholism. Regula's mother was herself a chronic drinker and had to be repeatedly hospitalized for depressive, manic, and paranoid episodes. Regula was really the second child of this marriage, after the first had died during birth. The mother never recovered from that loss, and Regula was compared with, and had to live up to, an impossible ideal: mother's fantasy image of the dead child; she was always only second best. "I lived in her shadow; if only *she* were alive! I had to hear that all the time." Concomitantly, there was deep fear in her mother that Regula would die as well; she was, not surprisingly, a colicky, fussy baby. A second daughter was born one year after Regula.

The marriage of the parents was dismal, and they divorced when the patient was about four years old. The father's new wife not only repeated the alcoholism, but also suffered from a seizure disorder, and often seriously mistreated the two stepchildren and the two additional ones. She undertook a number of suicide attempts. Once, when she had lain undiscovered, unconscious in a closet in the attic, it was Regula who had to plead with her father to call a physician. He wanted to let her die. The sister who had uncovered the stepmother had fled in hysterical panic. Both older children repeatedly had to run away from the chaotic household or were sent away, "for the sake of peace," for months, even years, and were shuttled back and forth between half a dozen homes, welcome nowhere.

Regula grew up in a web of missions: She had to replace the lost baby for her mother and console her; she was to sacrifice her own ambitions for the demands of her father but to take care not to surpass him; she had to appease a violent and irrational stepmother; she served as emissary for an arthritically immobilized grandmother and always derided as a humble second best for her socially more successful sister, dressed in the simple dresses her grandmother had made and given her; and later on she was the protector and only advocate for her stepbrother, ten years her junior. It was only one of the tasks in which she failed when the stepbrother, the father's much abused favorite, killed himself during his adolescence. Even today she is caught between a series of incompatible and superhuman missions—rescue missions of one kind or another—chronically failing, chronically berating herself, chronically in a depressive fury against herself.

Why would I talk about her in the present context of character perversion and tragic character though?

First, she dealt with a severely traumatic childhood mostly by depression. All her rage, her anger, her hatred, her contempt, her disappointment were monotonously turned against herself. A previous psychotherapist found, at least as the patient experienced it, no better way to approach this than by commenting upon her secret grandiosity and omnipotence, her "narcissism," and the great inward gratification and pleasure as revealed by her suffering: in the sadism satisfied on herself. Dutifully he related it to the transference, repeating and mimicking some favorite barbs of father's: "It has punctured her little heart." This confrontation with her narcissism and masochism increased, according to her account, her anger and allowed her to turn it back outward. But this occurred less by a reversal of her defense and by really making conscious what was warded off than by a transient provocation of aggression founded in a real injury, in fact a retraumatization, leading to a mobilization of rage without lasting therapeutic benefit.

I add a brief theoretical digression: It is often almost dogmatically held that for the "analytic process" it is necessary that such intense affects are reexperienced in the transference itself, in this instance the provoked rage and narcissistic injury. My attitude is: When it comes, it comes, and it needs to be dealt with, but to force it leads to what Arlow called a stilted way of analyzing (see Blum, 1983; Arlow 1995, 2002; also Anna Freud in Sandler and Freud, 1985). Moreover, the mere consciousness or venting of anger has little or no therapeutic value in and of itself. Its dynamic "web" is what counts. Here it was probably even counterproductive in the long run. This is consonant with the theoretical view of the nature of aggression—as always derivative: Like sexuality, aggression should be seen not as "continual, endogenous, internal pressure" (Mitchell, 1993, p. 363); rather "the biology of aggression is understood to operate not as a drive but as an individually constituted, prewired potential that is evoked by circumstances perceived subjectively as threatening or endangering" (p. 364). Thus, instead of "viewing aggression as constitutional and self-propelling (as Freud did)," this modern approach views "aggression as constitutional and reactive" (p. 372).

Second, she had not only manifested a quite interfering depression, but also a severe eating disturbance throughout her life which she calls a "food addiction," but more properly could be classified as periods of anorexia nervosa, reflecting an incessant obsession with thoughts of nurturance, food, and weight. Hence it came as no surprise that under the harsh sway of an implacable conscience, she had to bar herself from such vile indulgence not only by measures of rigorous asceticism, but with the help of prescribed amphetamines and thyroid hormones. For many years she had been dependent on those drugs in order to approach a little bit that ascetic ideal, a narcissistic ideal of purity, saintly abstemiousness, and Christlike self-sacrifice, without being able to reach it.

Third, her seemingly far more preferred younger sister dealt with the same issues by developing into a chronic alcoholic, poisoning her own family with her outward aggressivenes, her anger, her ruthless revenge, and her brutality toward her children, dealing with all attempts by Regula at helping intervention with: "I know that already; you don't have to tell me that. I do the best I can. Anyway, you always were the voice of doom." She (the sister) tried to forget herself not only by drinking, but also by her restless social activity. Often, Regula felt herself to be the victim of her sister's barbs.

What had become for the patient a demonically oppressive conscience holding absolute tyranny over her life had turned in her sister into a consistent defiance against all ethical constraints and a spiteful debunking of all inner and outer authority—what I describe in *Flight from Conscience* as the defense against the superego typical for substance abusers. It is as if the two sisters dealt with the same conflicts in a mirroring inversion.

Fourth, like many severely traumatized people, Regula too had a cardinal fear of the intensity of all her feelings, not only of anxiety or anger, of pain, grief, or envy, but also of pleasure, joy, hope, and sexual excitement. The positive feelings were in fact viewed as even more frighteningly flooding and uncontrollable than the negative ones: "I'm terrified I would overwhelm people with my feelings; they would not know how to take me. I think somebody is going to take me by the scruff of my neck and say: 'Who in the hell do you think you are? You think you know everything? Just shut your mouth and be quiet! You think you're right? You're not right! Control yourself!'" Thus, we see how the oppressive burden of her conscience, this inner overlord with his impossible commands and expectations for perfection, had also to serve as a kind of constraining guard against such flooding feelings and wishes, not so dissimilar to the alcohol that helped her sister to numb "those monsters within," as the latter had derisively called our patient's worries.

Fifth, "compassion, ecstasy, joy, mutuality—in short, love—the ability to give, to talk about it hits me in the pit of the stomach. I feel as if I had exposed myself and have to run and hide. Loving and caring leave me so vulnerable, and when you leave I feel so abandoned and bereft that I want to curl up and die in despair." It is much safer to be angry and controlled, particularly in the service of one of her rescue missions.

Aggression in the service of the superego, especially aggression turned against herself, is a most powerful and valuable defense against the overwhelming feelings and the drive wishes for closeness and union.

Sixth, her idealization of the therapist, another hallmark of narcissism, is just as pronounced as the radicalization of the ideal she is forever striving for, however failingly. In most of the sessions she cried much, very softly, but with a steady trickle of tears, in despair about her "badness and incorrigibility."

It was essential in her therapy that all these forms and aspects of narcissism (and ensuing aggression) were to be continually, but very tactfully questioned as defenses, examined as necessary protective attempts, not so much against the lurking anger, but as a protective shield against the constantly looming disappointment: "Just wait! He too will betray you!" She kept confessing: "I withdraw and wall myself off in my isolation, because otherwise I would be pushed away because of my dependency, laughed at for the mess of my flooding feelings, and chased away." Late in her analysis (778) she says: "My grandiosity lies in my aggressive, grandiose conscience, the attitude of the 'holier than thou.'" It is, she adds, fighting against her "miserable, wimpy character." In reality, her rabidly, immoderately critical conscience serves as a restraint against her being over-powered by her intensive feelings and caught unawares and overrun by her unstilled wishes.

Instead of confronting narcissism head on, it is far more helpful to lis-ten sympathetically to the voice of fear: the fear of being special and fear of expecting too much from the other, and hence the fear of helpless de-spair. And with that fear, the entire profound helplessness opens up—the traumatic state of anxiety. In other words, *narcissism* in its many manifes-tations should be constantly understood and treated as a *protection* against massive anxiety and against other overwhelming ("traumatic") feelings (not least among them sexual feelings), but among these anxieties the var-ious forms of shame are sans pareil. Narcissism is necessary as protection as long as the deep anxieties have not been specifically worked through. Narcissism as defense, especially also in the service of the superego, in-stead of narcissism as sin or prize—this is the shibboleth for the effective psychotherapy of severe neuroses, including, by the way, those that un-derlie substance abuse (see *Flight from Conscience*).

CONTRADICTORY IMPERATIVES

Over the course of one-and-a-half years, the analyst heard, almost inces-santly and in monotonous repetition, the recital of her tasks and their faulty delivery, all the assaults upon herself, all the self-devaluations. Only very hesitantly she permitted herself to utter also some critical thoughts toward him. But how specific the work has to be I would like to show with a brief example.

During one session (243), she and the therapist were very briefly inter-rupted by a janitor. In the following session she expressed her anger that he had not been able to protect her against the intrusion of a stranger and that he had not at least prolonged the session. At once she got scared about these thoughts and wanted to make them magically disappear. She broke off and turned instead to the thought that it was similar magical thinking when she was afraid she would get older than her father who had died al-most at her current age, or if she were superior to him in anything at all. "This would mean, however, I could not exist any longer than a year. This makes me even more depressed." After longer wanderings he interrupted her by making her aware of the *sequence* of thoughts. He remarked how she at first had seen herself as victim (by having been shortchanged by him), but then, after a brief protest against him, she had described how she was wishing to compete both *for* and *against* her father (for his love and with him), and especially to triumph over him by her accomplishments and her survival, how she then had to accuse herself anxiously for such prohibited impulses and to put herself down, and how this *double rivalry* (for some-body's love and against the success of the same person) probably also re-ferred to him (the analyst), how hard it was to reconcile these two opposed tendencies, and how they were then replaced and covered over by her self-abasement.

In the following session she said that had been a real "aha" experience; that she had had the feeling of "eureka." Yet, it did not go any farther.

One month later, two little episodes happened that permitted a reac-quisition of the gained and then lost insights and their deepening. Her daughter had come home from far away for a visit. Although the patient had taken time off, she could not entirely free herself from all her obliga-tions. As she hurried home between some professional duty and the ana-lytic hour, fearing that her daughter would be mad at her because of her absence, she fell, injured herself on the flat ground, and fainted.

The following day, it happened as she went shopping with her daugh-ter that by chance she had to pass the therapist on a narrow sidewalk. Al-though he was looking directly in her face and tried to greet her she looked right through him—simply did not notice him. As he examined this little incident of "scotomization," a hyperattentiveness for one aim at the exclusion of everything else, almost a kind of blindness (260/261), she was at first astounded and almost contrite; but when she considered the process more in detail, it turned out that she was deeply afraid her daugh-ter would scream at her if they would return from shopping somewhat later and the daughter would have to delay her jogging. It was as if noth-ing else, no other perception ought to rival with her attention *for* her daughter. At the same time she added herself that she also knew examples for her rivalry *with* her daughter, as glad as she would be to dismiss them under protest. The same was true for her relationship with her sister. All these examples had the meaning: "I don't want to compete." Most of all, in this "rivalry for somebody" (now especially for the therapist and for her daughter) the inner command becomes dictatorial: You have to do this or that at a certain time: "Under the dictatorial sway of time reality takes second place." *Time* becomes then the implacable voice of the inner de-mand, and the inner demand above all says the following: "I can only be loved if I don't pay any attention to anything else and to anybody else. The person I love does not tolerate any rival; I have to switch off every-thing else in order to avoid that person's jealousy—regardless how much this demanded exclusivity can damage me." Opposed to this one exclu-sivity and absoluteness of demand there are of course other demands of no less intense and radical quality. Moreover, her own personal claims contradict it as well.

There was her own imperative desire to be the only and exclusive one who would receive love and protection, attention and nourishment, the demand to triumph once and for all by exclusion over the rival, absolutely. This was being countered by an equally absolute superego command under whose dictatorial force she had felt compelled to surrender all competitive wishes. She responded to this inner compulsion by renouncing almost all (drive) claims and wants that had anything to do with competition (and which would fail to do so!?) and by supporting their gratification instead in others—in what Anna Freud described as altruistic surrender (1936).

VIOLATED

I add here some other brief excerpts helpful to cast a light on her dynamics.

A first comes from the end of the second year in the analysis. In the previous hours she has alluded to sexual feelings in regard to the analyst during masturbation. "Often there appears the image of a child reaching out its arms, but nobody is there. I'm so needy and greedy. I'm frowning to keep back the tears. I'm always so afraid I would overwhelm somebody with my needs because I'm so possessive, so clinging; I don't let the other have any space. Part of me tells me: it is alright to have these sexual fantasies; but the other part says it is no good to have them; they lead only to longings that cannot be fulfilled, and I will be hurt again. Better to keep it all down" (365). By the way, she mentions masturbation only very rarely and does not allow it to herself. When she sins against this prohibition she is terribly ashamed. In the context here, he has made an interpretation that she was trying to protect *him* from her sexual wishes.

In the following session (on a Monday) she begins right away: "I had very interesting experiences. They were so nerve shattering that I could not sleep. I left here Friday with several thoughts. . . . I mentioned the boarding school [at the age of ten] where I was severely punished by a nun for masturbating." She continues in fragmented sentences that she has had a feeling, not a real insight, that it is so crazy and that she wants to deny it, that she is only making this up, "it has not happened," that she needs protection without and within, because of what has occurred to her: "I was put in a situation where I was completely unprotected from the people outside and my feelings. I was in foster care on a farm when I was 3½ years old. After half a year we were removed from there by my mother, because the woman had cut the blankets and it was a dirty place. But all the feelings—it seems that what happened is: that I was violated there, in a very intrusive way. Every time I masturbated this woman took and put a soap up my rectum, so deeply that I could not get it out, and with that there was very much pain." While talking about this she cries so strongly that she cannot continue speaking.

Eventually she resumes: "I was thinking of my masochistic sexuality. I take the punishment upon me so that I can masturbate. It was the pain with it and the overwhelming helplessness and violation. The feelings are all there; the anxiety in the night was so great that I could hardly sleep." She adds how she felt similarly violated by her previous therapist when he had treated her sarcastically, "his needling me," his insensitivity. She adds under tears that it was not the thought but the feeling that had come up first, and then the image how she had been lying there, and the foster mother over her. "How easy my father could say that my heart was pierced! How vulnerable I must have been to all that criticism! I was very hurt inside and felt so alone and uncared for and unprotected. I thought also of my growling attitude as a defense, my frown—. As I returned to my mother I was screaming so hard that my throat hurt, and I took a washrag and was sucking it. I can really now get in touch with my anger, but only when I put everything together: I was so angry at my mother because she left me unprotected and I got violated, and from there comes all the rage" (366).

It had been the analyst's interpretation that had given her the assurance: "Here I am protected; I can trust," and with that had made possible the memory of the traumatic injury and unprotectedness with all the conflicting feelings, and the upwelling of the ensuing intense aggressions.

THE FUNCTION OF THE "INNER DWARF"

Another excerpt stems from the end of the fourth year of her analysis. She feels far more in control of her self-condemnation and her self-damaging acts, especially of the unreasonable giving-in when others impose on her; she is far less depressed, but a series of minor car accidents have happened, and they give her and the analyst pause. After observing the usual stereotypical sequences of self-jeering, he makes her aware that this scornful self-criticism appears after she has dared to utter some mildly critical remarks about her daughter, and if they might not be able to translate the attacks directed against herself into similar ones directed against the very demanding young lady? Instead of a direct response she mentions, toward the end of the hour, a so-far-withheld dream fragment: "I stand in a cemetery, on a hill. I see the stones covered with a piece of cloth, meaning I keep things covered up."

"Specifically the death wishes."

"Probably."

She begins the next hour in mordant anger because he has hinted at something in regard to her daughter of which she has not had any idea. She does not have any such feelings. "It was driving me so crazy that I began getting paranoid: that you are setting up a test to see how far I can be pushed, until I go over the edge." The anxiety has been overwhelming. She has often thought he should drop dead or jump into the lake, but she has never dared to say that because it was so irrational, but last night she has felt that he knows something she does not know, something in regard to her daughter. It does not refer to the daughter, but to *him*—those attacks against herself and criticism. He agrees very much with her and remarks that he has merely wanted to point out to her the sequence observed yesterday in order to find access from the Here-and-Now to this stereotypical self-condemnation, but that she is very correct in relating it to him. She calms down and adds that she has been so deeply *ashamed* about her death wishes against him that she has had to hide them for such a long time from him—the "piece of cloth" covering the tombstones. She has always idealized him so much, she says, yet she recognizes now that he too has feet of clay (763).

"There is always the fear that if I had not this punitive, controlling conscience I would get out of control, and yet I don't want to make it to that Dwarf that finds fault with everything . . . it is the anger that builds on my anger; it feeds on itself. It is my fear that the anger will lead to more anger, and more anger, and I would not be able to stop it. I don't know the reason for it, but am afraid I am unable to put controls on my feelings" (765).

He has, together with her, compared her implacable, contemptuous, and petty conscience, this inner figure of corrosive resentment, with Pär Lagerkvist's Dwarf (known to her). This inner "dwarf" had been needed as a regulating, controlling power to enable her to contain the affect storms of early childhood, to hold them back, to stop them. For no parent had shown capable to offer a holding environment; to the contrary, they themselves had been completely out of controls and bounds.

Yet, "the evil Dwarf" had not only the function to put a stop to the emotional storms, but also to the wishes of many kinds. How could that be any different if every self-assertion and every remonstrance of hers was answered by her mother: "You will yet be my death!" or "You drive me crazy!"—and the latter threat turned real, and the first was repeatedly enacted in suicide attempts? What magic belonged to her destructiveness?—"to have it occur so early in childhood when so much is still magical that the parents totally fragment in front of you! The power of my anger and aggression becomes so part of reality, and that becomes the core problem. And keeping myself thin, means I am weaker and smaller, that I am not so strong and powerful [i.e. dangerous]" (772).

Thus the malignant Dwarf's main attack point is her weight. If she goes over a specific, very low line she considers herself sentenced to death. Under no circumstance would she allow the analyst to touch on that! It is an absolute limit, and even if the analysis would fail over that, so be it! It turns out that, although there had been earlier phases of eating disorders (including problems of being overweight) her first really severe episode of anorexia had occurred after her brother's suicide. "I'm so afraid of dying that I take myself to the edge and play with fire, but I assure myself that I cannot get burned." In fact, in her adolescence she wanted to put her hand, like the ancient Roman hero and revolutionary Mucius Scaevola, in the fire and singe it in order to harden herself against the pain and to "get a thick skin" (she did not carry out the fantasy). "If I can put my hand in the fire and can stand it, I strengthen myself; and if I walk over coals and come through unscathed then I shall be strong. It is the same with my weight. To get down to 100 pounds is playing with death." After all, her last accident with her brand new car had happened on the way to the cemetery after she had bought her own funeral lot. "Out of the fear of death I am wooing death"—counterphobically. "I'm convinced that it was an identification with my brother [when I starved myself after his suicide]: he hardly ate and looked like a concentration camp prisoner. My father made me his protector, and yet he killed himself. I was angry at him, and I turned the anger against myself. I became his protector but at the same time I felt much rage at him that I denied: that he was the boy my father wanted, his heir, and he put me in the position to take care of him. It was his legacy that was impossible to carry out" (770).

The identification with the brother served, together with the act of turning against the self and the underlying and still prevalent reaction formation, to defend against her strong aggressions. This *identification as defense against murderous rage directed against the object of identification*, which we have also found in other patients described here, probably is a basic process in her pathology. It also plays a decisive role in the *transference of defense*: the reduction of her self-condemnation, as an identification with the analyst's tolerance, is paralleled by the stubborn refusal to question the absoluteness of her weight limit or most of the time even to mention it. The non-analysis of the conflict about weight and eating has thus become a power struggle in the transference—but remains hidden behind the idealization. He should wordlessly understand it and approve of it— and if he were to fail in that it would be his fault and his guilt. "For me it is a matter of life or death." In truth, it is so: her identity is founded upon her determination not to be voracious like her father, not to be obese like her mother or sister, not to be a drunkard like all her parents and stepparents. The loss of this counteridentity would be a self-betrayal she could not survive, a form of *lethal shame*: "Either I become heavy and strong and overweight, and cannot stop, and I have to kill myself because I am so ashamed. Or I vanish by fasting, in a kind of passive dying. Being a woman is something to be ashamed of. It makes one crazy; women are demeaned and demeaning. Better to be nothing than either one, man or woman." The dilemma is therefore: *absolute control or shame worthy of death*. She dreams of standing before a firing squad. A woman has the gun to shoot her, and Regula pleads for her life.

The therapist is now the one who is holding the weapon against her head and forces her into life threatening exposure: He is the carrier of her humiliation and disgrace because he shakes her rigid control of those forbidden wishes (771).

As mentioned, *altruistic renunciation* plays for her a crucial role. "I'm ashamed of my greediness. I prepare the food for others and then only take afterward what is left over: that I deserve to eat out of trash cans, the scraps." In a dream she steals food for others. She remembers that she had wanted to take away the bottle from her sister (meant of course is the milk bottle in early childhood, yet uncannily repeated in her vain efforts to stop her sister's alcoholism). That *wish to take away* must have been so powerful that she has surrendered its fulfillment to others, and most rigorously forbids it to herself. Basically, all drive gratifications follow henceforth this pattern and must be condemned and blocked.

The real phobia pertains, however, more to her weight than to the eating and to food itself, and it goes even more deeply: "It is not so much the weight and the eating, but the fear of death, and the wish for death; that is the basis."

"The covered tombstones."

"To feed the judge in me, to placate him, to give him his pound of flesh so that he allows me to live another day." This can only be done by the strictest observation of the weight limit. "The reprieve comes if I have not gained any weight; if I do, I do not have the right to eat." Were there phobias in childhood? Certainly: "There was a trapdoor under my bed, and if I stepped on it a man would grab me by my feet and pull me down. I had to leap from the door into my bed. I also was afraid that the black ragman would get me." She is very afraid of heights, "an extreme fear of being on a tall building: the enticement of jumping off and splattering myself on the pavement is great. Or that I trip and fall and would be squashed in the middle of the street. My mother wished that she would die and get it over with, to be freed from everything, and I feel the same." It is again the identification with the hated, feared, and loved mother (775).

But there is more to it: The feared *falling* from great heights is also, as we just heard, a wish to throw herself into the depths. The fear of falling, hidden behind the acrophobia, and thus the fear of the wish to jump down points toward a deep, perhaps generally valid equation: letting oneself fall = dying = being passive = dependency = defense against the dangerous wishes for self-assertion and competitive triumph. In her case it was the deep, *envious and jealous* desire to take something away from her sister, and still more deeply and broadly: the murderous rage, foremost against that rival, thereupon against all the adults who have so brutally abused her in her childlike openness and vulnerability. Yet such killing wishes were, because of their magical potency, far too dangerous. The defense by drive reversal, here specifically by turning from active into passive, is, just like its counterpart of turning passive into active, one of the very early forms of defense (Fraiberg, 1982; Sandler and Freud, 1985). *Falling* has therefore become one of the major symbols for masochism, and with this also its core in narcissism, the "delusion of omnipotence" (Novick and Novick, 1996a, 1996b).

By the way, Regula had other manifestations of this equation: At times of severe conflict she used to fall down and injure herself. As we have seen, she suffered many car accidents. When she is surprisingly attacked by a strong pain—stomach cramps or a sudden, though trivial arm injury—she tends to faint. On the other side, and as a counterpoint, she manages by self-hypnosis to tolerate even deep drilling in her teeth without anesthetic. The emergence from a narcosis she experienced as a state of absolute peace and blissful passivity.

In regard to this basic equation we can again observe Fenichel's "triple stratification": "By my restless activity and productivity I have to prove that I am not passive, even if I may appear pushy. This is so because my wish to be passive and dependent is so strong. Yet if I gave in to this I would be too vulnerable. I would just give up and die. I spent much of my life to prove that I had a reason for living, a right to live, by pushing and running and being productive. And when I defended myself as a small child against my sister and her provocations: 'How dare you attack the poor baby? You ruthless big monster! You are the oldest, the biggest, and the meanest!'" (779). The triple stratification is: deep, competitive aggression, in the form of jealousy and envy ("taking away"), covered over by a pervasive protective layer of passivity (the falling), and this in turn is veiled by her frantic busyness, her restless activity.

Another way out from this underlying conflict about "taking away" is the demand of the "inner Dwarf": to strive stubbornly after an ideal of purity that would be bare of the guiltful jealousy and envy, vacated of the magically dangerous, vengeful rage, and freed from the disgraceful similarity of her body, of its needs, and of the affects related to it, with her hated parents.

Third, the valence of dangerousness has been displaced from the greedy and envious seizing of what has been withheld from her—nourishment, love, sexuality—to food in general, from there to weight, and ultimately to death. And who, after all, would contest the reasonableness of the fear of death? Still, the initial phobia and the underlying conflict about "taking away" cannot be completely disguised.

And the denial necessary with this?

"I tried to stick up for my brother, and I failed, and I was not aware how I competed with him. My father had such grandiose ideas and dismissed all problems! Finally, reality faced him, and it was too grim, impossible to undo. He succumbed to it. I warned and warned and nobody wanted to listen. I create even now situations where I try to warn somebody, and I am not heard. What I say is dismissively treated and denied."

"Like Cassandra. And what *you* deny is the good in you."

"It is the mirror image to the denial of my sister."

"And of your father" (780).

It is the denial over which the malicious Dwarf, dwelling in her depression, presides.

THE INNER DRAMA—FOUR SELF-FIGURES

How does this doubleness of Dwarf and victim, and that other doubleness of false me and the "little real me" find together an inner drama, and "how do the evil Dwarf and the false, but socially acceptable me stand at the gate of myself and make people perceive me in distorted ways, how does the real me never get to be seen?" (789). Again, as in all cases of character perversion, we encounter such ego splits, often multiple ones.

Her entire adult existence is divided into an *ungenuine* and a *tormented* part. This is her double identity—analogous to Vera's identity split into a *depersonalized* and a *masochistic* part (*The Power of the Inner Judge*, Wurmser 2000a, chapters 3 and 4; see also above, the sixth criterion of character perversion, chapter 3). One is a life under the dictate of the "inner judge" who seeks to punish her incessantly and mercilessly for all the forbidden impulses; the other is a life of concealment, of masking, of global denial. "With the false me I pretend to be a good girl and to give in." The longer this lasts during the inner development, the more layers succumb to the self-denial: "Simply to give in and to play the part they want" (786). Basically, this is a denial of the conflict itself, manifested as more or less marked and extensive depersonalization.

She describes three "me" figures: "the *little free me*," "the other *me that wants to be accepted* and that should please the others—that I do what I think people expect of me," and the third "me," "the scolding, berating, *condemning me*." "And sometimes the free me steals some aggression from the berating me, and I want to do what I want, and I don't care about the others; but then the scolding me takes it back and hits the free me over the head with it." What is omitted here is really a fourth self-figure, the "fat, disgusting, bodily me," that is, the victim and counterpart to the third "me." With that we have two polarities: (1) the pseudo-identity, the "pleasing, false me," the conformist self versus the "genuine me," the defiant "little free me," and (2) the "malicious dwarf," that rabid inner voice, a particularly important expression of the superego, originally part of the defending ego, but one of archaic features and endowed with those most intensive aggressions that have been "borrowed" from the traumata, versus the "victim me" that is "heavy and unacceptable and derided and rejected," because it always "runs the risk of losing the control over the demands and of overeating, and of overdoing everything, out of control, being a mess" (787).

It is, she says, a drama with four inner persons whereby the "genuine (or real) me" is being held by the others as prisoner in a dark jail: "Closed off in a closet, in dark recesses sits the real me and does not get a chance" (788). The other selves are liars and ally themselves with each other; but the social surrounding knows only that "dwarf self" and the "façade-self" that play with each other. At times the dwarf pulls the victim-me to the stage and pretends that this is now the real person, and the victim plays along; it becomes the accomplice of the other two. "But the real me is the only one that has feelings, the only one that has hope. The real me is confused and perplexed, it feels so alone. It has not learned to deal with the others. It had always to live in the shadows of the other three. It expects to be chastised for something it has not known. So it has only learned to distrust itself and the others and does not know what to believe. No learning and recognition that comes from the outside can be used. It [the real self] acts as naive, confused, foreign, alien. It has been locked up for so long, that when it really gets out now it is in a sense of wonderment and fear. And sometimes it is so intimidated that it seems better to go back and to let the others take over" (788).

Her double existence expresses the ego split between the two attempted solutions of the same conflict, the one attempt by depersonalization, adaptation, and occasional rebellion (conformist versus free or genuine self), and the other, more archaic attempt at solution by global identification, massive introjection, turning of the aggression against the own person, and by denial and repression of all the competitive, sexual, and destructive wishes (dwarf self versus victim me).

The splitting of identity means a doubleness of two ways of being: one where the conflict is denied versus another way of being where this conflict is virulent and newly reenacted.

LOYALTY CONFLICT

Immediately after these profound self-recognitions another momentous insight occurred, which also opened up doors of understanding of a more general nature which had been closed before: It was a spontaneous insight of Regula when she was reacting to the imminent departure of her youngest son who went to visit his father, the former husband of the patient: "It hit me suddenly: this is an old feeling reaching far into the past and one I never solved. It is the question of loyalty between father and mother [who got divorced when the patient was four], that it was impossible to love both at the same time. I had to protect the image of my mother, and I did not want to give it up against my stepmother, in spite of all the pleading by my father. The terrible thing was: when I was loyal to the one, I had to give up the loyalty to the other. I was angry at my father for demanding that of me. He depended on me, my mother depended on me, I also wanted to depend on somebody. . . . And when I became so overwhelmed by panic [last night], I again felt nailed against the wall, trapped, unable to move and yet with an incredible storm of feelings. Like a dog, I took myself by the scruff of my neck and was shaking myself with reproaches against myself. . . . I was besides myself" (790). In this instance the major reason for the split identity (which was, as we saw, an extremely prevalent part of her pathology) suddenly became clear: loyalty was at the same time disloyalty. It was a "no-win situation" and completely confusing. How can such a paradox be resolved, such a radical loyalty conflict? That cannot be done without denial, of course. Two irreconcilable and absolute claims for truth and allegiance can only then become tolerable if the contradiction, though perceived, is disconfirmed by her conscience: "Only if I take over the responsibility myself, I can still do justice to both and be loyal toward both. If this fails it is all my fault!" The anxiety caused by such a loyalty conflict is overwhelming, the resentment and the rage about having been put into such an unsolvable quandary intolerable and yet inexpressible; it has to be turned in its entirety against the self. Only the false front: "I take the responsibility entirely upon myself and shall be the rescuer of both," can paper over the irreconcilable contradiction, yet at the price of a deep cleavage in the experience of reality (in the "experience," not in the "testing" of reality). As we have seen before, in depression everything good that the person has done or experienced has to be denied.

Basically, the denial pertains to the betrayal that has to be disavowed. But since every loyalty in such a loyalty conflict is eo ipso already a disloyalty to the other, it also amounts to a double, simultaneous betrayal that has to be ignored. Regula says accordingly that she was just completely confused, perplex, and full of anxiety. The radical denial by taking it all upon herself is the only and completely logical way out from that confusion and fright, from that state of utter bewilderment.

Each loyalty conflict is a kind of superego-split calling forth enormous affects. As explained in connection with *The Dwarf* (Wurmser, 1987, 1989), loyalty is more than an ordinary bond, more than an "object relationship": it sets up the other as a beloved authority over oneself toward whom one has to keep faith. It is a kind of superego relationship and *superego bond*. Contradictory loyalties tear apart one's innermost self as probably no other conflict does. Since loyalties are fundamentally unconditional and raise the demand for absolute, that is, uncompromising fidelity, opposite loyalty claims by parents who fiercely fight against each other evoke in the child the deepest anxieties, the sharpest resentment and helplessness, and a rage which can only be directed inward.

There is, however, also something like *loyalty to oneself*, first probably toward one's own feelings and wishes, later on toward one's ideals and values. In the loyalty conflict between two parents the loyalty toward oneself is at first sacrificed. How can "the little real Me" be anything but bewildered and concealed?

It is now not simply so that one can equate the one part-identity with one parent, and the second with the other. Rather, it turns out to be so that the "real Me" defends the commitment to the one who at any given moment is being attacked and deprecated. The "false Me" adjusts superficially; it is only under inner protest that it eventually submits to the authority that is at that moment in power. This entails treachery against the one who is defamed, who lacks power, who cannot defend himself or herself. And that treason, which is at the same time also self-betrayal, has to be castigated in the severest form—and where else than on the self? The greater the fidelity and the deeper the obligation for loyalty, the more severe the punishment one has to undergo, and the greater the reparation necessary. Treason is a type of action giving rise to massive shame as well as to intense guilt: one is ashamed about the disgrace of being a traitor, the weakness this entails, the horrible image of the self as an untrustworthy member of any form of bond, group, or community—and one is full of guilt for the suffering one has inflicted upon the person (or form of community) one has betrayed. It is this loyalty conflict that calls forth all the most intense affects.

Facing her mother, Regula defended her father, but it was by her father that she was bitterly punished and repeatedly chased out of the house when she refused to call her stepmother "mother," asserting: "I already have a mother!" In turn, when she was dragged away from her grandmother and brought back to her father, everything that reminded her of her grandmother was ridiculed.

When I think of the other patients I ask myself whether something similar had not occurred with them as well. It did not have to be as extreme as with Regula. Yet for many of them, there were great value conflicts, and with them personalized loyalty conflicts. If we also count the loyalty toward one's own self it becomes evident that basically the superego-split and the resulting split-identity (always? at least very often) amounts to a sharp, largely unconscious loyalty conflict. Strong loyalty conflicts represent severe traumatization—with all its consequences!

Loyalty is a kind of corresponding term to justice, insofar as they determine each other: if somebody in a stronger position, in a position of power and authority, is fair toward me, I am loyal toward him, and in turn, if I am loyal toward somebody who has some strength beyond mine, I can expect justice from him: I "deserve" this. The resentment reflects the conflict between perceived injustice (hence the thwarted claim for justice), and felt (or fulfilled or demanded) loyalty. In other words, it corresponds to the perception that, in spite of the felt or implemented loyalty, the expected "desserts," in particular the deserved respect, are being withheld. A strong form of resentment is being experienced as indignation or outrage.

Resentment itself therefore results from a loyalty conflict. One tries to deal with the shame and outrage about having been betrayed, that resentment should be removed, by a grand strategy of seizing power and by avenging the offense, hence by redressing the impaired balance of fairness. In short, resentment leads to a kind of revenge rooted in wounded loyalty and cloaked by justice. There exists thus a motivational sequence, perhaps some form of a "developmental line," of expectation of justice → loyalty → betrayal → shame → resentment → greed of power and vindictiveness, which, because of its origin in the injured sense of justice and honor, is presented as a moral claim, a superego demand. We have the phenomena of the resentment-laden conscience—on a mass basis: a morality rooted in resentment, as described by Nietzsche and Scheler (see chapter 5).

This axis of claimed justice → shame → resentment → morality can be discovered wherever an absolute (global) demand of conscience enlists the instruments of power and authority to make the other subservient. The power of categorical condemnation of others, often cruelly exerted, should extinguish the feeling of inner weakness and humiliation, and thus counteract the gnawing resentment. So much greed for power and abuse of power in religion, state, and institution, just as in family traditions, is fed by this deep sense of being insufficient and therefore disregarded, which originates in the offended need for justice and honor.

We have heard how central the conflict about the wishes "to take away" is for Regula, deeply frightening and warded off in different ways. We referred it both to repressed envy and jealousy, but it seems valuable to pay special attention to jealousy because this appears to be a particularly strong motive force in the various forms of "tragic character," both in literature and in the way I sketched it clinically. Elsewhere (Wurmser, 2006; Wurmser and Jarass, 2007 b) I give a far more differentiated psychodynamic study of this affect, including of its very early manifestation (in babies at the age of six months and before). Here I deal with it as part of the central conflicts of the "tragic character."

JEALOUSY AND THE PROBLEM OF THE EXCLUSIVE POSSESSION OF THE OTHER

Dimitry Karamazov states: "But to fall in love does not mean to love. One can fall in love and still hate" (Dostoyevsky, 1879–1880/1988/1990, Russ. p. 113, Engl. p. 104). This idea contains a very deep truth: Infatuation can harbor and veil very much aggression. It does not have to be that way, but the danger always lurks there. This can be extended to much of what is called love.[2]

Socrates starts his own inquiry into the nature of love in Plato's *Symposion* with the observation that one desires what one does not have, what one feels "in need of" and "deprived of"—*endeés*. As psychoanalysts we would say that there is in the core of love a yearning for something one profoundly feels lacking, a core feeling that we also detect both in envy and in jealousy.

A very important aspect to be considered in much of love is therefore the often quite unabashedly expressed wish for exclusive possession of the partner. In its midst, there crouches therefore often devouring, even murderous jealousy. It seems that this wish for exclusivity can be observed already in very small children. Newest experimental studies show clear reactions of jealousy in six-month-old infants in episodes "where the mothers directed positive attention toward a lifelike doll" (as compared with face-to-face play and still-face perturbation) (see Hart et al., 2004):

> Cross-context comparisons of affects and behaviors revealed that jealousy evocation responses were distinguished by diminished joy and heightened anger and intensity of negative emotionality, comparable to levels displayed during the still-face episode; heightened sadness, with durations exceeding those displayed during still-face exposure; and an approach response consisting of interest, looks at mother, and diminished distancing, which was more pronounced than that demonstrated during play.

Fascinatingly, this works in experiments when a lifelike baby doll is used, but not when "the mothers focused positive attention toward a book" (p. 58). Hart et al. therefore conclude: "Because infants were being ignored in both conditions, the results suggest that infants find maternal inattention even more perturbing if the object of maternal attention is another child." Moreover, "5-month-olds were found more upset when maternal attention was directed toward another infant than toward an adult (Draghi-Lorenz, 1998) (also: Masciuk and Kienapple, 1993)" (p. 58). It is also very fascinating to notice that the crucial element is "exclusiveness." The authors mention other observations

> that infants as young as 3 months old recognize when their mothers are focusing on social objects other than themselves, and operate in triangular situations by distributing their affect signals and attention between their conversing parents. These studies suggest that young infants are sensitive to even brief and unintentional instances of social exclusion, and utilize various approach responses toward establishing social exclusion. (p. 59)

As crucial as dyadic relationships are, the similarly critical relevance of triadic constellations from quite early infancy on is shown in these intense efforts by very young children to reestablish "dyadic relationships with attachment figures," after they had been replaced by a triad (p. 60).

In contrast to the still-face situation, there is the combination of sadness and "heightened interest and looks at mother and dimininished distancing, suggesting an approach response . . . the approach response associated with jealousy evocation was even more pronounced than that demonstrated during play" (p. 68). "Overall, these results indicate that expressions of sadness and looks at mother were specific to the jealous evocation situation" (p. 70). The better the relationship with mother is, the more pronounced the jealousy response!

Certainly this wish to take possession of the other person is an innate disposition. According to Freud, there is "normal" jealousy in love, besides the excessive, hence pathological, especially delusional jealousy.

Surprisingly however, jealousy is an affect that has attracted astonishingly little attention in psychoanalytic studies, given its centrality for the oedipal triangle. In the supervision of analyses, it strikes me how often manifest conflicts of closeness and distance which then are interpreted as symbiotic, in truth hide unconscious jealousy: the dyadic fends off the triadic (often the reverse also holds true, but this latter circumstance is readily acknowledged and not particularly repressed). This hidden jealousy is often overlooked, just as is the case with hidden shame (cf. M. Lansky's paper, "Hidden Shame," 2005a).

If we reflect more about "normal" jealousy, the question is justified: Doesn't this concept of its "normality" rest on a concept of infatuation or even of love that is founded on total possession and disregards the individuality of the other? There may be complex compromise formations between the claim for exclusivity and respect. Still, the double question remains hanging in the air: On the one side, how is trust, the core of love, possible if the claim for possession is dominant? On the other side, how is trust possible if because of such possessiveness the attractions and ties to other people have to be hidden, that is, if it has to come therefore to lies and secrecy?

If we put aside for the moment this form of love that is founded upon possession and power we have still to admit that in every close and emotionally intimate relationship there are areas of exclusivity from which any third person is barred. Put differently: Love has its own private zone. If it is violated by a third person, it generates shame, and if this happens in a particularly forceful way, the offense leads to strong indignation or impotent rage and despair. Similarly it is true that even in love one guards a reserve of privacy and devotion to oneself and to others besides the beloved. It is a main task of love to discover the right measure. Thus one may gently and tenderly try in every relationship to find the right balance between the opposing tendencies of total bestowal of love and the equally intense need for other deep relationships. Therefore, the basic question becomes then: How do we find the individually specific balance between exclusivity and sharing?

An important conclusion is that fidelity and exclusivity are not identical and have to be uncoupled from each other. There exists a deep and lasting fidelity to the other, beloved person but this faithfulness and loyalty does not have to entail exclusivity. The voice of jealousy does not want to accept this as true. No one of us is acquitted from this conflict, and if the reconciliation of these two sides fails, the most painful wound of being totally unloved opens up—of not being worthy at all of being loved. Unlovability is the core experience of shame. It comes together with desolate loneliness and sadness, and with that almost inevitably a wish to gain power over what seems to have been lost. In the tragic character, life is ruled by this dilemma: either total affection or total pain and total shame; either exclusivity of love and possession or total abandonment and unworth. This state is, however, a retraumatization. Very deep traumata hide behind it. Yet before I turn to this topic I would like to reflect on a deeper aspect of the claim for exclusivity in love.

In regard to this exclusivity in love we can add that the core feeling of jealousy, that of being excluded from the intimate twosomeness of others, the conviction: "I am the excluded third," and with that of the intense sense of loss: "I have lost what would give my life any meaning," is inevitably connected with humiliation: that is, shame lurks behind jealousy. In turn, the exertion of power and possession toward the other, which becomes so much part of jealousy, is a rape of the other person's individuality and marks with this a really incurred guilt: the possessive lover or spouse should feel guilty: he deprives the other of her essential humanness. In reverse, the "betrayal" of such exclusivity, the breaking of such love imposed as possessiveness incurs its own guilt: the victim of such a possessive love feels guilty when he or she tries to break that bond and escape from that prison of dehumanization.

Once these psychodynamic processes are internalized we are faced with a great superego polarity: the shame for being excluded against the guilt for the taking-over and hence the dehumanization of the other person, or for the rebellion against such an absolute claim. The tragic character breaks apart in this conflict between love and domination and the ensuing derivative conflicts. In our terms: ultimately, he experiences every intimate relationship in sadomasochistic categories.

Thus it appears that this one conflict is a kind of leitmotif for the tragic character: it is the *conflict between love and power*. It is manifested, for example, in the tipping over of the yearning for the beloved into the compulsion to control this other person completely and thus to functionalize and dehumanize the beloved.

THE INNER CONFLICT IN LOVE

Beside this large-scale conflict between love and power that I believe dominates much of human existence, we encounter a second conflict. To get to it we have to take a little detour.

Let's reflect upon what we really mean by love. What follows is meant to be something that is open to our introspection and the empathic observation of the dynamics of our patients, not as a great, encompassing theory about the deepest roots of motivation.

In earlier papers I used Aristotle's beautiful definition as a starting point: "Love means: I want you to be." I begin from the *Nicomachean Ethics* (1926/1968, chapter 9.4, 1166a):

> The feelings of love [*philiká, philíai*] are thus defined: the loving [*philón*, also: the friend] is one who wishes, and promotes by action, the real or apparent good of another [more precisely: the next one, *tou pélas*] for that other's sake; or it could also be said that [the loving] one is somebody who wants the beloved [*ton phílon*] to be and to live for his own sake—what mothers feel towards their children.

Here, I expand on this idea and differentiate it in this way: Love means:

1) It is a main wish and need of mine for you to be.
2) I want to be near you, and if you are far away I miss you very much.

3) I want you not to suffer any damage, and your well-being is as important to me as my own (the meaning of caring, corresponding to Aristotle's alternative definition).
4) Your own will (your autonomy), your identity, your being so as you are, is as essential for me as my own.
5) I want to share with you what I have, what is within, just as what is without.

However, a sixth part is added to this that is both important and highly problematic: "I want to merge with you on all levels, not only on the plane of the mind and the values and on that of the emotions, but also physically," because at that point, immediately a big contradiction opens up: Not only does that not apply for every form of love, for example, that between child and parent, or rather, we know since Freud, that it is very much the case that it exists, but should not and has to be defended against, or it is not so between friends where the sexual aspects have to remain completely sublimated, but it is true especially for many deep love relationships where the sexual wishes are very much present and stormy, cannot be defended against and are not unconscious at all, but where they are at the same time forbidden and have to be suppressed, precisely in order not to harm the beloved other. In such a case then the conflict may become intolerable, irreconcilable: it becomes tragic. With that, there exists in love a gaping, often utterly painful, inner contradiction that may lead to a dialectic reversal: where the genuine love is overpowered by the frustrated desire and switches over into anxiety and angry rebuff, or into jealousy.

This means that within the just described full essence of love, in all its six constituents, there arises its own adversary; and this foe standing up against love in the guise of a great biological and deep emotional force: sexual desire. Love stands then in conflict with such an important and ultimately undeniable part of itself: the impetuosity of sexual wishes, the "drive" par excellence.

This is then one of the fundamental tragic conflicts: the dialectical reversal of love into sexual desire with its inherent aggression, its possessive jealousy, and its shame. Understood in this way, this second conflict, the enmity between love and sexuality, may be only a veiled form of that first conflict, the struggle between love and power.

To put the contradiction very pointedly: Love celebrates individuality, sexuality destroys it. Love wants the singular being, sexuality wants to undo the boundaries and destroy what is singular. The tragic character is incapable of transforming this conflict into complementarity. This, however, is the goal of genuine maturation: to bring these two powers to reconciliation, to harmony, to mutual fulfillment—something very rare, but always alluring as the shining summit of being.

SELF-ASSERTION AND AGGRESSION

In quite similar ways, as we noted in the conflict within love, the striving for self-protection, the search for respect and for claiming one's own identity may generate within itself its own bitter foe: the desire for power and control and for destruction. This third conflict is also a basic dialectic: the defense of one's own dignity and one's feeling entitled to be seen as an individual, is perverted into furious defiance, the seeking for power and the aggression against the other. In this sequence, shame plays a decisive role. Who is filled with deep, hidden shame desperately tries to reestablish his identity and his pride, and this seems only possible by a compulsive pursuit of power whose ruthlessness destroys others.

If the other is being functionalized, instrumentalized for narcissistic purposes of power or services, it induces deep shame. So often in analysis the question: "Am I fair toward the other (e.g., my spouse)?" turns into the question: "Am I fair toward myself?" And very often this questioning needs to be reversed as well. Both questions are very important. This issue of justice needs to be taken up again shortly.

The tragic character condemns himself to partial or full death for these three unsolvable conflicts and pulls the others surrounding him down into his vortex of perdition. And it is just at that point that jealousy may become one of those dark powers that plow everything else away.

The tragic character breaks apart in these fundamental and existential conflicts. His (or her) conscience fights against, condemns, and most massively punishes both sexuality and aggression. But there is far more to this.

CONFLICTS OF VALUES IN THE CONSCIENCE

In a fourth dimension, tragic character is not thinkable without the conflicts in the superego: the unsolvable conflicts between loyalties and especially the shame-guilt dilemma.

I already referred to the polarity between the shame for being the excluded one and the guilt for taking possession of and thus objectifying (dehumanizing) the other person, but also the guilt in the victim of such dehumanization for the rebellion against it and the almost inescapable "betrayal" inherent in such defiance. I also at least implied the dilemmas of love against love, of fidelity against fidelity, of exclusivity against exclusivity—conflicts that hardly anybody ever entirely escapes from.

Moreover, as already mentioned in chapter 1, we are well acquainted with the following dilemma and the vicious circle it leads into: Subjectively, and often accurately, within family reality every separation and assertion of separateness and identity is experienced as if it were something utterly destructive, murderous, or at least as something treacherous, as a breach of faith: Leaving the parents is taken as if it were wounding, if not killing them. In the same way, being left is felt as if it were an unbearable pain and is equated with death. The necessary implication of this deep equation of separation = death lies in that every step toward autonomy and independence is burdened with heavy guilt; every act of self-will, even every success is punished as if it were insolence, condemned at first from without, then from within. Defiance of any kind is treated as a deathly sin. This *separation guilt* forms one pole. However, if this daring is abandoned and replaced by submission under the binding other, one's one self, one's dignity and identity is forsaken. Sacrificing one's self, for the sake of preserving a human bond, is ultimately experienced with self-contempt. The victim-self, the passive, dependent self, is viewed with disgust and deep shame. Sooner or later, such *dependency shame* has to lead to open or secret rage and defiance, and with that the circle is closed.

In earlier works, I have called these antitheses of shame and guilt and the loyalty conflicts the tragic dilemmas par excellence.

PATHOS—THE MORTAL WOUND

The image of the incurable and unstaunchable wound recurs in tragedies, operas, and the clinical material—most poignantly in Philoctetes's stinking wound in Sophocles's tragedy and in Prometheus's devoured liver, when he is hanging forged with iron fetters to the rocks of the Caucasus and gnawed on by Zeus's eagle (*Prometheus Bound* by Aeschylus).

Pathos, the term used by Aristotle time and again in regard to tragedy, means both "suffering" and "affect." Both are applicable for our patients. We find these overwhelming affects directly, in the core of their personality, we find them as symbolic images (of doom, perdition), and we find them enacted as concrete catastrophe.

The intensity of suffering is by rights considered by many as the hallmark of tragedy; it is also the stigma of these patients.

If we start off from the side of the overwhelming *wishes*, in many patients with severe neuroses we find such a desperate search, like Don Quixote's, braving mortal danger und punishment—a constantly driving force of yearning, of longing, a desperate search. In the context of addiction I spoke about the addictive search. It is a search that defies mortal danger and punishment—not quite a heroic quest as in the romantic myth, but of a much more desperate quality, rather a *tragic quest*. It is a flight from a mortal wound, an effort to make up for a basic defect, an abyss of despair. I would suspect that it is this "tragic wound" which the ancient Greeks from Homer through Euripides used to call Ate (Ἄτη)—the Goddess of blindness and disaster.[3] This mortal wound itself is not so often described in literature or in personal experience, but its manifestation as longing and yearning, as searching at any cost, dominates the scene, a kind of most radical "Heimweh" (nostalgia).

This yearning is most typically awakened in the overwhelming regressive experience of infatuation and rejection: a sense of depletion, total isolation, and separation where the alternative seems to be either regaining what was lost or death. This crisis of "mortal wound" and "desperate search" is most likely to break out openly in adolescence but then recurs throughout life. In truth, it usually can be traced back far into childhood to traumatic experiences of overstimulation and loss, hope and deep disappointment, and all the other wounding experiences I have mentioned. The Greek word "trauma" means, after all, wound.

Again, in literature as well as in clinical observation, the suffering is double: First, it consists in being overwhelmed by affects like yearning and blind love, towering rage and abysmal shame, devastating loneliness and inner deadness, horrifying guilt and terror; it is painful suffering to the extreme and is terror in its own right. We know an experience is, by definition, traumatic when the ego is overwhelmed by an unmanageable affect. I think this is one source of suffering, the one we see clinically, and which is expressed etymologically in the words "pathos," "pathema," and Latin "passio." Passion is indeed, at least partly, suffering; extreme passion is extreme pain, is traumatic pain and terror.

But, second, suffering is also the result of these passions, of these affects that break through all order and measure. The towering rage of Oedipus and Kreon, of Lear and Penthesilea, the devouring greed and ambition of the Macbeths, the lechery of *Troilus and Cressida*, the absolute dread about becoming dependent and ridiculous and thus to lose power and untouchability in *Hedda Gabler*, the ruthless creativity of Rubek in Ibsen's *When We Dead Awaken* and of *Masterbuilder Solness*, the "murder of love for profit," putting "utility" above love and genuineness, in *John Gabriel Borkman*—all these are examples for this doubleness of pathos: as overwhelming affective motivation, namely as rapacious affects that *cause* suffering and death. They dictate the lives against (the ego's) better knowledge; they overwhelm rational decision and attempts at moderation. It is precisely the rapaciousness, the devouring global nature of these passions that cause suffering and disaster for these characters and for their surroundings.

It appears appropriate, therefore, to call those persons "tragic characters" who are overwhelmed by such vehement affects, especially rage, love, terror, and greed, by anxiety, guilt, and shame. Disaster is an inevitable consequence of their unmanageable passion. An almost indispensable aspect of this suffering is that it cannot remain internal: The propensity to provoke an *external catastrophe* is, I think, part of the tragic experience, almost always present in literary tragedies (Aeschylus being an exception), always a menace and often an actuality in the clinical experience: suicide, the partner's suicide, inevitable rejection and total isolation, social humiliation, endless torture in an indissolvable marriage, inescapable guilt.

The tendency to bring about an external catastrophe is part of what strikes us as tragic. Precisely that which they dread most they bring about by the very act of avoidance: "The ridiculous and vile falls like a curse upon everything I touch," laments Hedda Gabler (Ibsen, 1989/1966, p. 432). "His defense brought about what he should have fought off," says Peter Szondi (1961/1978) in regard to Basilius in Calderón's *The Life a Dream*. The family drama of Laios and Oedipus is paradigmatic.

External catastrophe and death are, however, symbolic representation and confirmation of the self-condemnation (of the masochistic aspect in the tragic fate) inherent in the overwhelming guilt and shame, which in turn lead back to the overwhelming passions and limitless wishes, and lastly to the "wound in the core." Mostly, these overwhelming, "absolute" affects are, therefore, not simply the result of trauma, but they are recruited by, and put in the service of, the *absoluteness of conscience*, specifically of the opposing demands of conscience that are themselves of such totalitarian character.

Thus externalization should be considered a *conditio sine qua non* for this complex of the tragic experience. In some, the externalization, paired with a considerable dose of denial, is quite successful: the subject is largely free from pain. It is his surrounds who are made to suffer. Kubie used for this a homely metaphor. "There are two types of neurosis," he used to say, "the onion type and the garlic type. In the former, the person himself is mostly affected; in the second it is everybody around who notices it."

But I think we would not do full justice to this aspect of suffering if we did not go back to the root, to what I called the "wound in the core"—this basic affective state of pain and yearning, underlying the tragic conflict and all that follows. Shouldn't we talk in these patients about "primary pain"—as we talk about "primary anxiety"? What the origin of this source of suffering might be we cannot know at the outset: Which narcissistic injury, when, in whom, in what family constellation—that emerges only under careful exploration.

As mentioned, it is not so much a heroic quest, but rather a flight from the inwardly experienced mortal wound. The main means of rescue and healing of this terrible woundedness is often and repeatedly sought in love, but this love incurs the awful danger of being permeated and corroded by those three dialectically experienced forces, all forms of power: jealousy, sexual desire, and defense against shame.

The *object* of this desperate search may be an archaic imago or vision, a very specific image of a person, the very individually shaped face of a figure that arises from the deepest of the soul, unknown and yet familiar, enigmatically spellbinding, who would be experienced both as omnipotently protective or as ominously threatening (we encountered it in all the cases presented both in this work and in its companion volumes). The search may mean rescuing or reviving a "dead soul": the calling forth from the realm of Death or the reawakening of a lost being, of a soul that seems emotionally dead and mute. It might be the search for a specific landscape—as in the "Heimweh" mentioned or in the recurring landscapes of our dreams.

MERGER AND HUBRIS

The *aim* of the search might be the merger with an all-nourishing, all-powerful, and, above all, all-forgiving ideal, a person endowed with all epithets of beauty and charm. This fusion with a Dulcinea-like ideal would forever undo all separateness, a union so intensely experienced in the mystical ecstasy. The aim may be to wield unlimited power in the vain attempt to heal the mortal wound. Or it may lie in the destruction, the aggression against, and annihilation of, the obstacle that is perceived as causing the wound, the inner lack. The pain of the mortal wound is projected onto the "mortal enemy"—the Jew, the black, the spurning lover, the hidden conspiracy, the viciousness of society. Radical fear and radical pain call for radical violence, and thus the retribution both feared and provoked is equally radical.

It is, for example, the constellation of overwhelming anxiety, of terror and pain, that is experienced more or less consciously as the "tragic injury." It is followed by the search for an all-powerful protector and for redemption; it is a search for something absolute. This means by necessity a lack of measure (*Maßlosigkeit*) and transgression of boundaries: Who is searching for the absolute cannot respect the barriers of reality; he has to break them. This violation of the laws of nature and culture is imperative. It does not happen out of arbitrariness, but out of the soul's hidden depth, out of the search for the absolute that could afford protection and redemption from trauma and judgment. Yet, that inevitably also means a bold disregard of the rights of others and a breaching of limits—*hubris*. As Kaufmann (1969) rightly said: hubris is not pride, it is an "anarchical defiance of the bounds," a "wanton disregard for the rights of others" (pp.

74–76); it means insolence, an arrogant breaking of the laws of nature or society; it means a self-righteous breach of norms accompanied by self-justification.

However, this breaking of limits may also be a creative discovery, the exhilarating sense of being one with Nature, with the mystery of creation, the bliss of a great love, the merging through the senses in the psychedelic experience. Or it is the breach of the limits of order, rationality, and measure, the regression to the forbidden wishes of the oedipal tragedy, to the breaking of "law and order" by Antigone, Orestes, Prometheus.

In our patients we find both: the *creative* aspect of this regression and the *anarchic* and deadly side of it.

It is the tragic demandingness glorified for example by the Spanish poet and philosopher Miguel de Unamuno (1921/1954):

> The visible universe . . . , the universe that is created by the instinct of self-preservation, becomes all too narrow for me. It is like a cramped cell, against the bars of which my soul beats its wings in vain. Its lack of air stifles me. More, more and always more! I want to be myself, and yet without ceasing to be myself to be others as well, to merge myself into the totality of things visible and invisible, to extend myself into the illimitable of space and to prolong myself into the infinite of time. Not to be all and forever is as if not to be—at least, let me be my whole self, and be so forever and ever! And to be the whole of myself is to be everybody else. Either all or nothing! All or nothing! And what other meaning can the Shakespearean 'To be or not to be' have or that passage in 'Coriolanus' where it is said of Marcius: 'He wants nothing of a god but eternity'? Eternity, eternity!—that is the supreme desire! . . . nothing is real that is not eternal. (pp. 38–39)

Another aspect of conscience is equally overvalued and exaggerated (i.e., narcissistic): the *demand for justice* (we encountered it in all the patients described here, and even in the Dwarf). That "mortal wound" is, after all, basically also a deep sense of injustice. If we pursue a high value, or, in the simplest words, if we are "good," we also expect to be rewarded. At its deepest, the child generally wants to have the right both to be loved and to be respected. If one or both needs are thwarted it is not only felt to be an existential threat, but also a grave injustice. Not to be worthy of love and of respect—this engenders massive shame, and one of the most relevant consequences of this deep shame is the resentment. "I need to apologize for who I am," said one patient. "Nobody in life is showing up when they should. It is so unfair."

I already mentioned one basic law of tragic experience, tragic character, and tragic fate: that one brings about the very thing one is most afraid of and tries most to avoid. And how does that happen? By exaggerating the pursuit of *one* ideal that is preferred by far to all others and which is put as an absolute: "You are too absolute," says Volumnia to her son Coriolanus (Act III, Sc. 2). What does that come to? It has to lead to a disregard of all other ideals, which is in the "nature of things" impermissible; it has to force a tragic choice and with that the violation of obligations, inevitably bringing about condemnation in the form of guilt or of shame. It is the awful dilemma we just heard from Regula.

In short, in tragic experience, the entire existence stands under the shadow of unsolvable conflicts of conscience, of values, and of loyalties, or it is riven by the antagonism between *inner necessity* and *outer limitation* that condemns the individual to struggle and suffering. Out of this inner and outer wrestling, *deeper insight* might emerge, yet without that those absolute opposites can be reconciled and the suffering lifted.

Absoluteness, the hallmark of narcissism, both in the aspiration for the ideal and in the ensuing condemnation, becomes the decisively important tragic criterion. Absoluteness is necessarily joined by the denial of what does not fit the ideal, and this denial exacts its own huge price. The counterideals, the countervalues, and the counteridentity (all that is the sharpest opposite of what one wants to be) have to become just as absolute as the ideals and values and mark the tragic depth of existence. Denial itself thus takes on tragic significance. The attempt at escape becomes the downfall, the surface turns into the depth of anguish. It is an inescapable dialectic.

I conclude this part with another quote from Shakespeare, this one from *Troilus and Cressida*: "Take but degree away, untune that string,/And hark, what discord follows! Each thing meets/In mere oppugnancy. . . . Then everything includes itself in power,/Power into will, will into appetite,/And appetite, a universal wolf/So doubly seconded with will and power,/Must make perforce a universal prey/And last eat up himself" (Act I, Sc. 3).

THE WOUND AS REPRESENTATION OF TRAUMA

In the center of inner life of the tragic character stands trauma, wound. Fischer and Riedesser (2003), in their standard textbook of psychotraumatology, define trauma "as a vital experience of discrepancy between threatening situational factors and the individual's abilities of mastery, a discrepancy that is accompanied by feelings of helplessness and unprotected exposure and thus effects a lasting shock in the understanding of self and world" (p. 82). Trauma is thus not merely an external event, but always already the interaction of event and experience, of outside and inside.

Especially what Fischer and Riedesser call *relational trauma* (*Beziehungstrauma*) is hugely significant—not only soul-blindness and soul murder, but also a consistent way of double-bind messages cloaking the deep underlying family value and loyalty conflicts.

Together with the abysmally felt trauma, the feelings are overwhelming and unbearable. These affects impose on all the inner conflicts their insolubility: drive, defense, and superego assume the same absoluteness as those traumatogenic affects. The six attributes of affect regression are indispensable for an understanding of early trauma (expanding on what I wrote in chapter 2):

1) the feelings are globalized, total, that is, dedifferentiated;
2) they can only insufficiently or not at all be put into words: they are deverbalized or hyposymbolized;
3) they are experienced and expressed again in body language: resomatized;
4) they are accompanied by sexual excitement: sexualized;
5) they mobilize massive aggression that is largely turned against the own self; and finally,
6) trauma always means a form of cognitive regression in the sense of fragmentation, of incoherence, the splitting of consciousness in the sense of wide scale dissociation.

This horizontal principle of 'splitting up' [*Zerlegen*] the whole traumatic experience into single scenes and 'compartments of the revolving stage' that are kept as separate from each other as possible, is one of the principles of control enabling the person to adapt to the traumatic experience, to live with it, to keep it under control, and even to 'abreact' it to a certain degree: in the sense of a passive, not of an active repetition. (Fischer and Riedesser, 2003, p. 115, my translation)

These thoughts transcend individual psychology (see Wurmser, 2004b): A culture that abuses its children and inculcates blind obedience to authority creates the suicide bombers and mass murderers of totalitarian states and religions. It continually recreates new trauma, but is itself rooted in historic trauma, above all else in the sense of humiliation. It deflects the rage created by incessant shaming and reinforced by historical grievances toward an outward enemy who symbolizes those values that are antithetical to all that the culture claims as honor and deeply senses as humiliating deficiency. From a psychoanalytic point of view, the pathology of an archaic shame-oriented superego in society and culture at large, rooted in severe physical or emotional traumatization, is as important as historical injustices, economic deprivations, religious fanaticism, or the threat posed by modernity. On the one side, the shame part of the self is being projected onto the victim; it needs to be tortured and destroyed as symbol of one's own image of weakness and victimhood. On the other side, the superego itself as punishing and absolving, absolute authority is projected onto leader figures, and onto terror-inspiring and -organizing groups, and above all onto "God." Terrorism can thus be understood as an important form of externalization of the inner conflict with an archaic superego, which is guided by pervasive resentment—"inner" here meaning within the individual as well as within family, group, and large community. Terrorism's history is a tale of shame and resentment and their exploitation for power and profit. The inherent fanaticism is an absolutist way of thinking, rooted in the total affects of chronic traumatization, the ensuing globality of defenses and of the demands of the superego.

Even in social psychological inquiry, we can discern a psychodynamic connection, a kind of developmental line that leads from the expectation of justice to loyalty, then to the feeling of having been betrayed and thus to humiliation (I referred to it in regard to the Dwarf). This state of shame is followed by the corrosive feeling of suffered injustice, that is, resentment. In turn, such resentment manifests itself as a form of vengefulness and greed for power, yet, because of its origin in an offended sense of justice and honor, it presents itself as moral entitlement, as a kind of perverted demand of conscience. We see how entire communities, societies, and states are comprehensively ruled by such a resentment-laden conscience, of a morality that is drenched in envy, jealousy, and vindictiveness.

This developmental line is also important for the understanding of the tragic character, and hence for the questions of narcissism, masochism, and that which we commonly call borderline pathology, to which we now turn.

NARCISSISM, MASOCHISM, AND TRAGIC CHARACTER

Let's look somewhat more closely to the character defenses without getting locked in behind the iron bars of diagnostic categories!

Freud called overvaluation the narcissistic stigma in the choice of objects (1914, p. 91). It is, in my view, always part of neurosis. We could talk about the narcissistic dimension of neurosis. It is always just a matter of the extent and strength of such character formation. This overestimation and exaggeration always entails some violation of boundaries. Narcissism therefore refers to a too-much, to a transgression of boundaries in value, truth, and action, in other words, to a want of moderation in the pursuit of a certain value or of certain groups of values, to a blurring of the boundaries between acknowledgment of reality and denial, and to the disregard of the limitations in human relations and the injunctions of conscience. As we saw before, it is this transgression of boundaries that is meant by "hubris," one of the attributes of the protagonists in Greek tragedy. It refers to a "self-willedness" (Dostoyevsky's *svoyevolye*), or arrogant abuse of power that refuses to accept measure. The tragic character is immoderate (*maßlos*); the chorus, or now the therapist, represents measure.

At the same time, we generally observe in neurosis the phenomena of polarization, of dichotomizing, of what is commonly today meant by "splitting." The more severe the neurosis, the more severe the phenomena of splitting, and its reverse holds true as well. Thus we might speak about the borderline-dimension of neurosis; and again I talk here about the neurotic process in general, perhaps ultimately, though in milder form, in each one of us.

Accordingly, the *exclusivity and absoluteness* is one of the hallmarks of tragedy, tragic experience, and tragic character: the disjunction into unsolvable conflicts of conscience and irreconcilable contradictions of values. Exclusiveness always stands in conflict with other exclusiveness. Absolute values and demands are always incompatible with each other; their conflicts defy solution. This belongs to the essence of tragedy.

We recognize that the two groups of phenomena of want of measure ("narcissistic dimension") and exclusivity ("borderline dimension") are practically congruous with what I describe here psychodynamically as the tragic character, and what we know from the main persons in the works of tragedy. Of course, I think foremost of Greek tragedy. Yet, I encompass also Shakespeare's and Schiller's tragedies, Verdi's operas that were strongly influenced by both, Dostoyevsky's "tragic novels," and Ibsen's "present day dramas" (*nutid dramaer*).

Still, there is something third: we have to remind ourselves of the concentration upon *victimhood* and *blood sacrifice* in the tragic character, both in the form of self-sacrifice and sacrificing the other, suffered or carried out on behalf of a higher value. Historically, this theme of sacrifice is the starting point of the tragic play: the hero is being offered as sacrificial victim in lieu and as proxy for the torn god Dionysos. The image of the incurable wound forms the core of this idea of victimhood.

Being a victim, the motto "power through suffering," omnipotence with the help of the role of martyr, is, however, the dynamic meaning of masochism. The "art of living" is being constantly undermined and sabotaged. This victimhood, which always stands in the service of a morally exalted idea, of a core value and core ideal, is being conceptualized by us as masochism, and in particular of "moral masochism." This is the *masochistic dimension of neurosis.*

All three dimensions combine and are ways with whose help the tragic character tries in constant repetition to overcome the traumatization and the conflicts connected with it, and yet, because of their severity and insolubility, has to fail again and again—the repetition compulsion. It is especially the double inner necessity: to master the trauma and to solve the conflicts within the superego, that instigates and sustains this fruitless repetition.

WHY ARE WE SO ATTRACTED BY THE TRAGIC PHENOMENON IN ART?

The central thought in Schiller's essay of 1791 ("About the reason for pleasure in tragic objects," *Über den Grund des Vergnügens an tragischen Gegenständen*; 1911) is this: tragedy comprises all those cases in which a natural necessity is sacrificed to a moral (ethical) dictate or where one ethical necessity is sacrificed to another higher one. The victory of an ethical principle causes pleasure, even at the price of severe suffering and death.

What can we add now from a psychoanalytic perspective?

Whenever truth and loyalty enter into conflict with each other, loyalty usually wins out. The theme of demanded, but impossible exclusivity of love, loyalty, fidelity, and attachment dominates tragedy and opera, as well as the clinical picture. Absoluteness, faithfulness, and betrayal are the substance of tragedy—and with that the fatal insult, especially the humiliation and the sense of injustice if that exclusivity is not maintained, and the guilt if it comes to its "betrayal." Thus it always is the problem of a triangular conflict, hence that which we mean by the Oedipus complex in its widest sense. No one has been or is being spared from such conflicts. We all have suffered or are suffering under such conflicts of double love, or of double obligation, or of love against obligation, or of power against love, or of love against desire—conflicts whose poles always command exclusive adherence. Therefore we feel an inner closeness to the art forms of tragedy. It is always our own issue.

Art allows us to share these feelings and to confront them in this commonality. Music and theater are, immediately, shared passions: they are experienced together. Just like therapy, it is a form of loving dialogue that heals. In a somewhat more concealed way, this holds true for reading as well. Reading is only seemingly solitary, intrapsychic. It is in the greatest and most intimate sense a "com-municating" (etymologically: having one wall in common), "Mit-teilen," a twosomeness of author and reader, or perhaps even oftener: a threesomeness of author, reader, and main figures of the work. This sharing is a most important part of what we know as sublimation. The power of sublimation struggles with the power of exclusivity (absoluteness). This is, I believe, the *essence of the tragic experience*. We could call it the *tragic consciousness*. Not only is great art animated by this, but also all serious psychoanalytic working.

THE ANTI-TRAGIC

The "Philistine" is the antithesis to this tragic consciousness, not only of the tragic character who breaks down under the burden of the tragic. He shows the conventional attachment to things, the consistent turning to what is external, and does not want to know anything of the inner dimension of experience and of its inevitably tragic conflictedness. His motto is: "I do not want to be touched in my inmost being." Everything of significance is being shifted to the external, and thus the conflicts are screened out and bypassed, instead of being tackled.

If what is inward is being made to a thing, as it so often happens in the art world, it is like a betrayal of the soul: passion turned into business. Yet, this is only one form of the anti-tragic, namely the denial of the importance of the inner life, the psychophobia. More accurately: what should be within is being sought on the outside, and what is outside is being unhesitatingly transferred unto the mind—what childhood research today calls the equivalency principle (Fonagy and Target, 1996). It comes down to a lifting of the boundaries between inside and outside.

Speaking more generally, the anti-tragic may claim limitlessness and deny that the limitedness of life, knowledge, and power are really valid. Most of all, it denies inner conflict, avoids the inevitability and effectiveness of our inner contradictoriness and indissoluble oppositions. It sees the splitting as something inimical, strange, as something to be condemned, to be met with perhaps in psychotics or near-psychotics, but not something that applies to all humanity. And yet, tragedy tells us, and the tragic altogether calls out to us: *Nostra res agitur*—this tension, this basic conflict, this inclination to the esoteric, to the absolute, to the compulsive and to split reality, they all matter to us, they dwell in ourselves, they threaten us all the time. None of us can escape from them forever. It is human destiny that is shaped and marked by inner conflict and the flight from conflict because it grows out of the roots of the tragic.

SOME CONCLUDING REMARKS

I try to summarize now what I mean by a tragic character: It is a personality disturbance that for inner reasons brings about a fate that has many features in common with the protagonists of the art forms of tragedy because of which there has also been talk about "fate neurosis" (e.g., Helen Deutsch, 1930; L. Szondi, 1948):

1) that everything good is transformed into something negative;
2) how that which is feared most is being brought about by its avoidance;
3) how the affects show an excess, a too-much in intensity and spread, and an overpowering quality, in particular the negative affects;
4) how every passion has therefore to change into suffering;
5) how the overwhelming feeling of an incurable inner wound from pain, shame, yearning, and sadness keeps breaking open with every slight, rejection, and loss;
6) how love keeps tipping over into power, jealousy, and hatred;
7) how the identity appears to be deeply threatened by shame and how thus every relationship is quickly permeated by burning envy and resentment;
8) that conflicts between power and love, between love and sexuality, between protection of identity and destructivity, between shame and guilt, and between loyalty against loyalty quickly become insoluble;
9) that the self is being experienced as victim, the other as perpetrator, and that the surroundings are blamed for everything;
10) that his or her fate is marked by the failure in the pursuit of high values;
11) and most generally that there is a claim for totality in the feelings, in the attachments and desires, an absoluteness of the demands of conscience and expectations of the ideal, and therefore an excess of condemnation of the self and of the other.

I conclude with a saying ascribed to R. Yehoshua ben Korcha (probably a disciple of Rabbi Aqiva; Talmud tractate Sanhedrín 6b): "Is not it so: where there is judgment there is no peace, and where there is peace there is no judgment?"[4]

NOTES

1. The beginning of Schubert's *Winter Journey*: "Fremd bin ich eingezogen,/ Fremd zieh ich wieder aus" (W. Müller: *Die Winterreise*).
2. The following thoughts on jealousy and love are presented in far more detail in Wurmser, 2006 and Wurmser and Jarass, 2007b.
3. As inward temptation or as a blinding demoniac force from without.
4. *Wehaló bemaqóm sheyésh mishpát, en shalóm; uvemaqóm sheyésh shalóm en mishpát* (Steinsaltz, 1989–1999, Talmud vol. 15, Sanhedrín, 6B, p. 54, slightly modified).

7

"The Envy of the All-Powerful Goddess" and Womb Envy—Some Basic Equations

THE SILENT PLEDGE

The analysis of the following case, successfully terminated after 6½ years and 915 hours, is particularly hard to present because of its great complexity. The material could hardly be brought into a lucid order and under clearly defined themes, the course divided only unclearly into phases. Nonetheless, the case is instructive precisely because of the multiplicity of the dynamics and the more or less successful course in spite of the severity of manifest pathology. It seems therefore best for me to stay close to the clinical material and to develop the emerging insights and experiences as they emerged, *in statu nascendi*.

Moreover, in reviewing my earlier formulation of this case with newer insights, it occurs to me that a hitherto almost invisible magical lantern starts shining and illuminates the material in a new way, a new understanding that I can succinctly phrase as *the wish to be both sexes and hence the great power of the envy of femininity, womb envy* (Bettelheim, 1954/1962; Kubie, 1974; Eschbach, 2004/2007; Jarass and Wurmser, 2006/2007)—in this case against the background of a family dynamics drenched in mother and sister's deeply threatening *envy of masculinity*. What leads, however, beyond the literature is the additional insight how deeply this envy is rooted in shame (Lansky, 1997), and shame in turn in pervasive traumatization, with those hallmarks described in chapters 1 and 2.

But now in medias res!

A twenty-year-old, highly gifted student, living completely isolated and lonely, aimless and joyless, without interest, without sense of meaning for anything, has the following dream: "There were no people in it. I was in my apartment. I discovered a secret door leading to two additional rooms. The first was a bedroom with a small kitchen, sparsely furnished. In the corner there was a stove, and two or three air conditioners were piled up on each other. The next door led to a last room. It was like the first one. What was interesting was that the oven was on; there was a pot on it and a flame underneath. I thought how odd this was, because no one could have been there for a long time. It was the secret part of my apartment. Nobody had been there for years. It was very strange that the stove was on. I also could not understand how I could have twice the space within the confines of the rowhouse. I was thinking: This is great, but how could this be? I tried to see where I was situated, and I looked out the window. On the outside there was a street with many trees. It was a somewhat urban scene, but very different from where I live. The only thoughts, except for disbelief and curiosity about how this could be without a fifth dimension were: Now I could get another roommate and share the rent. And if I could not also use the two additional air conditioners?"

The evening before he had received a telephone call from his four-years-older sister that she and her boyfriend would come and visit him the next weekend. He did not want this. It would be an undesirable intrusion in his locked-in, isolated existence. Still, he had not rebuffed her outright but deferred his response to next Friday: "I burn the bridge when I get to it." He recognizes the meaning of both metaphors that are here condensed into one (crossing the bridge when one gets to it, and burning the bridges behind oneself). "No one can cross the bridge to myself." He had withdrawn totally into himself, he adds, into a world only known to him, existing perhaps only in his mind. Out of fear of his sister, he had withdrawn into another reality only he could see. He stresses how calm he had felt in that dream and how he had enjoyed himself, very much in contrast to his usual life, which was marked by unknown anxieties and meaninglessness. I ask him whether he has an idea what the flames might mean. This is one of the riddles in the dream, he replies. "There was such a calm setting, and yet they are the flames of rage burning in it. But this is just a stab in the dark. . . . It must have burned there for a long time—a very long-burning, forgotten fire. The whole thing was peaceful. The lid on the little pot was not properly set, it was crooked, and the content had long been boiled away; it was empty. Now I have a whacky thought: The fire and the warmth and the flame could represent my feelings toward my mother, and how these feelings have boiled away my soul."

"Which feelings?"

"The warmth and the love."

"The interest, the wish—you mention the mother. I also think of your sister."

"Yes."

"Why whacky?"

"Because I'm ashamed to make any statement."

"About love and warmth?"

"To take any kind of initiative, just as I don't say anything in class, out of the fear of ridicule."

"And more broadly: the shame about any personal feeling. And the burning is the same metaphor, as in the dream—"

"—and about the bridge. So that the warmth and the love can be very pleasant, but also very destructive."

"And dangerous."

"I think again of the dream: There is an interesting contrast between the heat of the flame in one room and the air conditioners in the other, in two different rooms. . . . I see it as a contrast to the warmth of the flame: the coldness."

"What do you make of it?" Long silence. I conclude: "The tremendous conflict toward mother and sister. We were just yesterday talking about how opposite your feelings were and are toward these two." He responds: "The ambivalence." It is the end of the hour (95).

TRAUMA, CONSCIENCE, AND NARCISSISM

Reuven is a tall young man, mostly smiling in embarrassment, almost cachectic and bent forward. Thanks to his excellent intelligence, he has up to now, without much effort, remained successful in his studies and had just concluded his undergraduate studies with distinction.

After a severe, long-lingering disappointment with a girl, he had, by and large, turned away from any sexual interests, engaging only at times in masturbation that included attempts to perform fellatio on himself—attempts usually resulting in very painful dislocations of his back and admitted only with deep shame.

Colleagues with whom I shared some of my observations considered him schizophrenic; this was certainly possible, but I did not see him that way because I failed to find unambiguous signs of real thought disorders or secondary symptoms. In spite of the severe and lifelong isolation, the factual lack of friends throughout his entire growing up, the almost total disinterest in any kind of work, his aimlessness and lack of libido, the very profound ambivalence vis-à-vis the three members of his immediate family and me—in spite of all this, I still had great reservations about diagnosing him as schizophrenic.

Undoubtedly, however, he presented the clinical picture of *severe narcissism*—in the sense of a "large-scale withdrawal of cathexis from the object world" and of a contemptuous uncaring attitude. Still, he was and is exceedingly conscientious, yet constantly expecting that everything he was doing would have to end in disappointment: "Behind the attitude of 'I don't care, it doesn't matter,' I care too much." His life stands under "the implicit promise: if I do everything I'm expected to do I will get a big reward even if I have to suffer a long time, and that those who are bad and enjoy the pleasures sooner or later will be punished." Although recognizing the falseness of this premise and the meaninglessness of building his life exclusively on this self-abnegating expectation, he is ruled by "absolute conscientiousness": "'If I'm only good enough I will be rewarded, and if I'm not it has to do with me: either it is all my fault, or nothing is worth anything anyway'" (98, my clarifying summary of his feelings)—what later on I came to call the *omnipotence of responsibility*—a character defense typical for those who have been severely traumatized as children and one we have already encountered in the patients described before.

His anxiety about not fulfilling his duty and what is expected of him is and remains therefore overwhelming, also in the transference, and his disinterest, his withdrawal, and his contempt, that is, all the narcissistic stigmata, serve the *defense by devaluation* against the possibility that he would be disappointed, anew and time and again, and too bitterly and too surprisingly, in his trusting expectation and hope. This is the basic theme of his life.

Consciously, his anxieties go back to his third or fourth year of life, when he retained his feces out of fear that rats were hiding in the toilet bowl and would bite him, and that, with the feces, his heart and other organs would also fall out and be flushed away. A little later, he believed his sister's claim that parents had children in order to kill them.

"This theory had a gap: the fact that others were not being killed. How could people otherwise survive? So I revised it: that it was true only for my parents and a few others that they would kill their children, but also not my sister. It was ideal for my sister to take revenge on me in this way by saying that the parents loved her and wanted to kill me."

Not surprisingly, he always was a very timid child, much ridiculed and mistreated in school. Only gradually it became known in the analysis that he was suffering under many compulsions: compulsive looking and blinking, moving his jaw back and forth, rearranging the position of his penis, opening his mouth in order to tense up his palate. All these compulsions appeared to him senseless, but he felt helplessly exposed to them. Just like the phobias, they can be traced back to his fourth year of life.

ACCUSATIONS

What was the chronic traumatization that was precipitated and perpetuated in this "bad conscience," in this "inner monster" and which, secondarily, manifested itself in the narcissistic problems and the schizoid, obsessive-compulsive, and phobic symptomatology?

In regard to the external history it has to be noted that the parents had a lot of vehement fighting with each other culminating in his mother's wild attacks of screaming and accusing. Reuven hated his father's frequent disciplinary demands and intrusions in his bedroom; during the arguments he took the side of his mother.

He also gives credence to his mother's and her sisters' claims that their late father had been a horrible ogre who had sexually abused all the girls in the family, a tradition allegedly continued by nearly all men in her family.

At the occasion of one of the two family sessions set up because of the serious and deteriorating situation of Reuven, I asked the mother about these allegations. She described all the misdeeds of her father that she and her sisters and nieces had deduced from their dreams and earliest childhood memories. My impression was that they most likely referred to some pedophilic acts of a very shy and timid old man who had been intimidated by his acerbic and dominant wife, acts that later on had turned into demonic crimes in order to allow this woman, Reuven's mother, to shift her own massive rage and resentment from her husband onto her dead father, as well as her own guilt feelings, which she soon admitted when she talked about her outbursts of hate and fury that had so terrified her children. Her eruptions of violent rage and hate still occur frequently today, especially against her husband and assume a more and more bizarre character, as if he were trying to murder her.

A repetitive episode from Reuven's early childhood serves as symbol for his entire life history: His mother used to lie down several times during the day. He was permitted to lie beside her on her bed, provided he would be absolutely still and would not move at all. In spite of his great effort, he always failed and was sent away: "In order to be with my mother I had to do the impossible. To reach what I wanted was impossible." The only path on which he could hope to attain it was *perfect passivity.* She bound her son intensively to herself, overstimulated him, and then frustrated him completely. "To enjoy something is evil. Striving after pleasure or joy, as in companionship or sexuality or drinking, meant I would become my own enemy." At the same time, every sign of annoyance or impatience on his side was being sharply punished. Already very early, this entire conflict and archaic relationship must have been fully internalized (120–21).

All pleasure is dangerous and must be disparaged and avoided. But the reverse is also true: that danger, anxiety, pain are lustful—in double transformation (698).

He also recalls that he had made himself responsible for the fights between his parents—again the omnipotence of responsibility—and believed that he had doomed his life because of this guilt: "I must have done something very bad that they would have wanted to take revenge on me and kill me." Hence he had immediately to undo all wishes, all impulses; the result was a near-total paralysis of will, a psychotic-like mask, and an almost absolute anhedonia.

Yet the image is not unambiguous. To the contrary, ambivalence splits all his experiences: When the parents were hugging or kissing each other he pushed himself between them, rose, and thus split them asunder in order not to be "left out" (192).

John Lennon's song "Mother" haunts him and does not leave his mind: "You had me, but I never had you. I wanted you, but you never wanted me. So I have to tell you: good-bye" (431).

"It is fundamental: I cannot have pleasure except vicariously: when somebody has pleasure in my pain. This is the sadomasochistic way that I have learned from my mother and my sister. The only way to be loved and to be liked is as somebody's victim. Only in that way can I have control and power" (488).

"I've learned very early: wanting to express myself and to show hunger for life would cause pain and disappointment. Even now I don't know what I am myself, who I really am, what I want out of life. I always was forced to subjugate myself, to deny myself, to swallow my self" (169).

"To get love I had to lose my identity, I had to sacrifice it, to lose myself into something bigger and better" (695).

SPLIT SCREENS

It would befit the obsessive-compulsive structure of his defenses, to strongly manifest the defense of isolation, and this is also how I understood at first what follows, but in reviewing it I ask myself whether he deals here with a very strong form of *dissociation hidden behind isolation*: a wholesale splitting off of entire personality parts, involving perception and cognition besides feelings, instead just of the simpler separation of affect from thought or of affect from affect.

For example, he declares after a long silence, which I interrupted, that he has been seeing simultaneously three things, like on three parallel TV screens: how he had been playing by a creek in the park of his early childhood; how he dislikes doing his homework for the phobia program, avoids it, and hates the entire program; and how angry he is at the continued studies program of the university, because they give easy credits and degrees. If I should ever hear that it had been blown up, he would be the main suspect. Pleasure about the explorations in childhood, displeasure about tasks and obligations, and massive rage stand, seemingly without connection, completely disjoined, at the same time side by side, are probably directly related to the analytic situation, and show the split feelings toward the same object (112). A dream follows in the next night where he experiences himself in three figures: as Reuven I jumping out of an airplane, whose parachute immediately opens; as Reuven II, who leaps besides the first, but who falls and falls without the parachute's opening; and as Reuven III, an outside observer watching with utmost alarm. Finally, the parachute opens five hundred feet from the ground. Reuven II falls into a dock area and through the roof of a boat into its interior. He is not breathing and would die, unless Reuven I gives him artificial respiration. Nobody else cares. He succeeds in resuscitating II, but the latter is severely injured. And yet all three are the same person. Reuven, the narrator, finds the dream crazy, and yet it soon becomes clearer that it is the case of a similar self-division as on the three screens: his identity as observer and explorer, his active self defending himself, but also the one that comes to the rescue, and his passive, gravely wounded self. His passivity really appears like a free fall toward death. In this way he symbolizes his current conflict in regard to his immediate future: Should he enter graduate school in a specific scientific field, or remain several months longer in his total inertia, or look for some low-level employment? All three possibilities disgust him, but he always seems to choose the second one as the safest (113).

In his childhood (ages four to nine) he had, similarly to this division in the dream, the following fantasy: "I wanted to be a different person. How would it be to take the place of this other person without having his thoughts and memories, but my own? To go in his house and to recognize no one and nothing, but to pretend that I am that person without being it. How could I gather information in order not to be exposed?" I believe that both forms of *depersonalization and split identity*—the one in the dream and the one in the childhood fantasy—are derived from severe *shame conflicts*.

Indeed, his feelings of shame about his appearance, about everything he has within and tries to express, are devastating and reminiscent of his early toilet phobia. "I always saw myself as an odd ball, estranged, as an outsider. Since kindergarten, I kept myself apart, I was special in an evil sense, unique in a negative way. I always felt the contempt and the disfavor of others and was tormented and ridiculed." Accordingly, he feels exposed and imperiled in the analysis. At the end of every hour, his pillow cover is drenched in sweat.

In the depersonalization, he seems to express, in the form of a compromise formation, both the wish to hide and to show himself: "I reveal myself, but as somebody very different from who I really am." And in the inward feeling of shame: "I look at myself from the outside and keep my distance both from my dangerous active side (the one that also would like to blow up a school) and from my passive dependent side that seems to hurtle down toward death. And this radical *self-distancing* is considered by others, and also by my analyst, as crazy and treated with contempt. In turn, I protect myself by my mask of contempt" (quasi-quote).

In regard to the *masturbation by self-fellatio* which he repeats from time to time in spite of the resulting neck and back pains, he states: "I never learn that it means much more pain than pleasure, and I'm very ashamed about it. . . . The fantasy is that I'm sucking on the penis of a man. But thinking of a man is, by itself, not exciting. This is not what I want, but when I'm sucking a disembodied penis, this is arousing. I identify with the woman who is performing it, and the self-fellatio satisfies this. Whose penis could be better than my own? I don't want to perform it on anybody else. It is acting out the fantasy. There is nobody I can trust for gratification. Nobody is there to gratify me."

"'I can only trust myself for pleasure. Everybody else is disappointing,'" I confirm (116). I think that it is the expression of a real *narcissistic perversion*, as a protective reversal of traumatization similar to the one we witnessed in Elazar: "Instead of being damaged, defective, and utterly humiliated in my impotence, I am complete, self-sufficient, and even grandiosely able to give myself whatever I want. Instead of anxiety and shame, I experience excitement and pleasure. Instead of being dependent on a disappointing object, I need only my own self, and I have it. I am mother and baby, man and woman, intrusive and receptive, active and passive at the same time." Later on, he also confesses that, in support of what he calls his "female identification fantasy" he resorts during masturbation to women's underwear and then wears it himself. For the purpose of this *masochistic-fetishistic perversion*, he temporarily appropriates from the dirty laundry the panties and pantyhose of a girl that lives in his house, although he has hardly any sexual attraction for her. The meaning of this is again a reversal, this time from passive to active: "If I actively play being both sexes at the same time and play suffering, I preempt being really passive, castrated, and tormented."

Under the mask of a severe narcissism I see in the patient a severely obsessive-compulsive, masochistic character with deepest phobic anxieties, intensive feelings of shame and social anxieties, and not only with very severe inhibitions, but also with a general ego-restriction toward entire segments of life rooted in traumatogenic dissociation. It is mostly this state of gravest ego-constriction that, together with the increasingly obtrusive narcissistic-fetishistic-masochistic perversion (evident in his sexual activity and fantasy, as well as in his character as a whole) evokes the impression of a psychosis. The anxieties and avoidances, the inhibitions and ego-restrictions stem from the ambivalence conflicts, which are even now omnipresent and point back to the earliest, admittedly traumatic childhood.

In the transference he often appears inaccessible, banished into an oppressively anxious silence that he is unable to break; my questions or remarks rather tend to aggravate it. There are hours during which he could say no more than five sentences. In other sessions he speaks rather freely. He views me, like his father, as a demanding, judging authority that is intrusive and may treat him with contempt and deride him. Yet his contempt and his sarcasm toward me are frequently very corrosive—in a kind of anticipatory turning from passive to active: Better I do it first, before he inflicts it on me! He readily recognizes this.

Although he does not therefore like to come to the analytic session, he sees in it his only hope (he had previously been in treatment about five times, although never in analytically oriented therapy). He misses no hour and always arrives punctually.

The passivity and complete inertia is dangerous, and its opposite, the aggression that easily develops into rage and indignation, is just as risky. He does not know what he should do beside remaining an observer. Yet this is a phony solution; it deepens his sense of unworth and thus his shame. It is exactly this interpretation that I now give him, with the clear message: "It cannot go on this way. This is too dangerous for you. And about the 'horror' you profess about continuing your studies and just as much about working, my heart really bleeds for you—especially after having worked with survivors from concentration camps" (114).

John Steiner (2006) speaks in a similar context of "verbal boundary violations": "Seduction can be done with words, cruelty inflicted with the tongue and moral condemnation with the tone of voice" (p. 316). Such attacks might be disguised as interpretations; he speaks therefore of interpretative enactments. My countertransference was a reenactment of Reuven's own superego shame-drenched attitude that by externalization had evoked and provoked the same in me (many would talk today here about projective identification; I prefer to talk about externalization of inner conflict and about role-responsiveness, see Sandler, 1993; Sandler and Freud, 1985). Perhaps, I also express with this taking over of such an "assigned" role what Steiner means: "It is sometimes startling how the patient prefers the analyst to make superego judgments about morality rather than ego-judgments about reality" (2006, p. 317)—"judging instead of exploring," in the very helpful formulation by Paul Gray (personal communication).

At the time, I tried to justify this sarcastic, very aggressive intervention to myself in this way: "It seems to me that I have to put a stop here to the expanding ego-restriction and the giving in to the phobic anxieties. However much he might take it as a superego intervention it seems to me a rational warning, an appeal to his observing and executive ego instead of a superego demand. If I let, without challenge, pass and deepen the passivity which he himself experiences as danger I fear I would turn into an accomplice of his anxieties and thus into a coconspirator of his extreme self-condemnation."

Later on it was clear to me that I was exasperated by his withdrawal from life and his almost total silence, felt helpless, and tried to shock him by this cruel and insensitive remark, expressing the helplessness in the countertransference. The form of intervention with its sarcastic tone was ineffectual and rather added to his profound and overwhelming self-chastisement. In a long dream he withdraws, in shame about the unfulfillable self-expectations, in a hole in the ground.

Subsequently, like several of my patients with severe neuroses (see, e.g., Wurmser 2000a, chapter 5, case Jacob), on my advice he entered for a limited time a program of behavioral therapy parallel to the analysis. This occurred because I felt after seven months that the analysis alone would not be able to break through his nearly total, basically phobic isolation and inertia and alter it in any lasting way; I was even concerned it might lead, with its strengthened introversion, to an increased encapsulation.

I was struck again in this case how well these two ways of approach complemented each other. A third approach was added when, about 3½ years after inception of analysis, the program prescribed medication in the form of Prozac (Fluoxetin).

For several years Reuven worked very successfully in a practical job, but without any satisfaction. He returned therefore full-time to a course of studies combining science with languages, but devoted himself to the courses in the former only with modest interest and success. At the same time he was employed about half-time and with much recognition at a state job. Around that time (3½ years into the analysis) he started a relationship with a colleague from the Far East, a girl who was much of the time friendly and submissive but quite often exploded, just like his own mother, in irrational fury, self-destruction, and self-humiliation. She was, in spite of severe abuse, still deeply attached to her mother, who reacted to her liaison with Reuven with death threats toward both and toward herself and with real violence.

It required endless deceptions and lies by the girlfriend to protect the relation against the attacks. Finally, the girl fled from home and only gradually resumed contact when her mother reluctantly assented to the bond. For about one year, Reuven and Jushu lived together until their marriage a few months before the end of the analysis. It was impressive to what extent his girlfriend also had a marked masochistic character attitude and sexual orientation. She eventually entered analysis herself; it led to considerable conflicts between her Confucian family tradition (in Christian disguise), with its accent on absolute loyalty toward the family and the ethos of truth and unmasking in psychoanalysis. Reuven saw himself pulled into this deep *value conflict*: Jushu's loyalty conflict between faithfulness toward her mother and her love for Reuven was intolerable. Reuven felt personally threatened (716).

Of course, the sequence was basically the other way around: This value conflict overshadowed the relationship from its inception, brought her into severe inner and outer conflicts and influenced the transference in her treatment.

In the later parts of treatment, Reuven had an extended circle of friends, and was, all in all, quite happy and relaxed. The symptoms or perverse inclinations (in the sense of sexual actions or masturbation fantasies) had also, except for a few remnants, vanished and played hardly any role in his fantasy life anymore. On the other side, the deeper masochistic-passive character tendencies were still at work for a long time and also showed in his indecisiveness about long-range plans. After concluding his scientific studies, which satisfied him little, he decided to start studying medicine while at the same time continuing his work for the state and, almost secretly, pursuing his interest in various languages. It was probably in accord with his still-prevalent masochistic orientation that it had been impossible for him to study what he liked most, to wit, languages.

His compulsions completely disappeared under the combined psychoanalytic and medication treatment. After about two years of Prozac he discontinued it step by step. It was very impressive to observe how the removal of compulsive acting and obsessive thinking, ostensibly due to the drug, remained effective since that.

In what follows I shall bring characteristic, thematically grouped excerpts from the analysis.

"I'M THE PRISONER OF MY CONSCIENCE"—MORAL MASOCHISM

The dilemma is this: "Fun and pleasure seem evil and wrong to me. I cannot admit that my wish to be good, not hedonistic could be wrong. My entire identity depended since my early childhood on this: not to be like the others. How could I now participate in parties where you get drunk and have sex with semiconscious girls? I don't want this and I want it, and I am afraid of it. And I would become my own enemy if I gave up my own values. And yet, I see how my sister and my cousins and my old friends, who have gone the way of using drugs and alcohol and failure in school and sexuality, are happy, satisfied, and successful while I, the good little boy, who has renounced everything, am miserable and getting nowhere fast, in a life without purpose and award. Was I wrong and was everybody else right? In a sense it was so. It is hard to admit or think that this could be flawed. It is so much part of me, no, it is me, it is my essence; without it I do not exist. It is so hard and painful for me. I saw the others as stupid and idiots and me as superior, as a genius. It is hard to concede that they are right and I wrong."

Thus the choice is between two extremes: an absolute asceticism renouncing all joy and drive gratification and condemning them as absolute evils, and an equally extreme and fantastic hedonism. Yet this choice in itself is of course wrong: the ideals and values in themselves are not wrong, but their absoluteness is: "I see much in black and white, and that is not how it is. As far back as I can remember, I had this dichotomizing view of the world: me against the world," without seeing that it also is part of himself that he is so busy condemning and scorning on the outside (144).

The intensity of his self-condemnation is overwhelming; the narcissistic fantasies and the mask of contempt are bulwarks against the despair and emptiness of his entire existence, caused by such radical condemnation. Hope, pleasure, and trust have been experienced from so early on and so radically as something thoroughly dangerous that his conscience has to condemn them from the beginning on as evil and that his life ever since shows itself as an unbroken chain of confirmations that he ought not to hope, not to enjoy himself, and not to trust the other. Neither praise nor affection means anything. He would like to give them credence, but they cannot be believed. Only disapproval, emptiness, and negativity mean something. The harsh conscience has let all joy be drained (167). *"I'm the prisoner of my conscience"* (175).

This dour, implacable conscience has to serve as totalitarian guardian against aggression. He is very much afraid of any expression of rage; it is an evil monster in him that must be locked up. It would destroy him and his surroundings (455).

"I paralyze myself to render the ugly monster of anger and shit harmless. Otherwise it would go on a murderous rampage."

"Or at least on one of torment and smearing" (633).

SEXUALITY AND ANALITY

Thus we always come back to the characteristic doubleness, back to inner conflict, particularly about his childhood sexuality: There was much sexual play with his sister and her girlfriends. He let himself be undressed and urinate in front of the fascinated young ladies, examine several of them and compare the size of the uncovered organs. It was discovered and led to punishments by mother and neighbors, but his sister, who was for him an adored and ardently loved goddess, seduced him always again to new adventures and arousals. He had to tickle her without coming to enjoy the promised reciprocity. Thus there was a whole lot of overstimulation, embedded in a sadistic context—like the mother's attacks of rageful screaming and the coalition between mother and sister with their secret language, "pig Latin," from which he was excluded (228).

From all this it again becomes evident how early the onset of his masochistic sexual orientation really was and to what extent it was a form of adaptation, an attempt to deal with traumatic overstimulation and failure, with aggression from without and inner helplessness, with anxiety, rage, and vengefulness.

The *identification with the victim* reaches very far back and is also today reflected in his vegetarianism. As a five-year-old he saw at their neighbor's a deer hung and disemboweled, a hollow torso. Another child claimed that the deer's meat was contained in the sausages, and he choked during the meal. This picture is intertwined with his deeply and convincingly held anxiety that he would be killed by his parents and with his anxiety that he would lose his inner organs. This would be the commensurate punishment for his own murderous wishes (212). The vision of the disemboweled deer expressed how he would be punished (345).

One of his very early sexual fantasies, reaching as far back as his fifth year, was that he would become part of the beloved girl, and specifically as feces of the idol, within her body. Even now this fantasy keeps reemerging. In a session three years after the beginning of analysis, he indulges in it once again. In this way he would be particularly near to the adored, closer than any other thing, in what he calls a "kind of *fecal jealousy.*" At the same time he is quite ashamed about this self-abasement and the anal excitement underlying it, in fact, about the *sexualization of the entire anal and fecal sphere*—the very thing which had of course originally also been warded off by the rat phobia (467).

And almost in the present, his anal orientation is reaffirmed: Jushu calls him *Bangu de Zhong*, the King of Farting: "My wish for union with the woman is almost something religious—a *mystical unification with the great female force,* of my puny self with the all-powerful goddess to whom I am totally submissive, totally passive, to do everything for her in order to be accepted. I become part of an 'oversoul': 'You should be a good victim and please her and not seek pleasure on your own, only fulfillment through this goddess.'"

"And in the most abject form: when you fantasized to be the feces of that goddess."

"Even the feces would be sacred, even that is closer to God than I am. It was a kind of *fecal envy*" (515).

Love for his father was also very anal—their shared time in the toilet as signs of closeness.

So the *feces become themselves treated as equal to persons*; on the one side he wants to dwell in the loved woman as her feces—a clearly masochistic fantasy of early childhood that is intensely pleasurable; and on the other side, he is afraid when he loses his own feces that something very essential of himself gets lost (210). The difference between person and thing is thus dramatically lifted—one of the central marks of character perversion (and perversion altogether). I would add: In particular, there is a deep need to wipe out the difference between male and female, a profound yearning to be both sexes at the same time.

"I spoke so much about my anal fears, but there was also much fascination and curiosity about it. I hated to defecate, but I peeked between my knees under the lid to get a view of my anus and to see the feces come out." It was a precursor to his self-fellatio (436).

He knows that his cleanliness training was particularly difficult and caused a lot of anger in his mother. Very long he kept on wetting pants and bed while suffering very early on from severe constipation. When he was four, he wet the bed about half of the nights, when he was six and seven, perhaps twice a week, when he was twelve, twice to thrice a month, since that, perhaps once a year. It happens even now occasionally (150).

At the same time he was, at the age of three or four, a compulsive questioner—a habit often engaged in during the hours during the early phases of the analysis.

There was, among others, the following archaic equation: the wish to defecate = all desires and all lust = great danger. In allusion to Nietzsche's "being free from versus being free to" he remarks: To have no feces (not to defecate) means purity, freedom from dirt = from evil = from all danger, especially also being free of *rage*—and yet he deeply suffers under this "compulsory freedom" (753).

From early times on, he tried to come to terms with the tremendous danger of his mother's nearly psychotic tantrums of fury and her unpredictability by forming a totally rigid, archaic, anal-masochistically centered conscience: "I am to blame. It stands in my power to prevent the catastrophe if I forbid myself everything which could provoke it." Defecation became the symbol for the dangerous wishes in him, and the rat stood as symbol of retaliation for them.

He pictures himself in his passivity "as a total parasite, an evil, slimy, sucking thing, an infant pushed away by his mother with disgust as a feces machine." Or he is "an ugly monster in a little prison cell that has kicked down the door, a shit machine in a deep well" (he had in fact once in his childhood punched through the bedroom door). At the same time he had known that his father had favored him over the sister. Therefore she had hated him so much, which posed the almost theological conundrum for him: "How could he like the shit machine over the goddess?" It was even more confusing since mother's affection and power counted far more. Once again: gain was loss (691).

In puberty he used to masturbate, mostly anally, with a bottle, again mixing lust and pain. There too, pain is always the stronger and more enduring thing (190). In this scene, he is dramatically both the aggressive male and the receptive and suffering female, or perhaps more accurately, the sadistic intruder like mother and the receptive, masochistic victim submitting in pleasure and pain to the tormentor with undefined gender roles.

THE COMPULSIONS

The compulsions described before all appear as failing efforts to correct something that causes shame. What is the original shame? It has obviously something to do with his penis because there it began; it is at the same time the "show piece" and the "shame piece," cause both of pride and of shame.

The compulsions began so that something that was "out of place, misaligned, incorrect" could be put into the right place and corrected. It started with the penis when he was about three years old; then it went to the hair around the anus, which had to be pulled out (ages five to seven); then to the eyes that seemed cold and dry and had to be squeezed shut. The problem with the eyes began as he held back his tears and had not wanted to be seen crying, when he was about seven; but it only became intense when he was twelve. As a last element came the "palate compulsion," where he tried to realign jaws and palate. Each of these compulsions remains in existence, but is put into a revised hierarchy of compulsions. They all are in turn a new source of shame, and the shame feeds on itself (206). "My entire life is a study in humiliation," especially the many public degradations he had to tolerate from his beloved and adored sister. It was she who revealed his early compulsions to the world, his "tics," his secret formulas, and also claimed that he had made crap at age four on the front lawn—a boldfaced lie, he contends.

The compulsions basically appear to be an endeavor forever renewed that keeps failing, "to put things right," that is, to undo the shame, but one that just leads to more shame: "I was an ashamed, scared little animal." The more fear of humiliation, the more compulsion. The demonstrations, on behalf of his sister, of his phallic glory and his squirting power were rather the outcome of the deeper shame referring to the penis than its origin. He saw himself as a weak, ridiculed, and shame-paralyzed child (201–206). Being male seemed itself a source of derision and humiliation: the result of the prevailing attitude of penis envy at home.

"FEMALE IDENTIFICATION FANTASY" AND FETISHISM

"I thought of the fetish off and on again (the underpants of the house-mate); it is a compulsive idea. I cannot get away from it although the masturbation with it is not as gratifying as the self-fellatio. The fantasy in it is that I'm the woman and being penetrated from behind, that I have the penis in me. The anal penis means power. The fantasy excludes other people. I'm man and woman, I'm self-contained, and I get around my anxiety of the woman. As soon as I think of being *with* a woman, the anxiety ruins the mood. This fantasy is self-contained and safe."

"It makes the woman unnecessary, it 'kills' her."

"Totally unnecessary!"

"This entire fetishistic-masochistic scenario is closely connected with the scene when you tried to sleep with your mother and with the other scene when you were together with your father when he was on the toilet having a bowel movement."

"To be close to somebody has too many drawbacks. I could be close to my mother when I was absolutely silent and immobile, which was impossible. And I could be close to my father only when he was shitting, and that was no fun for me. And now it's the same. It is not worth it."

"So you resorted to something inanimate."

"Or with my sister I had to be the victim. I never get what I want with a person. Most alluring with my father on the toilet was that I was sitting on the warm air vent. So the warmth again came from something inanimate. That I liked most."

"And this holds also for your interest in mathematics and physics. It's at a safe distance from people."

"It's frustrating. I want to be closer, and I cannot. I remember the picture: my father was sitting twenty-five minutes on the toilet, and I was sitting on the vent, and I remember how disappointing and cold it got when the heat would go off."

Besides, the fetishistic-transvestistic action was also strongly anal: he specifically chose the filthy underwear of a girl he found otherwise rather repelling (522).

During masturbation he discovers a peculiar inner split: on the one side he is, as part of his "female identification fantasy," his mother, and that is pleasurable: "That I was my mother, that was arousing." The figure of his father "does not enter into it at all." That comes only afterward when he thinks about it. "It is the woman who is on top, riding." At the very same time he observes the woman from behind. He is simultaneously observer and observed whereby the observed is at the same time he himself and his mother. In this way it comes to a kind of double doubleness, which he can magically and pleasurably unite within himself—thus undoing some basic differences of human existence: inside and outside, self and other, man and woman, perpetrator and victim, pleasure and pain, spectator and actor, human and inanimate, and ultimately dead and alive (526).

During the "female identification fantasy" he is being anally penetrated; rectum and vagina are equated: "With it there is both fear and excitement about the anal penetration. Anger and rage and attraction are twisted together and hard to separate." In a similar way, intense opposite feelings live in his mother in a bewildering mixture together. Love means hate, and disgust and sexuality go together. It is reflected in him: "There is fear and even shame that I have these desires, and that they would be exposed, that they are bad and dirty, and I would be ridiculed for them" (706).

It should also be added that in the actually performed self-fellatio he is both the nursing mother and the suckling baby, again both sexes. His penis becomes the breast.

CASTRATION ANXIETY

Four years into the analysis, he has, for the first time in his life, intercourse. He feels guilty that he had pushed Jushu into it. "When I touched her genitals I had the fantasy that she was a mutilated boy. The immature being in me asks: 'What is missing? What is wrong? The folds look as if something had been torn off.' That she had not been born without it, but that it had been ripped off, a hole with irregularities, something like a scar" (605).

"In the dream, my mother tried to urinate standing; she had a kind of penis, but it was not working very well. Then I shat all over the place, on the floor, the rim, the cover. I was very small and was crawling. Fecal material was over my skin, on my arms. I tried to wipe it off, but I couldn't." The dream follows intercourse during Jushu's menstruation. "When I looked on my penis it was all bloody. I had concerns to be mutilated myself."

"Which changed to anal imagery, from castration to smearing, from genital sexuality to anal sexuality."

"The best of all worlds."

"And what about mother's penis?"

"She had much power and control, also over my father, with her behavior."

"So the dream is a solace: Women are not mutilated or wounded, they do not bleed; they have a penis even if it doesn't work out that well, and the whole thing is fecal, anal—that your sexual experiences tap some of those early images, conflicts, and defense."

"The blood yesterday does not help my fears that I'm hurting her—the sadomasochistic perspective: that all pleasure comes at the cost of pain to somebody else" (611).

His sister delivers a boy by Cesarean section. In a dream "a huge alligator has bitten off the face of a girl." He has tried to prevent this horrible mutilation. It must be his "anger and rage at women, the wish to hurt and destroy them": "I take revenge on the woman for having castrated me." He has recently seen a movie about the castration of a man by his wife (*Pelle*). Because women are themselves mutilated and castrated—the sister's operation during delivery is another reminder of it—they have to castrate men. "The woman is missing something; therefore she wants to take it away from me." This is expressed in the phobias of his early childhood: that his inner organs would be taken away from him by the rats. And in the dream it is the reverse: "I take it away from her." More accurately: "Not I, but the alligator takes it away. To the contrary: I want to protect and save the girl!" Instead of the revenge on women, he is their rescuer: reaction formation.

He dreams of a friendly giraffe; he puts his whole arm in the giraffe's mouth, and the animal is biting without hurting. "It reminds me of having sex and of the consequences and danger: that it would shrivel up the penis. If I put the penis in her it would be bitten off." Women destroy in their passive-aggressive attitude, even if they seem harmless. "I can identify with them in the role of victim that really has the power."

"Power by suffering and passivity."

"But with angry teeth inside, ready to bite. That fits my mother well. She portrays herself as sufferer, but in her outbursts she bares her teeth."

"And perhaps this is also the way you see me; as long suffering who occasionally bares his teeth—when you see me as angry."

"And another similarity is there that you and my mother know secrets about me, and you can use that to inflict damage—the teeth bared in anger."

This masochistic imagery of being the victim of angry assaults follows a session in which he confessed that he had come to the hour with an acute infection and high fever although he knew it was shortly before my departure for Europe: he wanted to infect me and hoped I would get sick and could not leave for my vacation—and this as revenge for the likelihood that he anyway would have to pay for the hour canceled at such short notice: "He rips me off for $90, and I make him sick." I had remarked that the cruelty which his conscience meted out against him he was directing against others. He replied that it then came back upon him. If he was cruel against others he would have to expect the same from them. Thus it is a three-step-sequence: self-torment, directing the aggression against the other, retaliation feared from the other. And I add: "It may very well be some outer control: 'It is better if others constrain me than if I have to constrain myself'" (655).

WISH AND FEAR TO BE DEVOURED, AS BACKGROUND TO THE ISSUE OF CASTRATION

Again and again he returns to his mixed feelings toward women: anger, fear, and curiosity. "I think how, in my attitude to women, anger and attraction are so mixed, the wish to please and the wish to harm. And it is so toward all authority figures. I give the person power, and then I'm angry at the person for having power over me" (732). "The polarity in my mother is striking; it is replicated in the way I perceive women: she was and is at times seductive, warm, nice, loving and caring. Then, suddenly and unexpectedly, she is someone who rejects me, who refuses to talk with me at all, who is horrifying and raging, almost psychotic. Then again the idea: if I just behave right I can avoid setting off the witch in her, that love will come back" (720).

"The more I'm attracted to a woman, the stronger the anger and the wish to destroy her. I'm angry at her superficial beauty, about her pride and her power over me. It is as if desire and anger were twisted together in me."

"The equation: *violence = sexual excitement.*"

"This fits to my *double think: What is strongly desired must be held in utter contempt* . . . like my mother who holds all men in contempt. I'm afraid that all women hold me in contempt, and I try to prove to them that I don't deserve their contempt and anger, that I'm different." He placates them by becoming the woman himself (700).

In the night before the following session (701) he had a dream with a huge cockroach crawling on the kitchen counter. "Jushu screamed of anxiety about the black bug. I sprayed an insecticide on it, I pumped and pumped. But it continued moving and then ceased. I wasn't sure whether it was dead. Later it came back, and now they were two bugs, one very big and a smaller one, and they were copulating. Now they looked more like black praying mantis. The female was much bigger than the male that had mounted her. It was curious and repulsive. Then I went upstairs to the bedroom and put my belt on; it broke in two separate pieces."

At first he recalls events from the day before. A woman colleague had a bag of chocolate cookies and suddenly a big bug came out of it. Later he had been intimate with Jushu, but because she was menstruating she offered him fellatio. The glans of the penis became irritated: it was both pleasure and discomfort. Thinking back to the fornicating bugs he comments: "The female was so much bigger. The union means losing oneself and becoming part of a great being. This is a concept I've always had."

"That the woman is devouring you."

"Not so much in a destructive way but as assimilation. The difficulty I had in the dream was whether it was one or two. I want to merge and fear losing my individuality."

"And what about the first bug?"

"The anxiety that I would be immobilized by something, that my freedom would be taken away, that I could be an ugly creature which strikes fear in the heart of women, in Jushu, in my mother."

"And what about the pumping of the insecticide?"

"Sex with the penis."

"And the bug as the female genital: that it has some resemblance with it."

"That's true."

"Meaning: sex = killing, violence. And afterward the violence is turned against your self: that you identify with the despised female genital, the castrated one, namely in the female identification fantasy where you yourself become the bug, and then you are the ugly creature." (Silence)

"When I saw for the first time pictures of the female genitals, perhaps at age twelve, I couldn't believe it. I had always believed before that the vagina was the same as the anus. It seemed so strange, freak, something weird, so bizarre."

"So that it was not so much the absence of the penis, but the difference from the anus that struck you?"

"It seemed more like a penis than like an anus, but a mangled penis that was hanging down and twisted and grotesquely altered. I perceived the genitals as lying over the anal opening, a malformed thing."

"As the victim of some assault."

"Exactly. That the woman had been castrated and brutally so—butchered."

"And that the same thing could happen to you."

"Yes." (Long silence.)

I interrupt it: "And the female identification fantasy turns the threat into pleasure: the defense by sexualization."

"Against what?"

"Against the anxiety you could be mangled like the woman" (701).

"The destructive rage at my mother—that because of my anger and rage she is mangled and she bleeds, that I'm the cause of it."

"And you have to withhold the feces in order not to lose your own organs. . . . A much more soothing myth is that the parents want to kill the child than that you want to injure the mother. In this way it is systematically turned against yourself. The passivity, the female identification is a loud protest: I have not done it, I'm not guilty. To the contrary, I'm also wounded" (703).

"Everything seems to be an endless cycle of aggression and punishment."

"And reparation, atonement to attain forgiveness: like the bleeding of your mother that is followed by the fear of losing your own body contents."

"Because it [her bleeding, her mutilation] is my fault—that it was my anger and my rage. And this would be the payback."

"And also: the conscious fear that your parents would kill you."

"The relationship between my parents was very similar: aggression and payback, an endless cycle, a mutual sadomasochistic relationship."

"Alternating, and that both were exciting: injuring and being injured, attack and payback. Both had this sexual quality."

"And one follows the other, the cycle is continuous. At least the one part is pleasurable, and during the unpleasurable part it is known that the pleasurable one will come next, so that also the unpleasurable one is exciting, because it turns into pleasure" (705).

"'After having caused the damage I want to identify with her in order to repair it,'" I summarize.

"Repair through empathy."

"By identifying with the victim—but the victim of your own aggression" (709).

WEAKNESS IS POWER

"An overwhelming wish to sleep, it is a mother identification, playing her game, emulating her."

"'If I cannot *have* her, I can at least *be* her.'"

"Or that I can impress her when I imitate her. 'Imitation is the best form of flattery.' In many things I'm like her: I don't work much, I easily quit, I sleep a lot" (he clearly sells himself short here, at least, as to how he was behaving by this time).

"That you experience this identification like a curse."

"But also as a source of power."

"—yet one that fizzles out in weakness."

"Which turns into weakness. But weakness is power." He states this as if he had read Lao Tzu, which, as far as I know, has not been the case.

"A very illusory form of power," I say.

"Like that of the slave over the master. Illusions can be very powerful and are hard to break. When I was much younger, my most common complaint was that I was bored, that I had nothing interesting to do. What I want I cannot have, and what I have I don't want—very similar now with my studies and with Jushu."

"It means: 'My true wish can neither be fulfilled nor can I let go of it, whatever that wish might be.'"

"And if I have an idea of the wish: when it is reachable it loses its magic."

"Because it never is the true wish—the repressed wish. No conscious wish fulfills the unconscious need or needs."

"Sometimes I think: the true wish is to exact some revenge, to act on my anger."

"Perhaps like toward Joe [a professor who had gotten involved with female students and whom he avoided in a dream the day before; then there followed a dream scene with ducklings]—Joe who goes with the young chicks, that hated rival. You affront him by going to the other room."

"I felt such distaste that I couldn't be near him. But that meant I had to avoid the others as well whom I wanted to be with. His presence contaminated it [the meeting]."

"How do you interpret this?"

"A good question. Good and evil at the table. By exacting revenge on him, it backfires; I see myself as evil. I bend over backward not to be seen as evil."

"And who is the hated rival?"

"It could be my father, with mother."

"And good and evil may refer to both feelings toward your father: you go out of your way from the bad feelings, but they contaminate the good ones."

"That is very likely. He has his good side, and his repulsive side."

"And you wished to have [your] mother for yourself."

"And I saw it as his fault that my mother was so capricious. If I had her for myself I could satisfy her, and she would not behave that way. That the evil in him brings out the evil in her. It is his fault."

"As it is your doing in your fantasy that she is bleeding or mangled. When she suffers, it is his or your fault."

"The guy's fault."

"You mean also *her* father's" (Reuven's grandfather's).

"Exactly! She blames it on him and on her brother: The men are the root of her suffering. Which is perhaps not entirely invalid."

"And thus you protest with your female identification fantasy to her: I'm female, that means: I'm not guilty because I'm not a man!"

"And not evil."

"That is the myth; and it is contradicted by the rage that it is all so un-fair. And both are sexualized."

"To forego gender means to give up all desire. It fits to the toilet fears, the fear of anality. I had to forego also my feces: that is another thing that my mother doesn't like. She doesn't like men, and she doesn't like shit!"

"And they are the same: men = shit; and this equation is mightily rein-forced by your participation in his [father's] toilet activities."

"And his anality altogether. I never did this with my mother. For me it was so that she never did this! It was the mythical idea that only men shit. So I had to be constipated = I was no man; I had to forego my gender" (715).

He dreams that someone had defecated in the middle of the room, and on the table the family portrait is covered with cat feces. His own body in the picture is covered with it, but not his face, which he takes as a good omen. "An image: that my mother shows me her genitals. We have sex. It is a bizarre and disturbing fantasy. At the same time interesting and re-pulsive, horrible. Shit comes from the pussy. I had very early the fantasy that the female genital was the same as the anus."

"Like with the mangling: what was genital was transformed into some-thing anal" (718).

He keeps coming back to the center of his life philosophy: that love and violence are one. And very closely related to this basic equation is the just as fundamental premise: "What can be had cannot be enjoyed." In order to get something one cannot desire it. What one can have cannot be good. Then the image of the beating, furious mother: his mother, Jushu's mother, and of Jushu herself in her irrational outbursts (740).

It is therefore also the basic theme of his life, all-pervasive and deep: "Not to have any wishes and desires. They cause only more trouble. It is the power of suffering: Love is only possible if I torment her and myself. All needs and desires are bound up with the suffering and hence shame-filled." Here too there is a striking similarity to some basic thoughts of Lao Tzu.

But there is also deep embarrassment about her explosions: "In an old dream my mother was wearing a wiglet on the top of her head. It sprang to life and was flying through the air."

"That she flies so easily off the handle."

"That she blows the top" (752). Not only is it shame for her; he has to protect her by taking the blame largely on himself and on his father. It must have seemed too terrifying to contemplate the possibility of an episodic psychotic breakdown in her.

THE RAT: PROJECTED SADISM AND OVERSTIMULATION

In connection with a little sadistic play with a living mouse with which he had put Jushu and the two other female housemates into panic and which died of dread during the game, he keeps coming back to his central concern: All pleasure must be forbidden and punished and leads to underground guilt because of the existence of this deep undercurrent of sadism and that equation of love and torment. The anxiety about the rats that bite him is like the fantasy that the woman gets penetrated, that her genitals are invaded. "Every time that I see an attractive woman of my age I have intense feelings of anger, rage, hatred—"

"—and helplessness, and with that the need to gain sadistic domination" (722).

In the relationship with Jushu he experiences intensively both wish and anxiety about anal sadomasochistic fantasies: that due to his wishes, the woman is being mangled and castrated and how he has to expiate for them. Parallel with it is the wish to give himself sexually, anally, to his father; but with that it is his fearful turn to be mangled and castrated. Both strands unite in the female identification fantasy (725).

He speaks about his concealed resentment and hidden vindictiveness and expatiates about his interest in carnivorous plants: "Why I find them so fascinating: they are so passive-aggressive. They are passive, and yet they kill and destroy by deception and entrapping. I can identify with that very much. . . . I want to entrap the woman and get revenge on her. It is a masochistic vengeance, that angry monster that I keep inside and don't let out. . . . I take revenge by destroying her emotionally, by making her unhappy, by destroying her illusions."

"The reversal of what happened to you."

"Yes. The wish to castrate as I have been castrated. But how can one castrate someone who is already castrated?"

"By shaming."

"Yes."

"Because in truth the woman is not castrated" (729).

He dreams of a huge dog that allegedly is harmless but he knew that the dog would bite him in the genitals. It is a castrating beast, the angry, biting, dangerous monster within, that he is afraid of: how bitingly cruel he can be and has to annihilate everything good (730).

WOMB ENVY

In the following night he watches in a dream a TV scene where a girl gets infected by a housefly and swallows the egg of a tapeworm that starts growing within her and creates a lot of stomach ache. Her mother gives her a pill to cure her. His father, he recalls, used to joke that the orange and watermelon seeds would grow in him if he swallows them. That frightened him very much: "I have something in me that I cannot control—like the growing shit, the angry monster within."

"The baby growing within, the fear of pregnancy. The seed would come in through the mouth, and you wish to destroy the possible rival, and fear the punishment meted out to you."

"The fear of a potential sibling and that I would like to treat him with the same hate with which I had been treated as the younger sibling by my sister" (731).

At the same time, he discovers a pregnancy test at home. Does his mother want to get pregnant even at her age? He recalls, when he was seven to nine years old that the parents were talking about wanting to have another child. The seed growing inside would be like his anal fears: that something was growing within which was not part of him, and that he could not control: "The feces are an alien presence. In the self-induced constipation I tried to close the hole so that no more would come out." He is reminded of the woman's bringing forth blood (733).

In the same context he speaks about Jushu's enjoying her orgasm whereas he is often unable to reach it. What he does not have or loses is experienced as if it were taken away from him. It is as if she were withholding something from him, as if she were robbing him of it. "I see her as hungry, never satisfied, . . . I think of the part within myself: the angry spiteful monster. But I'm also hiding it from myself, by bending over backward in being nice."

In hindsight, I would think that hidden in these preoccupations with the woman's pleasures and, above all, in all the "female identification fantasies," he harbors a very strong womb envy: the wish to be like the woman, with her secret powers, especially now after his sister has given birth. This is born out of his own manifest pregnancy fantasies with the seeds growing within (see Benz, 1984; Barth, 1990; Eschbach, 2004/2007). And what follows may fit to it.

This imagery is promptly followed by dreams about rodents. In a big container full of rice and smaller ones with seeds, there are mice, rats, and hamsters. He is holding a little albino mouse hidden in his vest pocket. It is his friend and at times speaks with him. Then the ride goes over a swamp full of water snakes; he is sitting on the hood of the jeep. If they were to sink in, the snakes would bite and strangle them. He keeps on yelling to the driver that they are at the edge of a precipice. He is looking down into the water at the snakes and is both curious and fearful.

We both are wondering whether the dream does not reflect both his concern and excitement about a possible impregnation of his girlfriend, along the lines of fantasies of early childhood: eating the seeds and birth through the anus. He is yelling at the driver to be careful, but the feelings are a mixture of fascination, curiosity, and dread. The hood would refer to the condom and the conflict about contraception—and all against the background of the devouring-greedy, exclusive-jealous side of him as well as of her (734/5). Today, I would add his own unconscious wishes to bear children.

But the other interpretation of the *rat* refers to his *anal-sadistic conscience*.

In another dream he has to prepare ground meat for a banquet. Then he lives as a farmer in a backward agrarian society. "We, my father and I, sought a well for a plot of land we had leased, but the well keeper did not want to help us. I looked around and saw his old wife, sitting on the toilet, get up and flush. There was much blood in the bowl. I wanted to show it to my father; she might have a dangerous bowel disease. He immediately hushed me, not to say anything. I did not understand why not."

He again thinks of the mangled genitals of the woman and his guilt feeling about them—the wish to damage the woman and the guilt about it. He speaks about "the sphincter-like thing," the control of the flow, the flow of anger: that has to be stopped so that everything would stay "well."

I: "The well keeper is then the sphincter type conscience. It is a very ingenuous way of looking at it and close to the original phobia: that all these dangerous things could fall out."

"With catastrophic consequences—with blood in the water."

"As with mother."

"I think again of the female's genitals and a metal scraper to destroy it in order to save it," like a village in Vietnam. The transference meaning is added at the end of the session: he feels cheated and angry that he has to pay for a missed session, and his fear to express his anger. The "scraping" has more than one meaning here, and so does the rat! (739).

DEMANDED SELF-DENIAL AND SELF-SACRIFICE

He talks about the unreliability of the concept of truth and with that of the grave problems at home with shared perception and cognition. His father is really a nice guy, he says, but he, Reuven, has taken over mother's hatred against him. That hatred that she had felt at the time of her most ferocious rage had become his own: "And the same happens with the other accusations she makes: that her own mother was a cold monster who fed the children to her husband so that she did not have to be sexually involved with him—the picture of a conniving, evil woman. A couple of months later she is said to be a goodhearted Pollyanna whom we ought to love. It almost seems like betrayal: I'm told certain things, I believe them and paint an image, I embrace it, and then I'm told it's all wrong. The image that people paint when they are very angry or depressed—I have the feeling that the image is pretty accurate. Yet then I learn when these feelings are gone that the image is altered to one that is easier to live with, that is a fake. Then we are fooling ourselves with a fake, altered, rose-colored picture. That fits very well to my anal worldview: that all is shit, contaminated, bad, and that it has to be withheld. Yet eventually it has to come out. . . . My mother was very angry at my father, at all men, and to what extent she took that out on me!" Something similar is occurring in his relationship with Jushu.

I comment: "When the hidden hatred breaks through it seems all-consuming and total."

He describes how cruel Jushu's mother is, how she has to spoil every joy and pleasure not only for Jushu, but also for Jushu's sister and her husband and child: "She is very castrating." Both families, in spite of their radically different origins, have much in common: the alliance of the women against the men, their envy about pleasure and possession, more: their general enmity against pleasure and their need to spoil all joy. "My sister sees me as the instrument to take away all her pleasure. Before I had been born her relationship to my father was deep and strong. When I was born that love got decimated. For her it was all gone."

"And we know how she then took revenge on you by inculcating in you that children are killed and eaten by parents—and how she always baited you and then pushed you away. Now you take revenge on yourself for all pleasure and joy, in a deep identification with her."

"And the fantasy that the parents would kill me means my wish to bring the ultimate sacrifice for my sister. It is wish and fear."

"And that you then would finally be accepted by her."

"Only by making the supreme sacrifice. It is crazy."

"And it is still continued today that you have to work against all pleasure in you."

"Right. In some form of compensation."

"You eliminate your father from your life in order to be entirely with your mother and sister, in a kind of union. But with that, you try to become one with a woman who hates what is male altogether, and thus also the male in you. This makes it necessary that you not only take revenge on your own masculinity, but on your identity and pleasure."

"It is so crazy to want that bond. Nothing can be worth of such self-denial. But I believe there is in that union a very special power, and if I unite with this powerful woman [mother and sister] I could become part of that power. It is as if I sold my soul to the devil if I give up my masculinity to the female." He recalls a real event: "A man was in our car trying to steal the car radio.

When we came to the car he pulled out a knife. My mother stepped in-between and said to leave her husband alone and to get out. She took the chance from my father to be a man. The robber ran away" (754).

He dreams of riding an elevator, up and down. It is going always faster than he could think, and he is unable to stop it at the level he would like. He thinks he is also losing himself in his relationship with his girlfriend. He would have to relinquish his identity and merge with something greater and better, but that he polarizes everything: "Either I keep my identity, but am isolated and lonely, or I have the relationship and I lose myself. It was the same thing with defecating: I hold it all in, or every-thing comes out."

Acting and thinking do not agree: "In the dream I think too slowly and act too fast. In reality it is exactly the reverse. It refers to mother's and sis-ter's impulsive behavior." He wishes to join them instead of being so compulsive like his father. The wish to merge with the woman and to be-come her in the "female identification fantasy" means two things: the loss of his self and the anal intercourse with the man—the up and down in the elevator shaft: "The fantasy scheme 'backfires': the wish to be close to the woman and getting her approval means to become like her and then to become the victim of the man, of the penis" (755).

An image intrudes: that Jushu's sharp little knife is cutting off his penis. In order to be accepted by the women he has to hide his penis, has to be without penis and bleed: "Being without penis means to be good and to have power," I interpret. He adds that he has such a feeling of being par-alyzed—guilt has a paralyzing strength; not only guilt, but conflict alto-gether, especially about fantasized outbursts of rage (757).

THE WEB OF LIES

He dreams that he wants to go bowling with a childhood friend, but first needs to fill out all kinds of forms, to undergo a computer check, and to explain why he had lied to them. The friend with whom all contact had been broken is now, in the dream, bald.

"What are the impediments? What stands in the way? All the answers are so: that I'm not motivated, that I'm lazy and have the secret wish to fail."

"The question is rather: 'What is the conflict that burdens me most at the moment?'"

"That I'm angry and frustrated about myself. To have this anal view of the world makes everything worthless and does not permit any joy and pleasure; it changes all joy into a question of controlling things and per-verts it; it destroys all freedom."

"Perhaps the dream gives us some indication."

"I need to jump through all these hoops in order to get something that should be so easy and simple. I'm ashamed to tell the truth; but by lying I entangle myself in sticky snares, and it becomes difficult to extricate myself: Jushu's lying, always weaving these webs of deceit in her family. . . . That the bond to the woman weakens me as it did to the friend [who had submitted entirely to his girlfriend]. Bowling stands for intercourse. In order to go bowling I have to give up so much. It should be so easy, and yet it is such a hassle."

"That you are, rightly or wrongly, angry at Jushu, and then you turn the rage against yourself and are paralyzed in your work ability" (759).

A new tide of lies by his girlfriend: she does not want her family to learn that she is taking a trip with Reuven to the Grand Canyon—in order to hide her sexual relationship with him. It turns into a bitter fight between the two; she accuses him of exerting pressure on her in order to have sex. In reality, he says, she is far more interested in it than he. But now she claims she does not like sex with him at all, she does not want to have it anymore: "Or rather: She wants it so very much that she has decided to renounce it. She doesn't want to be penetrated. And it makes me feel so sad because it means I'm not a good lover, that she doesn't enjoy it and that I only abuse her. It makes me sad and disturbed. Then she plays out a coworker against me and wants to be with him instead of with me. And suddenly this long sharp knife appears in the bathroom. Jushu claims it does not come from her. Nobody wants to know where it comes from. As if to torment me, to cut off my penis, the anger of the woman who wants to mangle me. She doesn't want to have sex. She said afterward that she had said it in order to hurt me. During intercourse she wants me to put my hands on her neck as if I wanted to choke her or that I bite her. It is uncomfortable for me: in order to give her pleasure I have to inflict pain on her."

"And without it you torment each other emotionally."

"My lot in life is to be unhappy."

"That everything good has to be bought with suffering."

"With a disproportionately high price of suffering. . . . I have the very strong wish to withdraw from both, from pain and pleasure. I would like to cry. Yet when I allow it I lose Jushu. . . . I have the strong wish to withdraw, to hide, to bury myself. It's like a snake or a worm that sticks its head out of the ground and then is overwhelmed by everything; it digs back into the ground where it is dirty and dark. I have to hide my masculinity, my aggressive impulses, my anger."

"And what are they right now?"

"It's hard to put a finger on it: I direct them all against myself. I'm very angry at Jushu and at women for taking something away." (The metaphors in this brief statement are themselves telling).

"What?"

"I don't know. It's hard to distinguish these things. My pleasure? My happiness? It's not that. My soul, my individuality, my identity."

"Yes, it is all that."

"I felt I have traded away my identity, as a sacrifice for her happiness and pleasure, and then she says that it doesn't mean anything to her, she is not glad about it" (760).

"FECAL PENIS" AND LOSS OF SELF

Depression, sadness, misery persist. Another of his habitual dreams: "I had made several pieces of shit. They were all penis-shaped. It was most disturbing that they were all with the glans. They were all my penis, of the same size, but many of them. I found the image of finding my penis in the form of shit curious, but disturbing. I was with Jushu, and we had to go somewhere. She was in a hurry to leave while I kept on wiping my anus, because there were no signs that everything was clean and [that it would be] safe to leave. I was in conflict whether to listen to Jushu or to my ass-hole. Last night she wanted sex, wanted me, but then she didn't want it, was in a foul mood, wanting and not wanting."

"That pleasure immediately turns to pain."

"The wish to sleep in the hope that when I wake up things would change, to hibernate like a bear, to forget it, to awaken renewed and refreshed."

"What about that equation of penis and feces?"

"It makes me think of the [fear of] loss of my inner organs when I defecate. But the penis is external. That I could lose the penis by defecating. But that doesn't make any sense."

"Perhaps so: that you could lose the penis like stool—that you could lose so easily what is a part of you. And that, by magically holding back, you could prevent the loss."

He does not respond directly to the interpretation but talks about identifying with the victim, for example, with a female colleague who had failed in her studies. He is the only one who has been concerned and has actively tried to help her. No one cares about those who fall by the wayside. He quotes the old saying: "Those who can, do, those who cannot, teach." He has even neglected his language studies.

I: "So that even your potency has turned to feces."

After reports about further manipulations between Jushu and her family, he returns to the symbolic equation: *penis = masculinity = identity, self = feces* (an equation that evidently may be thought of in different sequences) and to the equation of depression with loss and devaluation of those equated factors (penis, self, etc.).

"And what about the conflict in the dream?"

"Inside against outside—that the inner problems create problems in my relationship with her."

I dare to give an amplification of the interpretation: "There are two other angles from which to look at the dream [I repeat the dream]: feces = power and anal control by withholding and devaluing, and feces = child, delivery"—again, "the boy's wish to have children" (Jacobson, 1950).

"That I have been born as mother's feces?"

"Or that if you were a woman [in the female identification fantasy] you could shit out a child—or holding it back, as in the pregnancy, on a very archaic level of fantasy."

"Right" (761).

THE ALL-POWERFUL VICTIM

The depression is lifted, he feels positive about most things, except for his studies. There are talks about a possible wedding, the expenditures for it, rings. His sister has offered Jushu her wedding gown. There are "incestuous elements" with this: to marry his sister, a very archaic desire, the sister as mother surrogate, thoughts to move even into the house of the parents and to take it over.

During a visit of his parents he shows his mother the carnivorous plants: "She found them ugly, disgusting, while I find them of striking beauty. They resemble snakes with forked tongues. For her to be pleased, things must be castrated: the plants, the son, the husband."

"The deep enmity against the penis."

"The plants are actually phallic looking."

"And the implication is, that the penis is attacking and devouring."

"A dangerous trap."

"Like her father, her husband, her son, and perhaps her brother; unless they are castrated they are dangerous."

"I think of a song; a fervent plea: if I fell in love, don't hurt me, don't castrate me. That fits very well with everything: Loving somebody means to suffer. It was so with my sister, it was so with my mother."

"And you were thinking of Jushu" (762).

He talks about his passivity in school and compares it with the one toward his mother: "I'm recreating an old thing, the pattern: If I'm totally passive I can sleep besides the woman I love. It is the old feeling: in order to get this closeness and intimacy I have to be helpless and powerless. Although I know that it isn't true I have the strong urge to follow the old pattern."

"And to replace the penis by feces, to become like a woman—what you literally did in the masturbation fantasies."

"And what was so appealing in it: that I was the castrated victim. And so it is today with work: I make myself into the victim—in order to gain something."

He is quite right: he alludes to what has been called "normal masochism," but here we remain with the original dyad where this dominant and devastating, basic passive-masochistic attitude is rooted.

"If you look at your mother, she appears, in spite of all the bluster, as exquisitely passive and a victim—at work, in her need to withdraw and to sleep, allegedly due to her headaches, experiencing herself as the victim of husband, father, and children. And you want not only to be loved by her, but to be her."

"She also never finished any school and immediately withdraws when things are not easy."

"Although she is very gifted and smart, she is ineffectual. And so are you" (this refers only to the current impasse, which he deplored at the beginning of the session).

"Every success goes to naught."

"And it is always somebody else's fault, like the evil grandfather's."

"I follow very well in her footsteps."

"It is also an issue of loyalty: not to follow your father, but her."

"In order to be liked by her, I have to be like her. This was always very important for me, also very consciously so: to be more like her than like my father" (763).

In all these "analyses" of the mother's character, I try to wander along a narrow crest: Precisely because he is, also very consciously, so deeply identified with her and has chosen her in many regards as his ideal, yet very much suffers from his identification with her, it seems to me important to try to understand the reality of his mother's personality.

On the other side, it is just as important not to succumb to the blaming and accusing that is so very much embodied by this mother figure and even today is being demonstrated to him: in the endless quarrels with her husband, in the accusations against her father and many other relatives who all are viewed in one way or another as sexual-sadistic miscreants and monsters. Moreover, this very blaming reconfirms the passive-dependent attitude and life orientation: the one who blames sees himself as the victim of the surroundings, of all the evil people and the cruelty of fate.

Repeatedly, I make him aware of this fine line between revealing reality, specifically in the sense of lifting the defense by denial, and the urge to accuse.

THE WISH TO SHOW HIMSELF AND
THE ANTICIPATION OF BEING SHAMED

In a dream the following night, he demonstrates stunts before his old class. During his performance, water starts sprinkling down from the ceiling and squirting, and everything becomes a mess. Teacher and children get up and leave. It is his fault, and he is left alone. The thinking goes to cleanliness training and to bedwetting: "I had a real problem with it. I was corked up in the anus and free-flowing on the other side, peeing without control."

"Why does the dream come now?"

"The scene of having to perform in school and to make a mess is a current issue with me, success and failure."

"Showing off that fails and leads to shame like the bedwetting."

"And today's midterm can lead to shame."

"Excitement tinged with anxiety—or maybe rather: anxiety tinged with excitement."

"Right." He fears he is a bad influence on Jushu; she too is working less and sleeps more. He is concerned that he has contaminated her. He is silent for a while. I return to the dream: "If we understand it correctly: you want to show off in the competition, in rivalry, but are afraid of failure and shame. So you give up, preemptively and first, what is dear to you: the success in performing. You bring about the shame before it would happen to you."

"And then it is under my control. This is very true."

"This is perhaps also in line with the dream last week: 'I have only feces and no penis.'"

"I degrade my penis first before it would be degraded by an outer force."

"Or taken away by somebody else."

"Flushed down the toilet. [After a long silence.] I think of giving away what is prized most. So it is with my language studies. Or I gave my guitar that I liked so much to Jushu's brother-in-law when he wanted it, in order to gain acceptance, approval."

His thoughts wander back to the exam. I remark that he used anticipation of shame in the dream in order to avoid the humiliation in reality—as a kind of consolation: It always turned out all right in reality anyway.

After a very long silence he responds: "I think again of competition, and not wanting to engage in it, of bike races and all those crashes, the danger in competition."

"That you would come out of competition mutilated, deprived of masculinity, like your father" (764).

A few nights later (769), it actually happens that he wets the bed, the first time after a good many years. The immediate connection in the hours is the topic of how easily sexual excitement turns into overstimulation and then into rage, devaluation, and the necessity to contain it, to shut it off. But deeper down it appears to be that conflict that has been preemptively "resolved" by the dream. Then his thoughts wander to the original traumatic situation: "If my mother doesn't like something she withdraws from it. If I dislike something I get angry and turn it [the anger] against myself, and so I'm back where I was: helpless, paralyzed, shut off, facing my unpredictable mother with her hate face."

THE BASIC MASOCHISTIC EQUATION

He went now with Jushu, despite all their fighting, on an early spring trip to the Grand Canyon. In spite of all her lies, her family found out about it, and they needed therefore a new house of cards for deception: that she had gone to a job interview to Arizona, without Reuven of course. He protested against these schemes, and she reproved him for it until he gave in and joined in the deceit. The web had to be spun because she was so scared she would be rejected by her family if they knew. For him it was very uncomfortable. Her mother believed her, but what bothered him a lot was the ease with which Jushu was lying. He was afraid she would do the same to him, however much she assured him she would never do so. This assurance might itself be an untruth, I say, quoting the German proverb: "*Wer einmal lügt, dem glaubt man nicht, und wenn er auch die Wahrheit spricht* (Who lies once is not believed even if he speaks the truth). Lying works like a poison."

He completely agrees. Yet, if she revealed the truth at home, the consequences would be so much more terrible than if she hid it. She was feeling helpless, he said, like the subject in a totalitarian system, which her family basically was. She also dreaded that he would leave her once she had a child. It was casting a pall over their sexual life. He was looking again at other women and felt attracted by them. Didn't that mean again in this sexual area as in everything else: "What can be had is devalued; and what cannot be had is desired and idealized?" he asked.

I replied: "It can be reduced to the equation: Only what is painful can be pleasurable, and in turn, what is pleasurable has to be bad. It is the basic equation of masochism" (765).

BACK TO THE RAT: OVERSTIMULATION

In a dream he is amusing himself playing "ski ball" with a friend; he is accumulating many coupons but is only getting a lot of cheap junk. He knocks over a gumball machine and tries to rebalance it. He keeps losing in the competitive game and is treated as a scapegoat. Yesterday he saw how a mother was screaming at a little child and beating it. It was reminding him of the rages of his mother, "the image of the explosive mother of my past."

I: "Terror in you and helplessness and counterrage, but also in-between the seductiveness, even sensuality."

He is thinking of how she prepared his lunch for school: "The pleasant side of my mother, the nurturer, but the castrator also, cutting the cucumbers, almost tit for tat; the two sides had to go together: to have security and nurturing I had to give up my masculinity."

"The self-assertion."

"The self—[in order] to be part of this higher power."

"And what role, do you think, might the symbol of the *rat* have played that was so important in your early childhood?"

"As castrator. It takes something away."

"And it devours."

"It bites."

I summarize: "Not only the penis, but the feces, the body content. The mother as devouring, not only castrating, and the self as bursting because it cannot stand the tension anymore, as being devoured by it. Both are being symbolized by the rat" (773). *Traumatic overstimulation* is symbolized by animals like rats and lions, by mythical figures like dragons and especially vampires, and by elements like fire or floods (Shengold, 1989; Hirsch, 2005).

In a dream, he is playing chess with me, is only "reactive" and loses most of his pieces; he knows he will lose and there will soon be checkmate, at best stalemate. Yet he keeps the queen hidden besides the king; she has to protect him. As in his family, she is the most powerful figure and the father a mere figurehead. He tries to create another queen out of a pawn: "This is my female identification fantasy; this little powerless pawn becomes the powerful queen. To be small, weak, but enduring, enables one to get the feminine power. . . . I think the analysis is a chess game that is hard to figure out. In the dream I have concerns: you are the enemy."

"And that you have to protect the queen against my attacks, that I am the enemy of your mother, and that this threatens your loyalty and bond to her."

"I talk about the dual role of the queen: she is the all-powerful protectress and she has to be protected herself." He thinks of Jushu and his mother. I point to the opposite feelings toward the "queen": "You want to be close to her, intimate, but you are afraid of being devoured by her, to be helpless, and you defend yourself with hatred and anger against her but that is dangerous too. And what is my role in this conflict?"

"The split loyalties?"

"I wonder whether the dream is not directly linked to my last comment yesterday?"

"About the rat: it hides in the toilet bowl, waits and attacks when the enemy is vulnerable. My strategy is similar: the queen is hidden and attacks only when he [the king] is threatened."

"When the king sits on the throne then the hidden rat comes, the queen, the most powerful figure. . . . I wonder if the dream may not have yet more to do with me and the analysis: the prolonged stalemate and the fear of losses?"

"I wish to reach the bottom without having to pay the emotional price" (774).

He is very unhappy about how he is doing in his courses. He is taking care of cooking; that is far more productive than the exams, "hiding in domestic surroundings so as not to face the outside world," being more in the woman's role. He also shares Jushu's profound chagrin about not having found the right place for them to rent. She yearns for a safe and permanent place. Then a dream: "Demonstration of an airbag device in a car. Somebody is driving recklessly and gets into a horrible crash. But the driver gets out of the wreck unharmed." Perhaps it refers to the analysis meaning both protection and air. I ask: "Hot air?" He talks more about double disappointment: house and study and that he is inviting a "crash" by his goofing off. "Pleasure and crash go together: the one has to follow the other. In order to avoid the crash I have to avoid fun."

"That all pleasure means at the same time pain."

"Right. That every pleasure has some kind of punishment tied to it."

"Or in the words of the last hour: that the good mother is also the devouring mother—or also: I don't want to compete; I castrate myself."

"When I was very young, my sister and I played with [my] mother's knitting needles. I was pretending to look with it into her ear and poked it too far in. It hurt her a lot, and I was very upset that I had done something very bad. I was penetrating her."

"And if we put the penis instead of the needle: How dangerous it is to be a man and to use the penis to penetrate the woman!"

"Right! It's followed by crash and punishment, and I still feel the guilt about that stupid incident with the needle! It is also interesting that this phallic, piercing thing was [my] mother's knitting needle. It means that she had the power, that she was the possessor."

"That she is a very phallic woman, and that the father is an airbag, castrated."

"And her angry piercing lets the balloon burst."

"Something similar to the work that happens here."

"I don't understand."

"The difficulty of carrying it through, of having results, of performing."

"I'm wondering whether there are also concerns about a crash here, when I perform here. In the dream the car was red—danger and blood."

"Aggression, murder, but also sexual excitement and overstimulation."

"And the name of the vehicle was Ford Probe: very phallic, it intrudes, goes in" (775).

"If I can have something I don't want it, and if I don't have it I do want it. And I'm unable to do it when the time is right, and when it is not good I want to do it."

"Another way to say it: that pain and pleasure are so intermingled that they are equated. And in yet another way: sex = violence = suffering."

"Perhaps what I was dreaming last night also belongs to it: I was wearing women's clothes. It was unclear whether I was a man or transformed into a woman. I was confused about my gender, confused about who I was and who I seemed to be. In the next dream I was with Jushu in the bathroom. I wanted to take the wet clothes out of the washing machine and put them into the dryer, but now this was changed also into a washer, so that we had two. The drainage hose was not attached and was squirting and made a mess. I put it in the toilet. It was strange: Why did we have two washers and no dryer? . . . Later in the dream Jushu had a vacuum cleaner, cleaning up, and she sucked everything up with it, was devouring everything."

"The biting, devouring vagina, and the squirting penis has to be removed."

"Everything that makes a mess, cleaning up all the dirty, bad things."

"And as we heard earlier: penis = feces."

"And the hose was black. Last night Jushu told me she wanted to have legs like mine: that hers are short and stubby and mine are long and thin. My sister was also jealous of my legs. It leads to the gender identity problem in the dream."

"The fear of the envious woman."

"Who wants something from me."

"And who ultimately becomes murderously devouring and biting, like the rat, the parents who are perceived as murderous—it is not only how your sister and mother *were*, but partly what you put in them."

"My interest in carnivorous plants is an acting out of the murderous devouring."

"As part of you—and the vegetarianism as a very strong counterposition: This is the last thing I would want to do!"

"A *disidentification*: that part of me wants to play their game, do to them what they have done to me," that is, very importantly turning passive to active.

"How do you link this up: the fear of the devouring woman with the equation of sex with violence and suffering and with what you have said: If I can have something I don't want it?"

He ponders: "Perhaps that the devourer is a pleasure taker and robs the other of his life."

I: "All love and closeness and pleasure are so bound up with someone who is extremely overstimulating, sexually as well as by violence, and inflicts pain, that everything assumes this devouring intensity."

He repeats his basic thesis: "'If I can have something I don't want it, and if I don't have it I do want it.' What could be had was only to be had with this devouring intensity. If it is there, the intensity is there, and it is not wanted."

"Or at least it is feared. You always shun it, and yet seek it. It is symbolized by the rat and the vacuum cleaner, or by the image of the devouring woman in general. This is a central connection for your whole life history. And when we look at your mother, she still appears to be so: *very overstimulating and very rejecting*, at the same time. And her accusation against her own father that he had abused the children in the family seems to me a projection of how seductive and at the same time rejecting she herself was."

"Right. [Silence.] I'm thinking of the carnivorous plants; they too are seductive, enticing and devouring creatures"

"And perhaps the silence itself is a protection against the overstimulating and devouring quality of what you experience,"—also meant of course as transference of defense.

"A way to turn off the stimulation" (777).

"WITHOUT THE VICTIM THE VICTIMIZER IS NOTHING"

He speaks of his fear of being bossed around and lorded over, castrated and devoured by the woman, now by Jushu, as it was with his mother and the father could offer no protection. He flees from it into homosexuality (in a dream), into work, to other friends (781).

In regard to career and profession, he feels helpless, buffeted about, dependent—and yet fears becoming active, independent, successful, and separate. "Being successful means it happens at the cost of the victim's failure."

"That everything is competitive."

"A balance sheet."

"A zero sum game. How very true it is for your family, at least as depicted: one as the victim, the other as the torturer."

"I subscribe to the belief: that the victim is the one who has the power." And stating, without noticing it, what Aristotle and Hegel had forged into a philosophical thesis: "Without the victim the victimizer is nothing" (784).

In what has just been quoted, we recognize the highly complex and derivative nature of what Freud designated as "feminine masochism" and what Reuven called "the female identification fantasy"—the manifold archaic equations and defensive processes that eventually result in that phenomenon.

THE "AGGRESSION BONE" AND ITS TRANSFORMATION INTO FECES

He permits himself to experience pleasure only as long as he excites his girlfriend during sex play and gives her pleasure while feeling himself to be the victim by subordinating his own gratification to hers. As soon as he is about to penetrate her and thinks that he inflicts pain on her by seeking his own satisfaction, he loses the erection—punished by his conscience. Active penetration is perceived as a cruel act and hence as very dangerous; it must be prevented. Activity, aggressive competition, and sadism are equated and anxiously prevented. He refers to the penis as the "aggression bone." Just as his penis becomes flaccid, his decisiveness and persistence slackens, for example, in his studies. The same is the case, he says, in his analysis when he is sinking into passivity and silence. He speaks of the wish as a three-to-five-year-old to be diapered by his sister, now by me, a "kind of proto-fetish": to be the baby and cared for, yet helpless, controlled by the woman—at all cost avoiding to compete or to appear aggressive, but being her victim, her slave, her helpless infant. He had tried to clean the bathtub with his behind to please his mother and to prove to her that this body part was not dirty and disgusting, but pure and good (785).

There is another severe blow-up of Jushu—as if she wanted to provoke him into abusing or abandoning her. The song occurs to him: "I don't want any part of this crazy love, I don't want no part at all." He is wondering how far his own conflicts about women contribute to it, his own hidden rage, his hatred, however much he tries to bend over backward—in his masochistic submissiveness, just as with his sister and mother while Jushu seeks her own redemption by her actively caused suffering (797).

After the operation on a small lipoma on his breast he talks of his un-easiness about the explosive atmosphere at home: "It's like a house of cards that will topple at any moment, like living on an earthquake fault, not knowing when and what, but something is going to happen"—as there was certainty in his childhood that they would kill him, it was only unsure when and how it would happen. "So much of my attraction to women is founded in anger, rage, and hatred that I ask myself: If I put that aside, will then also the attraction and the excitement vanish? Pain equals pleasure; violence equals sexuality. If I get rid of one, I'd lose the other." The dilemma is therefore this: In order to have a close relationship it is necessary to put anger and hate aside; but with that he would lose the woman because the relationship is so strongly based on sadomasochism.

"I saw the lump yesterday and associated it with fecal material: some-thing that grows in me, that is not good, and needs to be removed, a piece of shit, a contamination within me, and I needed help to get it out, as it was with my constipation. My mother showed Jushu pictures from my childhood, from the time I was three: I held my hands in front of the pe-nis, covering it."

"Protecting it."

"And checking."

"And we have also often heard of the fantasy equation feces = penis, and that both could be severed, cut off. The operation yesterday would then be equated with castration."

He deepens now the interpretation himself: "And with the same am-bivalence: the wish to get rid of it and to retain it—to keep it and to lose it. This is true for the shit as well as for the penis. Keeping the feces = keeping the penis; and defecation = castration. To lose the inner organs would then be transferred from the anxiety to lose the outer organs?"

I add: "And thirdly in the equation: *the self = penis = body content and feces.* A great threat was being felt against all three. The last in these three parts you could hold back. You came upon an ingenuous shift: since you could not protect your self and were constantly afraid you would lose your penis whenever you were close to women, you asserted your power and control where you could: with your feces."

"And my vegetarianism is not only a bending over backward against aggression, but eating meat means castrating, devouring somebody else's flesh—"

"—mutilating."

"I not only don't want to be a killer, but also not to be a mutilator."

"And also, essentially, the one who wants to respect the self of the other, to have regard for his feelings, even for the animal in its anxiety, as you wished to be protected in your self. Like Peer Gynt: the leading wish to be himself and the great fear of losing himself."

"As it stands in the Bible: Who clings to life loses it; who gives it to Christ will keep it forever. It is the irony I felt yesterday in the library: I wanted to buy a book on carnivorous plants which is out of print, in the hope that it never is loaned out and therefore would be sold. Sometimes they sell the books if there is no interest in them or they are in bad shape. I thought I'm my own enemy if I borrow the book: in order to have it I have to lose it, or: if the books are in a bad state, in order to have it I have to destroy it."

"Again, as you said: "Pain is pleasure; cruelty is sexuality. If I get rid of one, I lose the other" (801).

In a dream his superior at work in the state administration has died. Everybody seems to be happy about it and celebrates his demise while his corpse is not yet cold. "I felt very sad, sensing the loss. I'm not sure why I would mourn him because there is not much trust between him and me." In a second dream, Reuven is endlessly held back by a coworker while his girlfriend waits for him on the street. The colleague is obese, friendly, smart, and boring like Reuven's father and taxes his patience until he, Reuven, gets enraged and leaves. So are the opposite feelings toward his father and the analysis torn apart, separated out in two different dreams, compartmentalized: fondness and death wish, friendly affability and exasperating circumstantiality, patience and rage. This doubleness is repeated with Jushu: the colleague embodies also part of himself that torments his girlfriend while he himself suffers from it (803). Implicit are the references to me; looking back over it I wonder why I did not deepen the passing reference to it, the resistance against picking it up, a resistance by *distancing*.

He speaks of his "pleasure in saying anal, obscene words and telling scatological jokes to shock others," especially his girlfriend with it: "Striking out, disturbing people—it is a weapon." That goes very far back, "enjoying my power to make my parents angry." His aunt has told him how he, at age five, would run ferociously through the house yelling: "Fucker, fucker, fucker!" He is reminded how in kindergarten he made with crayons multicolored swirls, "designs," to little applause from his teacher. "The colors mixed together were pent up anger."

I add: "And the anal power, the power of dirt."

"The drawings were scatological, dirty, messy contamination."

"Instead of smearing of feces." He responds by his long silence.

I: "Silence is withholding, meaning: 'Don't smear!'"

He: "'Don't make a mess!' During toilet training I was afraid to sit on the toilet. I squatted over it, in the fear that something would be injured or get lost if I sat down. In the fantasy it was as if the rats were sitting under the rim and would bite just from there. When I was squatting they would not show themselves in the light of day and I would be protected.

My behind would be invading their territory, and then I would be vulnerable to their attack. Later this fear of being bitten by the rats was replaced by that of other invaders, for example, that I would be stuck by cactus spines in school."

"And that original image of fear stood for other invaders."

"It bothered me last night during intercourse that it was painful for Jushu. I was acting as this penetrator causing pain, that I have become what I have feared so very much: an invader and causer of pain" (804).

He equates the constipation of early childhood, the withholding, with the anxiety about being bitten, as expression of his fear of being intruded upon and penetrated. As in many dreams, here too are the opposite feelings or wishes toward the same object simultaneously present, but in *split and displaced* form (in a dream, e.g., in the death wish toward one cousin and assurances of affection toward his brother). The fantasy of his female identification is the pleasurable version of penetration, its wished side; the rat phobia on the toilet is its feared version. In the masturbation fantasy it is just the image of being penetrated and mistreated that is necessary for him to feel sexual pleasure. Thus, all important emotional experiences are deeply contradictory and split. The rent between pleasure and suffering goes, as it were, across his whole inner life. Every conflict appears to be resolved by this disjunction of what is antithetical, the avoidance of touching by the defense of isolation; actually, in this way it is perpetuated and in fact made insoluble.

THE "ROCKING SWAMP"

The cultural conflict with his girlfriend, the grand *Confucian antithesis of truth against loyalty*, troubles him profoundly. In her family, tax fraud, lying, deceit are rampant. For them it is a sign of shame and silliness to be honest about taxes. His own warnings, his Cassandra attitude, as he calls them, excite indignation. At the same time it is expected of him that, in the case of disaster, he would intervene as rescuer. For Jushu, loyalty toward her family is even today more important than truth. I mention the story of the Duke of She, in the *Lun Yü* of Confucius (1966), about the sheep-stealing father and Kung Tzu's praise of the son who puts piety toward the father over revealing the latter's theft of the sheep (13.18) (806).[1]

We talk about the atmosphere of mendacity and deception in his own family as in Jushu's, and I mention Ibsen's metaphor of "en gyngende myr" (a rocking swamp; in *The Pillars of Society*, 1989/1966, p. 37).

His own mother appears to disintegrate more and more. He asks himself: "What is real and what is not? My own background is thus based on role playing, on deception and acting. One moment my mother is yelling at my father and claims in all seriousness he wants to kill her; the next moment she is friendly and enthusiastic and fun and sweet with Jushu's nephew—Dr. Jekyll and Mr. Hyde. She has always been the purveyor of misinformation."

He talks about the multiple distortions when she used his minor surgical intervention as occasion to cancel a big family visit from far away. I remark on the capricious ways she is described as dealing with reality: "as an expert destroyer of reality" (808).

THE POWER OF SECRECY

He derides his own jealousy about Jushu's warm interest in Chopin, in his life and personality: "It is silly, but I find the music annoying."

"That you would be the excluded third."

"This reminds me of how often I feel this: in Jushu's family, in the alliance between my sister and my mother, socially in school. I feel excluded, pushed around, victimized."

"It runs like a red thread through your life. May not your interest in languages be linked: not to be excluded anymore?" [by understanding what others say].

"And the wish to exclude, to dissociate myself from what is here [the immediate surroundings] and to join what is strange, far away."

"Turning passive into active: 'I know your secrets, but you don't know mine!'"

"Knowledge is power. I was the excluded observer; I knew the people so well and nobody knew me. That I had secret power—as when I was feigning to sleep in order to listen better."

"You changed from being the excluded observer to being the one who had the secret power of knowing. In this way you excluded the others from your knowledge, by knowing more than they did, and they didn't even know that you knew" (813).

He dreams of skiing down a slippery slope, going at great speed into a huge pool, deep under water, and reemerging at the other side of the lake, flying through the air and grabbing branches, bouncing around; at the end the tree changes into drapery of his mother's room. He is dangling and swinging back and forth and falls down on the table, ripping the curtains and breaking the saltshaker. "It is ironic how I'm proud that I have saved myself, but at the same time I raise mother's ire. They are different layers of reality: I'm a good boy for having saved myself, but superficially for my mother it is something bad because I have broken her things."

"By saving yourself you break her."

"And she can only see the bad, the breaking."

"A deep truth. When you preserve your identity you shatter hers."

"And to preserve hers I have to shatter mine." Something similar is occurring right now with his girlfriend. "I'm walking like on eggshells to appease and soothe her, not to set her off, like mother. It's an icy slippery slope."

"And why the drapery?"

"The drapery is there so that the light doesn't come in. If I tear it I reveal it to the light: I expose my mother, her craziness, that her world is twisted."

"And the saltshaker?"

"It's phallic looking, a cone."

"That you feel guilty for having mangled mother's genitals?"

And swinging back and forth? It refers to his conflicts about marrying Jushu, his feelings about her family and their secret criminal past, all the lying, that "icy-slippery slope," the "gyngende myr" (815).

He talks about his worries that the "tax games" Jushu had, out of loyalty to her family, gotten involved in might drag him also down or at least would darken and devastate their shared future. Then an inner image: "A creepy bug, a centipede, similar to a female genital. I don't know why it comes to mind—that it is responsible for the mangling and can do it also to me, crawl in my groin and devour it and make my pubic area look like the bug—that it is similar and that it causes it: it replicates itself like a virus—and that it does this out of anger. It leaves its signature of destruction behind. I think of how women are frightened by creeping, crawling insects and snakes. They are phallic."

"And devouring."

"Jushu's mother is deadly afraid of mice. I would like to put it to good use, to throw it at her and have power" (817).

He thinks of engaging a band for their wedding with the telling name "Cloaca": "It's my urge to defile things; everything needs to be contaminated."

"To advertise your anal tradition."

"Their logo is a sphincter with a string of brown pearls."

"You recognize the aggression against the people around you: spitting shit."

"Exactly."

"Even the chaotic noise is anal, as defiance against these tight assed parents, on both sides, and against the corresponding part of yourself."

"That I have let my hair grow now for two years and didn't cut it is also defiance. To cut it would be a betrayal of myself. I spit shit at the conventions, against the tight asses . . . I'm angry against people who are blindly conventional. I get a perverse pleasure out of shocking them. That's why as a child I enjoyed the swearwords so much. That was power over them, verbal anality."

"Shitting through the mouth" (818).

He thinks of the obligatory white gloves at the now imminent wedding: "Isn't this a cover up—a pure lie over the dirty truth": all that rage and anger, the whole anality, the sadomasochism, all the lies and the violence in both families (833)? Here too the motto remains: "Who wins shall lose," reminiscent of Brand's double-meaning proclamation of masochistic triumph: " . . . that the greatest victory is defeat—*at største seir er nederlag*" (in Ibsen's verse drama *Brand*, 1866/1991, p. 77).

SUMMING UP—THE FEAR OF ENVY

Shortly before his wedding, he tries to summarize what, after almost six years, the analysis has brought him; it also is half a year before the termination of his studies in mathematical science that leave him quite dissatisfied. It is a time too where his parents let him know that he could not count on their further support for analysis.

There has been great progress in two regards, less so in a third, he says. In regard to the symptoms, particularly the compulsive actions and obsessive ideas, the depression, estrangement, and anhedonia, the improvement is dramatic. These symptoms have resolved themselves fully. In regard to the difficulties in human relations and in sexuality, even in his sexual fantasies, the masochistic-fetishistic perversion and the expressions of outer masochism (in contrast to inner, that is, "moral masochism") have largely abated, although this cannot be asserted with full assurance in regard to his tie to Jushu.

Only the third area, that of long-term career planning and of a certain passivity and dependency in his entire life orientation, particularly in living with Jushu (and later on in his marriage to her), is in need of bigger change: He has from his father the anality and from mother the passivity, the tendency to fail (835).

Success would mean separation and hence something prohibited (840). There is accustomed safety in avoiding rivalry and competition (846). Defeat would not only be his, but mine as well (847). Is it his revenge on me to prove to me my helplessness, in a reversal of roles—*in loco parentis*— and would not he hence also get around envying me since I am now bereft of power? (849) Yet *de facto*, he is, due to his indecisiveness, also largely financially dependent on his wife, is her "omnipotent baby" (852) and thus indirectly avenges himself on a woman, "the woman," by means of "anal stubbornness and defiance," although these words are too condemning (867).

What is probably at issue here is the *primacy of the inner or moral masochism* (that is, the character perversion) *over the manifest sexual perversion*. It reaches very far back into his early childhood, to the preoedipal relationship to his mother. Here too severe traumatization plays a decisive role, in his case, his mother's very frequent, terrible outbursts of rage and death threats, his father's weakness and the presumption that these explosions were his father's, and later his own fault.

Thus he feels forever tied to his mother, compelled to imitate her, as he says later on, shortly before the analysis has to be broken off after 6½ years and replaced by once-a-week psychotherapy. It is not merely out of loyalty but most of all for this reason: "to avoid her envy, because she is very envious." Therefore he finds it impossible to be successful, nor does he permit himself pleasure and gratification: his mother could envy him for it and react with her murderous rage to it (892): It is the envy of the all-powerful goddess: "that she is the omnipotent goddess. If we weak men only did what she wants! If she were right after all by wanting me to study medicine, she would be gloating about it." It makes it hard for him to take up the study of medicine although this attracts him most because of its fulfillment at the end: "I have a hard time getting enthused about anything" (875).

Later he has to prevent in a similar fashion the ever-vigilant jealousy of his sister, the second of his "goddesses." The phobic and obsessive-compulsive symptoms are ways to deal with those core conflicts and especially the fantasy equations described. In this context, the distinction made by Berliner (1947) is interesting and at least gives one perspective on the material presented: "Masochism develops from oral erotism and is the libidinal reaction to another person's sadism. Compulsion neurosis stems from anal erotism and from the subject's own sadism and the fear of its consequences, although masochistic motivations often assist in this development" (p. 470).

"The basic unconscious idea in the compulsive neurotic is: 'What have I done?' The aim is to avoid anxiety. The basic unconscious idea in the masochist is: 'What has been done to me?' The aim is to gain love. The compulsive neurotic is paying imaginary debts, not knowing what the real debt was . . . ; the masochist is presenting an old unpaid bill for affection" (p. 471).

I do not see them as opposites, but as very frequently conjoined, and I disagree with the derivation of masochism only from orality (see in contrast to Berliner, 1947, Novick and Novick, 1996a). Berliner's two "basic unconscious ideas" are one dynamic whole.

They can all be traced back to the masochistic submission under the cruelly abusive, envious and jealous woman, the mother and sister. This occurs mostly by turning the aggression against the self, by reaction formation and isolation, that is, the characteristic obsessive-compulsive forms of defense. They have to serve especially as affect defense: "Most in childhood was anticipated excitement which then inevitably was disappointed. *All feelings appear to me to be very dangerous"* (875). "Therefore I have to bend over backward to please her, to appease her. And I'm angry that I have to cater to her. I do my sister's bidding, and yet I hide enormous rage, the wish to do the opposite. I bend over backward, I cater to her, in an effort to hide my rage" (894). Jushu tells him that he is a joyless, anal person, but he fears that if he were to let go of this anality he would be free to let out the snarling monster within. He needs to keep it bound in its cage, otherwise it would break out as in his mother; "she could not contain her beast." Holding back the feces was meant to contain those dangerous monsters of the deep (899).

Added to this is the conviction that love and probably also sensual gratification are only possible through suffering and degradation. Danger, mutilation, and torment are sexually experienced (sexualized), and in turn sexual satisfaction in fantasy is linked to his subjugation and self-chastisement, lastly to his symbolic castration, in the "female identification fantasy." In reality, he feels guilty about his own sexual pleasure; for him it is far more important that Jushu could experience lust. Yet she insists that he torment her symbolically, above all that he would seemingly strangle her.

His only power lies likewise in passive submission: "I had to suffer to get my point across." Striving for pleasure is punished; striving for punishment is rewarded. This is the premise of "moral" masochism.

The extreme form of the outer as well as the "moral" masochism lies in the killing fantasy: "Only if they, the parents and the sister, kill me they love me. Only in death I am accepted. The only good Reuven is the dead Reuven. My wish to lie beside mother in bed meant to lie completely motionless, as if I were dead" (839).

Parallel to this, the *masochistic-fetishistic* fantasies and actions serve the same aim: to reconcile the envious goddess and to keep his own boundless rage entirely repressed. But this purpose is also attained by means other than those used in moral masochism: by the *dehumanization of the love object* (here the term "object" is for once justified) and the *splitting or doubling of the self* (see chapter 3, the starting point for the definition of character perversion): becoming, under his own stage management, a "castrated" and receptive woman while remaining at the same time the phallicly active, penetrating man, *being* the woman and *having* the woman (912), and, as we heard, the observed and the observer. Both are now feasible (839): What is essential is this self-duplication; but now, at the end of the sixth year of analysis, this kind of conflict solution has lost its appeal, is not interesting anymore.

As in the other cases, we are struck by the especially great role of envy. This is on the one side, in the form of the anxiety about his own envy, the inability to allow success to anybody else, in the analysis of course especially to me. On the other side, it is the much more powerful fear of the others' envy, especially the mother's and sister's, a dread that poisons every success, blocks all pleasure, forbids masculine self-assertion of any kind.

Out of all the connections, this appears to me dynamically the most important; it is the least accessible, the most repressed and has eluded up to now complete and full working through. I believe also that the superego again is the carrier of this most pernicious condemnation, not so much condemnation *for* his envy than condemnation *by* envy: *morality as expression of envy and resentment,* as we saw in Lagerkvist's *Dvärgen* (and in the case of Vera, see Wurmser, 2000a, chapters 3 and 4). This stance entails a resolute avoidance of all competition.

The manifest sexual perversion appears to be a defensive structure against this "moral" masochism. The character perversion is primarily based on a much broader foundation and proves to be much more resistant against therapy than the sexual perversion.

✳   ✳   ✳

We find the following main equations as unconscious fantasies underlying symptomatology and character pathology in Reuven. These six equations are, moreover, linked with each other as well and follow each other in approximately this sequence:

1) The basic equation of masochism: Only what hurts can give pleasure, and in turn what is pleasurable has to be bad.[2]
2) Love and violence are one, and with this: overstimulation = sexuality = violence (cruelty, vengefulness, envy, and jealousy) = suffering = penetration, and all desired as well as dreaded.
3) Male sexuality = active penetration = a dangerous, sadistic act = the destruction of the interior of mother = all activity = aggressive competition.
4) The rats biting him = being penetrated like a woman = the rat is his anal-sadistic conscience = turning the aggression (of the third equation) against the self, against his own interior. The fantasy of the female identification is the pleasurable version of the penetration, its wish side; the rat phobia on the toilet is its dreaded form.
5) The wish to defecate = all desires and pleasures = all kinds of aggressions = huge danger. In turn, not to defecate = purity, freedom of dirt, of evil = protection against all dangers, especially of rage = generalized defense against the drives.
6) The self, the identity = masculinity (as gender) = penis = body content, feces = pregnancy, child. Loss and devaluation of these members of the equation = depression. Holding back the feces means keeping the penis; defecation is equated with castration.[3]

We realize that the basis for all these archaic-mythical equations is the experience of overstimulation. Yet, this term itself is much too encompassing. I see it, together with Shengold, as an excess of sexual seductiveness and, probably more important: a huge surfeit of outer aggressions: of hostility, brutality, and especially of envy, jealousy, and resentment from without—for Reuven especially from his sister and mother. This *doubleness of sexualization and vehement aggression* leads to the equation of both (love = violence), to storms of extreme, global affects, and all this very early, most likely beginning in preverbal times. They have to lead to intolerable, unsolvable inner conflicts. Consequently, also all of the later conflicts tend to be radicalized, eventuating in those vicious circles and spirals that we very prominently encounter in all patients with severe neuroses.

Critically I may add now, in 2007, that the issue of *blood, bleeding, and menstruation,* in his view of the female and in his own female identification fantasy, and his own *fear of blood* may have been insufficiently observed. Wherever I formulated pain and hurt in the equations given above, we may have to add this element. This was at the time a blind spot in myself, a form of countertransference I have only now become aware of ("symbolic wounds," in the words of Bettelheim, 1954/1962). It is perhaps less the anticipated castration than the wished for and dreaded bleeding if he became a woman. The insufficient attention to this point has obviously not compromised the success of this treatment.

❊ ❊ ❊

It is his insight into the anxiety about the envy of the omnipotent goddess that enables him now to leap over the last hurdle. After concluding his scientific studies with a master's degree he decides to turn to the study of medicine and at once begins with the preparatory courses. He accomplishes this with much élan and success. In addition, he works several evenings a week as volunteer in the emergency room of a hospital. He also continues his work as a consultant to the state and looks for additional moonlighting jobs. It is obvious that the neurotic problems in the third area have been solved.

Certainly there are tensions in the marriage; they have after the end of analysis menacingly increased. Jushu's resentment about the outlook that for years she would have to be the financial mainstay breaks through from time to time in vehement despair and rage. Although he offers her alternatives, like a change in her work or loans, also more night work on his side, she insists that she is the one who is trapped and that he is but a parasite.

❊ ❊ ❊

Reading over the excerpts from Reuven's therapy I am struck how little space is given to the reflection on transference. And yet I remember that I have endeavored throughout to put the emerging fantasies and conflicts into connection with the relationship with me wherever it did not appear artificial and forced. This does not obtain here value and importance in the actual presentation of the most salient passages. In part, this may be due to the patient's great reluctance to utter feelings and fantasies about me, a kind of *archaic fear of touching,* as manifested also in the prominence of defense by isolation and intellectualization, and with that also in the anxiety to risk his extremely fragile identity in the emotional closeness to me. The "pathos of distance" (Nietzsche's very important term—see 1885/1976, p. 197; 1887/1976, pp. 251, 368; and 1888/1964, pp. 158, 244) was a necessity for him, just as intellectualization, used to master the overwhelming affect dangers caused by severe chronic traumatization, had become an indispensable control mechanism. I believe that, largely unconsciously, I was respecting in my countertransference this defensive attitude of his and refrained from questioning this "resistance" and thus from becoming as intrusive as his mother. Centrally, intense attention to transference issues can be experienced as shaming, strongly violating the sense of privacy and intimacy. Whether these considerations are justified or not will be answered differently, depending on the theoretical presuppositions. In this treatment especially what I have described (in Wurmser 2000a, chapter 2) as the often *unavoidable use of psychotherapeutic measures* (beyond the psychoanalytic ones in the proper sense) in the "wider scope analysis" of the severe neuroses (Gray, 1994) is true. Let us not forget that Reuven was a patient who commonly would not have been regarded as analyzable. In this case too, the work on the inner conflicts often took on a subtly pedagogical coloring. This certainly did not happen in the crude sense of an authoritarian oracular communication of knowledge as dogmatic truth, but as guidance to self-observation. That means, it was not so much a superego imposition as an *active support of the self-observing function* of the ego, especially by my drawing his attention again and again to the sequences within the sessions and in series of sessions.

It might also appear that in this way his passivity and dependency would be aided and abetted in the transference. However, the utterly stubborn silence in the earlier phases represented a countervailing danger, which I could only meet by a much more active kind of therapy, and this solely over time. Furthermore, he showed as a clinical result such a dramatic enlargement of autonomy and initiative that the transference danger of this kind can be seen as refuted. With all due skepsis, we might still hold in this regard that "one should not argue against success."

In spite of the ongoing life problems, we both have the feeling that the analytic work has reached its goal, that it has done what it can do. He has begun now to start his journey on his own. At the end of the last analytic session (915) he remarks that he has the impression in his work with patients that his sadomasochistic fantasies are actually assisting him to identify more with the victim and thus to feel more for the suffering other. He is appalled by the insensitivity and coldness with which some nurses and physicians treat the emergency room patients and mentions that repeatedly patients have thanked him for being the only one who has been nice to them.

In the years since, I have heard sporadically from him. He has been progressing very well in his life, has finished his studies, and become a successful physician. His marriage is now going very well, and he says he feels wonderful: pleasure has indeed become acceptable!

A concluding word:The fear of the envy of the other is one of the great motive powers in individual and social pathology. It crystallizes in the myth of the Evil Eye (about which more is going to be presented in our monograph *Jealousy and Envy*, Wurmser and Jarass, 2007).

Schiller's verses in *The Ring of Polycrates*, the story of the feared envy of the Gods, express this deep and pervasive human fear, which is rooted in traumatically experienced envy of others, in one's own envy, and in the projected version of a superego that directs now all the envy, jealousy, and resentment against the self:

Mir grauet vor der Götter Neide:
Des Lebens ungemischte Freude
Ward keinem Irdischen zuteil.[4]
(Schiller, 1911, vol. 1, pt. 1, p. 72)

NOTES

1. Cf. my paper on Confucius and Lao Tzu (Wurmser, 1990b, 1991, also in the second and third German editions of *The Mask of Shame*, Wurmser 1993/1997, appendix).

2. Asch (1988): "Eschewing gratification in the real world is a special morality of masochism" (p. 113).

3. Cf. Chasseguet-Smirgel, 1991, p. 407:

Once the anal-sadistic dimension is established it becomes a matter of brandishing a whip rather than of genital penetration, or inflicting pain, that is, of using a fecal penis which sullies and poisons rather than of giving pleasure with a penis which satisfies, nourishes, and repairs; of ruining, humiliating, and castrating rather than of engendering a baby who will grow and develop. At the same time, sexuality becomes a tool of vengeance (Stoller, 1975).

4. "I dread the Gods' envy: life's unmixed joy is given to no mortal."

8

❊

The Core Fantasies—"From Abyss to Abyss"

Going out from the insights gained especially in this fourth major case, we can now take an overview of the major fantasies that play a role in the material just presented as well as in the experiences quite generally with the severe neuroses.

There seems to be a relatively small number of particularly powerful, indeed nearly ubiquitous *core fantasies*, the knowledge and working-through of which is indispensable for the effective psychoanalytic work, precisely in their great specificity.

These fantasies may be "located" on any point and various gradation on the spectrum from preconscious to unconscious, or, to use Joseph and Anne-Marie Sandler's terminology, from the present unconscious to the past unconscious (1994) and with the various layers of defense both against them and built into them. They clearly show what Freud and the Sandlers describe as the censorship between consciousness and the present unconscious (the preconscious). They all show what is often now called relationships between inner objects or introjects (Raguse, 1995).

I describe here several groups of them whose examination I have found particularly useful.

SOME MASOCHISTIC CORE
FANTASIES AND FANTASY EQUATIONS

Power through Suffering and Magical Transformation

Almost emblematic for masochistic object relations is the largely preconscious motto "Power through suffering." The overriding importance of one such core fantasy has been made dramatically evident in several cases and can be seen in all the patients presented. I really owe the clearer understanding of this to the work of Jack and Kerry Kelly Novick (1996a) and their postulate of the "delusion of omnipotence" as a core of masochism.

In the sexual perversion of masochism, it is, however, the fantasy of the *magical transformation* hidden within the masochistic beating fantasy (Freud, 1919a). In the manifest masochistic perversion, the masochistic core fantasy is largely preconscious, though strongly warded off by feelings of shame: through suffering and humiliation, through staged beating, the patient tries to achieve love and respect on many developmental levels: "Only through pain can I preserve attachment, love, and sensuality." We found the same in the basic masochistic equation: "Only what hurts can be pleasurable, and in turn what gives pleasure has to be bad." What remains dynamically unconscious (in the "past unconscious") is its "alchemistic" meaning: the patient thus tries to alter magically, omnipotently, reality and bring about a series of massive denials and reversals, as we saw in the case of Elazar: "By my suffering I transform suffering into pleasure, anxiety into sexual excitement, hatred into love, separation into fusion, helplessness into power and revenge, guilt into forgiveness, shame into triumph, and so forth." All this has deep roots in early childhood and reflects the dynamics of severe early traumatization with its affect regression, protodefensive sexualization, aggressive defense, and traumatogenic shame (see chapters 1 and 2, and the second point below; see also Stein, 2005).

In the masochistic perversion, the suffering is conscious, the aim of the transformation is unconscious. In much severe, self-destructive acting out of a love addictive kind and perhaps of addictions also more generally, the suffering, including the superego aspects of it, are defended against. Only the seeming victory, the successful triumph, the narcissistic entitlement and grandiosity appear in manifest form. The analysis of this underlying masochistic fantasy and the conflicts behind it removes the compulsive acting out (see my parallel work *Flight from Conscience*).

Archaic Traumatogenic Equation

Closely connected with this is another archaic equation: sexuality and sexual exitement = violence, cruelty, explosive bursting = painful, intolerable tension = overwhelming, unbearable feelings. The other formulation just encountered corresponds: love and violence are one. In a slight variant: sexuality = cruel aggression = suffering = penetration, both desired and feared. This state and encompassing experience of overwhelming overstimulation is symbolized in images of consuming and devouring forces (persons, animals, fire, water), of cannibalistic acts, and embodied in the central symbol of the *rat*, as Shengold (1989) convincingly demonstrated. He also described how these oral forces (of gnawing and devouring) are concentrated in the area of the anus and its sphincter and in the body contents (equated with dirt). Other important pictures for this circle of experiences are the vagina dentata and the devouring penis, as well as the generalized fear of being disastrously penetrated and castrated. More generally, it is the fantasy of being consumed by flames, devoured, inundated. Derivative forms of this fantasy consist in the anxiety of being dismembered, dissolved, fragmented. In fantasy, the adult penis is seen "as an organ that can effectively discharge cannibalistic overexcitation and can bite. . . . These patients have frequently fantasies of *penis dentatus* as well as of *vagina dentata*" (Shengold, 1989, p. 107).

There exists a very close connection with the fantasies of the *primal scene*, this prototype of overstimulation.

Many assume that this archaic equation of pleasure and of aggression mostly directed against the self points back to preverbal times and then stamps the entire personality so pervasively and encompassingly that any possibility of change is quite limited. For example, John Gedö writes:

> the sequence of pleasurable stimulation changing to painful tension, rage, aggression directed against his own person, and depressive exhaustion came to characterize the patient's whole being. Whenever a pattern of this kind is built into the basic organization of the personality . . . the most we can hope to accomplish through treatment is to bring about a 'change in function' . . . for the behaviors in question. (1988, p. 144)

My experience allows some less pessimistic conclusions.

A mild version are the universal fantasies of having been sexually seduced and abused (fantasies whose importance of course in no way contradicts the reality character of actual seduction and abuse).

Penetration Fantasies

Closely and obviously linked are the following parallel fantasy equations: activity = active penetration = cruel act = aggressive competition = sadism. And correspondingly: passivity = being penetrated like the woman or as woman = being bitten, eaten = to be tormented, "bitten," by the anal-sadistic superego, poisoned, invaded. "The attachment to the painful aspects of the relationships, the equating of passivity with victimization, and the confusion of activity with aggression are emphases common to masochistic fantasies" (Grossman, 1986, p. 389).

Stand-ins are accordingly again devouring animals for this equation in its active or passive form, either pleasurable or terrifying. A variant of it is the one particularly prominent in bulimia/anorexia: Being penetrated = all forms of receptivity or passivity, particularly also receiving presents = "filling" the vagina = filling the mouth = filling the abdomen = getting pregnant = force endured from the other, from the penis, suffering = sexual excitement.

We observed also the following sequence, both microgenetically and ontogenetically: overstimulation = penetration by stimuli of a violent or sexual nature = diffuse, overwhelming excitement = images of being devoured and eaten. This equation leads to masturbation for discharge → punishment by castration = lack of the penis = defectiveness, feeling cheated.

The Anti-Shame Hero

The invasion of privacy is experienced as extreme shame, to be protected against by self-isolation, by Nietzsche's "pathos of distance" (see 1885/1976, p. 197; 1887/1976, pp. 251, 368; and 1888/1964, pp. 244, 158), a proud attitude of rebuff and impenetrability. Its sexualization is again an important aspect of it. A very important part in this is played by the idealization of untouchability, of being impenetrable and emotionally unmoved; this is revered as strength. The ideal of the anti-shame hero is opposed to the shame-self; the former is incessantly and compulsively sought on the outside. As soon as any weakness appears in this idealized figure, the disappointment is total, the devaluation ferocious, the disdain inherent in shame is now poured over the unfortunate other who has tumbled from the pedestal.

CASTRATION FANTASIES

A further important circle of fantasies is the one woven around castration and lack of penis: penis = self and identity = ability to see = pregnancy/child = being envied. And its frequent antithesis: loss of identity = shell existence = castration = bleeding (menstruation), loss of penis = blindness = confusion = shame, envy, and depression. And correspondingly: lack of penis = punishment by castration = defect = sign of inferiority and generalized deficiency and lack of substance = cause for shame, envy, and resentment. Hidden by this phallic construct is the deep fear, hatred, and envy of the Woman, the Great Mother; this layer is mostly very strongly defended against, and so is the secret wish to be both sexes. We deal here again with deep strata of the "past unconscious."

Connected with this, there is the web of fantasies around the magical revival of the genitals during masturbation, as a symbol of the resurrection of the self or the mother. Fantasies of rebirth are altogether very significant in many other versions; they link up with the following circles of fantasies.

Typically, in all severe forms of neuroses, and especially in character perversion, the underlying dangers and losses are sexualized, the various forms of anxiety and depressive affects are transformed very early into pleasurable excitement. The higher-level defense is specifically directed against this sexual reinterpretation and assumes strongly erotic traits but without becoming directly sexual: idealizing, infatuated, ecstatic. One pervasive form is the predominance of phallic conflicts, of castration anxiety, castration shame, and penis envy. At the place of the traumatically experienced "hole" in the human relation, of lovelessness, of affective coldness and soul-blindness in the environment, we encounter the preoccupation with the anatomical "hole" and the ostensible anatomical defectivity when there is a lack of a penis. The phallocentric orientation and the traumatically experienced difference of gender is a sexualizing defense against deeper affects of anxiety, sadness, and pain originating in the traumatic relationships of early childhood (Hägglund et al., 1976; Bach, 1994).

BLOOD FANTASIES

In this context, special attention needs to be given to fantasies swirling around bleeding and blood. Obviously they are very closely interwoven with issues of menstruation, circumcision, and the wishes of being both sexes. Right now, I would like to point to two versions of blood fantasies: fantasies around self-cutting and the vampire fantasies.

Self-Cutting

First to the fantasies underlying the rituals of self-cutting: The way the patient is ashamed of her weight, she feels shame about the content of her body, which is equated with dirt and has to be cleansed. This presumed dirt is a stand-in for deeper shame contents: her sexual fantasies, particularly their sadomasochistic coloring, her feeling defective, maybe also the fantasy of the hidden penis. Yet, there is not just shame. There is also guilt about every success. So it evolves in fantasy that self-cutting is a blood sacrifice to expiate and mitigate the feelings of guilt and shame, that is, to bring about atonement and purification.

Just as the deity should be moved by the blood sacrifice to forgive and so to redeem the supplicant, the other should accept the self-cutter because now she is, thanks to the blood sacrifice, not so burdened by guilt and shame anymore. With the help of cutting, she seeks a rebirth out of her paralyzing detachment. Cutting is thus a defense against depersonalization. It has the aim to make her alive again. Pain and blood are what is living; they break through the numbness—as magical transformation. The ritual of cutting herself is a self-injury that is magically transformed into rebirth and redemption. By letting the blood flow out she drains out of herself everything that is evil and bad. The venom is then on the outside, but she can be herself. The poison is all that which she feels ashamed and guilty about. Moreover, in the cutting itself she can feel ashamed for something that she *does*, not for what she *is*.

Blood Rituals

The blood rituals are also what creates community. Culturally, they are an essential way of communion, a sharing of flesh and blood. Cutting is the bridge out of the world of estrangement into the world of full presence, out of the world of forgetting her identity and continuity into the world of reestablishing continuity and being herself, out of the masochistic self-loss, of the identification with her mother and the total submission under the demanding-condemning voices of the inner judge into the expiation of guilt and shame by the blood sacrifice and into forgiveness.

Blood thus stands for impurity, just as the conviction that menstruating women are unclean is very widespread or the uncleanliness of the bleeding boy in the initiation rites by circumcision or subincision (Bettelheim, 1954/1962). In turn, blood sacrifice is an ancient form of seeking absolution; blood is used for "purification": "For it is the blood that makes atonement by reason of the life" (Leviticus, 17.11: "ki-haddám hu bannéfesh yekappér").

In the Bible, blood stands symbolically for the soul, for life: "For the life of the flesh is in the blood": (Leviticus, 17.11: "ki-néfesh habbassár baddám hi"), but also, in menstruation and birth, for ritual "uncleanliness" (or such *nidda* as sanctity and protection of the woman), and even for sexuality. Blood cleanses in the form of the sacrifice of atonement, the "sin offering" (*chatát*), or in the symbolic castration by circumcision although the meaning of circumcision has to be seen much more deeply than just against the background of castration anxiety, as Bettelheim (1954/1962) rightly stresses. According to some views quoted by him, "circumcision was originally performed as a sacrifice to a female goddess" (p. 95), as the biblical account also indicates where it is Moses's wife Tzipporah who circumcises him: "You are a bridegroom of blood to me (Exodus, 4.25: "ki chatán-damím ata li"). Bettelheim suggests that the sacrifice of the foreskin might be a gift that would assure a "share in women's great and secret power of procreation, a gift that only women can bestow because only women possess it" (1954/1962, p. 96). It is a rite of wished-for bi-sexuality and an expression of womb envy and recurs in important adolescent fantasies (see below).

Blood thus stands for the dangerous femaleness, for the huge power of the Great Mother. Blood is life and death.

Blood is both sacred and dangerous, pure and impure, life and death. May it be just this union of opposites that makes it also into a concretely presented symbol, on the one hand for sin and shame, and yet on the other for the punishment by the superego and their expiation? In short: blood thus signifies at the same time birth and killing, soul and body, spirituality and sexuality, sin and atonement, and most profoundly the union of cruelty and love, of aggression and sexuality, of pleasure and suffering. It should therefore mystically overcome the deep split of man's existence, his self-alienation, and thus also the exile of God from himself. In this way, the blood sacrifice restores again unity out of self-estrangement and inner division—the mythical-magical surmounting of inner conflict. Like milk, blood becomes in fantasy a powerful symbol for the original unity of being, for the primordial relation between mother and child before there is a split into subject and object, into self and other. It is "preobjectal," the "mother as environment" (Ogden, 1990; quoted by Raguse, 1995, p. 76).

Yet such grand symbolic transcendence of the separation of good and evil keeps changing, as devastating desymbolization, into the horrendous annihilation of the other.

Vampirism

There exists another kind of blood fantasy, which I encountered in a series of patients, female and male, and which faces us also in folk fantasy as presented in fairy tales, sagas, and movies: the frightful and lustful theme of the blood-sucking vampire. One patient used her cotton blanket throughout childhood as a protection against Dracula's assault. She used to wind it as a security blanket around her neck in order to give her time to call her mother for help. Outside of her sleeping room there was a terrace sheltering bats under its roof. She thought they would transform themselves into the threatening person with fangs and collared cape. Her father had once participated in a theater production of the Dracula story, and a big poster for that performance was stored in the closet. That picture evoked such panic in her that she refused to bring her father's hat from the closet. The image had been magically transformed into the thing itself. Her sisters took much fun in posting themselves in the darkness at both entrances to her bedroom and whispering to her: "I am Dracula; and

I come to suck your blood." Or her father would sit in the living room, staring at her without blinking, and would suddenly break the silence with a whispered, "I want to suck your blood." Often she had nightmares with similar content and sought help from her parents. When at her mother's advice she tried to imagine good scenes, these quickly turned into scenes of horror. Thus, even today she uses that blanket as a kind of pillow to shield her neck. The malicious laughter of the vampire reminds her of her father's laughing at the cost of others. "I think of fangs, neck, blood cape, and the evil laugh." She remembers how scared she was to stay with her father alone after dark. "Part of me is afraid that every man could be a Dracula type." The vampire represented simultaneously, in dramatically projected form, the gnawing feelings of jealousy and envy and her "biting" conscience (Gewissensbisse). But there is more to this complex of fantasies, for example, ideas of sadistic attacks by her father and the primal scene: first thrillingly fascinating, then terrifying, and then both together.

I would like to take up some thoughts from Mathias Hirsch's article "About Vampirism" (2005; I follow here Heidrun Jarass's excerpts, Jarass and Wurmser, 2007). In his dealing with the mythological meaning of vampirism, he mentions "incubus": "A ghost that at certain places throws himself upon people . . . that sits on their backs and lets himself be carried by them for a good stretch of way.[1] . . . It is only told that the victim of this Aufhocker remains in a state of great exhaustion as if a vampire had sucked out his life force and that he is only one inch away from death" (p. 128). In the continuation of his essay, Hirsch demonstrates how these myths link up with modern conceptions of psychoanalytic traumatology, according to which the traumatic relationship leads to a "sucking out of vitality," as already remarked by Ferenczi. "In such a scenario, it would be about robbing the life of a child by the adult, that is, the transition of a vital substance of a really needy object to the other who by rights should be the nourishing one" (p. 134). Hirsch gives examples for these interpersonal traumatizations: "depriving the child of the self-critical faculties by constant scolding about small acts of clumsiness, in the assumption that the child itself is unable to recognize that it has made a mistake; robbing the child of playfulness . . . the ability of thinking, affectivity, mental structures, parts of the self, could all become objects of such robbing. Britton calls 'vampire' the destructive container that keeps the child captive in 'the interior of the mother' whom it has to live for" (p. 137). We are reminded of Ferenczi's (1932) statement: [the abused child] "feels enormously confused, innocent and culpable at the same time—and his confidence in the testimony of his own senses is broken" (p. 519).

NARCISSISTIC FANTASIES

There is a broad range of fantasies that can be subsumed under this rather elastic title.

Lifting of Boundaries as Protection against the Superego

I paid special attention to the narcissistic core fantasy: "By blurring the boundaries, by overstepping the limits set, by achieving fusion with others, by excluding the differences between the sexes, I can attain liberation and redemption."

The entire fantasy world of overvaluation, boundary crossing, grandiose entitlements and idealizations is, in my experience, an attempt to find relief from an overweening superego, especially by magically overcoming helplessness in front of the inner and outer judge (obviously one particularly privileged form of "inner object"). Part of this important fantasy of omnipotence is that of the rescue mission: in order not to be helpless anymore, the child (and the child-self in the adult) prefers to ascribe guiltiness for the situation of terror to itself and to seek the life's goal and task in the identity of the Savior.

The main processes of narcissism as described by Kohut (1971, 1972, 1977), the idealization of the other, the grandiosity of the self, can very usefully be seen as defensive structures against aggression at the behest of some overwhelming superego pressure. Omitted from the schema of Kohut is not only the deep intertwining of narcissism with conflict, and with that the question to what extent these narcissistic fantasies specifically protect against conflicts about aggression and superego commands, but also a narcissistic fantasy of great prevalence: that of attaining completeness as a sexual being, the fantasy of the bisexual nature of the self (see below).

Omnipotence of Responsibility

Part of the important fantasy of omnipotence is that of the rescue mission (see above). It is the omnipotence of responsibility and with it the fantasy of perfection; inevitably, they cannot be fulfilled and this nonattainment leads to equally global forms of guilt and shame respectively. The characteristic sequence is: traumatogenic helplessness → omnipotence of responsibility and perfection → inevitable failure → absolute self-condemnation in the form of guilt or shame.

Beyond this sequence, it is especially striking to what extent it is the internalized parental expectations that are the carrier of these grandiose fantasies, carriers also very much of the *envy of the parents*. The issue may be that the parents envy the child or, in turn, that the child is used to fulfill the envious demands and aspirations vis-à-vis the surroundings, particularly the wider family. It is an insoluble contradiction for the child. In order to satisfy the first claim of parental envy, the child has to renounce all success ("wrecked by success"): "the successful child often faces the threat of experiencing some form of unconsciously desired, envious filicide" (Schafer, 1988, p. 86); this is the factor of "the real envy of the child felt by one or another parent" (ibid.). In order to obey the second demand, however, he finds no success big enough. It is less an issue of his own grandiosity than that of the exalted request that he has to fill.

Absoluteness

This omnipotence of responsibility is a special form of the absoluteness of the superego demands and ego ideal. I give a brief excerpt from an analytic dialogue to illustrate what I mean: The patient had been talking about the Either/Or, the black-white nature of her inner expectations and, as consequence, the intensity of self-condemnation.

"On some plane it is essential to my survival: being absolute: something that would be so clear as a standard I can measure things with. It's the only thing that I can trust, even when it is so high and unrealistic and unworkable. It keeps me shoved in the little corner: you are not good enough, you don't measure up. It feels impossible."

"So it is either the splendid ideal or the black hole."

"And my bouncing between the two, hitting the ceiling and crashing down in the hole."

"Why was being so absolute necessary for survival?"

"It helped to give structure to a world that was so unpredictable. . . . The absoluteness gave me the purpose for being."

Another version of such absoluteness is the fantasy of eternal love and eternal bliss, the Garden of Eden: a return to an ideally good mother, a limitless union in ecstasy.

Yet, the answer to the question "Where does such absoluteness come from?" needs to come from a deeper root. I think it comes from the total experience of affect in early childhood. Every severe trauma evokes such absoluteness of affect, and every new conflict or major stress reevokes it. The terror of war, of extermination camp, or of threatened annihilation is absolute—and it reemerges transgenerationally. Therefore the protection against such an absolute threat must have a similarly total character. For example, the protective fantasy may be: "I want to be totally loved and inseparably attached, without any limitation in time or boundary of connectedness and presence. Either there is total love or there is nothing!" Or: "I have to be absolutely good in order to be accepted by the other or by

God. I am not allowed to have any angry or sexual thought or fantasy." I also read in this way Psalm 42.8: "Abyss calls the abyss, to the roar of Your cataracts [*tehóm el tehóm qore leqól tzinnorécha*]. All Your breakers and billows have swept over me" (see Bible, JPS Tanakh, modif.): The abyss of despair calls for the abyss of love and protection and being one—the absoluteness both of trauma and of protective fantasy. Life becomes the extremes of Either-Or.

This fantasy of absoluteness and limitlessness, an illusion indeed of infinity, in threat and wish, in obligation and perfection is a shadow that hangs over much of pathology, both in the individual and in cultures. From all the fantasies I deal with here it seems to me like the "crown jewel," binding together trauma, affect, defense, and superego, and manifesting itself in a thousand variants.

Fantasies of Bisexuality

Fantasies of bisexuality are the largely unconscious fantasies of men who take on the tasks of conception and maternity and of women who do not want to be robbed of the phallus. It is the central importance in the fantasy life of many variants of androgynous figures (Jacobson, 1950; Bettelheim, 1954/1962; Kubie, 1974; Grunberger, 1979; Chasseguet-Smirgel, 1988a, 1988b; Barth, 1990; Eschbach 2004/2007; Janowitz 2005, 2007; see also the study of Otto Weininger by Sengoopta, 2000). For example, Bettelheim sees the function of initiation rites based on "the premise that one sex feels envy in regard to the sexual organs and functions of the other" (1954/1962, p. 19).

Peter Blos Jr. has specifically stressed this for the masochistic character pathology:

> If, for the male, castration anxiety is to be relinquished, the possibility of becoming female and having the female experience must be given up. If, for the female, penis envy is to be given up, the possibility that a real magical phallus exists must be abandoned. Neurotic sadomasochism—a flight by regression from the oedipal resolution—is an illusory way to sustain bisexuality and thereby avoid the intense disillusionment of being limited to one gender. Because bisexuality also implies that one is dependent on no one for sexual pleasures, to complete the oedipal passage requires, among other things, mourning the idealized fantasy of omnipotentiality and bodily completeness, and acknowledging dependence on another for sexual gratification. (Blos, 1991, p. 429)

The narcissistic core fantasy *denies all differences*: between sexes, between generations, between inner and outer, between dream and reality, and between before and afterward, hence the lapse of time altogether

(Grossman, 1996; Bass, 1997; see above, chapter 3); it culminates in Nietzsche's "eternal return of the same."

I already examined the fantasy of phallic monism (as presented by Bass, 1997) in detail in chapter 3. It is another example of the fantasy of eliminating all boundaries and differences, particularly that between the sexes.

Life Is Death, Death Is Life

Another part of this realm of narcissistic fantasies is the idolization of the dead, of death, of the inanimate. With the feeling of soul-blindness at home, there is an atmosphere of dehumanization of relationships in general, and of sexuality in particular. We have seen that perversion is dehumanized sexuality and sexualized dehumanization. In many people, in particular with some intellectuals, we observe a fascination with everything that has to do with death. This fascination with what is dead corresponds to a glorification of the objectification of the human relation by aesthetic and sexual transformation and distancing. Such creation of distance by aestheticization is a defense not only against the fear of death and castration, but also against the entire reality that is experienced as traumatic, in particular if one's own pain and yearning for love is not acknowledged by the other person. Indulging in fantasies of what is inanimate, robot-like, unfelt, engaging in manipulation, the "death realms of the soul" (Benedetti, *Todeslandschaften der Seele*, 1983/1987), the fantasy of the "dead mother" (Green, 1993)—all these are fantasy creations that have enormous defensive quality. The dehumanization proposed by Cooper (1988, 1991) is an extreme variant of this kind of fantasy: "I am dead and the other is dead, an inanimate thing; hence there is no danger anymore." Its extreme is the death cult of jihadism.

FANTASIES OF SHAME, RESENTMENT, AND REPARATION

Fantasies of Excessive Shame and of the Magical Look

Together with the family myth of expectations that are too high, the attempted realization of an envy-laden family fantasy, there has to be, of course, the devaluation of the real self, and with that the familiar world of *shame fantasies*, as in feelings that all looks are directed at oneself, that others see through the self and look with scorn and jeers and contempt at the self, up and till the ideas of reference: "Everybody is whispering about me and knows about my disgrace. I'm not like others, I'm apart, disgusting, stupid." One patient talked, in a masochistic version, of his Ikaros dream: to fly, to tempt the envy of the gods, and to crash.

As counterfantasies of narcissistic power, as an inner anti-shame strategy, we find dreams of magical protection, like robots, rays, powerful animals, or divinities, today also extraterrestrial beings from far-away stars that come to assistance and rescue, similar to the "helpers and servants [helperne og tjenerne]" in Ibsen's Masterbuilder Solness (1989/1966, p. 465).

Yet corresponding to these shame fantasies, there are those of the magical look. By looking, and to some lesser extent, by touching and hearing, we may unite with the other being or we may have the power of penetration and destruction.

Conversely, when we are being looked at, we are invaded, turned into stone, annihilated. In other words, seeing and being seen are turned into grand instruments of sexual and emotional union or into tools of power and death. To use Freud's late metaphor, the mythical forces of Eros and Thanatos turn into the powers of the divine or diabolic eye. A special version of this demonization of looking (and more generally of perceiving) is the widespread myth of the Evil Eye. Myths, however, are widely held fantasies that are given power over entire cultures and societies.

The Evil Eye embodies the sequence of shame → envy → self-condemnation. The Evil Eye is more than just projected envy, as usually described, for example by Freud (1919b), but it crucially encompasses its parallel affect of jealousy, their antecedent of shame and their superego derivatives and sanctions (see more on this in Jealousy and Envy, ed. Wurmser and Jarass, 2007, specifically the articles on the "Evil Eye" and the "Magical Look").

In deep strata of experience we might meet the fantasy that being close to somebody, seeing and touching the other, means to merge with him = to become similar, the same and identical with him. It is one of the basic laws of mythical thinking: closeness = common attributes = identity (Cassirer, 1923b/1958a, 1944/1962; see also Kafka, 1989). But what does this cognitive regression mean dynamically? I quote Ruth Stein (2005, p.789): "Perversion is avoidance of direct—straight, guileless—contact, owing to the fantasy, or the accumulated learning, according to which intimate contact is deadly and threatens with psychic obliteration. Contact may quickly become merger with an arch-fiend, terrifying in its cannibalistic or annihilating intentions" Thus any form of closeness, emotional or physical, becomes psychic death and has to be replaced by mechanical, robotlike rituals.

Resentment

As already encountered in chapter 4 of The Power of the Inner Judge (Wurmser, 2000a) and chapter 5 of this book, another important core fantasy, affect, and basic attitude is that of resentment, ressentiment, usually to a considerable extent not dynamically unconscious, but preconscious ("present unconscious"), yet still facing an intense barrier of censorship. Again, however, it reaches down to very early and deeply repressed roots. It is the feeling of injustice, the conviction of having been unfairly dealt some deficit: "I have been cheated. I have been loyal and expected justice, but I have been dealt with unjustly. I need more than others in order to balance this unfairness. Revenge is the reparation for the suffered lack of love and respect, it is repair for the fault and defect, it is an aide against shame and rage, jealousy and envy." This too may play on all levels of development, not just in regard to phallic or oedipal conflicts. Part of this is: "I have a defect, I am a born loser; because of my defect, I am empty and so demanding that nobody can stand to be with me." It is a fantasy both of shame and of resentment, leading to insidious attempts to rectify, in fantasy and often then also in action, the balance of justice, to redress the grievance by leveling, by deposing the unjust authority within or without. The politics of "revenge" (*revanche, vendetta, jihad*), of fanaticism, of violent protest, are fed by the deep sources of that resentment; of course, it always has at least a kernel of truth.

John Steiner (1993) gives eloquent expression to this topic in what appears to be a lecture of May 1993 with the title "Revenge, Resentment, Remorse and Reparation," the same title as chapter 7 of *Psychic Retreats*, but markedly different from the latter:

> The revenge has to be stifled and denied and as a result it is transformed into resentment. . . . The patient feels trapped in a deadly internal situation where he feels wronged but compensated for his suffering with freedom from guilt and responsibility. It is the object who has done wrong and who should feel remorse and guilt. In analysis development is blocked while the patient waits for the analyst to recognize the error of his ways and to agree that it is he and not the patient who needs to change . . . he lives in hope that in the future right will be done and he will be avenged.

The analyst's neutrality is felt as a betrayal. These are all crucial and enacted fantasies or, on a historical level, highly effective myths.

It has been especially noteworthy in our cases to what extent and how frequently it is the superego that becomes the carrier of this resentment, how much, in other words, the voice of conscience may express a vengeful sense of injustice. Envy and especially resentment vested in the superego mean: No pleasure or success can be granted to the self, just as one envied it in the other. The German (and Yiddish) allows more graphic expression of this idea: "Man kann sich selbst nichts gönnen, da man dem anderen nichts gönnt" (Yiddish: "Ich farginn mir nischt").

FANTASIES OF RIVALRY

Exclusivity

In connection with the intensive, especially oedipal competition, but at least as much in regard to sibling rivalries, we find, as a variant of the narcissistic core fantasy of transgressing the boundaries and tearing down the barriers, another inner construct of great frequency: "Instead of being the excluded and humiliated third, I am now the excluding and victorious first; instead of being painfully the one who does not know I am now in truth the warrant and holder of secrets, the one mysterious and hence powerful. Instead of being the envious little one and ashamed dumb one, I really am now the envied big one who unriddles all the mysteries." Another version of this same reversal from passive to active may put the entire sexual life under an incessantly repeated modus operandi: "Instead of being jealous I do everything in my power to make someone else jealous" (case Vera, in Wurmser, 2000a). Linked with this is the annihilation of the rivals, for example in Arlow's cave fantasy (1969a, 1969b): the destruction of further siblings in mother's body, their revenge, and the resulting claustrophobia.

Fantasies of Primal Scene and Primal Scene Equivalents

The exclusion complex has a lot to do with the repeated, traumatically received and construed primal scene, but it is also important to think of "primal scene equivalents": vehement fights and arguments between the parents that assume a sexual-sadistic connotation. Such experiences are very frequent and an enormously important form of chronic traumatization. More precisely, the observations of the battles on the outside are equated with *sexual-aggressive* overstimulation and overexcitement that occur during the witnessing or fantasizing of parental intercourse that is interpreted as a sadomasochistic scene (certainly one of the most eminent "model scenes," see Lichtenberg et al., 1996). This equation is accompanied by affective storms of jealousy and rage, by feelings of shame about being "the excluded third," but decisively also by sexual wishes, and leads to intensive anxiety and even panic reactions. Crucially, this entire complex of experiences and fantasies is warded off by superego sanctions in the form of massive self-condemnation, mostly as shame, and the sense of having been wronged: resentment. Thus, the primal scene fantasy serves as a crystallization point for manifold conflicts. Rescue and Savior fantasies, sometimes like some Christlike transferences, are important consequences of this core fantasy.

CLAUSTRUM

Then there is the large area of fantasies woven around limits, boundaries, and borders. Perhaps the large-scale appeal of the "borderline concept" may partly be due to this evoked complex of core fantasies. We already encountered another very important fantasy equation: that of the sense of being entrapped by a *claustrum* with all kinds of limitations, of restrictions, and the profound need to break out. *Border*, limit, barrier, enclosure represent an important group of symbols standing for inner authority, the superego. This need to burst out of the claustrum, literally and much more frequently metaphorically (Arlow, 1969a, 1969b), is a flight from conscience that fails. Connected with this is the deeper fantasy of the maternal womb or body as a sheltering cave promising union and bliss—fantasies, not memories (as Grunberger sees them, 1979). The oral meaning of such a claustrum is easily recognizable. But dynamically far more important is the equation of such a "devouring claustrum" with the superego and all its representations and representatives: "claustrum = limits = superego = confining external world."

Other dynamic meanings of the claustrum refer, as mentioned, to murderous fantasies toward the rivals still within the mother's body (and with that to fantasies about oral impregnation). Also the anal closure by the sphincter, especially in the context of intolerable overstimulation and tension, may be symbolized by the claustrum.

FANTASIES OF THE MURDEROUSNESS OF SEPARATION AND OF SELF-EXTINCTION IN CLOSENESS

In connection with the two "basic equations" (Wurmser 2000a, chapter 5) I repeatedly pointed to a dynamically prevalent double fantasy. In the deep ambivalence characteristic of the severe neuroses, separation is equated with hurt, crime, murder, and death: "If I separate I wound or kill the other; in turn, I will have to die for it." The issue of separation guilt—"about not having the right to one's own life"—is, as Modell (1965, 1984) has noted, an important motive in severe pathology. So is its antipode, dependency experienced as fusion, self-dissolution and self-loss, the massivity of dependency shame. Thus we encounter in our case studies, as deep, powerful fantasies, the following two antithetical equations: Separateness, being an individual with one's own will is absolutely evil: Success, self-affirmation = separating oneself = injuring and killing the other = dying = immense guilt. In contrast to it, submitting = passivity = dependency and weakness = loss of control, of identity, of one's self = shame and humiliation. Thus the two antithetical affects of extreme separation guilt and of equally deep dependency shame form one of the basic polarities in the structure of the conscience.

Part of this conflict is also addressed by Shengold:

> The analyst's investigation of the masochistic bond implicitly threatens to modify the tie to the sadistic parent, and faces the soul murder victim with the terrifying intensity of rageful wishes; these are felt capable of effecting a murder that will bring unbearable loss and aloneness. What is usually not conscious is the idealized fantasy that at the next sadomasochistic encounter the parent will this time emerge as the loving nurturer and rescuer who will magically erase the past, remove the murderous hatred, and make everything all right—in short, who will restore the prospect of paradise. (1989, p. 316)

THE FANTASY OF DIRT

Then there is the largely unattended fantasy of dirt, described by Kubie in an important paper (1937). He proposes a "psychological definition of dirt": "It is possible in this way to derive a psychological definition of dirt as being anything which either symbolically or in reality emerges from the body, or which has been sullied by contact with a body aperture" (1937, p. 391). He speaks of the astonishing fantasy (which was dwelled upon so much by Reuven) "that the body itself creates dirt, and is in fact a kind of animated, mobile dirt factory, exuding filth at every aperture, and that all that is necessary to turn something into dirt is that it should even momentarily enter the body through one of these apertures" (ibid.).

Part and consequence of this is the conviction: "Whatever comes out of me is filth. Thus what is within me is evil. If I am not touched I am rejected. I must be totally bad, inside and outside, if I can't even be touched and looked at. I must remain untouchable and invisible." It is one of the important fantasies of shame and underlies much of what often nowadays is described as alexithymia or "splitting."

There exist, as Kubie continues, unconscious hierarchies of filth and dirtiness whereby the reactions to semen and milk show the most striking ambivalence. What is soft, wet, slimy, and hairy is experienced as dirtier than what is solid, dry, and hairless. Old age represents the accumulation of unexcreted remnants of lifelong eating and drinking and is viewed as dirtier than youth. Pigmentation and dark hair are experienced as dirtier than blond hair and fair skin. Prominent body parts are cleaner than concavities and clefts. "The most important consequence of this hierarchy of fantasies is an unconscious, but universal conviction that the woman is dirtier than the man" (p. 396). The genitals themselves are unconsciously experienced as detachable excretory products (p. 403). We encountered this last part of the fantasy in the case of Reuven in the equation: identity = masculinity = penis = body content and feces, and their loss and devaluation = depression. Retaining the feces means keeping the penis; defecation is castration. The fantasy of the "fecal penis," which has been so much emphasized by the French analysts (Oliner, 1988), appears to be a special form of this.

Another version is Melanie Klein's (1932, 1952a, 1952b) fantasy construct that the body is full of destructive and evil contents. If they are permitted to exit the body they contaminate and poison the world and have to be immediately destroyed. Correspondingly, we then found in Reuven the double equation: The wish to defecate = to have and fulfill all desires and pleasures = great danger; and opposite to this: not to defecate = purity, freedom of dirt = of all evil = of all perils, especially also of rage.

Kubie also mentions: Since all excretions are seen as dirty and therefore the excretory zones and apertures should not be touched, the pleasure about these zones is experienced as filthy as well. If one touches oneself and masturbates, one dirties oneself and becomes sick so that "guilt, sickness, dirt, masturbation, contamination, intercourse, pregnancy, and cancer become intimately linked concepts" (1937, pp. 416–17).

I have repeatedly mentioned the "anal-narcissistic defensive attitude," a kind of global *affect blockage*. To this, Shengold quotes Robert Fliess (1956):

> "It is often as though the anal sphincter were charged with the mastery of regressive and archaic affect, intrinsic to whatever phase of development, because it is the strongest [sphincter]; and as though the ego chose anal-erotic elaboration upon instinctual strivings of whatever nature as the most reliable means of preserving its organization." (Shengold, 1989, p. 77)

Shengold adds: "The overuse of the emotional sphincter makes for a kind of anal-sadistic universe with all the contradictions that this entails" (p. 78). He refers to the "special resistance evoked by the cannibalistic vulnerability of the anal zone and especially the anal sphincter" and adds that "the anal and perianal area of erogeneity seems to be the principal intrapsychic site for the overwhelming stimulation (experienced as being eaten into and eaten up) that can lead to ego dissolution" (p. 87).

It is part of such "sphincter morality" that in at least some patients, excretion, both defecation and urination, may symbolically stand for the relief from intolerable superego pressure. It is as if it represented the accomplishment of a severe task and release from a heavy burden, followed by joy, if not some sexual excitement.

THE DOUBLE SELF

Another archaic, very important fantasy is that of the doubling of the self: that an illusion of protectedness and a transcendence of anxiety and particularly of shame could be reached then when the "true self" is split off from its masks, when it could be hidden, abducted, removed to some other, strange place, eventually to reemerge in powerful disguise.[2] This may lead to complicated scenarios in fantasy (Wurmser, 2000b).

Especially, this type of fantasy and much of the doubleness of many patients with identity disorders ("multiple personalities") is an important protective fantasy in the face of overwhelming traumatization: "It is not me who suffers something so horrible. It is my 'alter ego,' my body, my 'shell.' In reality I am somewhere else and am somebody different," as we noticed most eminently in Agnes.

This can be found in almost all strongly masochistic patients: that they show a splitting, a 'doubling' of their sense of reality. On the one side, it is the world as perceived on the outside, consensually validated, confirmed by the ego. On the other side, it is either a reality that is built up in order to deny the traumatization, that is, a reality built upon fantasies woven around denial, or it is a reality shaped and twisted by a totalitarian superego. It is in particular the conflict between the perceptual reality and the superego reality, which leads to an often dramatic cleavage of self and world, with all their consequences.

The dehumanization focused upon by Cooper (1988, 1991) as a core of perversion is indeed an extreme variant of this core fantasy of doubleness; "I'm dead and the other is dead, an inanimate thing; no danger exists anymore."

Another variant has been described for "soul murder":

> Only the mental image of a good parent who will rescue can help the child deal with the terrifying intensity of fear and rage that is the effect of the tormenting experiences. The alternative—to maintain the overwhelming stimulation and bad parental image—means annihilation of identity, of the feeling of the self. So the bad has to be registered as good. This is a mind-splitting or mind-fragmenting operation. To survive, such children must keep in some compartment of their minds the delusion of good parents and the delusive promise that all the terror, pain, and hate will be transformed into love. . . . This compartmentalized "vertical splitting" transcends diagnostic categories. (Shengold, 1989, p. 26–27)

Ellen Handler Spitz notices, in her analysis of Euripides's *Bakchai*, the perverse paradox, "the centrality of double vision to perversion" (1991, p. 219): "that paradox, both emotional and intellectual, can be conceived as the underlying traumatic state out of which perversion crystallizes"

(p. 215). "Under the disguise of the castrated image, he [Pentheus] preserves his intact phallus and masculine persona" (p. 219). "The bifur-
cated, dissociated world of perversion—where one fixed set of images is
hyperidealized at the expense of another set that remains too dangerous
to contemplate" (p. 220).

Yet, at the other end of the spectrum, we find the creative doubleness;
opposed to the painful repetition of the traumatic experiences in memory
and action, there is the mastery by a recognizing, insightful, re-creating
and transforming self-figure—as in Nietzsche's saying about the knowing
ascete's eye, which "sees the human being split into a suffering and an observing [being]";[3] he thus anticipates one of the central insights into the
psychoanalytic process, Sterba's "therapeutic splitting of the ego" into the
experiencing and the observing ego.

THE LOST CHILD

The dynamic relevance of the fantasy of falling, of empty space, with a
profound experience of discontinuity and disconnectedness, which we
very often encounter in the severe neuroses (see above in Regula) has recently been impressively described by Sheldon Bach (2001): "at the center
of Jeffrey's [the described patient's] multiple phobias and anxieties lay a
primary anxiety of being forgotten, a wordless fear of falling in an endless
tumble out of his mother's mind and into the oblivion of nonremem-
brance" (p. 741). As a child, he was well known as a lost child at Macy's
because his mother kept losing him during shopping. Also in the transference he always assumed that the analyst had forgotten what he had
told him. He needed to sit up in order to assure himself of the face of the
analyst and to reestablish the connection with him. The anxiety that he
would be lost in aimless thought culminated in the horrible fantasy that
he would endlessly fall through empty space. Bach talks of a disturbance
in the ability for "evocative constancy," that is, to evoke in one's mind the
other's image. With this, the establishment of stable representations and
of self- and object-constancy is impeded. "So this mutual holding in memory may well have life-and-death implications for both child and mother"
(p. 742). His fear was "specifically of not being remembered, as if the act
of being remembered by someone was very literally what was keeping
him alive" (ibid.). Understanding how the parents' minds work is an important task of growing up, and transference and countertransference can
valuably assist in this (p. 743). As is often the case, this patient notices the
abrupt changes of mood and attention in his mother, a striking lack of
continuity, which then is repeated in his interaction with the analyst and
his experience of self and world. His entire life seems to fall into pieces,

"into discrete and fragmented moments, which he experienced as unconnected to each other in any meaningful or unified way" (p. 745). This leads to "a pervasive sense that he was a dumb and unmemorable person" (p. 747). Bach then puts this in the beautiful metaphor that I repeatedly have found very helpful in supervision and treatment:

> a person's specific memories and experiences are like individual beads that can achieve continuity and gestalt form only when they are strung together to become a necklace. The string on which they are assembled is the child's continuous existence in the mind of the parent, which provides the continuity on which the beads of experiences are strung together and become the necklace of a connected life. (p. 748)

For these patients, the frequency of sessions is of particular importance: "that in order for a dismembered life to come together, the analyst must keep the patient alive in his or her own mind in a continuous way, and the patient must believe that the analyst holds the patient and keeps him or her alive in memory" (p. 749).

At the same time, the countermovement is relevant as well: the respect for the need to be left alone, to be unconnected, which Warren Poland called the respect for otherness (2000). Furthermore, it is essential to recognize that discontinuity and unconnectedness are themselves consequences of defensive processes in the family and that they are used also by the patient as a protection, particularly against rage and violence.

The experience of meaning and time emerge out of the feeling of connectedness created in one's mind by the acts of being remembered by the other: "For such a sense of meaning arises out of the connectedness of things and their relationships to each other in time, and when the links of this connectedness in time are broken, we are left with only empty moments in a frightening and meaningless void" (Bach, 2001, p. 754).

The patients may talk about "losing the thread" and thus themselves and fall into a trancelike state of confusion, where they feel incapable of keeping the other in memory, and are sure that they are equally unable to keep them in mind. "I cannot reach you," may be said in analysis. It is the fantasy of the lost child. This may be dramatically reenacted in the transference. As the title of Bach's article indicates, the lost child also loses himself.

Such trancelike self-loss is widespread in the severe neuroses, in particular also with addicts to alcohol or drugs who actively bring about with the help of the substance this state of self-loss and try in this way to control it. Getting lost is, as already mentioned, a family affair of defending against manifest aggressions. We also may witness in such families the flight into religion, in an effort to avoid concrete human encounter and indirectly also aggression.

✳   ✳   ✳

All these fantasies and complexes of fantasies, and many others that are less prominent, are pretty ubiquitous, appear in weak or in massive form, and are of course intertwined. They all lead, as bridges should, to the other bank, to the essential unconscious inner conflict. And here it is, of course, particularly the oedipal conflict, with its wishes for incest and murder. I have not listed it among the fantasies because it is rather, as described in chapter 4, one of the cardinal conflicts and enters to greater or smaller extent into the core fantasies spelled out.

The more extensive the neurotic process, that is, the more severe the neurosis, the more pronounced and extreme are these aspects, and the more intense and radical are the underlying conflicts causing these phenomena. These fantasies, the self- and object-images and the symbols standing for them, are derivative compromise formations and take part in the radicalization of feelings and wishes. Like the superego, they have become the carriers of global affects and partake in what is felt and described as repetition compulsion. Measure and what is absolute—the tragic truth lies in the insight into their irreconcilable opposition.

With no other chapter have I had such a feeling of open-endedness, of painful incompleteness: that I could go on finding other highly relevant fantasies. It is "finished, but not completed [*tam welo nishlam*]."[4]

NOTES

1. I am reminded of Gogol's story "Viy" (LW).
2. It is especially this last type of fantasy and much of the doubleness of many patients with "multiple personalities" that we reencounter in Nietzsche (cf. my separate study of Nietzsche: "Man of the Most Dangerous Curiosity," Wurmser 1997, 1999a).
3. "den Menschen zu einem Leidenden und zu einem Zuschauenden zerspaltet sieht" (Nietzsche, 1886/1976, *Morgenröte* [Dawn], 113, p. 95–96).
4. This is a statement put at the end of medieval manuscripts, as a sign of humility. It modifies by modesty what stands at the very end of the Torah: "*tam wenishlám; tehillá le'él boré olám*—finished and completed; praise be to God who keeps creating the world," referring to it in the presence, as a becoming.

9

*

Technique and Relationship in the Treatment of the Severe Neuroses

Denn nur, insofern wir mitempfinden, haben wir die Ehre,von einer Sache zu reden.
(Only to the extent that we have empathy [feel with and into the other] are we entitled [lit: do we have the honor] to talk about an issue [here: suicide][1])

Inwendig lernt kein Mensch sein Innerstes erkennen.
Denn er mißt nach eignem Maß
Sich bald zu klein und leider oft zu groß.
Der Mensch erkennt sich nur im Menschen, nur
Das Leben lehret jedem, was er sei.
(From within himself, no one learns to recognize his inmost being. For he measures himself, according to his own yardstick, sometimes too small and unfortunately often too large. The human being recognizes himself only in the other [lit.: in the human being]; only life teaches everyone who he is.)[2]

In this final chapter I would like not only to describe in more general ways how I conceive the technical aspects of my work with "patients suffering from severe neurosis" (itself a rather problematic expression, namely, far too medicalized and dealing with the illness as if it were a concrete entity), but also to raise some principal, more philosophical questions about the nature of our work with these persons. The treatment of these patients suffering from various forms of neuroses touches upon the core questions of psychoanalysis and its central polarities that I described in the preface and for which I suggested a flexible form of complementarity. Many of these questions I have addressed in chapter 2 of *The Power of the Inner Judge* (Wurmser, 2000a); some were studied throughout these two books, and several especially important issues are taken up again in this retrospective reflection.

Gray's remark (1994, p. 91) is particularly pertinent in regard to the issue of psychoanalysis versus psychotherapy, namely whether "the treatment has the broad therapeutic aim of reducing the patient's *potential* for anxiety, as differentiated from merely reducing anxiety." And in a more recent article he notes:

> More severe pathology might well require analysts to divert close process attention away from the immediate context and to make interpretive inferences or interventions referring to events outside the analytic situation, thereby mobilizing, for both analyst and patient, demands to adapt one's orientation to "outside" realities. If such safety concerns suddenly become the analyst's, as well as the patient's, the conditions ensuring safety and freedom from real consequences in the analytic situation no longer prevail. (Gray, 2000, p. 234)

Most of the patients I present in these three books (the current one, *The Power of the Inner Judge*, and *Flight from Conscience*) pose precisely those problems, and it has been an overriding challenge to combine the careful conflict-analytic, that is, strictly "psychoanalytic" approach with "psychotherapeutic" modifications, that is, interventions that are dictated by the severity of the clinical regression. The detailed description of the cases illustrates the dilemmas faced and the self-critical review, step by step, when useful.

It needs also to be said that technical ineptitude or severe personal shortfalls, for example by "acting-out," by soul-blind withholding, or by sarcasm, lead to bad psychotherapy or bad psychoanalysis, and the consequences can be disastrous. Often, bad treatment is worse than no treatment, and it also slams the door shut against the patient's seeking therapy again.

TEN MAJOR POINTS CONCERNING COMPLEMENTARITY

When I select now the following ten major points that have emerged from the work presented here and from my extensive supervision, mostly in Europe, we need to keep in mind that I would always like to see them in the dialectical way that permeates this book. However, this complementarity (I use this term interchangeably with "dialectic") "between the analyst's personal emotional presence and the analyst's role-determined behavior" (Hoffman, 1994, p. 197) is but one among a number of such complementary opposites.

Another, particularly eloquent statement of such dialectic is Warren Poland's (2000):

> This respectful attention on the analyst's part, this silent but active presence, this silence of engaged nonintrusiveness rather than of abstinence, this listening in a way other than to seek for what can be interpreted, complements the analyst's interpretive function. The two, interpreting and witnessing, go hand in hand, each facilitating the other. . . . We have long been familiar with analytic functions that are related to such witnessing. It may have its origin in empathic responsiveness or in offering a holding environment, but it is a function changed by maturation beyond those roots. Indeed, it reflects the patient's advancing self-other differentiation, both a growing self-definition and an increasing regard for otherness, seemingly separate processes that are intrinsically unitary. Thus, analytic witnessing, seen most easily in the termination phase of an analysis, brings into the open the connection between *self*-definition and the fabric of *inter*connection. (p. 18)

> Separation and respect for the other's autonomy are central to witnessing. . . . *Witnessing develops from holding but implies letting go.* It implies respecting the patient's essential aloneness. . . . For witnessing has its roots in interpreting as well as in holding. (p. 21)

> Any interpetation moves the relationship from one of seeming union to one of separateness, where, separate people touching, contact replaces merging. . . . Otherness is deeper than verbal communication. It is the analyst's recognition of being the patient's other—that is, the analyst's dawning and growing respect for the patient along the relational developmental line. The negation buried in an interpretation exposes and strengthens essential otherness. (p. 27)

Now to the substance.

Shared Reexperiencing of the Intense Traumatogenic Affects

Listening patiently to the *details of the traumatizations*, again and again, is, at least in my experience, inevitable—*the shared reexperiencing of the intense traumatogenic affects*—in contrast to what many claim in regard to the treatment of traumatized patients. Corresponding to the centrality of affect regression (Krystal, 1988) and the attachment to pathogenic affects (Valenstein, 1973), *abreaction or catharsis* assumes with these patients a considerable space in treatment. These affective storms may, however, have a multiplicity of functions and have always to be seen as an outcome of inner conflict, and specifically as mobilized in the transference situation. They are not a mere mechanical repetition of affects that have not been sufficiently experienced during the original trauma, although they are that also. They very often serve in the transference masochistic functions, and thus indirectly aggressive, controlling purposes toward the analyst or therapist: by incessantly displaying their victimhood, they are set up to evoke strong guilt feelings and rescue fantasies in the other person, and exert with this a powerful interpersonal effect: power through suffering, the martyr's great coercive power through guilt induction—as we know very well from history and current events. Also, the sexualization of all these victim experiences needs to be understood, although its interpretation requires special tact because the sense of shame is intense. Therefore, it is very important, sometimes for a very long time, to patiently listen, or, as Poland (2000) recently stated so well and I already quoted, to "witness" it, to be witness to a past that is being made present again and again.[3] Ofra Eshel (2005) describes the "presencing," which is close to what Poland calls witnessing: "For me, the magic, the wonder of psychoanalytic treatment in general, and the treatment of perversion in particular, is *the magic of the emotional connection created within a profound loneliness*" (p.1088), and she quotes Yeats: "Tread softly, because you tread on my dreams" (p. 1089).

Often the interpretive interventions may be best tolerated when they go out from the self-condemnation and, through this superego and defense analysis, approach their fear of aggression. The complementarity is obviously that between affective reliving and exploring with the goal of insight.

Patience, Tact, and Approaching Conflict from the Side of Defense

This last-mentioned anxiety about *aggressive* wishes, fantasies, and affects, and with that the defenses by turning against the own self, the identification with the aggressor, and in particular the introjection of this aggressor into the superego (see specifically *The Power of the Inner Judge*, Wurmser 2000a, p. 193; see also Inderbitzin and Levy, 1998), often require exceedingly patient and tactful treatment. In my view, this entails seeing aggression and other "drive" aspects (especially sexual wishes, narcissistic concerns) always as secondary, that is, as mobilized by inner or outer threats or losses, by pain and shame, and consistently to approach them from the side of the defense. It is a matter of therapeutic tact because the direct pronouncement of what is defended against is experienced by the recipient as reproof or as humiliation and thus increases the "resistance." That means that such drives that are defended against have to be interpreted indirectly, as feared, avoided, dangerous. This is particularly and forcefully so in regard to the aggression in the transference. However, aggression that may be indirectly expressed, but clearly is not in itself unconscious, for example a hidden attack, taunts and sneers, may very well be directly, though nonjudgmentally addressed.

I would be a little hard put to apply to this point the dialectical view, were it not so that, of course, every "good" interpretation acknowledges within itself precisely wish, defense, and anxiety, or, on other levels, the opposite values or inner necessities. The interpretation is in itself dialectical; the opposites are complementary. That they should be approached from the side of defense, that is, always in regard to inner conflict, is an a priori decision when we engage in analysis *sensu strictiori*, but such a decision is in itself complementary to a view of the mind and of its systematic investigation that does not think in terms of conflict, but rather of a model of growth, wholeness, and defect, or of one of learning and its failure (as it happens for example in Jungian forms of treatment or in self-psychology).

"Close Process Monitoring" and Large Scale Reconstructions

With these patients too, Gray's method of "close process monitoring," in the here and now of the session, of the observable shifts revealing ego-sequences of impulses and painful affects, anxiety and various defensive processes, especially as transference of defense, can be very rewarding and helpful. "We are here to listen to the inner voices within you"—more precisely: to that which threatens, altering and stifling these voices. "Analysts can achieve this [the analytic situation as a safe place] by explicitly narrowing their focus to observing, and demonstrating to the patient, how his or her mind functions in the immediacy of the task of speaking as freely as possible (*not* according to a fundamental "rule"). The analyst engages the patient's *conscious* demonstrable defense solutions to repeated encounters with conflicted drive derivatives" (Gray, 2000, p. 234). In my experience, such microscopic close process monitoring, especially of the superego and defensive processes, can very well be combined with larger-scale reconstructions of the macroscopic connections. I find the complementary use of both perspectives particularly helpful.

Caution with Transference Interpretations

It is an essential part of tact to be *cautious with transference interpretations*: "If analysis is a journey, the transference-countertransference engagement is the train, not the destination" (Poland, 1996, p. 285). Again and again, I have been struck in supervision (especially in Germany) how every content is very rapidly related to the therapist. Every piece of the narrative is immediately forced into a transference interpretation, mostly of a drive nature. The associative flow is interrupted, the immediate connections are disrupted. The patient feels misunderstood and, irritated, rebels against it ("Listen, this is about me, not always you!")—which is then even more forcefully treated as resistance. It surely belongs to what Arlow describes as "stilted listening" (1995) and about which he comments in 2002. He quotes Harold Blum (1983):

> "Extra-transference interpretation has a position and a value which is not simply ancillary, preparatory, and supplementary to transference interpretation. Transference analysis is essential, but extra-transference interpretation, including genetic interpretation and reconstruction, is also necessary, complementary, and synergistic."

Arlow adds: "To date it would appear that hardly anyone has challenged the one-sided, technically exclusive view of the centrality of transference interpretation" (Arlow, 2002, p. 1141) and he reports in his observations

> how exclusive concentration on possible transference derivatives skews the way analysts listen to their patients. As a result, an artificial insensitivity seems to impose itself on the discourse in the psychoanalytic situation. Often analysts permit outlandish statements and bizarre connections that would never escape comment in ordinary conversation to go by without notice or comment as they prospect instead for transference material. They are not listening *to* the material, they are listening *for* material, transference material.

Most painful experiences are bypassed and attention focused instead on some minor transference issue (p. 1141). He also finds that "what is often overlooked is that the manifest transference constitutes a defensively distorted set of derivative representations of the unconscious conflict as organized into some form of compromise fantasy. It is not necessarily a recapitulation of actual events of the past." (p. 1142). Rightly, in my view, Arlow criticizes:

> It is as if history is being repeated without reference to the notion that the complicated interpersonal relations are derivative compromise expressions of persistent unconscious conflicts. When transference is presented one-sidedly in this light, the process of pathogenesis is reduced to the effects of a set of untoward, deleterious interpersonal relations, a kind of harmful conditioning by insensitive or malignant caretakers." (p. 1142)

This is clearly borne out by the case dialogues presented in my work. Arlow comes to a conclusion that I have seen borne out again and again in my work with candidates both here and still more abroad:

> Focusing one-sidedly on the transference and disregarding how it emerges in the context of the defensive needs of the patient may transform the therapeutic process into a stilted, intellectualized, and dehumanized experience. . . . Transference phenomena have to be understood in terms of their function in the context in which they appear. . . . Transference phenomena must not be

torn out of their context; they should not be interpreted in isolation but rather as part of the continuum of the patient's associations. (pp. 1145, 1146–47, 1150)

From a somewhat different vantage point, the two German trauma experts Fischer and Riedesser (2003) arrive at similar views. I summarize them: "Neutrality no, abstinence yes" (p. 205). A deep emotional engagement and solidarity is a *conditio sine qua non* for the treatment: not to be distant or focusing on "systems" or "fantasies," but listening to the details of the real traumatization without falling into "therapeutic narcissism," without dwelling on accusation and victimhood. Yet, a "neutral" attitude toward victims of violence is a form of retraumatization (ibid.). "The reconstruction of the traumatic experience relieves the otherwise often emotionally overcharged (therapeutic) relationship" (p. 212). Of the greatest practical importance is the authors' stress on caution with direct transference interpretations. They tend to stoke the great affective pressure even more (p. 212).

The concentration upon the here-and-now, be it in the framework of affect-activating therapeutic approaches or in an exclusive "transference analysis," is contraindicated in trauma patients. The past subverts then the present without its being recognized or named. The therapist fails to help his patient in the differentiation of past and present. Psychotherapy with trauma patients that is restricted to the here-and-now of the therapeutic relationship runs the danger of being retraumatizing. It does not allow the patient to experience the therapeutic work relationship in optimal difference to the past and potentially exposes him to an unmitigated reexperiencing of the destructive experience. (p. 225)

On the other side, a mere reconstruction of the past without reference to the actual life situation and the transference relationship also fails the optimal difference and becomes an intellectualizing and rationalizing preoccupation with the past (ibid.).

I have often observed stagnations and threats of breaking off the treatment as a result of intrusive, ultimately "soul-blind" and shaming transference comments. It is crucial to deal very discretely and delicately with transference. As Lichtenberg et al. (1996) stress, content and process need to be distinguished: "In our view, all of the patient's communications within the analytic setting have transferential meaning; however, the meaning may not be related to the content but to the process of communicating" (p. 152). The patient describing an abusive experience does not mean to indicate that he experiences the analyst as abusive, but rather "as sufficiently safe and protective to be able to communicate the painful experience" (ibid.), that is, the communicative process itself is being seen as having transferential meaning. Similarly, Wallerstein (1997) juxtaposes his own view to Gill's. Gill claims: "If the therapist is attempting to deal with the analysis of the transference as completely and thoroughly as he can, the therapy is analysis. If he is not, it is psychotherapy" (in Wallerstein, 1997, p. 252). In contrast, Wallerstein states, "the interactions inherent in analysis are not always interpreted, don't always need to be, and in fact should not always be" (Wallerstein, 1997, p. 254; see also Wallerstein, 1984). The complementary understanding of what is being said and experienced by the patient as referring to a *reality outside* of the relationship to the analyst, be that now present or long past, and as referring on many distinct levels to the *interaction with the analyst* has to be reflected in a subtle back and forth of the analyst's comments.

For me, the hinge in all this is the question: Where is the acute conflict? How do I find access to the deeper layers of this acute conflict? How do I interpret the defense and what is defended against in a way that comes closest to the actual experience of the patient? In other words: The center of the common work is the inner conflict, not the relationship, or formulated differently, the inner conflict in regard to all emotionally intensely experienced relationships.

At the end of these considerations I shall come back to this point, but revisit it from a philosophical vantage point.

The great question with all these complementary opposites is always: what helps at any given moment more, both in understanding and in support, and what, when, how? And here the minds part company: some give much preference to one side, some to the other, and clinical experience bears them both out—to some extent. It also does not just depend on the personality of the patient and on the clinical moment, but very much on the personality of the analyst whether one predilection works out better than its obverse. And then, there is also the inner development of the therapist: I certainly have myself moved over the decades from a much stricter adherence to a technique of consistent conflict analysis to a more pronounced emotional participation—again not as an either-or, but as a more-or-less. This change was dictated, by and large, by necessity for the work with the severe neuroses. In line with one major idea of this book, here too absoluteness is a bane and a brief for disaster (on this see also Hoffman, 1994, p. 215, and the very interesting recent discussion by and around Greenberg, 2001: the criticism of all forms of "excess" in theoretical and practical positions).

Clarification

In regard to the overwhelming (post-)traumatic feelings, it has to be added that the new trauma research (Horowitz, 1986; Krystal, 1988; van der Kolk et al., 1996, 1998; Herman et al., 1989; Krause, 1997–1998; Fischer and Riedesser, 2003) puts the *naming* of what has happened, of what has been experienced, and above all of the affects, very much in the center and thus tries to reestablish the meaningful connections. It is nothing else than what Bibring (1954) described as one of the basic types of intervention in the psychoanalytic method itself: *clarification*. This approach accords well with that of cognitive behavioral therapy: "the promotion of both awareness and expression of emotions" and the "working on cognitive deficits," also the thematization of unempathic and concretistic thinking (Beisel and Leibl, 1997). Still, such naming and clarifying forms only one part of the whole endeavor and always can be traced back to, and put into connection with, inner conflict, again in complementary fashion. Emphatically, it is not a defect that needs to be pedagogically filled, or certainly not mainly that.

Superego Analysis

Superego analysis, working through the massiveness and irrationality of the inner judge, plays, as we have seen, a very big, very central role in the analysis and analytic psychotherapy of severely traumatized patients (and virtually all patients with severe neuroses are severely traumatized, particularly in the form of "relational traumata"). I put it very often in the metaphor of *driving a wedge* between the archaic superego with its annihilating absoluteness and the rest of the personality. Typically, these totalitarian commands have become completely ego-syntonic; the ego is identified with this inner tyrant. To reopen the combat, to reestablish the inner conflict between "inner dictator" and "self," is *conditio sine qua non*, a first step that often alone makes treatment possible. Many treatments I supervise do not even get off the ground because this identification has not been questioned.

But then the second step is the question: Why is this inner judge so powerful and so cruel? And the answer to that cannot be simple: Many jump quickly to a historic "explanation" by the evil voice of a parent and by the abuse suffered, but this is a short circuit. To be sure, as we have amply seen, much of this archaic nature of the authoritarian superego can be understood and intuitively grasped as resulting from the introjection of cruel parental imagos. Patient and therapist are therefore often quick to blame the harshness and unreasonableness of their inner judge, its contempt and resentment, on similar traits in the outer authorities they had, and often still have, to contend with (the concept of the "inner objects" also seduces to such an oversimplification). Yet this is only a part of the story, and commonly not even the most useful insight. For the more detailed work I refer back to chapter 1.

Especially in the transference, it is very valuable to watch out for those superego derived affects (more exactly speaking, affects relating to conflicts between the superego and both ego and id, but especially also the intrasystemic superego conflicts).

In the cases depicted here, another important superego defense can often be found: Every form of excitement is quickly turned into overstimulation, as part of the tendency to affect regression, and therefore inevitably leads to a crash, to a most painful disappointment. This traumatic, passively suffered sequence is now reversed, turned into something active; every joy, every gratification, everything good done or received has to be aborted and changed into something negative and bad—the prevention of pleasure. It seems as if an unconscious guilt would not allow them to be successful and to feel happy—and this is in fact the traditional understanding of this process ("negative therapeutic reaction," Freud, 1923).

In particular, for many patients, all of life is an unending and constantly repeated sequence of "comparing, competing, and condemning" ("the three c's"), a continuous fear of their own jealousy and envy and of the same being expected from the others, and hence unendingly a source of guilt (in case of success) or shame (when they fail)—the wandering on the crest between two abysses of condemnation (see Wurmser, 2003a, 2003b).

Yet the fear of that dangerous excitement and the shame about the built-in debacle appear to be even more important (although the one explanation does not exclude the other). In this way, the superego becomes the resolute and absolute guardian against pleasure and joy and the carrier of that envious resentment against all goodness. This process can be studied very well both in "close process monitoring" and in the more macroscopic reviews and become a very important part of the shared exploration of a form of most massive superego transference: The analyst may be seen, by his very advocacy of "exploring instead of judging," as tempting the patient into gratifications and thus has to be fought against with withering condemnation or, in reverse and often at the same time, he is feared as the one who would mercilessly condemn the patient for his success or pleasure—in particular, very much so in regard to all competition. Yet, this superego-dictated reverse attitude of "judging instead of exploring" (in Paul Gray's words; personal communication.), sometimes even in a circular fashion ("I judge myself for the judging"), can be seen as a kind of generalized and global attitude that seems to block all analytic endeavor. In turn, it is of great relief when this premise can be pulled into the spotlight.

In all this, there are some countertransference constellations of great importance: One is the identification of the analyst (or therapist) with the suffering victim-self of the patient, and against a tormenting, blaming superego within the patient and its external representatives. Thus it can easily come to an acting-out of a revolt by the analyst against his own superego if his conflicts involving aggression and superego have not been adequately addressed in his own analysis (Gray, 2000). The therapist is then sucked in and pulled into the renewed fight against his blaming and depressive parents. It is a variant of the rescue fantasy and rescue mission undertaken to still one's own powerfully mobilized guilt feelings.

With that incessant self-condemnation between the opposite demands of avoiding both success and failure, dependence as well as independence, the patient's despair and hidden accusation against the analyst (or therapist) for not being there to help can become intolerable. The analyst may then hide behind theoretical constructs, like the intractable force of "the repetition compulsion" or of "primary masochism," "primary aggression," and "Death Instinct," and resort to the premature conclusion that the patient is unanalyzable or untreatable altogether. More generally, the provocation of the authoritarian superego parts in ourselves is very often a very great temptation with the patients who massively "act out" (I deal with this more in detail in *Flight from Conscience*).

Another threatening countertransference problem that I find particularly daunting is when the sadistic and totally soul-blind inner authority is projected onto me and is continuously treated as if it were reality. This paranoid transference and the enactment of the superego projection in reality, for the moment incorrigible and unreflected, and constantly recurring, I find often almost intolerable and as crossing the lines of what I can accept (Wurmser 2003b; Steiner, 1993).

Acknowledgment of the Traumata

Denial and the resulting phenomena of splitting have to be seen as attempts to deal with the (mostly chronic) traumatization, to prevent its repetition, and to resolve the massive inner conflicts that always are part and parcel of such trauma. Superego pressure and superego conflicts are like a reprise of trauma and evoke the same tendency for dissociation. Denial does not have to be viewed eo ipso as expression of an especially malignant early disorder. Acknowledgment of the traumata as probable external truth and as certain inner truth is decisive. Sure, we cannot always concentrate on the inner conflict caused by the traumatization, although we keep coming back to it and understand the core affects and core fantasies accordingly (i.e., largely as part of conflict resolution). Still, we can be, and sometimes we must be, *advocates of reality* and even may tend to become in this way educational instead of remaining in the position of analyzing. The more severe the denials and the distortions are (particularly in the transference, in the sense of transference psychosis and insistently recurring, though intermittent delusional misappraisals), the more important may be the calm, thoughtful reflection about reality (see Wurmser,

2003a). Yet, the danger in such "confrontation with denied reality" is very similar to the confrontation with repressed drives and affects: it is humiliating and often deeply resented. In emergency situations it may indeed be necessary, but if it can be avoided, all the better! Avoided how? Even this can often be done in such a way that what may at first seem to require pedagogical interventions can be phrased analytically and remain part of the process of understanding conflict. In other words: With problems of current distortion of reality it may be very helpful to explore what these defenses of denial and externalization are deployed against. Stated more generally, almost no remark by the analyst is being experienced as a reproach or a slight if it is being addressed on the level of inner conflict: if we phrase it as struggle within between two sides, two parts of the self, for example the wish (for the self or the other) to be perfect, and how disappointing or painful or humiliating it is (again for the self or the other) to fall short of this ideal, and how one part wants to close the eyes against such awareness; or: how intolerable the absolute impotence and helplessness was (or is or threatens to be), that we can understand how important the fantasy of being totally responsible, that is, omnipotent, omniscient, perfect, would be, and that the guilt or shame feelings are the price that has to be paid for this inner need, and how much then this realization has to be disavowed, hidden behind the veil of blame: again "judging instead of exploring."

This power of denial can be particularly devastating when it is directed against the perception of crushing shame or overwhelming guilt and hides behind a façade of egocentric insouciance or blaming others (the "sociopath").[4] We observe such large-scale denial, by what the Kleinians would call "manic defense," especially in the cases of drug addiction (including alcoholism) and in the case of Dilecta (*Flight from Conscience*).

Still, this topic touches on a much larger polarity inherent in psychoanalytic technique: How far are we indeed to consider external reality, and how far is it our overriding or even only task to examine the inner life. Paul Gray states it very clearly: "the analyst's primary goal is always the analysis of the patient's psyche, not the patient's life" (1994, p. 9). In my work with the severe neuroses, the dialectic between the "inside" perceptual focus and the "outside" focus has been more helpful than a strict adherence just to the former. But it has been decisively important to keep returning to the former and to see indeed our primary task in that. Complementarity does not preclude preference here, and what is necessary as tactic may be superseded by what is strategic—meaning that the overall goal is the resolution of inner, not of outer conflict.

In this context, I also would like to add another comment about outer reality and its complementary role in the life of the mind. After the catastrophe of September 11, 2001, and the generalized fear and worry about how to understand what is happening on the outside, I have found my-self repeatedly in clinical situations, both with psychoanalytic and with psychotherapy patients that I did not only listen to their anxieties and what they meant in their inner contexts, but added comments of my own, on the basis of my knowledge of history and about the background of cur-rent events. This is clearly not psychoanalysis nor does it fit into the usual understanding of psychotherapy. And yet, I feel that a failure to address the concerns on a reality basis, in contrast to just viewing them as part of inner fantasy and inner conflict, would itself be a form of shared denial (see also Wurmser 2004b). At the same time, I keep asking myself: To what extent do I do that out of my own need, in order to deal with my own anx-iety, to restore some semblance of power and even continuity at a time of helplessness and shifting ground? It is a very delicate balance of "cui bono?"—for whose benefit?

Fantasies as a Counterforce to Traumatization

The wounds never heal completely, the traumata can never be undone en-tirely, the affects involved in them can never be extinguished altogether, nor can the conflicts ever be fully solved. Yet, it appears to me to be an es-sential part of psychotherapy, and even more so of psychoanalysis, to bind the intolerable experience into what is *creative* and conjoin it with common humanity, creating thus some distance from the profound sad-ness and the pain. By its very complexity, creativity integrates what is contradictory, by lifting what stands in conflict to a level where it becomes complementary. Not all patients are ready and capable of doing this. But this ability to sublimate is an invaluable help.

More generally stated, the *fantasies have to be seen as an enormous coun-terforce to traumatization*, even if they lead to a split between the real world and the world of fantasies, analogous to play—Winnicott's "'potential space' between 'me-extensions and the not-me'" (Target and Fonagy, 1996, p. 471). Taking the fantasies very seriously in psychoanalysis, or the "active imaginations" in treatment methods more strongly influenced by Jung (for example Reddemann, 1998), or the stimulation of "mentaliza-tion" by putting into words what has hitherto been unspeakable (Fonagy, 1997; Fonagy et al., 1993; Fonagy and Target, 1996; Target and Fonagy, 1996)—they all utilize in different ways this *vis medicatrix naturae* ("the healing power of nature"; see also Waelder, 1967/1976, p. 340) in order to pave the way for an encompassing synthesis between the intolerable and the creative in our existence.

Added to this should be something that has probably not escaped the reader of the case histories presented: the references to literature as part of the interpretive process (Wurmser, 1993, pp. 92–95). I consider this work in the creative space as a special form of transference sublimation, allowing the patient an additional tool of insight to deal with the otherwise inexorable compulsion to suffer. It is, for these severely traumatized patients, an expanded, sometimes even new form of mastery and competence (Novick and Novick, 1996a, 1996b, 2003a, 2003b), allowing them to break out of the self-tormenting vicious circle, "to step out of the masochistic carousel."

A first point is that this approach enlarges the interpretive possibilities by bringing together and making visible in imagination, with the help of complex new metaphors, the multiple levels of inner reality and affect constellations. The art of poetry lives in the power of metaphor; the art of interpretation is effective through metaphor; transference itself is, as etymology shows, a kind of metaphor (*meta-phorá* in Greek is literally "transference," "carrying over," "Über-tragung"). The combination of these three provides us with a mighty means for inner transformation. This idea of an enlarged power of interpretation and insights is suggested by the words of Goethe's Tasso, the suffering poet:

Sie ließ im Schmerz mir Melodie und Rede,
Die tiefste Fülle meiner Not zu klagen:
Und wenn der Mensch in seiner Qual verstummt,
Gab mir ein Gott zu sagen, wie ich leide.[5]

Second, the inner events, the inner conflicts, the power of dread and suffering are seen in a shared human context. Instead of the shame-filled isolation in neurosis, the patient experiences the universal nature of these problems of living in conflict. It is, like what I described in regard to "catharsis" (first point above), another important form of sharing, this time not only with the partner in the analytic dialogue alone, but with a broader cultural world.

Third, one of the most important aspects of psychoanalytic treatment is the resumption of the sublimatory process. Creativity is indeed one of the sturdy bridges leading from the state of helplessness and fantastic omnipotence to real power, in the best sense of this word, as mastery and competence (Novick and Novick, 1996a, 2003a, 2003b). This realm of creativity is a transitional world of simultaneous participation in fantasy and reality perception, in conflict and complementarity, in suffering and in its surmounting—all this in a form that presents something valid and shared. A transference of the participation in the creative work replaces the narcissistic transference with its absoluteness and exclusivity.

Fourth, there is the identification with the analyst, but more with a kind of suprapersonal "ideal analyst" who would transcend my presence and my life.

What I have just described in regard to allusions to the world of creativity can be said about humor (Bader, 1995). Both were amply used by Freud himself in his work.

The dangers are manifold: fortification of defenses like intellectualization, idealization as fending off of aggression in the transference by such "educational" measures, gratification of narcissistic wishes and exhibitionistic wants in me, the denting of "the rule of abstinence."

What about the strengthening of defenses, and with that of the resistance against work on the affects and their origins in conflicts? This may indeed happen, but there is a double problem: Certainly, there is the risk that the affects may be held back by such intellectualizing inroads. Yet, it behooves us to consider that we deal here with overwhelming, global affects stemming from severe traumata, affects also that in some instances have led to violence against the self or others. The measures recounted serve to get a grip on those huge affects by fantasy and symbolization and thus to make the conflicts more solvable—as a kind of guardrail protecting the patient from stumbling into the abyss. They have to be understood as being rather of a tactical than of a strategic nature—auxiliary means for the working through of conflict, not as a therapeutic main purpose. These global feelings are dealt with as parts of conflicts; they do not stand apart from them, in some crepuscular field of deficits. Everything that serves the working-through of conflicts by insight and affect is valuable. I am convinced that such an individually and prudently handled broadening of technique can be of great worth. Perhaps, this is one effective counterforce against the suffered dehumanization: the rediscovery of what is creative, and this occurring not in loneliness, but in the peculiar dialogue of psychoanalysis.

In regard to the issue of abstinence: More generally speaking, all treatment requires a prudent titration of gratification and frustration, of wish fulfillment and abstinence. I am reminded of a little story René Spitz reported when reminiscing about his analysis with Freud (I heard him, I believe, in 1975 in Denver): After a particularly good session, Freud handed him a cigar: "This deserves a reward." Bemused, Spitz asked: "But, Herr Professor, what about the rule of abstinence?"—because it happened shortly after Freud's introduction of the need for "Versagung." Freud answered: "I have set up the rule, I can break the rule."

Inner Participation—"Respect for Minds"

Accordingly, all rigidity and stereotypy in the approach, everything that can be experienced as impersonal, general, nonindividual, harbors the big danger that it is taken as a repetition of traumatic dehumanization and objectification (Eshel, 2005, with her emphasis on "presencing"). One great transference anxiety is, therefore, that of renewed soul-blindness and soul murder: not to be seen in one's own nature as a person, the sharp and quick alternation of overstimulation by intrusive warmth and of rejection, coldness, even cruelty. Again, we are reminded of the dialectic between "personal responsivity and analytic discipline . . . the patient's deepest need is for the synergy of my personal involvement and the relatively detached, theoretically informed, and interpretive aspect of my analytic attitude" (Hoffman, 1994, pp. 198, 214). Crastnopol (see Greenberg, 2001, p. 388) speaks of the "patient's struggle to be deeply seen by a fellow human being." And Poland (1996) beautifully says "the analyst's respect for the authenticity of the patient's self as a genuine other, equal in validity to the analyst's self, may be the most profound of all clinical psychoanalytic principles . . . work based on a ruthless dedication to honesty, the importance of psychic reality and the unconscious, and the possibility of freedom and growth through the mastery to be gained from insight are the most the analyst can offer to patients" (pp. 88–89).

That means that the treatment cannot be carried through without strong *inner participation*—without "a deep and lasting attachment to the patient," as Lawrence Friedman (1997) stresses. Fonagy (1997) enlarges and deepens this concept by that of "the respect for minds," the ability to put oneself into the other's way of thinking and feeling and to express this symbolically, by what Goethe in the sentence quoted in the epigraph at the head of this chapter, called "Mitempfinden":

> The internalization of the therapist's concern with mental states enhances the patient's capacity for similar concern towards his own experience. Respect for minds generates respect for self, respect for other and ultimately respect for the human community. It is this respect which drives and organizes the therapeutic endeavor and speaks with greatest clarity to our psychoanalytic heritage. (Fonagy, 1997, oral presentation)

In order for us to reduce the risk of retraumatization by objectification and categorization and the ensuing shame, our *emotional presence and our spontaneity*, our genuineness and humaneness are crucial. This attitude is just as important as the tactful, patient unveiling of the hidden and highly complicated connections, which enables our patients to break open the vicious circles, to mitigate the absoluteness and totality, and with that to overcome the repetition compulsion.

This means a necessary dialectic, a complementarity or bipolarity in our therapeutic attitude: On the one side, the emotional presence is required, an attitude of holding, of spontaneity, of warmth and participation. On the other side, what is at least as important, and what is specific to psychoanalysis, is the clear understanding, the tying together of the torn connections, the recognition of the deep, largely unconscious conflicts, that is, the entire *interpretive process*. Now it is the one, now it is the other, and, all in all, I still agree with Michels (in Greenberg, 2001, p. 408) "that exploration takes priority over action." Still, it is a steady back and forth of great subtlety. This is what the art and the craft of analysis consists of. With these severely ill patients, it cannot be done without the sense of engaging on a rescue mission nor without the clear consciousness of the rational ego. It is the need both for inner participation and for otherness on the side of the analyst (see Poland, 1996, 2000), for a certain measure of affect, but at the same time an attitude that does not lead to affective flooding on the analyst's (or therapist's) side. Neutrality is necessary vis-à-vis the inner conflict of the patient (Hoffer, 1985), but not neutrality vis-à-vis the person, quite to the contrary!

And yet, even the countertransferential mobilization of strong (even "flooding") affects, especially of sadness, even despair, sometimes of anger, can in cases of severe ego regression in the patient occasionally be helpful, especially when we are faced with incessant paranoid accusations or unmitigated enacted self-destructiveness (Wurmser, 2003a). "You feel too, only now I know that you really care," I have repeatedly heard from patients. Or the patient feels shocked by such a reaction into a more reflective, less delusional stance. I emphasize: this has been for me the rare exception, but it does not have to be a disaster. Is it ever desirable? Rarely perhaps, yes.

Shared Curiosity

Finally, it is curiosity, the *shared curiosity*, again in Friedman's words (1997): "If the historical path to treatment is any clue to its nature, then curiosity must certainly lie at its heart" (p. 23). Such curiosity is based on the presumption of the existence of "objective truth, truth undistorted by the analyst's and patient's preconceptions and wishful thinking" (p. 28). It is a curiosity that grows on the grounds of skeptical questioning.

One of Niels Bohr's favorite sayings was a couplet by Schiller: "*Nur die Fülle führt zur Klarheit/Und im Abgrund wohnt die Wahrheit*—Only fullness leads to clarity/And truth lies in the abyss" (Holton, 1973, p. 148). Lester Havens (1997, p. 49) quotes part of the beautiful saying of Henry James about the writer: "We work in the dark. We do what we can—we give what we have. Our doubt is our passion, and our passion is our task. The rest is the madness of art" (Henry James, from *The Art of Fiction and Other Essays*, quoted by Azar Nafisi, 2003, p. 248).

THE COMPLEMENTARITY AND POSSIBLE
OPPOSITION OF PSYCHOANALYTIC
TECHNIQUE AND EXISTENTIAL RELATIONSHIP

Where I go beyond authors like Arlow and Blum is in the explicit recognition of the contribution by the analyst or therapist to the real relationship, over and beyond its transference aspects, and even beyond questions of technique. The question arises: Is "technique" really all there is to our treating severely troubled human beings? Is there not inevitably something much more existential at work here? When we speak about our "presence" and about "witnessing," are we not going far beyond what is usually looked as "technique"?

True, even this real relationship is affected by conflict. There is, in fact, a profound and inevitable complementarity between the interpersonal reality and the intrapsychic reality. Analysis deals both with the dyad and with the monad; neither can be reduced to the other. And yet, both are transcended by the dialogic relationship (Litowitz, 2006) as will shortly become clearer. *The analytic relationship is always real, and it is also always transference.* Relational psychoanalysis and systematic study of inner dialogue determine each other, and are, so to speak, two sides of the same coin of examining human nature in the light of conflict and complementarity. But there is far more to this dialectic.

What follows emerged mostly from my collaboration with Heidrun Jarass on a number of very difficult cases (see our monograph *Jealousy and Envy*, 2007) and hence the deepened reflection about my own past work.

Lipton (1977a, 1977b) made us aware of the importance in analytic treatment of the real relationship besides the transference aspects. Of course, it is always possible to also understand these "technically," to reduce them for example to early aspects of the relationship to a trusted mother or to use Ogden's (1990) term of "mother as environment" and "psychological matrix" where mother and child form an "invisible unity" and the "ability is internalized to become a subject that can have objects" (Raguse, 1995, p. 76).

Especially in the treatment with so severely and chronically traumatized patients as some of the cases presented in my books, we may have to resort to a framework different from the one that is based on the theory of technique, and hence on the "analysis of transference." It is a difference of the philosophical vantage point.

We go out from the a priori assumption that inner life can best be understood by seeing all the inner processes as incessantly standing in conflict with each other and continually also complementing each other in spite of their contradictions. Without this philosophical presupposition, psychoanalysis would be unthinkable. It is being used and is useful in every moment of our work.

But it is not the only one. There is a second a priori presupposition: that all these insights are only truly mutative if they occur in the matrix of an emotionally intimate relationship, a deep trustful togetherness that far transcends intellectual insight. Here Buber's philosophy of dialogue appears to be particularly helpful. In no way should it supplant the understanding by conflict, it should only complement it. In other words, the intrapsychic and the interpersonal or relational way of understanding are dialectically bound to each other. One without the other does not do justice to the complexity of our work.

This is an inescapable conclusion from work that is as difficult and demanding as that described here.

I try to summarize Buber's thought in a few sentences (following in this the formulation in Dan Avnon's book *Martin Buber: The Hidden Dialogue*, 1998, p. 39. It is very difficult to translate the nuances of Buber's thinking into another language and to render the very poetic essence of what he tries to say.). Buber attempts to capture the core of his conception of the interpersonal by devising the "basic words" I-You and I-It. I quote Avnon:

> The 'I' of I-You indicates a quality of presence that considers self and other as elements of one, inclusive reality: *when* one addresses the other from an inclusive state of being that is present to the unity of creation and of being, *then* the interpersonal is permeated by an I-You mode of existence. This 'I' is not sensed as singular; it is the 'I' of being present to being. Such a relation to being . . . establishes in the interpersonal sphere a quality of relation that Buber refers to as the Between. In contradistinction, in an I-It attitude to being, the person tends to distance himself from the other, to create in the interpersonal a quality of relationship characterized by the person's desire to distinguish him- or herself by accentuating differences, by emphasizing the uniqueness of the 'I' in contrast to the other. The 'I' of I-It indicates a separation of self from what it encounters.

I try to translate some further relevant quotes from Buber's work: In the I-You relation, in the "relationship" (*Beziehung*) in this specific sense, the other is a person, "not a thing among things nor consisting of things, . . . relationship is mutuality,"[6] whereas the I-It relationship, what Buber calls "experience" (*Erfahrung*), is "distance from You" (*Erfahrung ist Du-Ferne*) (Buber, 1947, *Dialogisches Leben*, pp. 20–21). The dialectic is however inescapable:

> This is the sublime melancholy of our lot that in our world every You has to become an It. . . . For every You it is in its essence fated to become a thing or at least to keep entering into thingness [*in die Dinghaftigkeit einzugehn*]. . . .

The It is the eternal chrysalis, the You is the eternal butterfly—only that it is not so that these states are cleanly separable, but often, in their profound doubleness, a confusedly intertwined happening. (Buber, 1947, pp. 29–30)

Buber talks about "the drive to turn everything into the You, the drive to all-relatedness" (p. 38), just as he speaks later on of the "spiritual drive for the word [*der geistige Trieb zum Wort*]," (p. 439). This spiritual (*geistige*) side is also inborn and appears with the initial attempts at communication. Anticipating today's insights into early development, he states:

It is not so that the child would first perceive an object and then put himself into relation to it; rather, the striving for relationship comes first; it is the open hand which the other [*das Gegenüber*] nestles against. The relationship to this [Other], a wordless prototype for saying You, is the second. But the constitution of an object [a very free translation of *das Dingwerden*] is a late product that has emerged from the dividing out of the primal aliveness [again a free translation of *Urerlebnisse*], the separation of the conjoined part- ners—like the arising of the I [*Ichwerdung*]. *In the beginning there is the rela- tionship* [emphasis added, L.W.]: as category of the essence, as readiness, as receiving form, as model of the soul; the A priori of relatedness, *the inborn You* [italics by M. Buber]. The lived relationships are realizations of the inborn You in the encounter. That this [other] can be conceived of as the encounter- ing one [free translation of *als Gegenüber*] and taken into the exclusivity is founded in the relationship. (p. 39)

It is decisive for us that "in the You, the human being becomes an I [*Der Mensch wird am Du zum Ich*]" (p. 40). "The separate It of the institutions is a Golem, and the severed I of the feelings is an errantly fluttering soul bird. Neither of them knows the human being" (p. 54).

For us, the dialectic between the two, between I-You and I-It, is decisive: the real relationship on the level of I-You and the prominence of empathy is essential, but the very exact comprehending in concepts of conflict, defense, and unconsciousness is just as necessary. Especially for analysts who work effectively with severely traumatized patients, it is the deep inner related- ness that has a curative effect over a very long period. There are innumer- able such "Now-experiences" (Stern, 2004) that form part and parcel of the enduring dialogue, the lasting relationship, a very deep emotional partici- pation by the therapist in the suffering of the patient while again and again finding the necessary distance. It is both, a continuous dialectic between an I-You intimacy and an I-It separation, a back and forth of closeness and dis- tance, in delicate balance. Many times the search for such a balance fails, but, all in all, the right way of dialogue keeps being reestablished.

Perversion is, as we saw, dehumanized sexuality and sexualized dehu- manization (see above, chapter 3). To put it now also in the terms just introduced: character perversion changes everything that is personal and could partake in the I-You relationship into something used, functionalized, that is, into an I-It. Life turns into that hole about which Küchenhoff (1990), Green (1993), Stein (2005), and Eshel (2005) speak.

Where there is no dialogue, power and thus possessiveness replace love, and with that envy and jealousy rule relationships with everyone. The transference becomes filled with all the emotions that go with this, besides envy and jealousy, rage and revenge, and also, very much resentment. The vampire vested in the superego threatens to suck out not only the vitality of the patient, but of the therapist in the relationship as well. Technique is important, but it is not all-important. It is a means to an end. The end, however, is a different way of being: where the other is more than a thing among things.

It is a way of being beyond envy and jealousy, beyond furious self-condemnation and shame, and beyond the sadomasochistic functionalizing and dehumanizing of the self and of the other.

I conclude with a story from the Talmud that could be interpreted as an illustration of this dialectic—the multiplicity of being, vision, and interpretation. There was a bitter dispute between Rabbi Yochanan and his former pupil Resh Laqish, in which they deeply humiliated each other. Resh Laqish fell ill and his wife pleaded with Rabbi Yochanan, her brother, to forgive her husband the slight. He refused, and Resh Laqish died. Now Rabbi Yochanan was overtaken by remorse and grief.

> Said the Rabbis: 'Who shall go to ease his mind? Let R. Eleazar ben Pedath go, whose disquisitions are very subtle.' So he went and sat before him; and on every dictum uttered by R. Yochanan he observed: 'There is a Baraitha (a taught opinion from Mishnaic times) which supports you.' 'Are you as the son of Laqisha?' he complained: 'When I stated a law, the son of Laqisha used to raise twenty-four objections, to which I gave twenty-four answers, which consequently led to a fuller comprehension of the law; whilst you say: 'A Baraitha has been taught which supports you.' Do I not myself know that my dicta are right?' Thus he went on rending his garments and weeping: 'Where are you, o son of Laqisha, where are you, o son of Laqisha—*hecha at Bar Laqisha, hecha at Bar Laqisha!*' and he cried thus until his mind was turned. Thereupon the Rabbis prayed for him, and he died.[7]

NOTES

1. Goethe, *Die Leiden des jungen Werthers* (The Sufferings of Young Werther, 1961, vol. 13, p. 79).

2. Goethe, *Torquato Tasso*, Act II, Sc. 3., vv. 1239–43 (1961, vol. 10, pp. 170–71).

3. This enormously great creative power of witnessing is expressed in a metaphysically stunning remark from Talmudic times (in Sifré Deuteronomium 346, quoted in Finkelstein, 1936/1990), ascribed to Shim'on ben Yochai: "'You are My witnesses, and I am God.' This means: 'So long as you testify to Me, I am God; but if you cease to testify to Me, I am no longer God'" (p. 213, slightly modified). It also reflects, by the way, a symbolic, nonconcretistic understanding of God.

4. I am reminded of the figures of Daisy and her husband Tom Buchanan in F. Scott Fitzgerald's *The Great Gatsby*: "They were careless people, Tom and Daisy— they smashed up things and creatures and then retreated back into their money or their vast carelessness, or whatever it was that kept them together, and let other people clean up the mess they had made" (1925/1953, p. 180)—a strongly autobiographic description.

5. "In my pain, she [nature] left me melody and speech to lament the deepest fullness of my distress: And when man falls silent in his torment, a God gave me the gift to say how much I suffer" (*Torquato Tasso*, Act V, Sc. 5, vv. 3430–34; Goethe, 1961, vol. 10, p. 227).

6. "Stehe ich einem Menschen als meinem Du gegenüber, spreche das Grundwort Ich-Du zu ihm, ist er kein Ding unter Dingen und nicht aus Dingen bestehend."

7. Talmud Bava Metzia, 84a; (*Talmud*, 1962/1936, see Soncino edition, vol. 10, pp. 481–82; trans. H. Freedman, ed. I. Epstein).

References

Abrams, J. Z. (1995). *The women of the Talmud*. Northvale, NJ: Aronson.

Abrams, J. Z. (1999). *A beginner's guide to the Steinsaltz Talmud*. Northvale, NJ: Aronson.

Aeschylus. (1955). *Aeschyli septem quae supersunt tragoediae: Recensuit Gilbertus Murray*. Oxford: Oxford University Press.

Aristotle. (1926/1968). *Nicomachean ethics*. Loeb edition. Trans. H. Rackham. Cambridge, MA: Harvard University Press.

Aristotle. (1932/1967): *Politics*. Loeb edition. Trans. H. Rackham. Cambridge, MA: Harvard University Press.

Arlow, J. A. (1969a). Unconscious fantasy and disturbances of conscious experience. *Psychoanalytic Quarterly* 38: 1–27.

Arlow, J. A. (1969b). Fantasy, memory and reality testing. *Psychoanalytic Quarterly* 38: 28–51.

Arlow, J. A. (1971). "Character Perversion." In *Currents in Psychoanalysis*, ed. I. M. Marcus, pp. 317–36. New York: International Universities Press.

Arlow, J. A. (1995). Stilted listening: Psychoanalysis as discourse. *Psychoanalytic Quarterly* 64: 215–33.

Arlow, J. A. (2002). Transference as defense. *Journal of the American Psychoanalytic Association* 50: 1139–50.

Asch, S. S. (1988). The analytic concepts of masochism: A reevaluation. In *Masochism: Current psychoanalytic perspectives*, ed. R. A. Glick and D. I. Meyers, pp. 93–116. Hillsdale, NJ: Analytic Press.

Assmann, J. (2001). *Tod und Jenseits im alten Ägypten*. Munich: Beck.

Assmann, J. (2002). *The mind of Egypt: History and meaning in the time of the Pharaos*. New York: Metropolitan Books, Henry Holt.

Avnon, D. (1998). *Martin Buber: The hidden dialogue*. Lanham, MD: Rowman & Littlefield.

References

Bach, S. (1991). On sadomasochistic object relations. In *Perversions and near-perversions in clinical practice: New psychoanalytic perspectives*, ed. G. I. Fogel and W. A. Myers, pp. 75–92. New Haven, CT: Yale University Press.

Bach, S. (1994). *The language of perversion and the language of love*. Northvale, NJ: Aronson.

Bach, S. (2001). On being forgotten and forgetting one's self. *Psychoanalytic Quarterly* 70: 739–56.

Bader, M. J. (1995). Authenticity and the psychology of choice in the analyst. *Psychoanalytic Quarterly* 64: 282–305.

Barth, B. (1990). Die Darstellung der weiblichen Sexualität als Ausdruck männlichen Uterus-neides und dessen Abwehr. *Jahrbuch der Psychoanalyse* 26: 64–101.

Bass, A. (1997). The problem of concreteness. *Psychoanalytic Quarterly* 66: 642–82.

Beisel, S., and Leibl, C. (1997). Stationäre Verhaltenstherapie bei Eßstörungen. In *Psychotherapie der Eßstörungen*, ed. G. Reich and M. Cierpka. Stuttgart: Thieme.

Benedetti, G. (1983/1987). *Todeslandschaften der Seele*. Göttingen: Vandenhoeck & Ruprecht.

Benz, A. E. (1984). Der Gebärneid der Männer. *Psyche* 38: 307–28.

Berliner, B. (1947). On some psychodynamics of masochism. *Psychoanalytic Quarterly* 16: 459–71.

Bettelheim, B. (1954/1962). *Symbolic wounds: Puberty rites and the envious male*. New York: Collier.

Bible. (1999). Hebrew-English Tanakh. Philadelphia: JPS (Jewish Publication Society).

Bibring, E. (1954). Psychoanalysis and the dynamic psychotherapies. *Journal of the American Psychoanalytic Association* 2: 745–70.

Blos, P., Jr. (1991). Sadomasochism and the defense against recall of painful affect. *Journal of the American Psychoanalytic Association* 39: 417–30.

Blum, H. P. (1983). The position and value of extratransference interpretation. *Journal of the American Psychoanalytic Association* 31: 587–618.

Brenner, C. (1959). The masochistic character: Genesis and treatment. *Journal of the American Psychoanalytic Association* 7: 197–226.

Brenner, Ch. (1982). *The mind in conflict*. New York: International Universities Press.

Brenner, Ch. (2002). Conflict, compromise formation, and structural theory. *Psychoanalytic Quarterly* 71: 397–417.

Breuer, J., and Freud, S. (1893–1895). *Studies on hysteria*. Freud, Standard Edition 2, pp. 1–251. London: Hogarth Press.

Bristol, R. (2001). Obsessive-compulsive disorder (OCD): Manifestation, theory, and treatment. *Psychoanalytic Inquiry* 21: 133–44, 320–32.

Brontë, C. (1847, in 1994). *Jane Eyre*. In *The Brontës. Three great novels*. Oxford: Oxford University Press.

Brouček, F. J. (1991). *Shame and the self*. New York: Guilford.

Buber, M. (1947). *Dialogisches Leben: Gesammelte philosophische und pädagogische Schriften*. Zürich: Müller.

Camus, A. (1942/1986). *Le mythe de Sisyphe: Essai sur l'absurde*. Paris: Gallimard.

Cassirer, E. (1923a/1956). *Philosophie der symbolischen Formen, Bd. I*. Darmstadt: Wiss. Buchgesellschaft.

Cassirer, E. (1923b/1958a). *Philosophie der symbolischen Formen, Bd. II*. Darmstadt: Wiss. Buchgesellschaft.

Cassirer, E. (1929/1958b). *Philosophie der symbolischen Formen, Bd. III*. Darmstadt: Wiss. Buchgesellschaft.

Cassirer, E. (1944/1962). *An essay on man*. New Haven, CT: Yale University Press.

Chasseguet-Smirgel, J. (1988a). A woman's attempt at a perverse solution and its failure. *International Journal of Psycho-Analysis* 69: 149–61.

Chasseguet-Smirgel, J. (1988b). From the archaic matrix of the Oedipus complex to the fully developed Oedipus complex. *Psychoanalytic Quarterly* 57: 505–27.

Chasseguet-Smirgel, J. (1991). Sadomasochism in the perversions: Some thoughts on the destruction of reality. *Journal of the American Psychoanalytic Association* 39: 399–415.

Coen, S. J. (1981). Sexualization as a predominant mode of defense. *Journal of the American Psychoanalytic Association* 29: 893–920.

Coen, S. J. (1985). Perversion as a solution to intrapsychic conflict. *Journal of the American Psychoanalytic Association* 33 (Suppl.): 17–57.

Coen, S. J. (1987). Pathological jealousy. *International Journal of Psycho-Analysis* 68: 99–108.

Coen, S. J. (1988). Sadomasochistic excitement: Character disorder and perversion. In *Masochism: Current psychoanalytic perspectives*, ed. R. A. Glick and D. I. Meyers, pp. 43–60. Hillsdale, NJ: Analytic Press.

Confucius (Kung Fu Tse). (1921). *Kung Fu Tse: Gespräche. Lun Yü*. German trans. Richard Wilhelm. Jena: Diederichs.

Confucius (Kung Fu Tse). (1966). *Confucian Analects (Lun Yü)*. Original Chinese text. English trans. James Legge. New York: Paragon.

Cooper, A. M. (1988). The narcissistic-masochistic character. In *Masochism: Current psychoanalytic perspectives*, ed. R. A. Glick and D. I. Meyers, pp. 117–39. Hillsdale, NJ: Analytic Press.

Cooper, A. M. (1991). The unconscious core of perversion. In *Perversions and near-perversions in clinical practice: New psychoanalytic perspectives*, ed. G. I. Fogel and W. A. Myers, pp. 17–35. New Haven, CT: Yale University Press.

Deutsch, H. (1930, in 1965). Hysterical fate neurosis. In *Neuroses and character types. Clinical Psychoanalytic Studies*, pp. 14–28. New York: International Universities Press.

Dostoyevsky, F. M. (1864/1982/1960). *Notes from the underground*. Russian edition, Ann Arbor, MI: Ardis, 1982. Trans. Garnett/Yarmolinsky. Garden City: Doubleday/Anchor, 1960.

Dostoyevsky, F. M. (1872/1994). *Demons*. Russian edition, St. Petersburg: Gumanitarnoye Agenstvo "Akademičesky Projekt," 1994; English trans. R. Pevear and L. Volokhonsky. New York: Vintage Classics, Random House, 1994.

Dostoyevsky, F. M. (1874/1972/1981). *The adolescent*. Russian edition, Moscow: "Chudozhestvennaja literatura," 1972; English trans. A. MacAndrew. New York: Norton, 1981.

Dostoyevsky, F. M. (1879–1880/1988/1990). *The brothers Karamazov*. Russian edition, Moscow: "Chudozhestvennaja literatura," 1988; English trans. R. Pevear and L. Volokhonsky. San Francisco, CA: North Point Press, 1990.

Draghi-Lorenz, R. (1998). "Jealousy in the first year: Evidence of early interpersonal awareness." Lecture 11, Biennial International Conference on Infant Studies, Atlanta, Georgia.

Edvardson, C. (1998). *Gebranntes Kind sucht das Feuer*. Trans. A.-L. Kornitzky. Munich: Deutscher Taschenbuch Verlag.

Eickhoff, F.-W. (1996/2001). Über moralischen Masochismus und den Affekt des Ressentiments: Moral masochism and the affect of resentment. In *Mankind's oedipal destiny*, ed. P. Hartocollis. New York: International Universities Press.

Eliot, G. (1862–1863/1994). *Romola*. Oxford: Oxford University Press, 1994.

Eliot, G. (1876/1982). *Daniel Deronda*. London: Penguin, 1982.

Eschbach, Ch. (2004/2007). Womb envy in character development. Presented at a meeting of the American Psychoanalytic Association, San Francisco. To be published in L. Wurmser and H. Jarass, eds., *Jealousy and envy*. Psychoanalytic Inquiry Monograph, 2007.

Eshel, O. (2005). Pentheus rather than Oedipus: On perversion, survival and analytic 'presencing.' *International Journal of Psycho-Analysis* 86: 1071–97.

Fenichel, O. (1945). *Psychoanalytic theory of neurosis*. New York: Norton.

Ferenczi, S. (1932). Sprachverwirrung zwischen den Erwachsenen und dem Kind (Die Spracheder Zärtlichkeit und der Leidenschaft). In *Bausteine zur Psychoanalyse*, ed. Vilma Kovács, pp. 511–25. Bern, Switzerland: Huber.

Ferenczi, S. (1933/1949). The confusion of tongues: The language of tenderness and of passion. *International Journal of Psycho-Analysis* 30: 225–30. English translation of previous reference.

Finkelstein, L. (1936/1990). *Akiba: Scholar, saint, and martyr*. Northvale, NJ: Aronson.

Fischer, G., and Riedesser, P. (2003). *Lehrbuch der Psychotraumatologie*. Third, revised edition. Munich: Reinhardt.

Fitzgerald, F. S. (1925/1953). *The great Gatsby*. New York: Scribner.

Flack, J. C., and de Waal, F. B. M. (2000). 'Any animal whatever': Darwinian building blocks of morality in monkeys and apes. In *Journal of Consciousness Studies* 7 (1–2): 1–28, and Commentary discussion, pp. 31–65.

Fliess, R. (1956). *Erogeneity and libido*. New York: International Universities Press.

Fonagy, P. (1997). Attachment and borderline personality disorder: A theory and some evidence. Presented at a meeting of the American Psychoanalytic Association, December 1997, New York.

Fonagy, P., Moran, G. S., and Target, M. (1993). Aggression and the psychological self. *International Journal of Psycho-Analysis* 74: 471–86.

Fonagy, P., and Target, M. (1996). Playing with reality. *International Journal of Psycho-Analysis* 77: 217–234.

Fraiberg, S. (1982). Pathological defenses in infancy. *Psychoanalytic Quarterly* 51: 612–35.

Freud, A. (1936). *The ego and the mechanisms of defense: The writings of Anna Freud*. Vol. 2. New York: International Universities Press, 1971.

Freud, S. (1893/1895). *Studies on hysteria*. Standard Edition 2 (see under J. Breuer and S. Freud).

Freud, S. (1912). *Totem and taboo*. Standard Edition 13: 1–161.

Freud, S. (1914). *On narcissism: An introduction*. Standard Edition 14: 69–102.

Freud, S. (1919a). *A child is being beaten.* Standard Edition 17: 175–204.

Freud, S. (1919b). *The "uncanny."* Standard Edition 17: 217–52.

Freud, S. (1923). *The ego and the id.* Standard Edition 19: 3–66.

Freud, S. (1924). *The economic problem of masochism.* Standard Edition 19: 157–70.

Freud, S. (1930). *Civilization and its discontents.* Standard Edition 21: 59–145.

Freud, S. (1940a). *Splitting of the ego in the process of defence.* Standard Edition 23: 271–78.

Freud, S. (1940b). *An outline of psychoanalysis.* Standard Edition 23: 141–207.

Friedman, L. (1997). Ferrum, ignis, and medicina: Return to the crucible. *Journal of the American Psychoanalytic Association* 45: 21–36.

Gedö, J. (1988). Masochism and the repetition compulsion. In *Masochism: Current psychoanalytic perspectives,* ed. R. A. Glick and D. I. Meyers, pp. 139–50. Hillsdale, NJ: Analytic Press.

Gill, M. M. (1963). *Topography and systems in psychoanalytic theory.* Psychological Issues Monograph 10. New York: International Universities Press.

Gill, M. M. (1991). Indirect suggestion. In *Interpretation and interaction: Psychoanalysis or psychotherapy,* ed. J. D. Oremland, pp. 13–164. Hillsdale, NJ: Analytic Press.

Glenn, J. (1984). Psychic trauma and masochism. *Journal of the American Psychoanalytic Association* 32: 357–86.

Goethe, J. W. v. (1961). *Dtv Gesamtausgabe* [Complete Works]. Munich: Deutscher Taschenbuch Verlag.

Gray, P. (1994). *The ego and analysis of defense.* Northvale, NJ: Aronson.

Gray, P. (2000). On the receiving end: Facilitating the analysis of conflicted drive derivatives of aggression. *Journal of the American Psychoanalytic Association* 48: 219–36.

Green, A. (1993). *Le travail du négative.* Paris: Minuit.

Greenberg, J. (2001). The analyst's participation: A new look. With commentaries by P. J. Casement, M. Crastnopol, J. L. Kantrowitz, R. Michels, and B. Pizer. *Journal of the American Psychoanalytic Association* 49: 359–426.

Grossman, L. (1992). An example of 'character perversion' in a woman. *Psychoanalytic Quarterly* 61: 581–89.

Grossman, L. (1993). The perverse attitude toward reality. *Psychoanalytic Quarterly* 62: 422–36.

Grossman, L. (1996). 'Psychic reality' and reality testing in the analysis of perverse defences. *International Journal of Psycho-Analysis* 77: 509–17.

Grossman, W. I. (1986). Notes on masochism: A discussion of the history and development of a psychoanalytic concept. *Psychoanalytic Quarterly* 55: 379–413.

Grossman, W. I. (1991). Pain, aggression, fantasy, and concepts of sadomasochism. *Psychoanalytic Quarterly* 60: 22–52.

Gruen, A. (2000). *Der Fremde in uns.* Stuttgart: Klett-Cotta.

Grunberger, B. (1979) *Narcissism: Psychoanalytic essays.* New York: International Universities Press.

Hägglund, T.-B., Hägglund, V., and Ikonen, P. (1976). On the defensive nature of phallicity. In *Dying: A psychoanalytical study with special reference to individual creativity and defensive organization.* Monograph 6, Psychiatric Clinic, Helsinki University Central Hospital.

Hart, S. L., Carrington, H. A., Tronick, E. Z., and Carroll, S. R. (2004). When infants lose exclusive maternal attention: Is it jealousy? *Infancy* 6 (1): 57–78.

Hartmann, H., and Loewenstein, R. M. (1962). Notes on the superego. *Psychoanalytic Study of the Child* 17: 42–81.

Havens, L. (1997). Commentary to L. Friedman: "Ferrum, ignis, and medicina: Return to the crucible." *Journal of the American Psychoanalytic Association* 45: 49–51.

Haynal, A., Molnar, M., and de Puymège, G. (1980). *Le fanatisme: Histoire et psychanalyse*. Paris [?]: Editions Stock.

Herman, J. L., Perry, J. C., and van der Kolk, B. A. (1989). Childhood trauma in borderline personality disorder. *American Journal of Psychiatry* 146 (4): 490–502.

Henricks, R. G. (1989). *Lao-Tzu Te Tao Ching: A new translation based on the recently discovered Ma-wang-tui texts*. New York: Ballantine.

Hirsch, M. (2005). Über vampirismus. *Psyche* 59: 127–44.

Hoffer, A. (1985): Toward a definition of psychoanalytic neutrality. *Journal of the American Psychoanalytic Association*. 33: 771–96.

Hoffman, I. Z. (1994). Dialectical thinking and therapeutic action in the psychoanalytic process. *Psychoanalytic Quarterly* 63: 187–218.

Holton, G. (1973). *Thematic origins of scientific thought*. Cambridge, MA: Harvard University Press.

Horowitz, M. J. (1986). *Stress-response syndromes*. New York: Aronson.

Ibsen, H. (1866/1991). *Brand. Et dramatisk dikt* [Brand: A dramatic poem]. Oslo: Gyldendal.

Ibsen, H. (1867/1988). *Peer Gynt. Et dramatisk dikt*. Ed. D. Haakonsen. Oslo: Gyldendal.

Ibsen, H. (1989/1966). *Nutidsdramaer 1877–1899* [Dramas from the present]. Oslo: Norsk Forlag, Gyldendal. English trans. J. W. Mc Farlane. London: Oxford University Press, 1966.

Inderbitzin, L. B., and Levy S. T. (1998). Repetition compulsion revisited: Implications for technique. *Psychoanalytic Quarterly* 67: 32–53.

Jacobson, E. (1950). Development of the wish for a child in boys. *Psychoanalytic Study of the Child* 5: 139–52.

Jacobson, E. (1957). Denial and repression. *Journal of the American Psychoanalytic Association* 5: 61–92.

Janowitz, N. H. (2005). Lusting for death: Some unconscious meanings of martyrdom traditions. Lecture, meeting of the American Psychoanalytic Association, New York, January 2005.

Janowitz, N. H. (2007). Envy of maternal functions in sacrifice rituals. To be published in L. Wurmser and H. Jarass, eds., *Jealousy and envy*. Psychoanalytic Inquiry Monograph, 2007.

Jarass, H., and Wurmser, L. (2006/2007). "The burned hedgehog skin"—Father's envy and resentment against women perpetuated in the daughter's superego. Presented at a meeting of the American Psychoanalytic Association, New York, January 2006. To be published in L. Wurmser and H. Jarass, eds., *Jealousy and envy*. Psychoanalytic Inquiry Monograph, 2007.

Kafka, J. S. (1989). *Multiple realities in clinical practice*. New Haven, CT: Yale University Press.

Kant, I. (1784/1983). Idee zu einer allgemeinen Geschichte in weltbürgerlicher Absicht. In *Werke*, vol. 9. Darmstadt: Wissenschaftliche Buchgesellschaft.

Kant, I. (1797–1798/1983). Metaphysik der Sitten. In *Werke*, vol. 7. Darmstadt: Wissenschaftliche Buchgesellschaft.

Kaufmann, W. (1969). *Tragedy and philosophy*. Garden City: Doubleday.

Kernberg, O. F. (1988). Clinical dimensions of masochism. In *Masochism: Current psychoanalytic perspectives*, ed. R. A. Glick and D. I. Meyers, pp. 61–80. Hillsdale, NJ: Analytic Press.

Kernberg, O. F. (1991a). Aggression and love in the relationship of the couple. In *Perversions and near-perversions in clinical practice: New psychoanalytic perspectives*, ed. G. I. Fogel and W. A. Myers, pp. 153–75. New Haven, CT: Yale University Press.

Kernberg, O. F. (1991b). Sadomasochism, sexual excitement, and perversion. *Journal of the American Psychoanalytic Association* 39: 333–62.

Kilborne, B. (2002). *Disappearing persons: Shame and appearance*. Albany: State University of New York Press.

Klein, M. (1932). *The psychoanalysis of children*. London: Hogarth.

Klein, M. (1952a). *Development in psycho-analysis*. Ed. J. Riviere. London: Hogarth.

Klein, M. (1952b). The mutual influences in the development of ego and id [Discussion]. *Psychoanalytic Study of the Child* 7: 51–53.

Kohut, H. (1971). *The analysis of the self*. New York: International Universities Press.

Kohut, H. (1972). Thoughts on narcissism and narcissistic rage. *Psychoanalytic Study of the Child* 27: 360–400.

Kohut, H. (1977). *The restoration of the self*. New York: International Universities Press.

Körner, J. (2004). Ressentiments und Gegenressentiments: Psychoanalytische Betrachtungen. In *Ressentiment! Zur Kritik der Kultur*. Special issue, *Merkur* 58 (9–10): 924–33. Stuttgart: Klett-Cotta.

Krause, R. (1997–1998). *Allgemeine Psychoanalytische Krankheitslehre*. Vol. 1: *Grundlagen*, 1997; vol. 2: *Modelle*, 1998. Stuttgart: Kohlhammer.

Kris, A. O. (1985). Resistance in convergent and in divergent conflicts. *Psychoanalytic Quarterly* 54: 537–68.

Kris, A. O. (1988). Some clinical applications of the distinction between divergent and convergent conflicts. *International Journal of Psycho-Analysis* 69: 431–42.

Kris, A. O. (1987). Fixation and regression in relation to convergent and divergent conflicts. *Bulletin Anna Freud Centre* 10: 99–117.

Kris, E. (1975). *The selected papers*. New Haven, CT: Yale University Press.

Krystal, H. (1988). *Integration and self-healing: Affect, trauma, alexithymia*. Hillsdale, NJ: Analytic Press.

Krystal, H. (1998). Desomatization and the consequences of infantile trauma. *Psychoanalytic Inquiry* 17 (2): 126–50.

Kubie, L. S. (1937). The fantasy of dirt. *Psychoanalytic Quarterly* 6: 388–425.

Kubie, L. S. (1954). The fundamental nature of the destinction between normality and neurosis. *Psychoanalytic Quarterly* 23: 167–204.

Kubie, L. S. (1974). The drive to become both sexes. *Psychoanalytic Quarterly* 43: 349–426.

Küchenhoff, J. (1990). Die Repräsentation früher Traumata in der Übertragung. *Forum der Psychoanalyse* 6 (1): 15–31.

Kummer, H. (1977/1978). Morality as a biological phenomenon. In *Life Sciences Research Report 9*, ed. G. S. Stent. Weinheim, Germany, and Deerfield Beach, FL: Verlag Chemie.

Lagerkvist, P. (1925/1982). *Gäst hos verkligheten*. Stockholm: Bonniers.

Lagerkvist, P. (1944). *Dvärgen* [The Dwarf]. Stockholm: Bonniers. English trans. Alexandra Dick. New York: Hill and Wang, 1985.

Lagerkvist, P. (1950/1984). *Barabbas*. Stockholm: Bonniers.

Lagerkvist, P. (1966). *Pilgrimen*. Stockholm, Bonniers.

Lagerlöf, S. (1904/1989). *Herr Arnes peningar*. Stockholm: Bonniers/Norbok.

Lakatos, I., and Musgrave, A. (1970). *Criticism and the growth of knowledge*. Cambridge: Cambridge University Press.

Lansky, M. R. (1984). The explanation of impulsive action. Presented at the December meeting of the American Psychoanalytic Association, New York. Published in *Fathers who fail: Shame and psychopathology in the family system*, pp. 93–112. Hillsdale, NJ: Analytic Press.

Lansky, M. R. (1992). *Fathers who fail*. Hillsdale, NJ: Analytic Press.

Lansky, M. R. (1997). Envy as process. In *The widening scope of shame*, ed. M. R. Lansky and A. P. Morrison. Hillsdale, NJ: Analytic Press.

Lansky, M. R. (2001). The problem of forgiveness in *The Tempest*. *Journal of the American Psychoanalytic Association* 49: 1005–34.

Lansky, M. R. (2003). Conscience and the project of a psychoanalytic science of human nature: Clarification of the usefulness of the superego concept. *Psychoanalytic Inquiry* 24: 151–74.

Lansky, M. R. (2005a). Hidden shame. *Journal of the American Psychoanalytic Association* 53 (3): 865–90.

Lansky, M. R. (2005b). The impossibility of forgiveness: Shame fantasies as instigators of vengefulness in Euripides' *Medea*. *Journal of the American Psychoanalytic Association* 53: 437–64.

Lansky, M. R. (2006). Discussion of contributions to symposium on "Shame." New York, March 4–5. Committee of Psychoanalytic and Psychotherapeutic Publications and Organizations.

Levi, Primo. (1958/1992). *Ist das ein Mensch?* Munich, Deutscher Taschenbuch Verlag.

Lichtenberg, J. D. (1986). The relevance of observations of infants for clinical work with adults. Paper presented at the meeting of the Swiss Psychoanalytic Society, Zürich, May 26, 1986.

Lichtenberg, J. D. (1989). *Psychoanalysis and motivation*. Hillsdale, NJ: Analytic Press.

Lichtenberg, J. D. (2004). Commentary on "The superego—A vital or supplanted concept?" *Psychoanalytic Inquiry* 24: 328–39.

Lichtenberg, J. D., Lachman, F. M., and Fosshage, J. L. (1996). *The clinical exchange*. Hillsdale, NJ: Analytic Press.

Lifton, R. J. (1986). *The Nazi doctors*. New York: Basic Books.

Lipton, S. D. (1977a). The advantages of Freud's technique as shown in his analysis of the Rat Man. *International Journal of Psycho-Analysis* 58: 255–74.

Lipton, S. D. (1977b). Clinical observations on resistance to the transference. *International Journal of Psycho-Analysis* 58: 463–72.

Litowitz, B. (2006). The second person. Gertrude and Ernst Ticho Memorial Lecture, presented at a meeting of the American Psychoanalytic Association, June 16, Washington, D.C.

Loewenstein, R. M. (1957). A contribution to the psychoanalytic theory of masochism. *Journal of the American Psychoanalytic Association* 5: 197–234.

Maleson, F. G. (1984). The multiple meanings of masochism in psychoanalytic discourse. *Journal of the American Psychoanalytic Association* 32: 325–56.

Masciuk, S., and Kienapple, K. (1993). The emergence of jealousy in children 4 months to 7 years of age. *Journal of Social and Personal Relationships* 10: 421–35.

Meyers, H. C. (1988). A consideration of treatment techniques in relation to the functions of masochism. In *Masochism: Current psychoanalytic perspectives*, ed. R. A. Glick and D. I. Meyers, pp. 175–88. Hillsdale, NJ: Analytic Press.

Meyers, H. C. (1991). Perversion in fantasy and furtive enactments. In *Perversions and near-perversions in clinical practice: New psychoanalytic perspectives*, ed. G. I. Fogel and W. A. Myers, pp. 93–108. New Haven, CT: Yale University Press.

Midrash Rabbah. (1983). 10 vols. English trans. H. Freedman. London: Soncino; Hebrew edition, Jerusalem: Lewin-Epstein, n.d.

Milch, W. E., and Orange, D. M. (2004). Conscience as the reappearance of the other in self-experience: On using the concepts of superego and conscience in self psychology. *Psychoanalytic Inquiry* 24: 206–31.

Miller, A. (1987). *Timebends: A life.* New York and London: Penguin Books, 1995.

Mitchell, S. (1993). Aggression and the endangered self. *Psychoanalytic Quarterly* 62: 351–82.

Mochulsky, K. (1947/1967). *Dostoevsky: His life and work.* Trans. M. A. Minihan. Princeton, NJ: Princeton University Press, 1967/1973.

Modell, A. H. (1965). On having the right to a life: An aspect of the superego's development. *International Journal of Psycho-Analysis* 46: 323–31.

Modell, A. H. (1984). *Psychoanalysis in a new context.* New York: International Universities Press.

Nafisi, A. (2003). *Reading* Lolita *in Tehran: A memoir in books.* New York: Random House.

Nietzsche, F. (1885/ 1976) *Jenseits von Gut und Böse.* Stuttgart: Kröner.

Nietzsche, F. (1886/1976). *Morgenröte.* Stuttgart: Kröner.

Nietzsche, F. (1887/1976). *Zur Genealogie der Moral.* Stuttgart: Kröner.

Nietzsche, F. (1888/1964) *Götzendämmerung, Der Antichrist, Ecce Homo. Gedichte.* Stuttgart: Kröner.

Novick, J., and Novick, K. K. (1996a). *Fearful symmetry: The development and treatment of sadomasochism.* Northvale, NJ: Aronson.

Novick, J., and Novick, K. K. (1996b). A developmental perspective on omnipotence. *Journal of Clinical Psychoanalysis* 5: 131–75.

Novick, J., and Novick, K. K. (2003a). Two systems of self-esteem regulation and the differential application of psychoanalytic technique. *Amererican Journal of Psychoanalysis* 63: 1–20.

Novick, J., and Novick, K. K. (2003b). The superego and the two-system model. *Psychoanalytic Inquiry* 24: 232–56.

Ogden, T. H. (1990). *The matrix of the mind: Object relations and the psychoanalytic dialogue.* Northvale, NJ: Aronson.

Oliner, M. M. (1988). *Cultivating Freud's garden in France*. Northvale, NJ: Aronson.

Panel on "Sadism and Masochism in Neurosis and Symptom Formation." Fall Meeting of the American Psychoanalytic Association, New York, December 17, 1988.

Papoušek, H., and Papoušek, M. (1975). Cognitive aspects of preverbal social interaction between human infants and adults. In *Parent-infant interactions*. New York: Associated Scientific Publishers.

Person, E. S. (1995). *By force of fantasy*. New York: Penguin.

Phillips, S. M. (2006). Paul Gray's narrowing scope. *Journal of the American Psychoanalytic Association* 54: 137–70.

Plato. (1967). *Platonis Opera*. 5 vols. Ed. J. Burnet. Oxford Classical Texts. Oxford: Clarendon Press. English translation in *Great books of the western world*, vol. 7, ed. R. M. Hutchins, trans. B. Jowell and J. Harward. Chicago: Encyclopaedia Britannica, 1952.

Poland, W. S. (1996). Melting the darkness: The dyad and principles of clinical practice. Northvale, NJ: Aronson.

Poland, W. S. (2000). Witnessing and otherness. *Journal of the American Psychoanalytic Association* 48: 17–34.

Pritchard, J. B. (1958). *Archaeology and the Old Testament*. Princeton, NJ: Princeton University Press.

Raguse, H. (1995). Internalisierung und Symbolisierung—Überlegungen zum kleinianischen Verständnis der Verinnerlichung. In *Internalisierung und Strukturbildung*, ed. G. Schneider and G. H. Seidler, pp. 71–94. Opladen: Westdeutscher Verlag.

Rangell, L. (1982), The self in psychoanalytic theory. *Journal of the American Psychoanalytic Association* 30: 863–92.

Rapaport, D. (1953/1967). Some metapsychologial considerations concerning activity and passivity. In *Collected papers of D. Rapaport*, ed. M. M. Gill, pp. 530–68. New York: Basic Books.

Rashi. (1946). In *Pentateuch*, trans. M. Rosenbaum and A. M. Silbermann. London: Shapiro, Vallentine & Co.

Reddemann, L. (1998). Traumaorientierte Therapie und Imagination. Lecture, Lengerich, Sept. 12, 1998.

Reed, G. S. (1997). The analyst's interpretation as fetish. *Journal of the American Psychoanalytic Association* 45 (4): 1153–81.

Reed, G. S. (2001). The disregarded analyst and the transgressive process: Discontinuity, countertransference, and the framing of the negative. *Journal of the American Psychoanalytic Association* 49: 909–31.

Renik, O. (1992). Use of the analyst as a fetish. *Psychoanalytic Quarterly* 61: 542–63.

Renik, O. (1995). The ideal of the anonymous analyst and the problem of self-disclosure. *Psychoanalytic Quarterly* 64: 466–95.

Renik, O. (1996). The perils of neutrality. *Psychoanalytic Quarterly* 65: 495–517.

Robert, P. (1985). *Micro Robert en Poche. Dictionnaire du français primordial*. Stuttgart: Klett.

Roth, G. (2001). *Fühlen, Denken, Handeln: Wie das Gehirn unser Verhalten steuert*. Frankfurt: Suhrkamp.

Rothstein, A. (1991). Sadomasochism in the neuroses conceived of as a pathological compromise formation. *Journal of the American Psychoanalytic Association* 39: 363–76.

Rubenstein, R. L. (1978). *The cunning of history: The Holocaust and the American future.* New York: Harper Colophon.

Sandemose, A. (1933/1980). *En flykting korsar sitt spår* [En flyktin krysser sitt spor]. Trans. into Swedish by C. Johnson. Harrisonsburg, VA: Donelley, 1980.

Sandler, J. (1976a). Dreams, unconscious fantasies and 'identity of perception.' *International Review Psycho-Analysis* 3: 33–42.

Sandler, J. (1976b). Countertransference and role-responsiveness. *International Review Psycho-Analysis* 3: 43–48.

Sandler, J. (1993). On communication from patient to analyst: Not everything is projective identification. *International Journal of Psycho-Analysis* 74: 1097–108.

Sandler, J. (ed). (1989). *Projection identification, projective identification.* London: Karnac Classics.

Sandler, J., with Freud, A. (1985). *The analysis of defense: The ego and the mechanisms of defense revisited.* New York: International Universities Press.

Sandler, J., Holder, A., and Meers, D. (1963). The ego ideal and the ideal self. *Psychoanalytic Study of the Child* 18: 139–58.

Sandler, J., and Sandler, A.-M. (1994). Phantasy and its transformations: A contemporary Freudian view. *International Journal of Psycho-Analysis* 75: 387–94.

Schafer, R. (1988). Those wrecked by success. In *Masochism: Current psychoanalytic perspectives,* ed. R. A. Glick and D. I. Meyers, pp. 81–92. Hillsdale, NJ: Analytic Press.

Scheler, M. (1915/1954). Das Ressentiment im Aufbau der Moralen. In *Vom Umsturz der Werte. Gesammelte Werke,* vol. 3, pp. 33–147. Bern: Francke, 1955.

Schiller, F. v. (1911). *Sämtliche Werke* [Complete works in 4 volumes], ed. P. Merker. Leipzig: Reclam.

Schore, A. (1997). A century after Freud's project: Is a rapprochement between psychoanalysis and neurobiology at hand? *Journal of the American Psychoanalytic Association* 45: 807–41.

Seibt, G. (2004). Das Paria-Volk: Nietzsche, Weber und die Juden. In *Ressentiment! Zur Kritikder Kultur.* Sonderheft *Merkur* 58 (9–10): 791–802. Stuttgart: Klett-Cotta.

Sengoopta, Ch. (2000). *Otto Weininger: Sex, science, and self in imperial Vienna.* Chicago: University of Chicago Press.

Shakespeare, W. (1952). *The Complete Works.* Ed. G. B. Harrison. New York: Harcourt, Brace & World.

Shengold, L. (1989). *Soul murder: The effects of childhood abuse and deprivation.* New Haven, CT: Yale University Press.

Sophocles. *Sophoclis Fabulae.* Oxford Classical Texts. Ed. A. C. Pearson. Oxford: Clarendon Press.

Spitz, E. H. (1991). Reflections on the smile of Dionysus: Theatricality, specularity, and the perverse. In *Perversions and near-perversions in clinical practice: New psychoanalytic perspectives,* ed. G. I. Fogel and W. A. Myers, pp. 207–31. New Haven, CT: Yale University Press.

Stein, R. (2005). Why perversion? *International Journal of Psycho-Analysis* 86: 775–800.

Steiner, J. (1993). *Psychic retreats*. London: Routledge.

Steiner, J. (2006). Interpretative enactments and the analytic setting. *International Journal of Psycho-Analysis* 87: 315–28.

Steinsaltz, A. (1989–1999). *The Talmud*. Trans. I. Berman, D. Strauss, et al. New York: Random House.

Stern, D. N. (2004). *The present moment in psychotherapy and in everyday life*. New York: Norton.

Stoller, R. J. (1975). *Perversion: The erotic form of hatred*. New York: Pantheon.

Stoller, R. J. (1991). The term perversion. In *Perversions and near-perversions in clinical practice: New psychoanalytic perspectives*, ed. G. I. Fogel and W. A. Myers, pp. 36–56. New Haven, CT: Yale University Press.

Szondi, L. (1948). *Schicksalsanalyse*. Basel: (no publisher).

Szondi, P. (1961/1978). Versuch über das Tragische. In *Schriften*, vol. 1. Frankfurt: Suhrkamp.

Talmud. (1962/1936). *Talmud: Hebrew/Aramaic edition of the Babylonian Talmud*, ed. Rabbi M. Zioni. Jerusalem: Bne Braq. English translation, ed. I. Epstein. London: Soncino, 1936.

Target, M., and Fonagy, P. (1996). Playing with reality II. *International Journal of Psycho-Analysis* 77: 459–80.

Titus, H. H., Smith, M. S., Nolan, R. T. (1986) *Living issues in philosophy*. Belmont, CA: Wadsworth.

Tugendhat, E. (1955). Partikularismus und Universalismus. In *Das Fremde*, ed. M. Egnér, pp. 21–30. Egnér-Prize paper. Zürich: Margrit Egnér Stiftung.

Unamuno, M. de. (1921/1954). *Tragic sense of life*. Trans. J. E. Crawford Flitch. New York: Dover.

Valenstein, A. F. (1973). On attachment to painful feelings and the negative therapeutic reaction. *Psychoanalytic Study of the Child* 28: 365–92.

van der Kolk, B. A., Pelcovitz, D, Roth, S., Mandel, F. S., McFarlane, A., and Herman, J. L. (1996). Dissociation, somatization, and affect dysregulation: The complexity of adaptation to trauma. *Special Supplement to the American Journal of Psychiatry* 153 (7): 83–93.

van der Kolk, B. A. (1998). Die sozialen und neurobiologischen Dimensionen des Zwanges, Traumata zu wiederholen. Paper presented at the Congress, "Trauma und Kreative Lösungen," March 5–7, 1998, Cologne, Germany.

Waelder, R. (1951). The structure of paranoid ideas: A critical survey of various theories. In *Psychoanalysis: Observation, theory, application*, ed. S. A. Guttman, pp. 207–28. New York: International Universities Press.

Waelder, R. (1967/1976). Inhibitions, symptoms, and anxiety. In *Psychoanalysis: Observation, theory, application*, ed. S. A. Guttman, pp. 338–60. New York: International Universities Press.

Waelder, R. (1976). *Psychoanalysis: Observation, theory, application; Selected papers*, ed. S. A. Guttman. New York: International Universities Press.

Wallerstein, R. S. (1984). The analysis of the transference: A matter of emphasis or of theory reformulation? *Psychoanalytic Inquiry* 4: 325–54.

Wallerstein, R. S. (1997). Merton Gill, psychotherapy, and psychoanalysis. *Journal of the American Psychoanalytic Association* 45: 233–56.

Wellendorf, F. (1995). "Zur Psychoanalyse der Geschwisterbeziehung." *Forum der Psychoanalyse* 11 (4): 295–310.

Wurmser, L. (1977). A defense of the use of metaphor in analytic theory formation. *Psychoanalytic Quarterly* 46: 466–98.

Wurmser, L. (1978/1995). *The hidden dimension: Psychodynamics in compulsive drug use*. Northvale, NJ: Aronson.

Wurmser, L. (1981/1994). *The mask of shame*. Baltimore: Johns Hopkins University Press. Republ. Northvale, NJ: Aronson, 1994.

Wurmser, L. (1987). "My poisoned blood." The spirit of resentment: Comments on Pär Lagerkvist's "The Dwarf." Paper presented at the Study Group "Psychoanalysis and creativity" (J. Lichtenberg), January 24, 1987, and at the psychiatric hospital St. Sigfrid Sjukhuset, Växjö, Sweden, January 31, 1987.

Wurmser, L. (1989). *Die zerbrochene Wirklichkeit: Psychoanalyse als das Studium von Konflikt und Komplementarität* [Broken reality: Psychoanalysis as the study of conflict and complementarity]. Heidelberg: Springer.

Wurmser, L. (1990a, 1993, 1997). *Die Maske der Scham: Die Psychoanalyse von Schamaf-fekten und Schamkonflikten* [The mask of shame: The psychoanalysis of shame affects and shame conflicts]. Heidelberg: Springer.

Wurmser, L. (1990b). The question of conflict in Chinese thought, specifically in Confucius: Some psychoanalytic considerations. *Journal of the Korean Psychoanalytic Study Group* 1: 115–30.

Wurmser, L. (1990c). "Man of the most dangerous curiosity"—Nietzsche's "fruitful and frightful vision" and his war against shame. Paper presented at Study Group "Psychoanalysis and Creativity," J. Lichtenberg, Bethesda, MD, April 7.

Wurmser, L. (1991). The question of conflict in Lao Tzu: Some psychoanalytic considerations. *Journal of the Korean Psychoanalytic Study Group* 2: 112–33.

Wurmser, L. (1993/1997). *Das Rätsel des Masochismus: Psychoanalytische Untersuchungen von Gewissenszwang und Leidenssucht* [The riddle of masochism: Psychoanalytic studies of the compulsion of conscience and the addiction to suffering]. Heidelberg: Springer.

Wurmser, L. (1997). Nietzsche's war against shame and resentment. In *The widening scope of shame*, ed. M. R. Lansky and A. P. Morrison, pp. 181–204. Hillsdale, NJ: Analytic Press.

Wurmser, L. (1999a). "Man of the most dangerous curiosity"—Nietzsche's "fruitful vision" and his war against shame. In *Scenes of shame*, ed. J. Adamson and H. Clark, pp. 111–46. Albany: State University of New York Press.

Wurmser, L. (1999b). *Magische Verwandlung und tragische Verwandlung: Die Behandlung der schweren Neurose* [Magic transformation and tragic transformation: The treatment of severe neurosis]. Göttingen: Vandenhoeck & Ruprecht.

Wurmser, L. (2000a). *The power of the inner judge*. Northvale, NJ: Aronson.

Wurmser, L. (2000b). Magic transformation and tragic transformation—Splitting of ego and superego in severely traumatized patients. *Clinical Social Work Journal* 28: 385–401.

Wurmser, L. (2001). *Ideen- und Wertewelt des Judentums: Eine psychoanalytische Sicht*. Göttingen: Vandenhoeck & Ruprecht.

Wurmser, L. (2002). The dynamics of anti-semitism, xenophobia and intolerance: A psychoanalytic view. Paper presented at a meeting of the American Psychoanalytic Association, Philadelphia.

Wurmser, L. (2003a). 'The annihilating power of absoluteness'—Superego analysis in the severe neuroses, especially in character perversion. *Psychoanalytic Psychology* 20: 214–35.

Wurmser, L. (2003b). "Abyss calls out to abyss"—Oedipal shame, invisibility, and broken identity. *American Journal of Psychoanalysis* 63: 299–316.

Wurmser, L., ed. (2004a). The superego—A vital or supplanted concept? *Psychoanalytic Inquiry* 24 (2): 141–340.

Wurmser, L. (2004b). Psychoanalytic reflections on 9/11, terrorism, and genocidal prejudice—Their roots and sequels [Book Essay]. *Journal of the American Psychoanalytic Association* 52: 911–26.

Wurmser, L. (2006). Pathologische Eifersucht. Dilemma von Liebe und Macht. *Forum der Psychoanalyse* 22: 3–22.

Wurmser, L. *Flight from conscience*. Forthcoming.

Wurmser, L., and Jarass, H. (2007a). *Jealousy and envy: New views about two powerful feelings*. Psychoanalytic Inquiry Monograph, forthcoming 2007.

Wurmser, L., and Jarass, H. (2007b). Pathological jealousy: The perversion of love. In *Jealousy and envy*. Psychoanalytic Inquiry Monograph, forthcoming 2007.

Zimmer, R. (2003). Perverse modes of thought. *Psychoanalytic Quarterly* 72: 905–38.

Index

About the Author

Léon Wurmser, M.D., is clinical professor of psychiatry at the University of West Virginia and training and supervising analyst at the New York Freudian Society. Former professor of psychiatry and director of the Alcohol and Drug Abuse Program at the University of Maryland, he has also taught extensively throughout Europe. Dr. Wurmser trained as a psychiatrist in his native Switzerland and received his psychoanalytic training in this country. Author of 300 articles and coeditor of the six-volume textbook *Psychiatric Foundations in Medicine*, he has written several books such as *The Hidden Dimension and The Mask of Shame*. Dr. Wurmser is a recipient of the 1997 Margrit Egner Foundation Award in recognition of outstanding work in anthropologic psychology and philosophy. He maintains a private practice in psychotherapy in Towson, Maryland.